Charles Darwin
A Biography

Editor

Emery Denson

Scribbles

Year of Publication 2018

ISBN : 9789352979622

Book Published by
Scribbles
(An Imprint of Alpha Editions)

email - alphaedis@gmail.com

Produced by: PediaPress GmbH
Limburg an der Lahn
Germany
http://pediapress.com/

The content within this book was generated collaboratively by volunteers. Please be advised that nothing found here has necessarily been reviewed by people with the expertise required to provide you with complete, accurate or reliable information. Some information in this book may be misleading or simply wrong. Alpha Editions and PediaPress does not guarantee the validity of the information found here. If you need specific advice (for example, medical, legal, financial, or risk management) please seek a professional who is licensed or knowledgeable in that area.
Sources, licenses and contributors of the articles and images are listed in the section entitled "References". Parts of the books may be licensed under the GNU Free Documentation License. A copy of this license is included in the section entitled "GNU Free Documentation License"
The views and characters expressed in the book are those of the contributors and his/her imagination and do not represent the views of the Publisher.

Contents

Articles   **1**
    Introduction 1

Darwin Family   **3**
    Darwin–Wedgwood family 3

Charles Darwin's Education   **25**
    Charles Darwin's education 25

Survey voyage on HMS Beagle   **45**
    Second voyage of HMS Beagle 45

Inception of Darwin's evolutionary theory   **81**
    Inception of Darwin's theory 81

Charles Darwin's health   **105**
    Health of Charles Darwin 105

Development of Darwin's theory   **123**
    Development of Darwin's theory 123

Publication of the theory of natural selection   **141**
    Publication of Darwin's theory 141

Responses to publication   **159**
    Reactions to On the Origin of Species 159

Descent of Man, sexual selection, and botany — 183
Darwin from Orchids to Variation 183
Darwin from Descent of Man to Emotions 196

Darwin from Insectivorous Plants to Worms — 209
Darwin from Insectivorous Plants to Worms 209

Commemoration — 231
Commemoration of Charles Darwin 231
List of things named after Charles Darwin 237
List of taxa described by Charles Darwin 239

Religious views — 243
Religious views of Charles Darwin 243

Evolutionary social movements — 271
Darwinism 271
Eugenics 279
Social Darwinism 298

Works — 311
Charles Darwin bibliography 311

Appendix — 315
References 315
Article Sources and Contributors 330
Image Sources, Licenses and Contributors 332

Article Licenses — 335

Index — 337

Introduction

Charles Robert Darwin, was an English naturalist, geologist and biologist, best known for his contributions to the science of evolution. He established that all species of life have descended over time from common ancestors and, in a joint publication with Alfred Russel Wallace, introduced his scientific theory that this branching pattern of evolution resulted from a process that he called natural selection, in which the struggle for existence has a similar effect to the artificial selection involved in selective breeding.

Darwin published his theory of evolution with compelling evidence in his 1859 book On the Origin of Species, overcoming scientific rejection of earlier concepts of transmutation of species. By the 1870s, the scientific community and a majority of the educated public had accepted evolution as a fact. However, many favoured competing explanations and it was not until the emergence of the modern evolutionary synthesis from the 1930s to the 1950s that a broad consensus developed in which natural selection was the basic mechanism of evolution. Darwin's scientific discovery is the unifying theory of the life sciences, explaining the diversity of life.

Darwin's early interest in nature led him to neglect his medical education at the University of Edinburgh; instead, he helped to investigate marine invertebrates. Studies at the University of Cambridge (Christ's College) encouraged his passion for natural science. His five-year voyage on HMS Beagle established him as an eminent geologist whose observations and theories supported Charles Lyell's uniformitarian ideas, and publication of his journal of the voyage made him famous as a popular author.

Puzzled by the geographical distribution of wildlife and fossils he collected on the voyage, Darwin began detailed investigations, and in 1838 conceived his theory of natural selection. Although he discussed his ideas with several naturalists, he needed time for extensive research and his geological work had priority. He was writing up his theory in 1858 when Alfred Russel Wallace sent him an essay that described the same idea, prompting immediate joint publication of both of their theories. Darwin's work established evolutionary descent with modification as the dominant scientific explanation of diversification in nature. In 1871 he examined human evolution and sexual selection in The Descent of Man, and Selection in Relation to Sex, followed by The Expression of the Emotions in Man and Animals (1872). His research on plants was published in a series of books, and in his final book, The Formation of Vegetable Mould, through the Actions of Worms (1881), he examined earthworms and their effect on soil.

Darwin has been described as one of the most influential figures in human history, and he was honoured by burial in Westminster Abbey.

Darwin Family

Darwin–Wedgwood family

The **Darwin–Wedgwood family** is composed of two interrelated English families, descending from prominent 18th-century doctor Erasmus Darwin, and Josiah Wedgwood, founder of the pottery company, Josiah Wedgwood and Sons. Its most notable member was Charles Darwin, a grandson of both. The family included at least ten Fellows of the Royal Society and several artists and poets (including the composer Ralph Vaughan Williams). Presented below are brief biographical descriptions and genealogical information with links to articles on the members. The individuals are listed by year of birth and grouped into generations. The relationship to Francis Galton and his immediate ancestors is also given. Note that the data tree below does not include all descendants or even all prominent descendants.

The first generation

Josiah Wedgwood

Josiah Wedgwood (1730–1795) was a noted pottery businessman and a friend of Erasmus Darwin. During 1780, on the death of his long-time business partner Thomas Bentley, Josiah asked Darwin for help in managing the business. As a result of the close association that grew up between the Wedgwood and Darwin families, one of Josiah's daughters later married Erasmus's son Robert. One of the children of that marriage, Charles Darwin, also married a Wedgwood – Emma, Josiah's granddaughter. Robert's inheritance of Josiah's money enabled him to fund Charles Darwin's chosen vocation in natural history that resulted in the inception of Darwin's theory of evolution. Subsequently Emma's inheritance made the Darwins a wealthy family.

Josiah Wedgwood married Sarah Wedgwood (1734–1815), and they had seven children, including:

Figure 1: *Josiah Wedgwood (1730–1795)*

- Susannah Wedgwood (1765–1817) (later Darwin; see below)
- Josiah Wedgwood (1769–1843) (see below)
- Thomas Wedgwood (1771–1805) (see below)

Erasmus Darwin

Erasmus Darwin (1731–1802) was a physician, botanist and poet from Lichfield, whose lengthy botanical poems gave insights into medicine and natural history, and described an evolutionist theory that anticipated both Jean-Baptiste Lamarck and his grandson Charles. He married twice, first during 1757 to Mary Howard (1740–1770), who died from alcohol-induced liver failure aged 31. She gave birth to:

- Charles Darwin (1758–1778) (not Charles Robert Darwin)
- Erasmus Darwin the Younger (1759–1799)
- Elizabeth Darwin, 1763 (survived 4 months)
- Robert Waring Darwin (see below)
- William Alvey Darwin, (1767) (survived 19 days)

He then had an extra-marital affair with a Miss Parker, producing two daughters:

- Susanna Parker (1772–1856)

Figure 2: *Erasmus Darwin (1731–1802).*

- Mary Parker (1774–1859)

He then became smitten with Elizabeth Collier Sacheveral-Pole, who was married to Colonel Sacheveral-Pole and was the natural daughter of the Charles Colyear, 2nd Earl of Portmore. Sacheveral-Pole died soon afterwards, and Erasmus married Elizabeth and they bore an additional seven children:

- Edward Darwin, (1782–1829)
- Frances Anne Violetta Darwin, (1783–1874); married Samuel Tertius Galton; mother of Francis Galton (see below)
- Emma Georgina Elizabeth Darwin (born 1784)
- Sir Francis Sacheverel Darwin (1786–1859)
- John Darwin (1787–1865)
- Henry Darwin (born 1789)
- Harriot Darwin (1790–1825); later Harriott Maling.

Samuel "John" Galton

Samuel "John" Galton FRS (1753–1832) was an arms manufacturer from Birmingham. He married Lucy Barclay (1757–1817), daughter of Robert Barclay Allardice, MP, 5th of Urie. They had the eight children:

- Mary Anne Galton (1778–1856), married Lambert Schimmelpenninck in 1806
- Sophia Galton (1782–1863) married Charles Brewin in 1833

Figure 3: *Samuel "John" Galton.*

- Samuel Tertius Galton (1783–1844) (whose son Francis Galton was also notable).
- Theodore Galton (1784–1810)
- Adele Galton (1784–1869) married John Kaye Booth, MD during 1827, dsp.
- Hubert John Barclay Galton (1789–1864).
- Ewen Cameron Galton, (1791–1800), died aged 9.
- John Howard Galton (1794–1862), father of Douglas Strutt Galton.

The second generation

Robert Darwin

The son of Erasmus Darwin, Robert Darwin was a noted physician from Shrewsbury,[1] whose own income as a physician, together with astute investment of his inherited wealth, enabled him to fund his son Charles Darwin's place on the Voyage of the Beagle and then gave him the private income needed to support Charles' chosen vocation in natural history that led to the inception of Darwin's theory of evolution. He married Susannah Wedgwood, daughter of Josiah Wedgwood (see above), and they had the following children.

Figure 4: *Robert Darwin (1766–1848).*

- Marianne Darwin (1798–?), married Henry Parker (1788–1858) during 1824.
- Caroline Sarah Darwin (1800–1888), married Josiah Wedgwood (grandson of the first Josiah Wedgwood)
- Susan Elizabeth Darwin (1803–1866)
- Erasmus Alvey Darwin (1804–1881)
- Charles Robert Darwin (1809–1882) (see below)
- Emily Catherine Darwin (1810–1866), was Charles Langton's second wife.

Josiah Wedgwood

Josiah Wedgwood (1769 – 1843) was the son of the first Josiah Wedgwood, and Member of Parliament for Stoke-on-Trent. He married Elizabeth Allen (1764–1846) and they had nine children:

- Sarah Elizabeth Wedgwood (1793-1880).
- Josiah Wedgwood; (1795 – 1880) married Caroline Darwin, daughter of Robert Darwin and Susannah Wedgwood. They are grandparents of Ralph Vaughan Williams.
- Mary Ann Wedgwood (1796-1798).

Figure 5: *Josiah Wedgwood (1769–1843)*

- Charlotte Wedgwood (1797–1862) was Charles Langton's first wife. After her death he married her cousin, Emily Catherine Darwin; she is the ancestor of Hugh Massingberd, see below.
- Henry Allen Wedgwood (1799–1885).
- Francis Wedgwood (1800–1888); married 26 April 1832 at Rolleston on Dove, Staffordshire Frances Mosley daughter of Rev. John Peploe Mosley and Sarah Maria Paget and granddaughter of Sir John Parker Mosley and Elizabeth Bayley; and was the grandfather of Josiah Wedgwood, 1st Baron Wedgwood and great-grandfather of CV Wedgwood and Camilla Wedgwood.
- Hensleigh Wedgwood (1803–1891), etymologist, philologist and barrister, author of *A Dictionary of English Etymology* father of Frances Julia Wedgwood (1833–1913), and grandfather of Bishop J. I. Wedgwood. His wife, his first cousin on his mother's side, Frances (Fanny) Wedgwood née Mackintosh (1800–1889, daughter of James Mackintosh), was a good friend and correspondent of Harriet Martineau.
- Frances (Fanny) Wedgwood (1806-1832).
- Emma Wedgwood (1808–1896); married Charles Darwin, son of Robert Darwin and Susannah Wedgwood.

Thomas Wedgwood

Thomas Wedgwood (1771–1805). Pioneer in developing photography. Son of Josiah Wedgwood.

Figure 6: *Samuel Tertius Galton.*

Samuel Tertius Galton

Samuel Tertius Galton married Frances Anne Violetta Darwin, (1783–1874) daughter of Erasmus Darwin, see above. They had three sons and four daughters including:

- Erasmus Galton (1815–1909), Lord of the Manor of Loxton.
- Francis Galton (1822–1911) – Inventor, polymath and father of eugenics. He married Louisa Jane Butler (1822–1897) during 1853 but their union was childless.

Sir Francis Sacheverel Darwin

Sir Francis Sacheverel Darwin was the son of Erasmus Darwin and Elizabeth (née Collier), daughter of Charles Colyear, 2nd Earl of Portmore. Francis was an accomplished travel writer, explorer and naturalist and bravely studied the ravages of the plague on Smyrna at great personal risk. He was the only one to return of his friends who went to the East. A physician to George III, he was knighted by George IV.

On 16 December 1815 he married Jane Harriet Ryle (11 December 1794 – 19 April 1866) at St. George, Hanover Square London. They had many children including:

Figure 7: *Sir Francis Sacheverel Darwin.*

- Mary Jane Darwin (12 February 1817 – 1872), married Charles Carill-Worsley of Platt Hall, near Manchester, in 1840. (Their daughter, Elizabeth, who married Nicolas Tindal, later Tindal-Carill-Worsley, was the mother of Charles and Ralph Tindal-Carill-Worsley – see under 5th generation).
- Frances Sarah Darwin (19 July 1822 – 1881), married Gustavus Barton in 1845, widowed 1846 and remarried to Marcus Huish during 1849. She is the stepmother of the art dealer Marcus Bourne Huish.
- Edward Levett Darwin (12 April 1821 – 23 April 1901), married Harriett Jessopp during 1850. A solicitor in Matlock Bath, Derbyshire, Edward Levett Darwin was the author, using the pseudonym "High Elms", of *Gameskeeper's Manual*, a guide for tending game on large estates which shows keen observation of the habits of various animals.

Figure 8: *Charles Darwin.*

The third generation

Charles Darwin

The most prominent member of the family, Charles Darwin, proposed the first coherent theory of evolution by means of natural and sexual selection.

Charles Robert Darwin (1809–1882) was a son of Robert Waring Darwin and Susannah Wedgwood. He married Emma Wedgwood, (1808–1896) a daughter of Josiah Wedgwood II and Elizabeth Allen. Charles's mother, Susannah, was a sister to Emma's father, Josiah II. Thus, Charles and Emma were first cousins.

The Darwins had ten children, three of whom died before reaching maturity.

- William Erasmus Darwin (1839–1914); graduate of Christ's College Cambridge, he was a banker in Southampton. He married an American Sara Sedgwick (1839–1902), but they did not have any children.
- Anne Elizabeth Darwin (1841–1851) died in Great Malvern aged ten and her death caused her father much grief.
- Mary Eleanor Darwin (1842–1842) died as a baby.

Figure 9: *Emma Darwin (née Wedgwood).*

- Henrietta Emma "Etty" Darwin (1843–1927); although she married Richard Litchfield during 1871, the couple never had any children. Etty Darwin edited her mother's private papers (published during 1904) and assisted her father with his work.
- George Howard Darwin (1845–1912) (see below)
- Elizabeth (Bessy) Darwin (1847–1926); never married and did not have any progeny.
- Francis Darwin (1848–1925) (see below).
- Leonard Darwin (1850–1943) (see below).
- Horace Darwin (1851–1928) (see below).
- Charles Waring Darwin (1856–1858) was the tenth child and sixth son of Charles and Emma Darwin. His early death from scarlet fever kept Charles Darwin from attending the first publication of his theory at the joint reading of papers by Alfred Russel Wallace and himself at the meeting of the Linnean Society on 1 July 1858. Wallace was not present either; he was on an expedition.

Figure 10: *William Darwin Fox (1805–1880)*

Ancestry of Charles Darwin

Ancestors of Darwin–Wedgwood family

Other notables from the same period

William Darwin Fox

The Rev. William Darwin Fox (1805–1880) was a second cousin of Charles Darwin and an amateur entomologist, naturalist and palaeontologist. Fox became a lifelong friend of Charles Darwin after their first meeting at Christ's College, Cambridge. He married Harriet Fletcher, who gave him five children, and after her death married Ellen Sophia Woodd, who provided the remainder of his 17 children.

After his graduation from Cambridge during 1829, Fox was appointed as the Vicar of Osmaston and during 1838 became the Rector of Delamere, a living he retained until his retirement during 1873.

The fourth generation

George Howard Darwin

George Howard Darwin (1845–1912) was an astronomer and mathematician. He married Martha (Maud) du Puy of Philadelphia. They had five children:
- Charles Galton Darwin (see below).
- William Robert Darwin (married Sarah Monica Slingsby).
- Gwendoline "Gwen" Darwin, artist; (see below).
- Leonard Darwin 1899.
- Margaret Elizabeth Darwin (married Sir Geoffrey Keynes, bibliophile) (see below).

Francis Darwin

Francis Darwin (1848–1925) was the botanist son of Charles Darwin and Emma Darwin (née Wedgwood). Francis Darwin married Amy Ruck during 1874, who died during 1876 after the birth of their son Bernard Darwin, an author on golf – see below. Francis married Ellen Crofts during September 1883 and they had a daughter Frances Crofts, who married and became known as the poet Frances Cornford (see below). During 1913 he married his third wife Florence Henrietta Darwin (née Fisher); there were no children of this marriage, but he became step-father to Fredegond Shove née Maitland and Ermengard Maitland.

He is buried at the Parish of the Ascension Burial Ground in Cambridge,[2] where he is interred in the same grave as his daughter Frances Cornford. His third wife and his brother Sir Horace Darwin and his wife Lady 'Ida' are interred in the same graveyard, as well as his step-daughter Fredegond Shove but not her sister Ermengard Maitland.

Leonard Darwin

Leonard Darwin (1850–1943) was variously an army officer, Member of Parliament and eugenicist who corresponded with Ronald Fisher, thus being the link between the two great evolutionary biologists.

Horace Darwin

Horace Darwin (1851–1928) and Ida Darwin (1854–1946) had the following children:
- Nora Darwin, married Sir Alan Barlow (see below).
- Ruth Darwin.
- Erasmus Darwin.

He is buried at the Parish of the Ascension Burial Ground in Cambridge, with his wife. His brother Sir Francis Darwin is interred in the same graveyard.

The fifth generation

Charles Galton Darwin

Charles Galton Darwin 1887–1962 was the son of George Howard Darwin (see above) and was a noted physicist of the age, and Director of the National Physics Laboratory. His son George Pember Darwin (1928–2001) married Angela Huxley, great granddaughter of Thomas Huxley.

Gwen Raverat (née Darwin)

Gwen Raverat (1885–1957) was the daughter of George Howard Darwin and was an artist. She married the French artist Jacques Raverat during 1911 and had daughters Elizabeth Hambro and Sophie Pryor, later Gurney. Her childhood memoir, *Period Piece*, contains illustrations of and anecdotes about many of the Darwin—Wedgwood clan.

Margaret Keynes (née Darwin)

Margaret Keynes (1890–1974) was the daughter of George Howard Darwin, (see above). She married Geoffrey Keynes, brother of the economist John Maynard Keynes (see Keynes family) and had sons Richard Keynes, Quentin Keynes, Milo Keynes and Stephen Keynes, and a daughter Harriet Frances.

Bernard Darwin

Bernard Darwin (1876–1961) was a golf writer. He married Elinor Monsell (died 1954) during 1906, and they had a son Robert Vere Darwin (7 May 1910 – 30 January 1974), and daughters Ursula Mommens (20 August 1908 – 30 January 2010), and Nicola Mary Elizabeth Darwin, later Hughes (1916–1976).

Frances Cornford (née Darwin)

Frances Cornford (1886–1960) Poet, daughter of Francis Darwin, see above, known to the family as 'FCC'; she was married to Francis Cornford, known to the family as 'FMC'. She is buried at the Parish of the Ascension Burial Ground in Cambridge, where she is in the same grave as her father Sir Francis Darwin. Her late husband, Francis, was cremated at Cambridge Crematorium on 6 January 1943, and his ashes are presumed to be interred in the same grave.

Ralph Vaughan Williams

Ralph Vaughan Williams (1872–1958), British composer. His maternal grandmother, Caroline Sarah Darwin, was Charles Darwin's older sister, and his maternal grandfather, Josiah Wedgwood III, was the older brother of Darwin's wife Emma.

Nora Barlow (née Darwin)

Nora Darwin (1885–1989), the daughter of Horace Darwin (see above), married Sir Alan Barlow. She also edited the *Autobiography of Charles Darwin* (<templatestyles src="Module:Citation/CS1/styles.css" />ISBN 0393310698 (hardback) and <templatestyles src="Module:Citation/CS1/styles.css" />ISBN 0-393-00487-2 (paperback)). They had the following six children:

- Joan Helen Barlow, (26 May 1912 – 21 February 1954).
- Sir Thomas Erasmus Barlow, (23 January 1914 – 12 October 2003), Royal Navy officer.
- Erasmus Darwin Barlow (1915–2005).
- Andrew Dalmahoy Barlow (1916–2006).
- Professor Horace Basil Barlow (born 1921). (see below)
- Hilda Horatia Barlow (born 14 September 1919) married psychoanalyst John Hunter Padel; their daughter is the poet Ruth Padel (see below).

Josiah Wedgwood, 1st Baron Wedgwood

Josiah Wedgwood (1872–1943), great-great-grandson of Josiah Wedgwood I, was a Liberal and Labour MP, and served in the military during the Second Boer War and the First World War. He was granted a peerage during 1942.

Charles Tindal-Carill-Worsley

Capt Charles Tindal-Carill-Worsley, RN, (died 1920) a great grandson of Sir Francis Sacheverel Darwin, served on the Royal Yacht HMY Victoria and Albert III during the reign of King Edward VII, before a successful career in the First World War, where he was commander of HMS Prince George during the Gallipoli Campaign of 1915 He was appointed Chevalier of the Legion of Honour by the President of France during 1918.

Ralph Tindal-Carill-Worsley

Cmdr Ralph Tindal-Carill-Worsley, RN, (1886–1966), brother of Charles, naval officer and bon viveur, served on the Royal Yacht with his brother, before serving in the Battle of Jutland in World War I. He retired from the Royal Navy after the First World War but was recalled during World War II, when he was commandant of a training school for WRENS[3] (members of the Women's Royal Naval Service). He married Kathleen, daughter of Simon Mangan of Dunboyne Castle, Lord Lieutenant of Meath and a first cousin of Brig. General Paul Kenna, VC, and had three children.

Sir Ralph Wedgwood, 1st Baronet

Sir Ralph L. Wedgwood, 1st Baronet CB CMG (2 March 1874 – 5 September 1956), railway executive, son of Clement Wedgwood.

The sixth generation

Erasmus Darwin Barlow

Erasmus Darwin Barlow (1915–2005) was a psychiatrist, physiologist and businessman. Son of Nora Barlow.

Horace Barlow

Horace Barlow (born 1921) was Professor of Physiology, Berkeley, California, US; Royal Society Research Professor, Physiological Laboratory, Cambridge (1973–87).

John Cornford

John Cornford (1915–1936), was a poet and member of the International Brigades died during the Spanish Civil War. Son of Francis and Frances Cornford, see above.

Christopher Cornford

Christopher Cornford (1917–1993), was an artist and writer. Son of Francis and Frances Cornford, see above.

George Erasmus Darwin (Ras)

George Erasmus Darwin (1927-2017) was a metallurgist and was the father of Robert Darwin, Chris Darwin and Sarah Darwin.

Henry Galton Darwin

Henry Galton Darwin (1929–1992) was a lawyer and diplomat. Son of Charles Galton Darwin.

Robin Darwin

Robert Vere "Robin" Darwin (1910–1974) was an artist. He is the son of Bernard Darwin, see above.

Quentin Keynes

Quentin Keynes (1921–2003) was a bibliophile and explorer. Son of Margaret Keynes, née Darwin, see above.

Richard Keynes

Professor Richard Darwin Keynes FRS (1919–2010) was a British physiologist. Son of Margaret Keynes, née Darwin, see above.

Ursula Mommens

Ursula Mommens (née Darwin, first married name Trevelyan) (1908–2010) was a well-known potter. Daughter of Bernard Darwin, see above. Her son by Julian Trevelyan is the movie-maker Philip Trevelyan.

Geoffrey Tindal-Carill-Worsley

Air Commodore Geoffrey Tindal-Carill-Worsley (1908–1996) was a Royal Air Force officer during the Second World War. Nephew of Charles and Ralph Tindal-Carill-Worsley.

Nicolas Tindal-Carill-Worsley

Group Captain Nicolas Tindal-Carill-Worsley (1911–2006) was a RAF bomber pilot during the Second World War (known as Nicolas Tindal). Son of Ralph Tindal-Carill-Worsley.

Camilla Wedgwood

Camilla Wedgwood (1901–1955), anthropologist, was the daughter of Josiah Wedgwood, 1st Baron Wedgwood (see above).

Cicely Veronica (CV) Wedgwood

Cicely Veronica Wedgwood (1910–1997), historian. Daughter of Ralph Wedgwood

The seventh generation

Martin Thomas Barlow

Martin T. Barlow (born 1953) is a mathematician; son of Andrew Dalmahoy Barlow.

Phyllida Barlow

Phyllida Barlow (born 1944) is a sculptor and art academic; daughter of Erasmus Darwin Barlow.

Matthew Chapman

Matthew Chapman (born 1950), screenwriter, author, grandson of Frances Cornford, see above.

Adam Cornford

Adam Cornford (born 1950), is a poet and essayist. Son of Christopher Cornford, see above.

Robert George Darwin

Robert George Darwin (born 1959), computer scientist, son of George Erasmus Darwin, brother of Chris Darwin and Sarah Darwin, see below.

Carola Darwin

Carola Darwin (born 1967), musician, granddaughter of Charles Galton Darwin, see above, and sister of Emma Darwin the novelist, see below.

Chris Darwin

Chris Darwin (born 1961), conservationist and adventurer, son of George Erasmus Darwin, see above, and brother of Sarah Darwin and Robert Darwin, see below.

Emma Darwin

Emma Darwin (Novelist) (born 1964), novelist, granddaughter of Charles Galton Darwin, see above.

Sarah Darwin

Sarah Darwin (born 1964), botanist, daughter of George Erasmus Darwin, see above, and sister of Chris Darwin and Robert Darwin, see above.

Randal Keynes

Randal Keynes (born 1948), conservationist and author, son of Richard Keynes, see above.

Simon Keynes

Simon Keynes (born 1952), Elrington and Bosworth Professor of Anglo-Saxon in the Department of Anglo-Saxon, Norse, and Celtic at Cambridge University, son of Richard Keynes, see above, and brother of Randal Keynes, see above.

Hugh Massingberd

Hugh Massingberd (1947–2007) was an obituaries editor for the *Daily Telegraph*, a journalist and the author of many books on genealogy and architectural history. He was the great grandson of Emily Langton Massingberd, and the great great grandson of Charlotte Langton (née Wedgwood), sister of Emma Darwin (Charles Darwin's wife) and granddaughter of Josiah Wedgwood I.[4,5]

Ruth Padel

Ruth Padel (born 1946), poet, granddaughter of Sir Alan and Lady (Nora) Barlow (née Darwin), see above.

R. Sebastian 'Bas' Pease

R. Sebastian 'Bas' Pease (1922–2004), physicist, Director of Culham Laboratory for Plasma Physics and Nuclear Fusion (1968–1981), manager of the British chapter of the Pugwash Conferences on Science and World Affairs, grandson of the fourth Josiah Wedgwood (see above). His sister, Jocelyn Richenda 'Chenda' Gammell Pease (1925–2003), married Andrew Huxley.

William Pryor

William Pryor (born 1945), memoirist, entrepreneur, screenwriter, grandson of Gwen Raverat (née Darwin), see above. He featured as a contestant on Dragons Den during 2017.

Lucy Rawlinson

Lucy Rawlinson (née Pryor) (born 1948), painter (as Lucy Raverat), granddaughter of Gwen Raverat (née Darwin), see above.

The eighth generation

Skandar Keynes

Skandar Keynes (born 1991), actor, played Edmund in The Chronicles of Narnia (film series), son of Randal Keynes.

Paula Darwin

Paula Darwin (born 1997) Daughter of Robert Darwin.

Ralph Wedgwood

Ralph Wedgwood, philosopher, great-grandson of Ralph L. Wedgwood.[6]

Neneh Darwin

Neneh Darwin (born 1991), Australian environment campaigner.

Intermarriage

There was a notable history of intermarriage within the family. During the period being discussed, Josiah Wedgwood married his third cousin Sarah Wedgwood; Charles Darwin married his first cousin Emma Wedgwood; his sister, Caroline Darwin, married Emma's brother (and Caroline's first cousin), Josiah Wedgwood III. There were other instances of cousin marriage as well. Cousin marriage was not uncommon in Britain during the 19th century though why is debated: poorer communications, keeping wealth within the family, more opportunity of evaluating a relative of the opposite sex as a suitable marriage partner (unmarried young women of the upper and upper middle classes were closely chaperoned when meeting men outside the family during the 19th century), more security for the woman as she would not be leaving her family (though legal rights for married women increased during the century, as a rule her property became his and she had little legal recourse if he chose to abuse her).

Coat of arms

These arms were granted to Reginald Darwin, of Fern, Derbyshire, for himself and certain descendants of his father, Sir Francis Sacheverel Darwin, and his uncle Robert Waring Darwin (Father of Charles), on 6 March 1890. As Charles Darwin was part of the destination, they have been used in association with him, despite being granted after his death. Something similar is used by Darwin College, Cambridge.

Coat of arms of Reginal Darwin

Notes	The arms of Reginald Darwin (1818 – 1892) and his heirs consist of:
Crest	Upon a wreath of the colours, in front of a demi-griffin Vert, holding between the claws an escallop Or, three escallops fesswise Argent.
Escutcheon	Argent, on a bend Gules cottised Vert, between two mullets each within an annulet Gules, three escallops Or.
Motto	Cave et aude (*Beware and dare*)

References

- Milner, Richard (1994). *Charles Darwin: Evolution of a Naturalist*. Makers of Modern Science. New York City: Facts on File, Inc. ISBN 0-8160-2557-6.<templatestyles src="Module:Citation/CS1/styles.css"></templatestyles>
- Freeman, Richard Broke (1982). "The Darwin family". *Biological Journal of the Linnean Society*. **17** (1): 9–21. doi:10.1111/j.1095-8312.1982.tb02010.x[7].<templatestyles src="Module:Citation/CS1/styles.css"></templatestyles>
- Berra, Tim; Alvarez, Gonzalo; Shannon, Kate (September 2010). "The Galton–Darwin–Wedgwood Pedigree of H. H. Laughlin"[8]. *Biological Journal of the Linnean Society*. **101** (1): 228–241. doi:10.1111/j.1095-8312.2010.01529.x[9]. Retrieved 16 July 2015.<templatestyles src="Module:Citation/CS1/styles.css"></templatestyles>

External links

- http://www.wedgwood.org.uk/Darwin.html
- http://darwin-online.org.uk/content/frameset?itemID=F1319&viewtype=image&pageseq=6

Charles Darwin's Education

Charles Darwin's education

Charles Darwin's education gave him a foundation in the doctrine of Creation prevalent throughout the West at the time, as well as knowledge of medicine and theology. More significantly, it led to his interest in natural history, which culminated in his taking part in the second voyage of the *Beagle* and the eventual inception of his theory of natural selection. Although Darwin changed his field of interest several times in these formative years, many of his later discoveries and beliefs were foreshadowed by the influences he had as a youth.

Background and influences

Born in 1809, Charles Darwin grew up in a conservative era when repression of revolutionary Radicalism had displaced the 18th century Enlightenment. The Church of England dominated the English scientific establishment. The Church saw natural history as revealing God's underlying plan and as supporting the existing social hierarchy. It rejected Enlightenment philosophers such as David Hume who had argued for naturalism and against belief in God.

The discovery of fossils of extinct species was explained by theories such as catastrophism. Catastrophism claimed that animals and plants were periodically annihilated as a result of natural catastrophes and then replaced by new species created *ex nihilo* (out of nothing). The extinct organisms could then be observed in the fossil record, and their replacements were considered to be immutable.

Darwin's extended family of Darwins and Wedgwoods was strongly Unitarian. One of his grandfathers, Erasmus Darwin, was a successful physician, and was followed in this by his sons Charles Darwin, who died while still a promising medical student at the University of Edinburgh in 1778, and Doctor Robert Darwin, Darwin's father, who named his son after his deceased brother.

Figure 11: *Erasmus Darwin, Charles Darwin's paternal grandfather, helped influence Darwin's later religious views.*

Erasmus was a freethinker who hypothesized that all warm-blooded animals sprang from a single living "filament" long, long ago. He further proposed evolution by acquired characteristics, anticipating the theory later developed by Jean-Baptiste Lamarck. Although Charles was born after his grandfather Erasmus died, his father Robert found the texts an invaluable medical guide and Charles read them as a student. Doctor Robert also followed Erasmus in being a freethinker, but as a wealthy society physician was more discreet and attended the Church of England patronised by his clients.

Childhood

Charles Robert Darwin was born in Shrewsbury, Shropshire, England on 12 February 1809 at his family home, the Mount, He was the fifth of six children of wealthy society doctor and financier Robert Darwin, and Susannah Darwin (*née* Wedgwood). Both families were largely Unitarian, though the Wedgwoods were adopting Anglicanism. Robert Darwin, himself quietly a freethinker, had baby Charles baptised on 15 November 1809 in the Anglican St Chad's Church, Shrewsbury, but Charles and his siblings attended the Unitarian chapel with their mother.[10]

Figure 12: *The seven-year-old Charles Darwin in 1816, a year before the sudden loss of his mother.*

As a young child at The Mount, Darwin avidly collected animal shells, postal franks, bird's eggs, pebbles and minerals. He was very fond of gardening, an interest his father shared and encouraged, and would follow the family gardener around. Early in 1817, soon after becoming eight years old, he started at the small local school run by a Unitarian minister, the Reverend George Case. At home, Charles learned to ride ponies, shoot and fish. Influenced by his father's fashionable interest in natural history, he tried to make out the names of plants, and was given by his father two elementary natural history books. Childhood games included inventing and writing out complex secret codes. Charles would tell elaborate stories to his family and friends "for the pure pleasure of attracting attention & surprise", including hoaxes such as pretending to find apples he'd hidden earlier, and what he later called the "monstrous fable" which persuaded his schoolfriend that the colour of primula flowers could be changed by dosing them with special water. However, his father benignly ignored these passing games, and Charles later recounted that he stopped them because no-one paid any attention.

In July 1817 his mother died after the sudden onset of violent stomach pains and amidst the grief his older sisters had to take charge, with their father continuing to dominate the household whenever he returned from his doctor's rounds. To the $8\ ^1/_2$-year-old Charles this situation was not a great change, as his mother had frequently been ill and her available time taken up by social duties, so his upbringing had largely been in the hands of his three older sisters who were nearly adults by then. In later years he had difficulty in remembering his mother, and his only memory of her death and funeral was of the children being sent for and going into her room, and his "Father meeting us crying afterwards".

As had been planned previously, in September 1818 Charles joined his older brother Erasmus Alvey Darwin (nicknamed "Eras") in staying as a boarder at the Shrewsbury School, where he loathed the required rote learning, and would try to visit home when he could. He continued collecting minerals and insects, and family holidays in Wales brought Charles new opportunities, but an older sister ruled that "it was not right to kill insects" for his collections, and he had to find dead ones. He read Gilbert White's *The Natural History and Antiquities of Selborne* and took up birdwatching. Eras took an interest in chemistry and Charles became his assistant, with the two using a garden shed at their home fitted out as a laboratory and extending their interests to crystallography. When Eras went on to a medical course at the University of Cambridge, Charles continued to rush home to the shed on weekends, and for this received the nickname "Gas". The headmaster was not amused at this diversion from studying the classics, calling him a *poco curante* (trifler) in front of the boys. At fifteen, his interest shifted to hunting and bird-shooting at local estates, particularly at Maer in Staffordshire, the home of his relatives, the Wedgwoods. His exasperated father once told him off, saying "You care for nothing but shooting, dogs, and rat-catching, and you will be a disgrace to yourself and all your family."

His father decided that he should leave school earlier than usual, and in 1825 at the age of sixteen Charles was to go along with his brother who was to attend the University of Edinburgh for a year to obtain medical qualifications. Charles spent the summer as an apprentice doctor, helping his father with treating the poor of Shropshire. He had half a dozen patients of his own, and would note their symptoms for his father to make up the prescriptions.

University of Edinburgh

Darwin went to Edinburgh University in October 1825 to study medicine, accompanied by Eras doing his external hospital study. The brothers took lodgings at 11 Lothian Street, near the University. The city was in an uproar over political and religious controversies, and the competitive system where professors were dependent on attracting student fees for income meant that the university was riven with argumentative feuds and conflicts. The monopoly held by established medical professors was challenged by private independent

Charles Darwin's education

Figure 13: *Darwin attended the University of Edinburgh to study medicine, at a time when the new buildings it occupied (the Old College) were still under construction. South College Street, to the left of the picture, connects to Lothian Street.*

Figure 14: *Plaque in Lothian Street, indicating where Darwin lived while studying at Edinburgh*

schools, with new ideas of teaching by dissecting corpses giving clandestine trade to bodysnatchers (just shortly before the Burke and Hare scandal).

He attended the official university lectures, but complained that most were stupid and boring, and found himself too sensitive to the sight of blood. He was disgusted by the dull and outdated anatomy lectures of professor Alexander Monro *tertius*, and later regretted his failure to persevere and learn dissection. Munro's lectures included vehement opposition to George Combe's daringly materialist ideas of phrenology. As the exception to the general dullness, the spectacular chemistry lectures of Thomas Charles Hope were greatly enjoyed by the brothers, but they did not join a student society giving hands-on experience. Darwin regularly attended clinical wards in the hospital despite his great distress about some of the cases, but could only bear to attend surgical operations twice, rushing away before they were completed due to his distress at the brutality of surgery before anaesthetics. He was long haunted by the memory, particularly of an operation on a child.

The brothers kept each other company, and made extensive use of the library. Darwin's reading included novels and Boswell's *Life of Johnson*. He had brought natural history books with him, including a copy of *A Naturalist's Companion* by George Graves, bought in August in anticipation of seeing the seaside, and he borrowed similar books from the library. The brothers went for regular Sunday walks on the shores of the Firth of Forth and Darwin kept a diary recording their finds, which included a sea mouse and a cuttlefish.

Darwin wrote home that "I am going to learn to stuff birds, from a blackamoor... he only charges one guinea, for an hour every day for two months". These lessons in taxidermy were with the freed black slave John Edmonstone, who also lived in Lothian Street. Darwin often sat with him to hear tales of the South American rain-forest of Guyana, and later remembered him as "a very pleasant and intelligent man."

During his summer holiday Charles read *Zoönomia* by his grandfather Erasmus Darwin, which his father valued for medical guidance but which also proposed evolution by acquired characteristics. In June he went on a walking tour in North Wales.

Lamarckian anatomy

In his second year Charles became active in student societies for naturalists. The 21-year-old radical demagogue William A. F. Browne and the 19-year-old John Coldstream both proposed Darwin for membership of the Plinian Society on 21 November 1826. John Coldstream came from an evangelical background and shared Darwin's fascination with sea life. Darwin was elected to its Council on 5 December, and at the same meeting Browne presented an attack on Charles Bell's *Anatomy and Physiology of Expression* (which in 1872 Darwin would target in *The Expression of the Emotions in Man and Animals*).

Darwin became a keen student of Robert Edmond Grant, a Lamarckian anatomist. Grant had cited Erasmus Darwin in his doctoral thesis and shared the evolutionist ideas of Étienne Geoffroy Saint-Hilaire on evolution by acquired characteristics. Charles joined Grant in pioneering investigations of the life cycle of marine invertebrates on the shores of the Firth of Forth. Darwin and Grant collected tiny animals from the rock pools and walked along the rocky shore at Prestonpans, where Grant lived during the winter at Walford House. Grant began taking Darwin as a guest to professor Robert Jameson's Wernerian Natural History Society. There Charles saw John James Audubon lecturing on the habits of North American birds. In the April–October 1826 edition of the quarterly *Edinburgh New Philosophical Journal* edited by Jameson, an anonymous paper praised "Mr. Lamarck, one of the most sagacious naturalists of our day" for having "expressed himself in the most unambiguous manner. He admits, on the one hand, the existence of the simplest infusory animals; on the other, the existence of the simplest worms, by means of spontaneous generation, that is, by an aggregation process of animal elements; and maintains, that all other animals, by the operation of external circumstances, are evolved from these in a double series, and in a gradual manner."[11] – this was the first use of the word "evolved" in a modern sense. Though some have attributed authorship to Jameson, this is hotly contested and others see Grant as having written it, as the first significant statement to relate Lamarck's concepts to the geological record of living organisms of the past.

Darwin made a discovery new to science when he observed cilia moving the microscopic larvae of a species of the bryozoan *Flustra*. He rushed to tell Grant, confirming Grant's belief that the larvae of these marine animals were free swimming, but was upset when Grant claimed rights to the work. Darwin also made the discovery that black spores often found in oyster shells were the eggs of a skate leech, and was disappointed when Grant announced both finds to the *Wernerian* on 24 March 1827 without giving Darwin credit, though Grant in his publication about the leech eggs in the *Edinburgh Journal of Science* later that year acknowledged "The merit of having first ascertained them to belong to that animal is due to my zealous young friend Mr Charles Darwin of Shrewsbury", the first time Darwin's name appeared in print. Darwin made a presentation of both discoveries to the Plinian Society on 27 March, his first public presentation. Later in the meeting Browne argued that mind and consciousness were simply aspects of brain activity, not "souls" or spiritual entities separate from the body. A furious debate ensued, and later someone deleted all mention of this materialist heresy from the minutes. This was Darwin's first exposure to militant freethought and the storm it stirred up.

During their walks Grant expounded his ideas to Darwin, and on one occasion dropped his guard and praised Lamarck's views on evolution. He explained his radical theory of *homology*, an extension of the idea of *unity of plan* in vogue in Paris at the time. He argued that all animals had similar organs differing only in complexity and, controversially, that this showed their common descent. Grant had announced to the *Wernerian* his identification of the pancreas in a pinned-out sea-slug, showing an organ molluscs shared with mammals. He assumed that as the earth cooled, changing conditions drove life towards higher, hotter blooded forms, as shown by a progressive sequence of fossils, and that study of eggs of the simplest creatures would help reveal *monads*, elementary living particles. While this showed that naturalists could try to "lift the veil that hangs over the origin and progress of the organic world", Darwin was troubled by Grant's atheism and could see that transmutation was far from respectable. Darwin later recalled "I listened in silent astonishment, and as far as I can judge, without any effect on my mind. I had previously read the Zoönomia of my grandfather, in which similar views are maintained, but without producing any effect on me."

Shortly afterwards Coldstream graduated and went to Paris for his hospital study, where he suffered a mental breakdown, struggling with "the foul mass of corruption within my own bosom", held captive to his body by "corroding desires" and "lustful imaginations". The doctor's report was that though Coldstream had led "a blameless life", he was "more or less in the dark on the vital question of religion, and was troubled with doubts arising from certain Materialist views, which are, alas!, too common among medical students".

Geology and *Origin of the Species*

Darwin also took the popular natural history course of Professor Robert Jameson, learning about stratigraphic geology. Jameson was a Neptunian geologist who taught that strata had precipitated from a universal ocean: he held debates with chemistry professor Thomas Charles Hope who held that granites had crystallised from molten crust, ideas influenced by the Plutonism of James Hutton who had been Hope's friend. Jameson's view was that "It would be a misfortune if we all had the same way of thinking... Dr Hope is decidedly opposed to me, and I am opposed to Dr Hope, and between us we make the subject interesting." Darwin liked Hope and found Jameson a boring speaker. It is not known what he made of Jameson's closing lectures on the *"Origin of the Species of Animals"*. Darwin enjoyed practicals in the Museum and course field trips, learning the sequence of strata. The Museum of Edinburgh University was Jameson's preserve and was then one of the largest in Europe. Darwin assisted and made full use of the collections, spending hours studying, taking notes and stuffing animal specimens.

Figure 15: *The coat of arms of Christ's College, Cambridge, a college of the University of Cambridge where Darwin was enrolled to become a clergyman.*

Even medical lectures proved of some use. In January 1826 Darwin had written home complaining of "a long stupid lecture" from Dr. Andrew Duncan *secundus* about medicine, but the lectures introduced him to Augustin de Candolle's *natural system* of classification and emphasis on the "war" between competing species. However, he loathed medicine and left in April 1827 without a degree.

He toured Scotland, went on to Belfast and Dublin and in May made his first trip to London to visit his sister Caroline. They joined his uncle Josiah Wedgwood II on a trip to France. There Charles fended for himself for a few weeks in Paris with Browne and Coldstream who was recovering having "found joy and peace in believing". Charles rejoined his relations and then returned to his home at Shrewsbury, Shropshire by July.

University of Cambridge

His father was unhappy that his younger son would not become a physician and "was very properly vehement against my turning an idle sporting man, which then seemed my probable destination." He therefore enrolled Charles at Christ's College, Cambridge in 1827 for a Bachelor of Arts degree as the qualification required before taking a specialised divinity course and becoming an Anglican parson. He enrolled for an *ordinary* degree, as at that time only capable mathematicians would take the Tripos. At that time the only way to get an honours degree was the mathematical Tripos examination, or the classical Tripos created in 1822, which was only open to those who already had high honours in mathematics, or those who were the sons of peers.

This was a respectable career for a gentleman at a time when most naturalists in England were clergymen in the tradition of Gilbert White, who saw it as part of their duties to "explore the wonders of God's creation". Charles had concerns about being able to declare his belief in all the dogmas of the Church of England, so as well as hunting and fishing, he studied divinity books. He was particularly convinced by the reasoning of the Revd. John Bird Sumner's *Evidences of Christianity*. John Bird Summer wrote that Jesus's religion was "wonderfully suitable... to our ideas of happiness in this & the next world" and there was "no other way... of explaining the series of evidence & probability." His Classics had lapsed since school, and he spent the autumn term at home studying Greek with a tutor. Darwin was accepted as a "pensioner", having paid his fees, on 15 October 1827, but did not attend Cambridge until the Lent Term which began on 13 January 1828. Eras returned from Edinburgh ready to sit his Bachelor of Medicine exam, and in the new year he and Charles set out together for Cambridge. Darwin came into residence in Cambridge on 26 January 1828, and matriculated at the University's Senate House on 26 February.

His tutors at Christ's College, Cambridge were to include Joseph Shaw in 1828, John Graham (in 1829 - 1830) and Edward John Ash in 1830 - 1831. One of his university friends was Frederick Watkins, (1808 - 1888).

Beetle collecting

Arriving at the University of Cambridge in January 1828, Darwin found this elite theological training institution governed by complex rules much more congenial than his experiences at Edinburgh. No rooms were available at Christ's College, so he took lodgings above a tobacconists in Sidney Street, across the road. Extramural activities were important, and while Darwin did not take up sports or debating, his interests included music and his main passion was the current national craze for the (competitive) collecting of beetles. Trainee clergymen scoured Cambridgeshire for specimens, referring to *An Introduction to Entomology* by William Kirby and William Spence. Charles joined his older cousin William Darwin Fox who was already a skilled collector and like him got a small dog. The two and their dogs became inseparable. They explored the countryside as Darwin learnt about natural history from his cousin. Darwin became obsessed with winning the student accolade and collected avidly. Once he stripped bark from a dead tree and caught a ground beetle in each hand, then saw the rare Crucifix Ground Beetle, *Panagaeus cruxmajor*. With the habits of an egg-collector, he popped one ground beetle in his mouth to free his hand, but it ejected some intensely acrid fluid which burnt his tongue and Darwin was forced to spit it out. He lost all three.[12] The specimens he did not lose had to be mounted and identified, and his knowledge from Edinburgh of Lamarck proved useful. Fox introduced him for advice on identification to the Revd. John Stevens Henslow, professor of botany, and Darwin began attending his soirées, a club for budding naturalists. Here he could meet other professors including the geologist the Revd. Adam Sedgwick and the new mineralogist the Revd. William Whewell.

In the summer Darwin paid visits to Squire Owen, and romance seemed to be blossoming with the squire's daughter Fanny. Darwin joined other Cambridge friends on a three-month "reading party" at Barmouth on the coast of Wales to revise their studies with private tutors. For Charles it was an "Entomo-Mathematical expedition". Though he badly needed to catch up with his mathematics, the insect collecting predominated along with pleasant diversions such as hillwalking, boating and fly fishing. He went on daily walks with his close friend, the older student John Maurice Herbert who he dubbed "Cherbury" after Herbert of Cherbury, the father of English Deism. Herbert assisted with the insect collecting, but the usual outcome was that Darwin would examine Herbert's collecting bottle and say "Well, old Cherbury, none of these will do." In September Darwin wrote to tell "My dear old *Cherbury*" that his own catches had included "some of the rarest of the British Insects, & their being found near Barmouth is quite unknown to the Entomological world: I think I shall write & inform some of the crack Entomologists." He described these *"extremely rare"* insects and asked Herbert to oblige him by collecting some more of them.

Second year doldrums

At the start of his second year Charles became the tenant of the rooms at Christ's College which traditionally had been occupied by the theologian William Paley. He now had breakfast every day with his older cousin William Darwin Fox. This was Fox's last term before his BA exam, and he now had to cram desperately to make up for lost time. At the Christmas holiday Charles visited London with Eras, toured the scientific institutions "where Naturalists are gregarious" and through his friend the Revd. Frederick William Hope met other insect collectors. These included James Stephens, author of *Illustrations of British Entomology".*

The January term brought miserable weather and a struggle to keep up with his studies. Around this time, he had an earnest conversation with John Herbert about going into Holy Orders, and asked him whether he could answer yes to the question that the Bishop would put in the ordination service, "Do you trust that you are inwardly moved by the Holy Spirit". When Herbert said that he could not, Darwin replied "Neither can I, and therefore I cannot take orders" to become an ordained priest. Even his interest in insect collecting waned. He fell out with one of the two locals he employed to catch beetles when he found that the local was giving first choice to a rival collector. In the doldrums, he joined a crowd of drinking pals in a frequent "debauch". He put in some hard riding. On one night he and three friends saw the sky lit up and "rode like incarnate devils" eleven miles to see the blaze. They arrived back at two in the morning and violated curfew. He was risking "rustication", temporary expulsion. Such behaviour would be noticed by the Proctors, university officials appointed from the colleges who patrolled the town in plain gowns to police the students.

Student resentment against two unpopular Proctors built up, and on 9 April 1829 a tumult broke out. Charles described how the Senior Proctor was "most gloriously hissed.. & pelted with mud", being "driven so furious" that his servant "dared not go near him for an hour." The Proctors had noted some faces in the mob, and four were rusticated and one fined for being out-of-gown and shouting abuse. Outraged by this leniency, the Proctors quit *en masse* and printed their resignation to post up around the colleges. Though the unpopular Proctors were gone, Charles was jolted into thinking of the consequences of law-breaking.

In the Spring, Darwin enrolled for John Stevens Henslow's lectures on botany. Professor Henslow's first "public herborizing expedition" of the year took place in May, an outing on which students assisted with collection of plants. However, Darwin made no mention of Henslow in his letters to Fox. On 18 May Darwin wrote to Fox enthusing about his success with beetle collecting, "I think I beat Jenyns in Colymbetes", contrasted with his lack of application to studies: "my time is solely occupied in riding & Entomologizing".

Cambridge was briefly visited on 21 May by the Radicals Richard Carlile and the Revd. Robert Taylor, both recently jailed for blasphemy, on an "infidel home missionary tour" which caused several days of controversy. Taylor was later nicknamed "the Devil's Chaplain", a phrase remembered by Darwin.

Charles had been sending records of the insects he had caught to the entomologist James Francis Stephens, and was thrilled when Stevens published about thirty of these records in *Illustrations of British entomology; or, a synopsis of indigenous insects etc.* which was printed in parts, with the first description under Darwin's name appearing in an appendix dated 15 June 1829.

That summer, amongst horse riding and beetle collecting, Charles visited his cousin Fox, and this time Charles was teaching entomology to his older cousin. Home at Shrewsbury, Shropshire, he saw his brother Erasmus whose "delicate frame" led to him now giving up medicine and retiring at the age of 26. The brothers visited the Birmingham Music Festival for what Charles described as the "most glorious" experience.

Third year, theology and natural history

Back at Cambridge, Charles studied hard for his *Little Go* preliminary exam, as a fail would mean a re-sit the following year. He dropped his drinking companions and resumed attending Henslow's Friday evening soirées. For the exam he slogged away at Greek and Latin, and studied William Paley's *Evidences of Christianity*, becoming so delighted with Paley's logic that he learnt it well. This was a text he also had to study for his finals, and he was "convinced that I could have written out the whole of the *Evidences* with perfect correctness, but not of course in the clear language of Paley." Later, on the *Beagle* expedition, he saw evidence which challenged Paley's rose-tinted view, but at this time he was convinced that the Christian revelation established "a future state of reward and punishment" which "gives order for confusion: makes the moral world of a piece with the natural". As with Cambridge University, God gave authority and assigned stations in life, misconduct was penalised and excellence bountifully rewarded. Charles took the one-day verbal examination on 24 March 1830. There were three hours in the morning on the classics and three in the afternoon on the New Testament and Paley. The next day he was delighted to be informed that he had passed.

Several of his friends celebrated their examination successes by dining in each other's rooms in rotation in a weekly club commonly known as the *Glutton Club*. This name was proposed to ridicule another group whose Greek title meant "fond of dainties", but who dined out on "Mutton Chops, or Beans & Bacon". The *Glutton Club* attempted to live up to their title by experimentally dining on "birds and beasts which were before unknown to human palate" and tried hawk and bittern, but gave up after eating an old brown owl, "which was indescribable". They had more amusement from concluding each meeting with "a game of mild vingt-et-un".

Over Easter Charles stayed at Cambridge, mounting and cataloguing his beetle collection. He then became an enthusiastic member of the botany course which the "good natured & agreeable" professor Henslow taught five days a week in the Botanic Gardens and on field trips. Henslow's outings were attended by 78 men including professor Whewell. Charles became the "favourite pupil", known as "the man who walks with Henslow", helping to find specimens and to set up "practicals" dissecting plants. He became interested in pollen. One day he watched through a microscope and saw "transparent cones" emerge from the side of a geranium pollen grain. Then one burst spraying out "numberless granules". Henslow explained that the granules were indeed the constituent atoms of pollen, but they had no intrinsic vital power – life was endowed from outside and ultimately derived its power from God, whatever more "speculative" naturalists argued regarding self-activating power. Darwin had been taught otherwise by Grant, and reflected quietly on this, biding his time.

For the summer holidays Darwin arranged to meet Fox at The Mount, but Darwin's father had been ill and family tensions led to a row. Charles went off with the Revd. Hope and other friends for three weeks "entomologizing" in North Wales, hunting for beetles and trout fishing. He went partridge shooting at Maer before returning home.

Fourth year finals and later attitude towards mathematics

Back at Cambridge, his final exams loomed. A "desperate" Charles focused on his studies and got private tuition from Henslow whose subjects were mathematics and theology. This term he had to study Euclid and learn Paley's *Principles of Moral and Political Philosophy*, though this old text was becoming outdated. It opposed arguments for increased democracy, but saw no divine right of rule for the sovereign or the state, only "expediency". Government could be opposed if grievances outweighed the danger and expense to society. The judgement was "Every man for himself". These ideas had suited the conditions of reasonable rule prevailing when the text was published in 1785, but in 1830 they were dangerous ideas. At this time the French king was deposed by middle class republicans and given refuge in England by the Tory government. In response, radical street protests demanded suffrage, equality and freedom of religion. Then in November the Tory administration collapsed and the Whigs took over. Paley's text even supported abolition of the *Thirty-nine Articles of the Anglican faith* which every student at Cambridge (and Oxford University) was required to sign. Henslow insisted that "he should be grieved if a single word... was altered" and emphasised the need to respect authority. This happened even as campaigns of civil disobedience spread to starving agricultural labourers and villages close to Cambridge suffered riots and arson attacks.

In the third week of January 1831 Charles sat his final exam. There were three days of written papers covering the Classics, the two Paley texts and John Locke's *An Essay Concerning Human Understanding*, then mathematics and physics. At the end of the week when the results were posted he was dazed and proud to have come 10th out of a pass list of 178 doing the *ordinary* degree. Charles shone in theology and scraped through in the other subjects. He was also exhausted and depressed, writing to Fox "I do not know why the degree should make one so miserable." In later life he recalled Paley and Euclid being the only part of the course which was useful to him, and "By answering well

Figure 16: *Statue of Darwin during his last months at Christ's College (age 22). Sculpted by Anthony Smith, the statue features some of the books Darwin was reading at this time; Humboldt's Personal Narrative, Paley's Natural Theology, Herschel's Preliminary Discourse on Natural Philosophy and James Stephens' Illustrations of British Entomology.*

the examination questions in Paley, by doing Euclid well, and by not failing miserably in Classics, I gained a good place among the οἱ πολλοί, or crowd of men who do not go in for honours."

On the specific issue of his mathematical education, Darwin came to regret his lack of ability and application: "I attempted mathematics, and even went during the summer of 1828 with a private tutor (a very dull man) to Barmouth, but I got on very slowly. The work was repugnant to me, chiefly from my not being able to see any meaning in the early steps in algebra. This impatience was very foolish, and in after years I have deeply regretted that I did not proceed far enough at least to understand something of the great leading principles of mathematics, for men thus endowed seem to have an extra sense".[13]

Natural theology and geology

Residence requirements kept Darwin in Cambridge till June. He resumed his beetle collecting, took career advice from Henslow, and read William Paley's *Natural Theology or Evidences of the Existence and Attributes of the Deity* which set out to refute David Hume's argument that "design" by a Creator was merely a human projection onto the forces of nature. Paley saw a rational proof of God's existence in the complexity and perfect adaptation to needs of living beings exquisitely fitted to their places in a happy world, while attacking the evolutionary ideas of Erasmus Darwin as coinciding with atheistic schemes and lacking evidence. Paley's benevolent God acted in nature though uniform and universal laws, not arbitrary miracles or changes of laws, and this use of secondary laws provided a theodicy explaining the problem of evil by separating nature from direct divine action. This convinced Charles and encouraged his interest in science. He later wrote "I do not think I hardly ever admired a book more than Paley's *Natural Theology*: I could almost formerly have said it by heart."

He read John Herschel's new *Preliminary Discourse on the Study of Natural Philosophy*, learning that nature was governed by laws, and the highest aim of natural philosophy was to understand them through an orderly process of induction, balancing observation and theorising. This was part of the liberal Christianity of Darwin's tutors, who saw no disharmony between honest inductive science and religion. Such science was religion, and could not be heretical. Darwin also read Alexander von Humboldt's *Personal Narrative*, and the two books were immensely influential, stirring up in him "a burning zeal to add even the most humble contribution to the noble structure of Natural Science." As a young graduate, Henslow had geologised on the Isle of Wight and the Isle of Man, and he too had longed to visit Africa. Marriage and his position at the university now made the prospect remote, but he still had an unfulfilled ambition to "explore regions but little known, and enrich science with new species."

At home for Easter in early April, Darwin told his cousin Fox of "a scheme I have almost hatched" to visit the Canary Islands and see Tenerife as recommended by Humboldt. On returning to Cambridge, he wrote to his sister that "my head is running about the Tropics: in the morning I go and gaze at Palm trees in the hot-house and come home and read Humboldt: my enthusiasm is so great that I cannot hardly sit still on my chair. Henslow & other Dons give us great credit for our plan: Henslow promises to cram me in geology". He was studying Spanish language, and was in "a Tropical glow". Henslow introduced Darwin to the great geologist the Revd. Adam Sedgwick who had been his own tutor, and shared views on religion, politics and morals. Darwin was fired up by Sedgwick's Spring course of "equestrian outings" with its vistas of the grandeur of God's creation, so much of which was yet unexplored. He exclaimed, "What a capital hand is Sedgewick for drawing large cheques upon the Bank of Time!". When Sedgwick mentioned the effects of a local spring from a chalk hill depositing lime on twigs, Charles rode out to find the spring and threw a bush in, then later brought back the white coated spray which Sedgwick exhibited in class, inspiring others to do the same.

Darwin continued plotting his "Canary scheme", and on 11 May he told Fox "My other friends most sincerely wish me there I plague them so with talking about tropical scenery &c &c.". His father gave him "a 200£ note" to pay his college debts. In addition, "Some goodnatured Cambridge man has made me a most magnificent anonymous present of a Microscope: did ever hear of such a delightful piece of luck? one would like to know who it was, just to feel obliged to him." Darwin later found that the gift was from his friend John Herbert.

In mid June Darwin returned home to Shrewsbury, and continued "working like a tiger" for the Canary scheme, "at present Spanish & Geology, the former I find as intensely stupid, as the latter most interesting". By then his most likely companion on the trip was the tutor Marmaduke Ramsay. Darwin was "trying to make a map" of Shropshire, "but dont find it so easy as I expected." He ordered a clinometer, and on 11 July wrote to tell Henslow that it had arrived and he had tried it out in his bedroom. "As yet I have only indulged in hypotheses; but they are such powerful ones, that I suppose, if they were put into action but for one day, the world would come to an end." In efforts to learn the basics of geology he extended his mapping of strata as far away as Llanymynech, some 16 miles (26 km) from Shrewsbury, using the terminology he had learnt in Edinburgh from Robert Jameson. Already he was anxious that he had not heard from Sedgwick, and when he investigated ship sailings he found that they were only available in certain months. For this reason, the trip to Teneriffe had to be postponed to the following June, and it looked increasingly unlikely that Henslow would come on the trip. Darwin wrote to one of his student friends that he was "at present mad about Geology" and had plans to ride through Wales then meet with other students at Barmouth.

On 4 August 1831 Sedgwick arrived in his gig at The Mount, Shrewsbury, to take Charles as his assistant on a short geological expedition mapping strata in Wales. That evening Charles told of a tropical shell found in a nearby gravel pit and was impressed when Sedgwick responded that it must have been thrown away there, as it contradicted the known geology of the area. This made him realise "that science consists in grouping facts so that general laws or conclusions may be drawn from them." Sedgwick aimed to investigate and correct possible errors in George Greenough's geological map of 1820, and to trace the fossil record to the earliest times to rebut the uniformitarian ideas just published by Charles Lyell. On the morning of 5 August they went from Shrewsbury to Llangollen, and on 11 August reached Penrhyn Quarry. After less than a week of doing hard practical work Charles had learnt how to identify specimens, interpret strata and generalise from his observations. Then he went off on his own to collect samples and investigate the Vale of Clwyd, looking in vain for the Old Red Sandstone shown by Greenough. They met up in Colwyn, and Sedgwick's pleasure at the confirmation that the map was incorrect made Darwin "exceedingly proud". They went on to Capel Curig where Charles struck out on his own across 30 miles (50 km) of "some strange wild places" to Barmouth. He had parted from Sedgwick by 20 August, and travelled via Ffestiniog.

Voyage on the Beagle

Arriving at Barmouth on the evening of 23 August, Charles met up with a "reading party" of Cambridge friends for a time before he left on the morning of 29 August, to go back to Shrewsbury and on to partridge shooting with his Wedgwood relatives at Maer Hall. He was grieved to have received a message that Ramsay had died. This upset Darwin's plans for a visit in the following year to Tenerife. He arrived home at The Mount, Shrewsbury, on 29 August, and found a letter from Henslow. The Cambridge Fellow George Peacock had heard from Francis Beaufort of plans for the second survey voyage of HMS *Beagle*, and had written to Henslow proposing Leonard Jenyns as "a proper person to go out as a naturalist with this expedition", or if he was unavailable seeking recommendations for an alternative to take up this "glorious opportunity". When Jenyns decided not to leave his parish, he and Henslow thought of Darwin. Henslow's letter, read by Peacock and forwarded to Darwin, expected him to eagerly catch at the likely offer of a two-year trip to Terra del Fuego & home by the East Indies, not as "a *finished* Naturalist", but as a *gentleman* "amply qualified for collecting, observing, & noting any thing worthy to be noted in Natural History". The appointment was more as a companion to Captain Robert FitzRoy, than as a mere collector. Henslow wrote "I assure you I think you are the very man they are in search of".

His father thought the voyage a waste of his son's time and strongly objected. Dejected, Charles declined the offer, and went to Maer for the partridge shooting with a note from his father to "Uncle Jos" Wedgwood. This contained a prescription for a bowel ailment and a note saying that Charles had quite given up the proposed "voyage of discovery", but "if you think differently from me I shall wish him to follow your advice." Charles' hopes were revived by this unexpected news, and his relatives came out in favour of the voyage. He outlined his father's objections, and sat up that night drafting a reply with his uncle. Jos wrote suggesting that Charles would be likely to "acquire and strengthen, habits of application", and "Natural History... is very suitable to a Clergyman." Though "useless as regards his profession", for "a man of enlarged curiosity, it affords him such an opportunity of seeing men and things as happens to few". The Admiralty would look after him well, but "you & Charles... must decide."

Charles begged "one favour... a decided answer, yes or no." This reply was sent post-haste early on the morning of 1 September and Charles went shooting. About 10 o'clock he received word from his uncle that they should go to The Mount at once. When they arrived a few hours later, Charles' father had decided that he would give "all the assistance in my power".

References

- Darwin, Charles (1958). Barlow, Nora, ed. *The autobiography of Charles Darwin 1809–1882. With the original omissions restored. Edited and with appendix and notes by his granddaughter*. London: : Collins.<templatestyles src="Module:Citation/CS1/styles.css"></templatestyles>.
- Browne, E. Janet (1995). *Charles Darwin: vol. 1 Voyaging*. London: Jonathan Cape. ISBN 1-84413-314-1.<templatestyles src="Module:Citation/CS1/styles.css"></templatestyles>
- Desmond, Adrian; Moore, James (1991). *Darwin*. London: Michael Joseph, Penguin Group. ISBN 0-7181-3430-3.<templatestyles src="Module:Citation/CS1/styles.css"></templatestyles>
- Herbert, Sandra (2005), *Charles Darwin, Geologist*, Ithaca, N.Y: Cornell University Press, ISBN 0-8014-4348-2<templatestyles src="Module:Citation/CS1/styles.css"></templatestyles>
- [[William Paley[14]], *Natural Theology; or, Evidences of the Existence and Attributes of the Deity* (Full text)]Wikipedia:Link rot
- van Wyhe, John (2008). "Charles Darwin: gentleman naturalist: A biographical sketch"[15]. Darwin Online. Retrieved 17 November 2008.<templatestyles src="Module:Citation/CS1/styles.css"></templatestyles>
- von Sydow, Momme (2005). "Darwin – A Christian Undermining Christianity? On Self-Undermining Dynamics of Ideas Between Belief and Science"[16] (PDF). In Knight, David M.; Eddy, Matthew D. *Science and Beliefs: From Natural Philosophy to Natural Science, 1700–1900*. Burlington: Ashgate. pp. 141–156. ISBN 0-7546-3996-7. Retrieved 24 April 2014.<templatestyles src="Module:Citation/CS1/styles.css"></templatestyles>

External links

- The Complete Works of Charles Darwin Online – Darwin Online[17]; Darwin's publications, private papers and bibliography, supplementary works including biographies, obituaries and reviews. Free to use, includes items not in public domain.
- Works by Charles Darwin[18] at Project Gutenberg; public domain

- Darwin Correspondence Project[19] Text and notes for most of his letters

Survey voyage on HMS Beagle

Second voyage of HMS Beagle

The **second voyage of HMS** *Beagle*, from 27 December 1831 to 2 October 1836, was the second survey expedition of HMS *Beagle*, under captain Robert FitzRoy who had taken over command of the ship on its first voyage after the previous captain committed suicide. FitzRoy had already thought of the advantages of having an expert in geology on board, and sought a gentleman naturalist to accompany them as a supernumerary. The young graduate Charles Darwin had hoped to see the tropics before becoming a parson, and accepted the opportunity. He was greatly influenced by reading Charles Lyell's *Principles of Geology* during the voyage. By the end of the expedition, Darwin had already made his name as a geologist and fossil collector, and the publication of his journal which became known as *The Voyage of the Beagle* gave him wide renown as a writer.

Beagle sailed across the Atlantic Ocean, and then carried out detailed hydrographic surveys around the coasts of the southern part of South America, returning via Tahiti and Australia after having circumnavigated the Earth. While the expedition was originally planned to last two years, it lasted almost five.

Darwin spent most of this time exploring on land: three years and three months on land, 18 months at sea. Early in the voyage he decided that he could write a book about geology, and he showed a gift for theorising. At Punta Alta he made a major find of gigantic fossils of extinct mammals, then known from only a very few specimens. He ably collected and made detailed observations of plants and animals, with results that shook his belief that species were fixed and provided the basis for ideas which came to him when back in England, and led to his theory of evolution by natural selection.

Figure 17: *Beagle anchoring at Tierra del Fuego in 1832; painting by the ship's draughtsman Conrad Martens.*

Aims of the expedition

The main purpose of the expedition was to conduct a hydrographic survey of the coasts of the southern part of South America. This was a continuation and correction of the work of previous surveys, in order to produce accurate nautical charts showing navigational and sea depth information for the navy and for commerce.

An Admiralty memorandum set out the detailed instructions. The first requirement was to resolve disagreements in the earlier surveys about the longitude of Rio de Janeiro, which was essential as the base point for meridian distances. The accurate marine chronometers needed to determine longitude had only become affordable since 1800; *Beagle* carried 22 chronometers to allow corrections. The ship was to stop at specified points for four-day rating of the chronometers and to check them by astronomical observations: it was essential to take observations at Porto Praya and Fernando de Noronha to calibrate against the previous surveys of Owen and Foster. It was important to survey the extent of the Abrolhos Archipelago reefs, shown incorrectly in Roussin's survey, then proceed to Rio de Janeiro to decide the exact longitude of Villegagnon Island.

The real work of the survey was then to commence south of the Río de la Plata, with return trips to Montevideo for supplies; details were given of priorities, including surveying Tierra del Fuego and approaches to harbours on

Figure 18: *Ship's chronometer from HMS Beagle*

the Falkland Islands. The west coast was then to be surveyed as far north as time and resources permitted. The commander would then determine his own route west: season permitting, he could survey the Galápagos Islands. Then *Beagle* was to proceed to Point Venus, Tahiti and on to Port Jackson, Australia which were known points to verify the chronometers.

No time was to be wasted on elaborate drawings; charts and plans should have notes and simple views of the land as seen from the sea showing measured heights of hills. Continued records of tides and meteorological conditions were also required. An additional suggestion was for a geological survey of a circular coral atoll in the Pacific Ocean including its profile and of tidal flows, to investigate the formation of such coral reefs.

Context and preparations

The previous survey expedition to South America involved HMS *Adventure* and HMS *Beagle* under the overall command of the Australian Commander Phillip Parker King. During the survey *Beagle*'s captain, Pringle Stokes, committed suicide and command of the ship was given to the young aristocrat Robert FitzRoy, a nephew of George FitzRoy, 4th Duke of Grafton. When a ship's boat was taken by native Fuegians, FitzRoy took some of them hostage.

After their return to Devonport dockyard on 14 October 1830 Captain King retired.

The 26-year-old FitzRoy had hopes of commanding a second expedition to continue the South American survey, but when he heard that the Lords of the Admiralty no longer supported this, he grew concerned about how to return the Fuegians who had been taught English with the idea that they could become missionaries. He made an agreement with the owner of a small merchant-vessel to take himself and five others back to South America, but a kind uncle heard of this and contacted the Admiralty. Soon afterwards FitzRoy heard that he was to be appointed commander of HMS *Chanticleer* to go to Tierra del Fuego, but due to her poor condition *Beagle* was substituted. On 27 June 1831 FitzRoy was commissioned as commander of the voyage, and Lieutenants John Clements Wickham and Bartholomew James Sulivan were appointed.

Captain Francis Beaufort, the Hydrographer of the Admiralty, was invited to decide on the use that could be made of the voyage to continue the survey, and he discussed with FitzRoy plans for a voyage of several years, including a continuation of the trip around the world to establish median distances. *Beagle* was commissioned on 4 July 1831 under the command of Captain Robert FitzRoy, who promptly spared no expense in having *Beagle* extensively refitted. *Beagle* was immediately taken into dock for extensive rebuilding and refitting. As she required a new deck, FitzRoy had the upper deck raised considerably, by 8 inches (200 mm) aft and 12 inches (300 mm) forward. The *Cherokee*-class brig-sloops had the reputation of being "coffin brigs", which handled badly and were prone to sinking. By helping the decks to drain more quickly with less water collecting in the gunnels, the raised deck gave *Beagle* better handling and made her less liable to become top-heavy and capsize. Additional sheathing to the hull added about seven tons to her burthen and perhaps fifteen to her displacement.

The ship was one of the first to test the lightning conductor invented by William Snow Harris. FitzRoy obtained five examples of the *Sympiesometer*, a kind of mercury-free barometer patented by Alexander Adie and favoured by FitzRoy as giving the accurate readings required by the Admiralty.

In addition to its officers and crew, *Beagle* carried several supernumeraries, passengers without an official position. FitzRoy employed a mathematical instrument maker to maintain his 22 marine chronometers kept in his cabin, as well as engaging the artist/draughtsman Augustus Earle to go in a private capacity. The three Fuegians taken on the previous voyage were going to be returned to Tierra del Fuego on *Beagle* together with the missionary Richard Matthews.

Naturalist and geologist

For Beaufort and the leading Cambridge "gentlemen of science" the opportunity for a naturalist to join the expedition fitted with their drive to revitalise British government policy on science. This elite disdained research done for money and felt that natural philosophy was for gentlemen, not tradesmen. The officer class of the Army and Navy provided a way to ascend this hierarchy; it was commonly the Ship's Surgeon who collected specimens on voyages, and Robert McCormick had secured the official position of surgeon on *Beagle* after taking part in earlier expeditions and studying natural history. A sizeable collection had considerable social value, attracting wide public interest, and McCormick aspired to fame as an exploring naturalist. Collections made by the Ship's Surgeon and other officers were government property, though the Admiralty was not consistent on this, and went to important London establishments, usually the British Museum. The Admiralty instructions for the first voyage had required officers "to use their best diligence in increasing the Collections in each ship: the whole of which must be understood to belong to the Public", but on the second voyage this requirement was omitted, and the officers were free to keep all the specimens for themselves.

FitzRoy's narrative recalls that, when investigating islands on the first voyage, he had regretted that no-one on board had expertise on mineralogy or geology to make use of the opportunity of "ascertaining the nature of the rocks and earths" of the areas surveyed, and resolved that if on a similar expedition, he would "endeavour to carry out a person qualified to examine the land; while the officers, and myself, would attend to hydrography." This clearly indicated a need for a naturalist qualified to examine geology, who would spend considerable periods onshore away from the ship. McCormick lacked expertise in geology, and had to attend to his duties on the ship.[20]

FitzRoy knew that commanding a ship could involve stress and loneliness; he was fully aware of the suicide of Captain Stokes, and his own uncle Viscount Castlereagh had committed suicide under stress of overwork. For the first time he would be fully in charge with no commanding officer or second captain to consult, and it has been suggested that he felt the need for a gentleman companion who shared his scientific interests and could dine with him as an equal. There is no direct evidence to support this. Henslow described the position "more as a companion than a mere collector", but this was an assurance that FitzRoy would treat his guest as a gentleman naturalist. Several other ships at this period carried unpaid civilians as naturalists.[21]

Early in August, FitzRoy discussed this position with Beaufort, who had a scientific network of friends at the University of Cambridge. At Beaufort's request, mathematics lecturer George Peacock wrote from London to Professor

John Stevens Henslow about this "rare opportunity for a naturalist", saying that an "offer has been made to me to recommend a proper person to go out as a naturalist with this expedition", and suggesting the Reverend Leonard Jenyns. Though Jenyns nearly accepted, and even packed his clothes, he had concerns about his obligations as vicar of Swaffham Bulbeck and his health, so declined. Henslow briefly thought of going, but his wife "looked so miserable" that he quickly dropped the idea. Both recommended the 22-year-old Charles Darwin who had just completed the ordinary Bachelor of Arts degree which was a prerequisite for his intended career as a parson, and was on a geology field trip with Adam Sedgwick.

Offer of place to Darwin

Darwin fitted well the expectations of a gentleman natural philosopher, and was well trained as a naturalist.[22] When he had studied geology in his second year at Edinburgh he had found it dull, but from Easter to August 1831 he learned a great deal with Adam Sedgwick and developed a strong interest during their geological field trip. On 24 August Henslow wrote to Darwin:

> ...that I consider you to be the best qualified person I know of who is likely to undertake such a situation— I state this not on the supposition of yr. being a finished Naturalist, but as amply qualified for collecting, observing, & noting any thing worthy to be noted in Natural History. Peacock has the appointment at his disposal & if he can not find a man willing to take the office, the opportunity will probably be lost— Capt. F. wants a man (I understand) more as a companion than a mere collector & would not take any one however good a Naturalist who was not recommended to him likewise as a gentleman. ... there never was a finer chance for a man of zeal & spirit... Don't put on any modest doubts or fears about your disqualifications for I assure you I think you are the very man they are in search of.

The letter went first to George Peacock, who quickly forwarded it to Darwin with further details, confirming that the "ship sails about the end of September". Peacock had discussed the offer with Beaufort, "he entirely approves of it & you may consider the situation as at your absolute disposal". When Darwin returned home late on 29 August and opened the letters, his father objected strongly to the voyage so the next day he wrote declining the offer, and left to go shooting at the estate of his uncle Josiah Wedgwood II. With Wedgwood's help, Darwin's father was persuaded to relent and fund his son's expedition, and on Thursday 1 September Darwin wrote accepting Peacock's offer. That day, Beaufort wrote to tell FitzRoy that his friend Peacock had "succeeded in getting a 'Savant' for you—A Mr Darwin grandson of the well known philosopher and poet—full of zeal and enterprize and having contemplated a voyage on his own account to S. America". On Friday Darwin left for Cambridge, where he spent Saturday with Henslow getting advice on preparations, and references to experts.

Alexander Charles Wood (an undergraduate whose tutor was Peacock) wrote from Cambridge to his cousin FitzRoy to recommend Darwin. Around midday on Sunday 4 September Wood received FitzRoy's response, "straightforward and gentlemanlike" but strongly against Darwin joining the expedition; both Darwin and Henslow then "gave up the scheme". Darwin went to London anyway, and next morning met FitzRoy who explained that he had promised the place to his friend Mr. Chester, (possibly the novelist Harry Chester) but Chester had turned it down in a letter received not five minutes before Darwin arrived. FitzRoy emphasised the difficulties including cramped conditions and plain food. Darwin would be on the Admiralty's books to get provisions (worth £40 a year) and, like the ship's officers and captain, would pay £30 a year towards the mess bill. Including outfitting, the cost to him was unlikely to reach £500. The ship would sail on 10 October, and would probably be away for three years. They talked and dined together, and soon found each other agreeable. The Tory FitzRoy had been cautious at the prospect of companionship with this unknown young gentleman of Whig background, and later admitted that his letter to Wood was "to throw cold water on the scheme" in "a sudden horror of the chances of having somebody he should not like on board". He half-seriously told Darwin later that, as "an ardent disciple of Lavater", he had nearly rejected Darwin on the phrenological basis that the shape (or physiognomy) of Darwin's nose indicated a lack of determination.[23]

Darwin's preparations

While he continued to get acquainted with Fitzroy, going shopping together, Darwin rushed around to arrange his supplies and equipment, getting advice from experts on specimen preservation such as William Yarrell at the Zoological Society of London, Robert Brown at the British Museum, Captain Phillip Parker King who led the first expedition, and invertebrate anatomist Robert Edmond Grant who had tutored Darwin at Edinburgh. Yarrell gave invaluable advice, and bargained with shopkeepers so Darwin paid £50 for two pistols and a rifle, while FitzRoy had spent £400 on firearms. On Sunday 11 September, FitzRoy and Darwin took the steam packet for Portsmouth. Darwin was not seasick, and had a pleasant "sail of three days". For the first time he saw the "very small" cramped ship, met the officers, and was glad to get a large cabin, shared with the assistant surveyor John Lort Stokes. On Friday Darwin rushed back to London, "250 miles in 24 hours", and on via Cambridge to arrive in Shrewsbury on 22 September for a last quick visit to family and friends, leaving for London on 2 October. Delays to *Beagle* gave Darwin an extra week to consult experts and complete packing his baggage. After sending his heavy goods down by steam packet, he took the coach along with Augustus Earle, and arrived at Devonport on 24 October.

The geologist Charles Lyell asked FitzRoy to record observations on geological features such as erratic boulders. Before they left England, FitzRoy gave Darwin a copy of the first volume of Lyell's *Principles of Geology* which explained features as the outcome of a gradual process taking place over extremely long periods of time. In his autobiography Darwin recalled Henslow giving advice at this time to obtain and study the book, "but on no account to accept the views therein advocated".

Darwin's position as a naturalist on board was as a self-funded guest with no official appointment, and he could leave the voyage at any suitable stage. At the outset George Peacock had advised that "The Admiralty are not disposed to give a salary, though they will furnish you with an official appointment & every accomodation [sic]: if a salary should be required however I am inclined to think that it would be granted". Far from wanting this, Darwin's concern was to maintain control over his collection. He was even reluctant to be on the Admiralty's books for victuals until he got assurances from FitzRoy and Beaufort that this would not affect his rights to assign his specimens. Darwin did not want his collection to go to the British Museum as he had heard that specimens from the first *Beagle* voyage were still waiting to be described. Beaufort assured him that he "should have no difficulty" as long as he "presented them to some public body" such as the Zoological or Geological societies. Darwin himself thought his new finds should go to the "largest & most central collection", not the Cambridge Philosophical Society museum that Henslow was setting up at Cambridge, but after getting Henslow's willing agreement to take delivery of the consignments of specimens, Darwin replied that he hoped to give some to the Cambridge museum.

Darwin's work on the expedition

The captain had to record his survey in painstaking paperwork, and Darwin too kept a daily log as well as detailed notebooks of his finds and speculations, and a diary which became his journal. Darwin's notebooks show a complete professionalism that he had probably learnt at the University of Edinburgh when making natural history notes while exploring the shores of the Firth of Forth with his brother Erasmus in 1826 and studying marine invertebrates with Robert Edmund Grant for a few months in 1827. Darwin had also collected beetles at Cambridge, but he was a novice in all other areas of natural history. During the voyage Darwin investigated small invertebrates, while collecting specimens of other creatures for experts to examine and describe once *Beagle* had returned to England. More than half of his carefully organised zoology notes deal with marine invertebrates, and the notes record closely reasoned

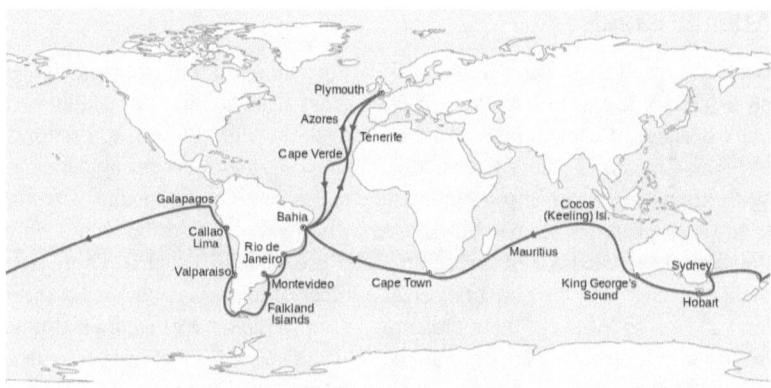

Figure 19: *The voyage of Beagle*

interpretations of what he found about their complex internal anatomy while dissecting specimens under his microscope, and of little experiments on their response to stimulation. His onshore observations included intense, analytical comments on possible reasons for the behaviour, distribution, and relation to their environment of the creatures he saw. He made good use of the ship's excellent library of books on natural history, but continually questioned their correctness.

Geology was Darwin's "principal pursuit" on the expedition and his notes on that subject were almost four times larger than his zoology notes, although he kept extensive records on both. During the voyage, he wrote to his sister that "there is nothing like geology; the pleasure of the first days partridge shooting or first days hunting cannot be compared to finding a fine group of fossil bones, which tell their story of former times with almost a living tongue". To him, investigating geology brought reasoning into play and gave him opportunities for theorising.

Voyage

Charles Darwin had been told that *Beagle* was expected to sail about the end of September 1831, but fitting out took longer. The Admiralty Instructions were received on 14 November, and on 23 November she was moved to anchorage, ready to depart. Repeated Westerly gales caused delays, and forced them to turn back after departing on 10 and 21 December. Drunkenness at Christmas lost another day. Finally, on the morning of 27 December, *Beagle* left its anchorage in the Barn Pool, under Mount Edgecumbe on the west side of Plymouth Sound and set out on its surveying expedition.

Atlantic islands

Beagle touched at Madeira for a confirmed position without stopping. Then on 6 January it reached Tenerife in the Canary Islands, but was quarantined there because of cholera in England. Although tantalisingly near to the town of Santa Cruz, to Darwin's intense disappointment, they were denied landing. With improving weather conditions, they sailed on. On 10 January Darwin tried out a plankton net he had devised to be towed behind the ship – only the second recorded use of such a net (after use by John Vaughan Thompson in 1816). Next day, he noted the great number of animals collected far from land and wrote "Many of these creatures so low in the scale of nature are most exquisite in their forms & rich colours. — It creates a feeling of wonder that so much beauty should be apparently created for such little purpose."

Six days later they made their first landing at Porto Praya on the volcanic island of St. Jago in the Cape Verde Islands. It is here that Darwin's description in his published *Journal* begins. His initial impression was of a desolate and sterile volcanic island, but after visiting the town he came to a deep valley where he "first saw the glory of tropical vegetation" and had "a glorious day", finding overwhelming novelty in the sights and sounds. FitzRoy set up tents and an observatory on Quail Island to determine the exact position of the islands, while Darwin collected numerous sea animals, delighting in vivid tropical corals in tidal pools, and investigating the geology of Quail Island.[24] Though Daubeny's book in *Beagle*'s library described the volcanic geology of the Canary Islands, it said that the structure of the Cape Verde Islands was "too imperfectly known". Darwin saw Quail Island as his key to understanding the structure of St. Jago, and made careful studies of its stratigraphy in the way he had learnt from Adam Sedgwick. He collected specimens and described a white layer of hard white rock formed from crushed coral and seashells lying between layers of black volcanic rocks, and noted a similar white layer running horizontally in the black cliffs of St. Jago at 40 feet (12 m) above sea level. The seashells were, as far as he could tell, "the same as those of present day". He speculated that in geologically recent times a lava flow had covered this shell sand on the sea bed, and then the strata had slowly risen to their present level. Charles Lyell's *Principles of Geology* presented a thesis of gradual rising and falling of the Earth's crust illustrated by the changing levels of the Temple of Serapis. Darwin implicitly supported Lyell by remarking that "Dr. Daubeny when mentioning the present state of the temple of Serapis. doubts the possibility of a surface of country being raised without cracking buildings on it. – I feel sure at St Jago in some places a town might have been raised without injuring a house." In a letter to Henslow he wrote that "The geology was preeminently interesting & I believe quite new: there are some facts on a large scale of upraised coast ... that would interest Mr. Lyell. While still on the island, Darwin was inspired to think of writing a book on geology, and later wrote of "seeing a thing never seen by Lyell, one yet saw it partially through his eyes".[25]

Customarily the ship's surgeon took the position of naturalist, and *Beagle*'s surgeon Robert McCormick sought fame and fortune as an explorer. When they first met at the start of the voyage, Darwin had commented that "My friend [McCormick] is an ass, but we jog on very amicably". They walked into the countryside of St. Jago together, and Darwin, influenced by Lyell, found the surgeon's approach old-fashioned. They found a remarkable baobab tree, which FitzRoy measured and sketched. Darwin went on subsequent "riding expeditions" with Benjamin Bynoe and Rowlett to visit Ribeira Grande and St Domingo. FitzRoy extended their stay to 23 days, to complete his measurements of magnetism. Darwin subsequently wrote to Henslow that his collecting included "several specimens of an Octopus, which possessed a most marvellous power of changing its colours; equalling any chamaelion, & evidently accommodating the changes to the colour of the ground which it passed over.—yellowish green, dark brown & red were the prevailing colours: this fact appears to be new, as far as I can find out." Henslow replied that "The fact is not new, but any fresh observations will be highly important."

McCormick increasingly resented the favours FitzRoy gave to assist Darwin with collecting. On 16 February, FitzRoy landed a small party including himself and Darwin on St. Paul's rocks, finding the seabirds so tame that they could be killed easily, while an exasperated McCormick was left circling the islets in a second small boat. That evening novices were greeted by a pseudo-Neptune, and in the morning they crossed the equator with the traditional line-crossing ceremony.

Darwin had a special position as guest and social equal of the captain, so junior officers called him "sir" until the captain dubbed Darwin *Philos* for "ship's philosopher", and this became his suitably respectful nickname.

Surveying South America

In South America, *Beagle* carried out its survey work going to and fro to along the coasts to allow careful measurement and rechecking. Darwin made long journeys inland with travelling companions from the locality. He spent much of the time away from the ship, returning by prearrangement when *Beagle* returned to ports where mail could be received and Darwin's notes, journals, and collections sent back to England. He had ensured that his collections were his own and they were shipped back to Henslow in Cambridge to await his return. Several others on board including FitzRoy and other officers were able amateur naturalists, and they gave Darwin generous assistance as well as making collections for the Crown, which the Admiralty placed in the British Museum.

Tropical paradise and slavery

Due to heavy surf they only stayed at Fernando de Noronha for a day to make the required observations, and Fitzroy decided to make for Bahia, Brazil, to rate the chronometers and take on water. On 28 February they reached the continent, arriving at the magnificent sight of the town now known as Salvador, with large ships at harbour scattered across the bay. On the next day, Darwin was in "transports of pleasure" walking by himself in the tropical forest, and in "long naturalizing walks" with others continued to "add raptures to the former raptures". He found the sights of slavery offensive and when FitzRoy defended the practice by describing a visit to a slaveowner whose slaves replied "no" on being asked by their master if they wished to be freed, Darwin suggested that answers in such circumstances were worthless. Enraged that his word had been questioned, FitzRoy lost his temper and banned Darwin from his company. The officers had nicknamed such outbursts "hot coffee," and within hours FitzRoy apologised and asked Darwin to remain. Later, FitzRoy had to remain silent when Captain Paget visited them and recounted "facts about slavery so revolting" that refuted his claim. Surveying of sandbanks around the harbour was completed on 18 March, and the ship made its way down the coast to survey the extent and depths of the Abrolhos reefs, completing and correcting Roussin's survey.

On 4 April they entered the harbour of Rio de Janeiro, to make observations of longitude from Villegagnon Island. Darwin took in the sights of the city then made an expedition into the interior, returning to the ship on 24 April. By then Robert McCormick had left the ship, with permission from the admiral in command, and returned to England. Assistant Surgeon Benjamin Bynoe was made acting surgeon in his place. McCormick felt "very much disappointed in my expectations of carrying out my natural history pursuits, every obstacle having been placed in the way of my getting on shore and making collections" while the gentleman Darwin received all the invitations from dignitaries onshore and was given facilities to pack his collections.

On 26 April Darwin moved into a house he had rented at Botafogo, and stayed there with three others when *Beagle* left on 10 May to recheck observations at Bahia. FitzRoy had found a discrepancy of 4 miles (6.4 km) in the meridian distance of longitude between his measurements and those of Albin Roussin, and decided to go back. A seaman, a ship's boy and a young midshipman had caught a fever after visiting the Macacu River, and died. When the ship returned to Rio on 3 June, FitzRoy confirmed that his measurements of Bahia and of the Abrolhos reefs were correct, and sent these corrections to Roussin. They sailed from Rio on 5 July.

Figure 20: *A caricature of the scene on the quarter deck while anchored at Bahia Blanca, painted around 24 September 1832. Darwin is the central figure in a top hat, Fitzroy the second figure to his left. The watercolour is attributed to the shipboard artist Augustus Earle.*

Fossil finds

After storms, *Beagle* reached Montevideo on 26 July 1832, and took observations for the chronometers. An attempt to call at Buenos Aires for information was thwarted by officials, then FitzRoy agreed a request for ship's crew (and Darwin) to briefly occupy a Montevideo fort to dispel a revolution. On 22 August, after taking soundings in Samborombón Bay, *Beagle* began survey work down the coast from Cape San Antonio, Buenos Aires Province, Argentina.

At Bahía Blanca, in the southern part of present Buenos Aires Province, Darwin rode inland into Patagonia with gauchos: he saw them use bolas to bring down "ostriches" (rheas), and ate roast armadillo. With FitzRoy, he went for "a very pleasant cruize about the bay" on 22 September, and about ten miles (16 km) from the ship they stopped for a while at Punta Alta. In low cliffs near the point Darwin found conglomerate rocks containing numerous shells and fossilised teeth and bones of gigantic extinct mammals,[26] in strata near an earth layer with shells and armadillo fossils, suggesting to him quiet tidal deposits rather than a catastrophe.[27] With assistance (possibly from the young sailor Syms Covington acting as his servant) Darwin collected numerous fossils over several days, amusing others with "the cargoes of apparent rubbish which he frequently brought on board".

Much of the second day was taken up with excavating a large skull which Darwin found embedded in soft rock, and seemed to him to be allied to the rhinoceros. On 8 October he returned to the site, and found a jawbone and tooth which he was able to identify using Bory de Saint-Vincent's *Dictionnaire classique*. He wrote home describing this and the large skull as *Megatherium* fossils, or perhaps *Megalonyx*, and excitedly noted that the only specimens in Europe were locked away in the King's collection at Madrid. In the same layer he found a large surface of polygonal plates of bony armour. His immediate thought was that they came from an enormous armadillo like the small creatures common in the area, but from Cuvier's misleading description of the Madrid specimen and a recent newspaper report about a fossil found by Woodbine Parish, Darwin thought that the bony armour identified the fossil as *Megatherium*. With FitzRoy, Darwin went about 30 miles (48 km) across the bay to Monte Hermoso on 19 October, and found numerous fossils of smaller rodents in contrast to the huge Edentatal mammals of Punta Alta. In November at Buenos Aires he "purchased fragments of some enormous bones" which he "was assured belonged to the former giants!!", and subsequently took any chance to get fossils "by gold or galloping".

At Montevideo in November the mail from home included a copy of the second volume of Charles Lyell's *Principles of Geology*, a refutation of Lamarckism in which there was no shared ancestry of different species or overall progress to match the gradual geological change, but a continuing cycle in which species mysteriously appeared, closely adapted to their "centres of creation", then became extinct when the environment changed to their disadvantage.

Tierra del Fuego

They reached Tierra del Fuego on 18 December 1832 and Darwin was taken aback at what he perceived as the crude savagery of the Yaghan natives, in stark contrast to the "civilised" behaviour of the three Fuegians they were returning as missionaries (who had been given the names York Minster, Fuegia Basket and Jemmy Button). He described his first meeting with the native Fuegians as being "without exception the most curious and interesting spectacle I ever beheld: I could not have believed how wide was the difference between savage and civilised man: it is greater than between a wild and domesticated animal, inasmuch as in man there is a greater power of improvement." In contrast, he said of Jemmy that "It seems yet wonderful to me, when I think over all his many good qualities, that he should have been of the same race, and doubtless partaken of the same character, with the miserable, degraded savages whom we first met here." (Four decades later, he recalled these impressions in *The Descent of Man* to support his argument that just as humans had descended from "a lower form", civilised society had arisen by graduations from a more

Figure 21: *Native of the Tierra del Fuego.*[28]

primitive state. He recalled how closely the Fuegians on board *Beagle* "resembled us in disposition and in most of our mental faculties.")

At the island of "Buttons Land" on 23 January 1833 they set up a mission post, with huts, gardens, furniture and crockery, but when they returned nine days later the possessions had been looted and divided up equally by the natives. Matthews gave up, rejoining the ship and leaving the three civilised Fuegians to continue the missionary work. *Beagle* went on to the Falkland Islands arriving just after the British return. Darwin studied the relationships of species to habitats and found ancient fossils like those he had found in Wales. Fitzroy bought a schooner to assist with the surveying, and they returned to Patagonia where this was fitted with a new copper bottom and renamed *Adventure*. Darwin was assisted by Syms Covington in preserving specimens and his collecting was so successful that with FitzRoy's agreement he took on Covington as a full-time servant for £30 a year.

Gauchos, rheas, fossils and geology

The two ships sailed to the Río Negro in Argentina and on 8 August 1833 Darwin left on another journey inland with the gauchos. On 12 August he met General Juan Manuel de Rosas who was then leading a punitive expedition in his military campaign against native "Indians", and obtained a passport from him. As they crossed the pampas the gauchos and Indians told Darwin of a rare smaller species of rhea. After three days at Bahía Blanca he grew tired of waiting for *Beagle* and on 21 August revisited Punta Alta where he reviewed the geology of the site in light of his new knowledge, wondering if the bones were older than the seashells. He was very successful with searching for bones, and on 1 September found a near complete skeleton with its bones still in position.

He set off again and on 1 October searching the cliffs of the Carcarañá River found "an enormous gnawing tooth" then in a cliff of the Paraná River saw "two great groups of immense bones" which were too soft to collect but a tooth fragment identified them as mastodons. Illness delayed him at Santa Fe, and after seeing the fossilised casing of a huge armadillo embedded in rock, he was puzzled to find a horse tooth in the same rock layer, since horses had been introduced to the continent with European migration. They took a riverboat down the Paraná River to Buenos Aires but became entangled in a revolution as rebels allied to Rosas blockaded the city. The passport helped and with Covington he managed to escape in a boatload of refugees. They rejoined *Beagle* at Montevideo.

As surveys were still in progress Darwin set off on another 400-mile (640 km) "galloping" trip in Banda Oriental to see the Uruguay River and visit the Estancia of Mr Keen near Mercedes on the Río Negro. On 25 November he "heard of some giants bones, which as usual turned out to be those of the Megatherium" but could only extract a few broken fragments, then on the next day visited a nearby house and bought for about two shillings "a head of a Megatherium which must have been when found quite perfect", though the teeth had since been broken and the lower jaw had been lost. Mr Keen arranged to ship the skull down river to Buenos Aires. At Las Piedras a clergyman let him see fossils including a club-like tail which he sketched and called an "extraordinary weapon".[29] His notes included a page showing his realisation that the cliff banks of the rivers exposed two strata formed in an estuary interrupted by an undersea stratum, indicating that the land had risen and fallen.[30]

Back at Montevideo, Darwin was introduced to Conrad Martens, the replacement artist brought on board *Beagle* after Augustus Earle had to leave due to health problems. They sailed south, putting in at Port Desire on 23 December, and the following day Darwin shot a guanaco which provided them with a Christmas meal. Early in the new year, Martens shot a rhea which they enjoyed eating before Darwin realised that this was the elusive smaller rhea, and preserved the remains. On 9 January 1834, 110 miles (180 km) further south, they reached Port St Julian and exploring the local geology in cliffs near the harbour Darwin found fossils of pieces of spine and a hind leg of "some large animal, I fancy a Mastodon". On 26 January they entered the Straits of Magellan and at St. Gregory's Bay they met half-civilised Patagonian "giants" over

Second voyage of HMS Beagle 61

Figure 22: *Illustration of Darwin's rhea, published in 1841 in John Gould's description of birds collected on Beagle's voyage.*

6 ft (1.8 m) tall, described by Darwin as "excellent practical naturalists". One told him that the smaller rheas were the only species this far south, while the larger rheas kept to the north, the species meeting around the Rio Negro.

After further surveying in Tierra del Fuego they returned on 5 March 1834 to visit the missionaries, but found the huts deserted. Then canoes approached and they found that one of the natives was Jemmy Button, who had lost his possessions and had settled into the native ways, taking a wife. Darwin had never seen "so complete & grievous a change". Jemmy came on board and dined using his cutlery properly, speaking English as well as ever, then assured them that he "had not the least wish to return to England" and was "happy and contented", leaving them gifts of otter skins and arrowheads before returning to the canoe to join his wife. Of the first visit Darwin had written that "Viewing such men, one can hardly make oneself believe that they are fellow creatures placed in the same world. .... It is a common subject of conjecture; what pleasure in life some of the less gifted animals can enjoy? How much more reasonably it may be asked with respect to these men", yet Jemmy had readily adapted to civilisation and then chosen to return to his primitive ways. This raised awkward questions; it jarred with Charles Lyell's sheltered views, expressed in volume 2 of his *Principles of Geology*, that human races "showed only a slight deviation from a common standard", and that acceptance of transmutation meant renouncing man's "belief in the high genealogy of his species".

About this time Darwin wrote *Reflection on reading my Geological notes*, the first of a series of essays included in his notes. He speculated on possible causes of the land repeatedly being raised, and on a history of life in Patagonia as a sequence of named species.

They returned to the Falkland Islands on 16 March just after an incident where gauchos and Indians had butchered senior members of Vernet's settlement, and helped to put the revolt down. Darwin noted the immense number of organisms dependent on the kelp forests. He received word from Henslow that his first dispatch of specimens had reached Cambridge, with the South American fossils being prized by the expert William Clift as showing hitherto unknown species and features of the Megatherium, and displayed by William Buckland and Clift before the cream of British science, making Darwin's reputation.

Beagle now sailed to southern Patagonia, and on 19 April an expedition including FitzRoy and Darwin set off to take boats as far as possible up the Santa Cruz river, with all involved taking turn in teams dragging the boats upstream. The river cut through a series of rises then plateaux forming wide plains covered with shells and shingle, and Darwin discussed with FitzRoy his interpretation that these terraces had been shores that had gradually raised in accordance with Lyell's theories. Several of the smaller rheas were seen in the distance, but were too elusive to catch. The expedition approached the Andes but had to turn back.

Darwin summarised his speculation in his essay on the *Elevation of Patagonia*. Though tentative, it challenged Lyell's ideas. Darwin drew on measurements by *Beagle*'s officers as well as his own measurements to propose that the plains had been raised in successive stages by forces acting over a wide area, rather than smaller scale actions in a continuous movement. However, he supported Lyell in finding evidence to dismiss a sudden deluge when normal processes were suddenly speeded. Seashells he had found far inland still showing their colour suggested to him that the process had been relatively recent, and could have affected human history.

West coast of South America

Beagle and *Adventure* now surveyed the Straits of Magellan before sailing north round up the west coast, reaching the island of Chiloé in the wet and heavily wooded Chiloé Archipelago on 28 June 1834. They then spent the next six months surveying the coast and islands southwards. On Chiloé, Darwin found fragments of black lignite and petrified wood, at least two of which

Figure 23: *The Bell mountain, Cerro La Campana, which Darwin ascended on 17 August 1834.*

the British Geological Survey discovered in 2011 locked away in their collection labeled "unregistered fossil plants". Exchanged with Joseph Dalton Hooker about ten years later, one slide was signed "Chiloe, C. Darwin Esq".

They arrived at Valparaiso on 23 July. After several walks in the area, Darwin obtained horses and on 14 August set off up the volcanic Andes with a companion. Three days later they spent an enjoyable day on the summit of the Bell mountain. Darwin visited a copper mine and spent five days scrambling in the mountains before going on to Santiago, Chile. On his way back, he fell ill on 20 September and had to spend a month in bed. It is possible that he contracted Chagas' disease here, leading to his health problems after his return to England, but this diagnosis of his symptoms is disputed. He learnt that the Admiralty had reprimanded FitzRoy for buying *Adventure*. FitzRoy had taken it badly, selling the ship and announcing they would go back to recheck his survey, then had resigned his command doubting his sanity, but was persuaded by his officers to withdraw his resignation and proceed. The artist Conrad Martens left the ship and took passage to Australia.

After waiting for Darwin, *Beagle* sailed on 11 November to survey the Chonos Archipelago. From here they saw the eruption of the volcano Osorno in the Andes. They sailed north, and Darwin wondered about the fossils he had

Figure 24: *Concepción after the earthquake, as drawn by Lieutenant John Clements Wickham of Beagle.*

found. The giant *Mastodon*s and *Megatherium*s were extinct, but he had found no geological signs of a "diluvial debacle" or of the changed circumstances that, in Lyell's view, led to species no longer being adapted to the position they were created to fit. He agreed with Lyell's idea of "the gradual birth & death of species" but, unlike Lyell, Darwin was willing to believe Giovanni Battista Brocchi's idea that extinct species had somehow aged and died out.

They arrived at the port of Valdivia on 8 February 1835, then twelve days later Darwin was on shore when he experienced a severe earthquake and returned to find the port town badly damaged. They sailed two hundred miles (320 km) north to Concepción, and arrived on 4 March to find that the same earthquake had devastated the city by repeated shocks and a tsunami, with even the cathedral in ruins. Darwin noted the horrors of death and destruction, and FitzRoy carefully established that mussel beds were now above high tide, giving clear evidence of the ground rising some 9 ft (2.7 m) which he confirmed a month later. They had actually experienced the gradual process of the continent emerging from the ocean as Lyell had indicated.

Back in Valparaiso, Darwin set out on another trek up the Andes and on 21 March reached the continental divide at 13,000 ft (4,000 m): even here he found fossil seashells in the rocks. He felt the glorious view "was like watching a thunderstorm, or hearing in the full Orchestra a Chorus of the Messiah." After going on to Mendoza they were returning by a different pass when they found a petrified forest of fossilised trees, crystallised in a sandstone escarpment showing him that they had been on a Pacific beach when the land sank, burying them in sand which had been compressed into rock, then had gradually been raised with the continent to stand at 7,000 ft (2,100 m) in the mountains. On returning to Valparaiso with half a mule's load of specimens he wrote to his father that his findings, if accepted, would be crucial to the theory of the formation of the world. After another gruelling expedition in the Andes while *Beagle* was refitted he rejoined it and sailed to Lima, but found an armed insurrection in progress and had to stay with the ship. Here he was writing up his notes when he realised that Lyell's idea that coral atolls were on the rims of rising extinct volcanoes made less sense than the volcanoes gradually sinking so that the coral reefs around the island kept building themselves close to sea level and became an atoll as the volcano disappeared below. This was a theory he would examine when they reached such islands.

Galápagos Islands

A week out of Lima, *Beagle* reached the Galápagos Islands on 15 September 1835. The next day Captain FitzRoy dropped anchor near the site of the modern town of Puerto Baquerizo Moreno on Chatham Island. At the location that is now known as Frigatebird Hill/Cerro Tijeretas, Darwin spent his first hour on shore in the Galapagos islands.[31]

Darwin eagerly looked forward to seeing newly formed volcanic islands, and took every opportunity to go ashore while *Beagle* was methodically moved round to chart the coast. He found broken black rocky volcanic lava scorching under the hot sun, and made detailed geological notes of features including volcanic cones like chimneys which reminded him of the iron foundries of industrial Staffordshire. He was disappointed that he did not see active volcanoes or find strata showing uplift as he had hoped, though one of the officers found broken oyster-shells high above the sea on one of the islands. Abundant giant Galápagos tortoises appeared to him almost antediluvian, and large black marine iguanas seemed "most disgusting, clumsy Lizards" well suited to their habitat – he noted that someone had called them "imps of darkness". Darwin had learnt from Henslow about studying the geographical distribution of species, and particularly of linked species on oceanic islands and on nearby continents, so he endeavoured to collect plants in flower. He found widespread "wretched-looking" thin scrub thickets of only ten species, and very few insects. Birds were remarkably unafraid of humans, and in his first field note he recorded that a mockingbird was similar to those he had seen on the continent.

Beagle sailed on to Charles Island. By chance they were greeted by the Englishman Nicholas Lawson, acting Governor of Galápagos for the Republic of the Equator, who accompanied them up to the penal colony. It was said that tortoises differed in the shape of the shells from island to island, and Darwin noted Lawson's statement that on seeing a tortoise he could "pronounce with

Figure 25: *The various Galápagos mockingbirds Darwin caught resembled the Chilean mockingbird Mimus thenka, but differed from island to island.*

certainty from which island it has been brought". Though Darwin remembered this later, he did not pay much attention at the time. However, he found a mockingbird and "fortunately happened to observe" that it differed from the Chatham Island specimen, so from then on carefully noted where mockingbirds had been caught. He industriously collected all the animals, plants, insects & reptiles, and speculated about finding "from future comparison to what district or 'centre of creation' the organized beings of this archipelago must be attached." At this stage his thoughts reflected Lyell's rejection of transmutation of species.

They went on to Albemarle Island, where Darwin saw a small jet of smoke from a recently active volcano. On 1 October he landed near Tagus Cove and explored Beagle Crater.[32] There he saw his first Galapagos land iguanas. Water pits were disappointingly inadequate for drinking, but attracted swarms of small birds and Darwin made his only note of the finches he was not bothering to label by island. He caught a third species of mockingbird.

After passing the northern islands of Abingdon, Tower and Bindloe, Darwin was put ashore at James Island for nine days together with the surgeon Benjamin Bynoe and their servants, and they busily collected all sorts of specimens while *Beagle* went back to Chatham Island for fresh water.

After further surveying, *Beagle* set sail for Tahiti on 20 October 1835. Darwin wrote up his notes, and to his astonishment found that all the mockingbirds caught on Charles, Albemarle, James and Chatham Islands differed from island to island. He wrote "This birds which is so closely allied to the Thenca of Chili (Callandra of B. Ayres) is singular from existing as varieties or distinct species in the different Isds.— I have four specimens from as many Isds.— These will be found to be 2 or 3 varieties.— Each variety is constant in its own Island....".

Tahiti to Australia

They sailed on, dining on Galapagos tortoises, and passed the atoll of Honden Island on 9 November. They passed through the Low Islands archipelago, with Darwin remarking that they had "a very uninteresting appearance; a long brilliantly white beach is capped by a low bright line of green vegetation." Arriving at Tahiti on 15 November he soon found interest in luxuriant vegetation and the pleasant intelligent natives who showed the benefits of Christianity, refuting allegations he had read about tyrannical missionaries overturning indigenous cultures.

On 19 December they reached New Zealand where Darwin thought the tattooed Māori to be savages with character of a much lower order than the Tahitians, and noted that they and their homes were "filthily dirty and offensive". He saw missionaries bringing improvement in character as well as new farming practices with an exemplary "English farm" employing natives. Richard Matthews was left here with his elder brother Joseph Matthews who was a missionary at Kaitaia. Darwin and FitzRoy were agreed that missionaries had been unfairly misrepresented in tracts, particularly one written by the artist Augustus Earle which he had left on the ship. Darwin also noted many English residents of the most worthless character, including runaway convicts from New South Wales. By 30 December he was glad to leave New Zealand.

The first sight of Australia on 12 January 1836 reminded him of Patagonia, but inland the country improved and he was soon filled with admiration at the bustling city of Sydney. On a journey into the interior he came across a group of aborigines who looked "good-humoured & pleasant & they appeared far from such utterly degraded beings as usually represented". They gave him a display of spear throwing for a shilling, and he reflected sadly on how their numbers were rapidly decreasing. At a large sheep farm he joined a hunting party and caught his first marsupial, a "potoroo" (rat-kangaroo). Reflecting on the strange animals of the country, he thought that an unbeliever "might exclaim 'Surely two distinct Creators must have been [at] work; their object however has been the same & certainly the end in each case is complete'," yet an antlion he was watching was very similar to its European counterpart. That evening he saw the even stranger platypus and noticed that its bill was soft, unlike the preserved specimens he had seen. Aboriginal stories that they laid eggs were believed by few Europeans.

Beagle visited Hobart, Tasmania, where Darwin was impressed by the agreeable high society of the settlers, but noted that the island's "Aboriginal blacks are all removed & kept (in reality as prisoners) in a Promontory, the neck of which is guarded. I believe it was not possible to avoid this cruel step; although without doubt the misconduct of the Whites first led to the Necessity." They then sailed to King George's Sound in south west Australia, a dismal settlement then being replaced by the Swan River Colony. Darwin was impressed by the "good disposition of the aboriginal blacks... Although true Savages, it is impossible not to feel an inclination to like such quiet good-natured men." He provided boiled rice for an aboriginal "Corrobery" dancing party performed by the men of two tribes to the great pleasure of the women and children, a "most rude barbarous scene" in which everyone appeared in high spirits, "all moving in hideous harmony" and "perfectly at their ease". *Beagle*'s departure in a storm was delayed when she ran aground. She was refloated and got on her way.

Keeling Island homewards

FitzRoy's instructions from the Admiralty required a detailed geological survey of a circular coral atoll to investigate how coral reefs formed, particularly whether they rose from the bottom of the sea or from the summits of extinct volcanoes, and the effects of tides measured with specially constructed gauges. He chose the Keeling Islands in the Indian Ocean, and on arrival on 1 April the entire crew set to work. Darwin found a coconut economy, serving both the small settlement and wildlife. There was a limited range of native plants and no land birds, but hermit crabs everywhere. The lagoons teemed with a rich variety of invertebrates and fish, and he examined the atoll's structure in view of the theory he had developed in Lima, of encircling reefs becoming atolls as an island sank. This idea was supported by the numerous soundings FitzRoy had taken showing a steep slope outside the reef with no living corals below 20–30 fathoms (10–15 m).

Arriving at Mauritius on 29 April 1836, Darwin was impressed by the civilised prosperity of the French colony which had come under British rule. He toured the island, examining its volcanic mountains and fringing coral reefs. The Surveyor-general Captain Lloyd took him on the only elephant on the island to see an elevated coral plain. By then FitzRoy was writing the official *Narrative* of the *Beagle* voyages, and after reading Darwin's diary he proposed incorporating it into the account, a suggestion Darwin discussed with his family.

Beagle reached the Cape of Good Hope on 31 May. In Cape Town Darwin received a letter dated 29 December from his sister Caroline telling him that his fame was spreading. On 18 November 1835 Sedgwick had read extracts from Darwin's geological notes to the Geological Society of London, and this had been reported in *The Athenæum* on 21 November. On 25 December their father received a letter from Henslow which said that Darwin would become one of the premier naturalists of the time, and enclosed some copies of a book of extracts of Darwin's letters on South American geology which had been printed for private distribution. Their father "did not move from his seat till he had read every word of *your* book & he was very much gratified – he liked so much the simple clear way you gave your information".[33] Darwin was horrified that his careless words were in print, but *No hay remedio* (it can't be helped). He explored the geology of the area, reaching conclusions about slate formation and the injection of granite seams as liquid which differed from the ideas of Lyell and Sedgwick. The zoologist Andrew Smith showed him formations, and later discussed the large animals living on sparse vegetation, showing that a lack of luxuriant vegetation did not explain the extinction of the giant creatures in South America.

Around 15 June Darwin and FitzRoy visited the noted astronomer Sir John Herschel. In his diary Darwin called this "the most memorable event which, for a long period, I have had the good fortune to enjoy." His zeal for science had been stirred at Cambridge by reading Herschel's book on philosophy of science, which had guided his theorising during the voyage. Their discussion is not recorded, but a few months earlier, on 20 February 1836, Herschel had written to Lyell praising his *Principles of Geology* as a work which would bring "a complete revolution in [its] subject, by altering entirely the point of view in which it must thenceforward be contemplated." and opening a way for bold speculation on "that mystery of mysteries, the replacement of extinct species by others." Herschel himself thought catastrophic extinction and renewal "an inadequate conception of the Creator", and by analogy with other intermediate causes "the origination of fresh species, could it ever come under our cognizance, would be found to be a natural in contradistinction to a miraculous process".

In Cape Town missionaries were being accused of causing racial tension and profiteering, and after *Beagle* set to sea on 18 June FitzRoy wrote an open letter to the evangelical *South African Christian Recorder* on the *Moral State of Tahiti* incorporating extracts from both his and Darwin's diaries to defend the reputation of missionaries. This was given to a passing ship which took it to Cape Town to become FitzRoy's (and Darwin's) first published work.

On 8 July they stopped at St. Helena for six days. Darwin took lodgings near Napoleon's tomb, and when writing to Henslow asking to be proposed for the Geological Society, mentioned his suspicions "that differently from most Volcanic Islds. its structure is rather complicated. It seems strange, that this little centre of a distinct creation should, as is asserted, bear marks of recent elevation." With a guide he wandered over the island, noting its complex sloping strata showing fault lines, interlaced with volcanic dykes. He examined beds high on the hill which had been taken as seashells showing that St. Helena had risen from the ocean in recent times, but Darwin identified them as extinct species of land-shells. He noted that woodland had been destroyed by goats and hogs which had run wild since being introduced in 1502, and native vegetation only predominated on high steep ridges, having been replaced by imported species.

At this stage Darwin had an acute interest in island biogeography, and his description of St Helena as "a little centre of creation" in his geological diary reflects Charles Lyell's speculation in Volume 2 of *Principles of Geology* that the island would have acted as a "focus of creative force". He later recalled believing in the permanence of species, but "as far as I can remember, vague doubts occasionally flitted across my mind". When organising his *Ornithological Notes* between mid June and August, Darwin expanded on his initial notes on the Galapagos mockingbird *Mimus thenca*:

> These birds are closely allied in appearance to the Thenca of Chile or Callandra of la Plata. ... In each Isld. each kind is exclusively found: habits of all are indistinguishable. When I recollect, the fact that the form of the body, shape of scales & general size, the Spaniards can at once pronounce, from which Island any Tortoise may have been brought. When I see these Islands in sight of each other, & [but del.] possessed of but a scanty stock of animals, tenanted by these birds, but slightly differing in structure & filling the same place in Nature, I must suspect they are only varieties.
> The only fact of a similar kind of which I am aware, is the constant asserted difference — between the wolf-like Fox of East & West Falkland Islds.
> If there is the slightest foundation for these remarks the zoology of Archipelagoes — will be well worth examining; for such facts [would inserted] undermine the stability of Species.

The term "would" before "undermine" had been added after writing what is now noted as the first expression of his doubts about species being immutable, which led to him becoming convinced about the transmutation of species and hence evolution. In opposing transmutation, Lyell had proposed that varieties arose due to changes in environment, but these varieties lived in similar conditions though each on its own island. Darwin had just reviewed similar inconsistencies with mainland bird genera such as *Pteroptochos*. Though his suspicions about the Falkland Island fox may have been unsupported, the differences in Galápagos tortoises between islands were remembered, and he later wrote that he had been greatly struck from around March 1836 by the character of South

American fossils and of species on the Galapagos Archipelago, noting "These facts origin (especially latter) of all my views".

Beagle reached Ascension Island on 19 July 1836, and Darwin was delighted to receive letters from his sisters with news that Sedgwick had written "He is doing admirably in S. America, & has already sent home a Collection above all praise.— It was the best thing in the world for him that he went out on the Voyage of Discovery— There was some risk of his turning out an idle man: but his character will now be fixed, & if God spare his life, he will have a great name among the Naturalists of Europe." Darwin later recalled how he "clambered over the mountains... with a bounding step and made the volcanic rocks resound under my geological hammer!." He agreed with the saying attributed to the people of St Helena that "We know we live on a rock, but the poor people at Ascension live on a cinder", and noted the care taken to sustain "houses, gardens & fields placed near the summit of the central mountain". (In the 1840s Darwin worked with Hooker, who proposed in 1847 that the Royal Navy import tree species, a project started in 1850 which led to the creation of an artificial cloud forest.)

On 23 July they set off again longing to reach home, but FitzRoy wanted to ensure the accuracy of his longitude measurements and so took the ship across the Atlantic back to Bahia in Brazil to take check readings. Darwin was glad to see the beauties of the jungle for a last time, but now compared "the stately Mango trees with the Horse Chesnuts of England." The return trip was delayed for a further 11 days when weather forced *Beagle* to shelter further up the coast at Pernambuco, where Darwin examined rocks for signs of elevation, noted "Mangroves like rank grass" and investigated marine invertebrates at various depths on the sandbar. *Beagle* departed for home on 17 August. After a stormy passage including a stop for supplies at the Azores, the Beagle finally reached Falmouth, Cornwall, England on 2 October 1836. A plaque now commemorates his arrival point in Falmouth, Cornwall.

Return

Upon his return, Darwin was quick to take the coach home, arriving late at night on 4 October 1836 at The Mount House, the family home in Shrewsbury, Shropshire. Darwin reportedly headed straight to bed and greeted his family at breakfast. After ten days of catching up with family he went on to Cambridge and sought Henslow's advice on organising the description and cataloguing of his collections.

Darwin's father gave him an allowance that enabled him to put aside other careers, and as a scientific celebrity with a reputation established by his fossils and Henslow's publication of his letters on South American geology, he toured

Figure 26: *In 1837 HMS Beagle set off on a survey of Australia, shown here in an 1841 watercolour by Owen Stanley.*

London's society institutions. By this time he was part of the "scientific establishment", collaborating with expert naturalists to describe his specimens, and working on ideas he had been developing during the voyage. Charles Lyell gave him enthusiastic backing. In December 1836, Darwin presented a talk to the Cambridge Philosophical Society. He wrote a paper proving that Chile, and the South American continent, was slowly rising, which he read to the Geological Society of London on 4 January 1837.

Darwin thought of having his diary published mixed in with FitzRoy's account, but his relatives including Emma and Hensleigh Wedgwood urged that it be published separately. On 30 December the question was settled by FitzRoy taking the advice of William Broderip that Darwin's journal should form the third volume of the *Narrative*. Darwin set to work reorganising and trimming his diary, and incorporating scientific material from his notes. He completed his *Journal and Remarks* (now commonly known as *The Voyage of the Beagle*) in August 1837, but FitzRoy was slower and the three volumes were published in August 1839.

Syms Covington stayed with Darwin as his servant, then on 25 February 1839 (shortly after Darwin's marriage) Covington parted on good terms and migrated to Australia.

Expert publications on Darwin's collections

Darwin had shown great ability as a collector and had done the best he could with the reference books he had on ship. It was now the province of recognised expert specialists to establish which specimens were unknown, and make their considered taxonomic decisions on defining and naming new species.

Fossils

Richard Owen had expertise in comparative anatomy and his professional judgements revealed a succession of similar species in the same locality, giving Darwin insights which he would later recall as being central to his new views. Owen met Darwin on 29 October 1836 and quickly took on the task of describing these new fossils. At that time the only fully described fossil mammals from South America were three species of *Mastodon* and the gigantic *Megatherium*. On 9 November Darwin wrote to his sister that "Some of them are turning out great treasures." The near complete skeleton from Punta Alta was apparently very closely allied to anteaters, but of the extraordinary size of a small horse. The rhinoceros sized head bought for two shillings near Mercedes was not a megatherium, but "as far as they can guess, must have been a gnawing animal. Conceive a Rat or a Hare of such a size— What famous Cats they ought to have had in those days!" Over the following years Owen published descriptions of the most important fossils, naming several as new species.

The fossils from Punta Alta included a nearly perfect head and three fragments of heads of the *Megatherium Cuvierii*, the jaw of a related species which Owen named *Mylodon Darwinii*, and jaws of *Megalonyx Jeffersonii*. The near complete skeleton was named *Scelidotherium* by Owen, who found it had most of its bones nearly in their proper relative positions. At the nearby Monte Hermoso beds the numerous rodents included species allied to the Brazilian tuco-tuco and the capybara.

Owen decided that the fossils of polygonal plates of bony armour found at several locations were not from the Megatherium as Cuvier's description implied, but from a huge armadillo as Darwin had briefly thought. Owen found a description of an earlier unnamed specimen which he named *Glyptodon clavipes* in 1839. Darwin's find from Punta Alta, a large surface about 3 by 2 ft (0.91 by 0.61 m) doubled over with toe bones still inside the folded armour, was identified as a slightly smaller *Glyptodont* named *Hoplophorus* by Lund in the same year.

The huge skull from near Mercedes was named *Toxodon* by Owen, and he showed that the "enormous gnawing tooth" from the cliffs of the Carcarañá River was a molar from this species. The finds near Mercedes also included a

Figure 27: *A Scelidotherium skeleton in Paris.*

large fragment of *Glyptodont* armour and a head which Owen initially identified as a *Glossotherium*, but later decided was a *Mylodon*. Owen found fragments of the jaw and a tooth of another *Toxodon* in the fossils from Punta Alta.

The fossils from near Santa Fé included the horse tooth which had puzzled Darwin as it had been previously thought that horses had only come to the Americas in the 16th century, close to a *Toxodon* tooth and a tooth of *Mastodon andium* (now *Cuvieronius hyodon*). Owen confirmed that the horse tooth was of an extinct South American species which he named *Equus curvidens*, and its age was confirmed by a corroded horse tooth among the Punta Alta fossils. This discovery was later explained as part of the evolution of the horse.

The "soft as cheese" *Mastodon* bones at the Paraná River were identified as two gigantic skeletons of *Mastodon andium*, and mastodon teeth were also identified from Santa Fé and the Carcarañá River. The pieces of spine and a hind leg from Port S. Julian which Darwin had thought came from "some large animal, I fancy a Mastodon" gave Owen difficulties, as the creature which he named *Macrauchenia* appeared to be a "gigantic and most extraordinary pachyderm", allied to the *Palaeotherium*, but with affinities to the llama and the camel. The fossils at Punta Alta included a pachyderm tooth which was thought probably came from *Macrauchenia*.

References

- Babbage, Charles (1838), *The Ninth Bridgewater Treatise*[34] (2nd ed.), London: John Murray, retrieved 2009-02-02<templatestyles src="Module:Citation/CS1/styles.css"></templatestyles>
- Barlow, Nora ed. (1933), *Charles Darwin's diary of the voyage of H.M.S. Beagle*[35], Cambridge: University Press, retrieved 2009-01-29<templatestyles src="Module:Citation/CS1/styles.css"></templatestyles>
- Barlow, Nora ed. (1945), *Charles Darwin and the voyage of the Beagle*[36], London: Pilot Press, retrieved 2009-01-29<templatestyles src="Module:Citation/CS1/styles.css"></templatestyles>
- Barlow, Nora ed. (1963), "With introduction, notes and appendix by the editor"[37], *Bulletin of the British Museum (Natural History)*, **2** (7), pp. 201–278, retrieved 2009-01-29 | contribution= ignored (help)<templatestyles src="Module:Citation/CS1/styles.css"></templatestyles>
- Barlow, Nora ed. (1967), *Darwin and Henslow. The growth of an idea*[38], London: Bentham-Moxon Trust, John Murray, retrieved 2009-01-29<templatestyles src="Module:Citation/CS1/styles.css"></templatestyles>
- Browne, Janet; Neve, Michael (1989), "Introduction", in Darwin, Charles, *Voyage of the Beagle: Charles Darwin's Journal of researches*, London: Penguin Books, ISBN 0-14-043268-X<templatestyles src="Module:Citation/CS1/styles.css"></templatestyles>
- Browne, E. Janet (1995), *Charles Darwin: vol. 1 Voyaging*, London: Jonathan Cape, ISBN 1-84413-314-1<templatestyles src="Module:Citation/CS1/styles.css"></templatestyles>
- Darwin, Charles (1835), *Extracts from letters to Professor Henslow*[39], Cambridge: [privately printed], retrieved 2009-01-27<templatestyles src="Module:Citation/CS1/styles.css"></templatestyles>
- Darwin, Charles (1836), "Geological notes made during a survey of the east and west coasts of S. America, in the years 1832, 1833, 1834 and 1835, with an account of a transverse section of the Cordilleras of the Andes between Valparaiso and Mendoza. (Read 18 November 1835)"[40], *Proceedings of the Geological Society of London*, **2**: 210–212, retrieved 2013-02-23<templatestyles src="Module:Citation/CS1/styles.css"></templatestyles>
- Darwin, Charles (1839), *Narrative of the surveying voyages of His Majesty's Ships Adventure and Beagle between the years 1826 and 1836, describing their examination of the southern shores of South America, and the Beagle's circumnaviga-*

tion of the globe. Journal and remarks. 1832–1836.[41], **III**, London: Henry Colburn, retrieved 2009-01-27<templatestyles src="Module:Citation/CS1/styles.css"></templatestyles>
- Darwin, Charles (1842), *The Structure and Distribution of Coral Reefs. Being the first part of the geology of the voyage of the Beagle, under the command of Capt. Fitzroy, R.N. during the years 1832 to 1836*[42], London: Smith Elder and Co., retrieved 2009-01-29<templatestyles src="Module:Citation/CS1/styles.css"></templatestyles>
- Darwin, Charles (1844), *Geological Observations on the Volcanic Islands visited during the Voyage of H.M.S. Beagle, together with some brief notices of the geology of Australia and the Cape of Good Hope. Being the second part of the geology of the voyage of the Beagle, under the command of Capt. Fitzroy, R.N. during the years 1832 to 1836*[43], London: Smith Elder and Co., retrieved 2009-01-29<templatestyles src="Module:Citation/CS1/styles.css"></templatestyles>
- Darwin, Charles (1845), *Journal of Researches into the natural history and geology of the countries visited during the voyage of H.M.S. Beagle round the world, under the command of Capt. Fitz Roy, R.N. 2d edition*, London: John Murray | access-date= requires | url= (help)<templatestyles src="Module:Citation/CS1/styles.css"></templatestyles>
- Darwin, Charles (1846), *Geological Observations on South America. Being the third part of the geology of the voyage of the Beagle, under the command of Capt. Fitzroy, R.N. during the years 1832 to 1836*[44], London: Smith Elder and Co., retrieved 2009-01-27<templatestyles src="Module:Citation/CS1/styles.css"></templatestyles>
- Darwin, Charles (1871), *The Descent of Man, and Selection in Relation to Sex* (1st ed.), London: John Murray | access-date= requires | url= (help)<templatestyles src="Module:Citation/CS1/styles.css"></templatestyles>
- Darwin, Charles (1958), Barlow, Nora, ed., *The Autobiography of Charles Darwin 1809–1882. With the original omissions restored. Edited and with appendix and notes by his granddaughter Nora Barlow*, London: Collins | access-date= requires | url= (help)<templatestyles src="Module:Citation/CS1/styles.css"></templatestyles>
- Desmond, Adrian; Moore, James (1991), *Darwin*, London: Michael Joseph, Penguin Group, ISBN 0-7181-3430-3<templatestyles src="Module:Citation/CS1/styles.css"></templatestyles>
- Eldredge, Niles (2006), "Confessions of a Darwinist"[45], *The Virginia Quarterly Review* (Spring 2006), pp. 32–53, retrieved 2009-01-27<templatestyles src="Module:Citation/CS1/styles.css"></templatestyles>

- FitzRoy, Robert (1836), "*Sketch of the Surveying Voyages of his Majesty's Ships Adventure and Beagle*, 1825–1836. Commanded by Captains P. P. King, P. Stokes, and R. Fitz-Roy, Royal Navy. (Communicated by John Barrow)"[46], *Journal of the Geological Society of London*, **6**: 311–343, retrieved 2012-05-14<templatestyles src="Module:Citation/CS1/styles.css"></templatestyles>
- FitzRoy, Robert (1839), *Narrative of the surveying voyages of His Majesty's Ships Adventure and Beagle between the years 1826 and 1836, describing their examination of the southern shores of South America, and the Beagle's circumnavigation of the globe. Proceedings of the second expedition, 1831–36, under the command of Captain Robert Fitz-Roy, R.N.*[47], **II**, London: Henry Colburn, retrieved 2009-01-27<templatestyles src="Module:Citation/CS1/styles.css"></templatestyles>
- FitzRoy, Robert (1839), *Narrative of the surveying voyages of His Majesty's Ships Adventure and Beagle between the years 1826 and 1836, describing their examination of the southern shores of South America, and the Beagle's circumnavigation of the globe*[48], Appendix to Volume II, London: Henry Colburn, retrieved 2009-01-27<templatestyles src="Module:Citation/CS1/styles.css"></templatestyles>
- Freeman, R. B. (2007), *Charles Darwin: A companion. 2d online edition, compiled by Sue Asscher and edited by John van Wyhe*.[49] (2d online edition, compiled by Sue Asscher and edited by John van Wyhe ed.), Darwin Online, retrieved 2010-08-01<templatestyles src="Module:Citation/CS1/styles.css"></templatestyles>
- Gould, John (1839), Darwin, C. R., ed., *Birds Part 3 No. 4*[50], The zoology of the voyage of H.M.S. Beagle, London: Smith Elder and Co., retrieved 2009-04-18<templatestyles src="Module:Citation/CS1/styles.css"></templatestyles>
- Herbert, Sandra (1991), "Charles Darwin as a prospective geological author"[51], *British Journal for the History of Science*, **24**, pp. 159–192, doi:10.1017/s0007087400027060[52], retrieved 2009-01-29<templatestyles src="Module:Citation/CS1/styles.css"></templatestyles>
- Herbert, Sandra (1995), "From Charles Darwin's portfolio: An early essay on South American geology and species. 14, no. 1, pp."[53], *Earth Sciences History*, **14** (1), pp. 23–36, doi:10.17704/eshi.14.1.76570264u727jh36[54], retrieved 2009-01-29<templatestyles src="Module:Citation/CS1/styles.css"></templatestyles>
- Hodge, Jonathan (2009), "Darwin, the Galapagos and his changing thoughts about species origins: 1835–1837"[55], *Proceedings of the California Academy of Sciences*, **61** (Supplement II, No. 7): 89–106, retrieved 2012-02-19<templatestyles

- src="Module:Citation/CS1/styles.css"></templatestyles>
- Keynes, Richard (2000), *Charles Darwin's zoology notes & specimen lists from H.M.S. Beagle.*[56], Cambridge University Press, retrieved 2009-01-27<templatestyles src="Module:Citation/CS1/styles.css"></templatestyles>
- Keynes, Richard (2001), *Charles Darwin's Beagle Diary*[57], Cambridge University Press, retrieved 2009-01-27<templatestyles src="Module:Citation/CS1/styles.css"></templatestyles>
- King, P. P. (1839), FitzRoy, Robert, ed., *Narrative of the surveying voyages of His Majesty's Ships Adventure and Beagle between the years 1826 and 1836, describing their examination of the southern shores of South America, and the Beagle's circumnavigation of the globe. Proceedings of the first expedition, 1826–30, under the command of Captain P. Parker King, R.N., F.R.S.*[58], **I**, London: Henry Colburn, retrieved 2009-01-27<templatestyles src="Module:Citation/CS1/styles.css"></templatestyles>
- Owen, Richard (1837), "A description of the Cranium of the Toxodon Platensis, a gigantic extinct mammiferous species, referrible by its dentition to the Rodentia, but with affinities to the Pachydermata and the Herbivorous Cetacea [Read 19 April]"[59], *Proceedings of the Geological Society of London* (2), pp. 541–542, retrieved 2009-01-27<templatestyles src="Module:Citation/CS1/styles.css"></templatestyles>
- Owen, Richard (1840), Darwin, C. R., ed., *Fossil Mammalia Part 1*[60], The zoology of the voyage of H.M.S. Beagle, London: Smith Elder and Co., retrieved 2009-01-27<templatestyles src="Module:Citation/CS1/styles.css"></templatestyles>
- Poulton, Edward Bagnall (1896), *Charles Darwin and the theory of natural selection*[60], London: Cassell & Co., retrieved 2009-01-27<templatestyles src="Module:Citation/CS1/styles.css"></templatestyles>
- van Wyhe, John (27 March 2007), "Mind the gap: Did Darwin avoid publishing his theory for many years?"[61], *Notes and Records of the Royal Society*, **61**: 177–205, doi:10.1098/rsnr.2006.0171[62], retrieved 2009-02-02<templatestyles src="Module:Citation/CS1/styles.css"></templatestyles>
- van Wyhe, John (2013), ""My appointment received the sanction of the Admiralty": Why Charles Darwin really was the naturalist on HMS Beagle"[63] (PDF), *Studies in History and Philosophy of Science Part C: Studies in History and Philosophy of Biological and Biomedical Sciences*, Elsevier BV, **44** (3): 316–326, doi:10.1016/j.shpsc.2013.03.022[64], retrieved 2016-09-23<templatestyles src="Module:Citation/CS1/styles.css"></templatestyles>

- von Wartenberg, Henry (2010), *Charles Darwin al sur del sur: Detrás de sus huellas dos siglos después*, Buenos Aires<templatestyles src="Module:Citation/CS1/styles.css"></templatestyles>

External links

- "Darwin, a naturalist's voyage around world"[65]. CNRS, Paris, France. Retrieved 2009-11-09.<templatestyles src="Module:Citation/CS1/styles.css"></templatestyles>
- "AboutDarwin.com – Beagle Voyage"[66]. Retrieved 2007-11-21.<templatestyles src="Module:Citation/CS1/styles.css"></templatestyles>
- Rookmaaker, Kees (2009), *Darwin's itinerary on the voyage of the Beagle*[67], Darwin Online, retrieved 2009-08-18<templatestyles src="Module:Citation/CS1/styles.css"></templatestyles>
- Grant K. Thalia and, Estes Gregory B. (2009), *Darwin's itinerary in Galapagos*[68]<templatestyles src="Module:Citation/CS1/styles.css"></templatestyles>

Further reading

- The Complete Works of Charles Darwin Online – Darwin Online[69]; Darwin's publications, private papers and bibliography, supplementary works including biographies, obituaries and reviews. Free to use, includes items not in public domain.
- Works by Charles Darwin[70] at Project Gutenberg; public domain
- Darwin Correspondence Project[71] Text and notes for most of his letters
- Darwin in Galapagos: Footsteps to a New World –[72]

Inception of Darwin's evolutionary theory

Inception of Darwin's theory

The **inception of Darwin's theory** occurred during an intensively busy period which began when Charles Darwin returned from the survey voyage of the *Beagle*, with his reputation as a fossil collector and geologist already established. He was given an allowance from his father to become a gentleman naturalist rather than a clergyman, and his first tasks were to find suitable experts to describe his collections, write out his *Journal and Remarks*, and present papers on his findings to the Geological Society of London.

At Darwin's geological début, the anatomist Richard Owen's reports on the fossils showed that extinct species were related to current species in the same locality, and the ornithologist John Gould showed that bird specimens from the Galápagos Islands were of distinct species related to places, not just varieties. These points convinced Darwin that transmutation of species must be occurring, and in his *Red Notebook* he jotted down his first evolutionary ideas. He began specific transmutation notebooks with speculations on variation in offspring "to adapt & alter the race to *changing* world", and sketched an "irregularly branched" genealogical branching of a single evolutionary tree.

Animal observations of an orangutan at the zoo showed how human its expressions looked, confirming his thoughts from the *Beagle* voyage that there was little gulf between man and animals. He investigated animal breeding and found parallels to nature removing runts and keeping the fit, with farmers deliberately selecting breeding animals so that through "a thousand intermediate forms" their descendants were significantly changed. His speculations on instincts and mental traits suggested habits, beliefs and facial expressions having evolved, and considered the social implications. While this was his "prime hobby", he was struggling with an immense workload and began suffering from his illness. Having taken a break from work, his thoughts of marriage turned to his cousin Emma Wedgwood.

Reading about Malthus and natural law led him to apply to his search for the Creator's laws Malthusian logic of social thinking of struggle for survival with no handouts, and he "had at last got a theory by which to work". He proposed to Emma, and was accepted. In his theory, he compared breeders selecting traits to natural selection from variants thrown up by "chance", and continued to look to the countryside for supporting information. On 24 January 1839 he was elected as Fellow of the Royal Society, and on the 29th married Emma. The development of Darwin's theory followed.

Background

Darwin was not the first to propose that species of organisms could become modified over time. In the third edition of *On the Origin of Species* Darwin provided a *historical sketch* of his predecessors in writing of descent with modification or natural selection, including those whom he had only learned of after the 1859 publication of *The Origin*. His account essentially deals with 19th-century authors; "Passing over authors from the classical period to that of Buffon, with whose writings I am not familiar, Lamarck was the first man whose conclusions on this subject excited much attention." However, in a footnote he remarks on how his grandfather, Dr. Erasmus Darwin, Goethe and Geoffroy Saint Hilaire came to the same conclusion on the origin of species in the years 1794–95, anticipating Lamarck.

After his early life in a Unitarian family, Charles Darwin developed his interest in natural history. At Edinburgh University his work as a student of Robert Edmund Grant involved him in pioneering investigations of the ideas of Lamarck and Erasmus Darwin on *homology* showing common descent, but he also saw how controversial and troubling such theories were. Robert Jameson's course taught Darwin stratigraphic geology, and closed with lectures on the "Origin of the Species of Animals". At Christ's College, Cambridge to qualify as an Anglican clergyman, Darwin became passionate about beetle collecting, then shone in John Stevens Henslow's botany course. He was convinced by Paley's *Natural Theology* which set out the Teleological argument that complexity of "design" in nature proved God's role as Creator, and by the views of Paley and John Herschel that creation was by laws which science could discover, not by intermittent miracles. The geology course of Adam Sedgwick and summer work mapping strata in Wales emphasised that life on earth went back over eons of time.

Then on his voyage on the *Beagle* Darwin became convinced by Charles Lyell's uniformitarian theory of gradual geological process, and puzzled over how various theories of creation fitted the evidence he saw.

Return to celebrity and science

When the Beagle returned, Darwin was quick to take the coach home and arrived at the family home of The Mount House in Shrewsbury, Shropshire, late at night on 4 October 1836. He went straight to bed, then greeted his family at breakfast and began catching up with news of his family and of the country: "all England appears changed". The Reform Bill had brought what the Tory Duke of Wellington described as a shift in power from decent Tory Anglicans to Whig manufacturers, shopkeepers and atheists. Educated people were discussing the writings of Thomas Malthus on population outstripping resources as the *New Poor Law* described by opponents as "a Malthusian bill designed to force the poor to emigrate, to work for lower wages, to live on a coarser sort of food" brought the construction of workhouses in the southern counties despite riots and arson. The government had not yet dared introduce these measures to London and the industrial north, and recession was bringing threats of mass unemployment.

Darwin wrote to Henslow that he was still "giddy with joy & confusion... I want your advice on so many points, indeed I am in the clouds" and on 15 October went on to Cambridge to get advice from Henslow and Sedgwick on the task of organising the description and cataloguing of his collections accumulated from the Beagle expedition. Henslow took on the plants, and Darwin was given introductions to the best London naturalists with a warning that they would already be busy with other work.

Charles went on to stay with his brother Erasmus in London, near the scientific institutions which were in the throes of renovation, while the city itself was being torn up to install new sewers and gas lighting. He went round the British Museum, the Royal College of Surgeons, the Linnean, the Zoological Society and Geological Society, trying to get the experts to take on his collections. Henslow had already established his former pupil's reputation during the Beagle expedition by giving selected naturalists access to fossil specimens sent back as well as having Darwin's geological writings privately printed for distribution. Darwin went "in most exciting dissipation amongst the Dons in science", and as Charles Bunbury reported, "[he] seems to be a universal collector" finding new species "to the surprise of all the big wigs". While geologists were quick to take on the rock samples, zoologists already had more specimens arriving than they could deal with. Their institutions were in turmoil as democrats argued for reforms replacing the aristocratic amateurs with professional salaried scientists as in the French research institutes. At the Zoological Society the reformers were led by Darwin's tutor from Edinburgh days, Robert Edmund Grant. Darwin now had an allowance plus stocks from his father, bringing him around £400 per year, and his sympathies were with the amateur clerical "Dons in science" of Cambridge.

Owen and fossils

The geologist Charles Lyell invited Darwin to dinner on 29 October 1836. Over dinner Lyell listened eagerly to Darwin's stories (which supported Lyell's uniformitarianism) and introduced him to Richard Owen and William Broderip, Tories who had just been involved in voting Grant out of a position at the Zoological Society. Owen was rapidly ousting Grant as the country's leading anatomist. Darwin went to visit him at his Royal College of Surgeons, and Owen agreed to work on some animal specimens in spirits and the fossil bones. Owen shared Darwin's enthusiasm. He was a proponent of German ideas of "organising energy" and vehemently opposed to Grant's evolution. At around this time Grant was one of the few to volunteer his help with cataloguing the collection. Darwin turned down the offer, not wanting to be associated with a disreputable radical who denounced his Cambridge friends.

On 12 November Darwin visited his Wedgwood relatives at Maer Hall and they encouraged him to publish a book of his travels based on his diary, an idea his sisters picked up when he visited his home.

On 2 December he returned to London and began finding takers for his specimens, with Thomas Bell and the Revd. William Buckland interested in the reptiles. Darwin's reputation was being made by the giant mammal fossils. Owen's first surprising revelation was that a hippopotamus sized fossil skull 2 feet 4 inches (710 mm) long which Darwin had bought for about two shillings near Mercedes while on a "galloping" trip 120 miles (190 km) from Montevideo was of an extinct rodent-like creature resembling a giant capybara, which Owen named *Toxodon*. Darwin wrote to his sister Caroline that "[the fossils] are turning out great treasures" and of the *Toxodon*, "There is another head, as large as a Rhinoceros which as far as they can guess, must have been a gnawing animal. Conceive a Rat or a Hare of such a size – What famous Cats they ought to have had in those days!" The College of Surgeons distributed casts of the fossils to the major scientific institutions.

Darwin paid a visit to his brother Erasmus's lady friend the literary Whig Miss Harriet Martineau who had strong views on egalitarianism and whose writings had popularised the ideas of Thomas Malthus. Around this time, she was writing her *Society in America* which included discussion of the geological "process of world making" that she had seen on her visit to the Niagara Falls. He sat there for almost an hour. "She was very agreeable and managed to talk on a most wonderful number of subjects, considering the limited time. I was astonished to find how little ugly she is, but as it appears to me, she is overwhelmed with her own projects, her own thoughts and own abilities. Erasmus palliated all this, by maintaining one ought not to look at her as a woman." In her autobiography, she later recalled Charles as being "simple, childlike, painstaking, effective".[73]

Geological début, species related to places

Unhappy with life in a "dirty odious London" he returned to Cambridge on 13 December then wrote his first paper, showing that the Chilean coast and the South American land-mass was rising slowly, and discussed his ideas with Lyell. To Lyell's delight, Darwin went further in balancing the rising continent with sinking mountains forming the basis of coral atolls. Darwin briefly returned to London to read his paper to the Geological Society on 4 January 1837. Despite Darwin's nerves about his début, the talk was so well received that he felt "like a peacock admiring his tail".

On the same day Darwin presented 80 mammal and 450 bird specimens to the Zoological Society. The Mammalia were ably taken on by George R. Waterhouse.

While the birds seemed almost an afterthought the ornithologist John Gould took them on and was quick to notice the significance of specimens from the Galápagos Islands. He startlingly revealed at the next meeting on 10 January that what Darwin had taken to be wrens, blackbirds and slightly differing finches were "a series of ground finches which are so peculiar" as to form "an entirely new group" of 11 species. The story of what we now call "Darwin's finches" was covered by the daily newspapers, though Darwin was in Cambridge and did not get details at this stage. In the minutes of the meeting the number was extended to 12 species.

Owen was finding unexpected relationships from the fossils: the batch included the horse sized Scelidotherium which appeared to be closely allied to the anteater, a gigantic ground sloth, and an ox-sized armoured armadillo which he called Glyptodon. The Patagonian spine and leg bones from Port St Julian which Darwin had thought might be from a Mastodon were apparently from a gigantic guanaco or Llama, or perhaps camel, which Owen named *Macrauchenia*. Lyell saw a "law of succession" with mammals being replaced by their own kind on each continent, and on 17 February used his presidential address at the Geological Society to present Owen's findings to date on Darwin's fossils, pointing out this inference that extinct species were related to current species in the same locality. He invited Darwin to come along, and the speech drew Darwin's attention to the question of why past and present species in one place should be so closely related. At the same meeting Darwin was elected to the Council of the Society. For Lyell this was "a glorious addition to my society of geologists", gentlemen (and amateurs of independent means) with duty only to scientific integrity, social stability and responsible religion, for Darwin it meant joining the respectable élite of eminent geologists developing a science dealing with the age of the earth and the Days of Creation.

Darwin had already been invited by FitzRoy to contribute his *Journal*, based on his field notes, as the natural history section of the captain's account of the Beagle's voyage, and this ended up keeping him fully occupied from 13 March to the end of September. He also plunged into writing a book on South American Geology, putting his and Lyell's ideas forward against the cataclysmic explanation of mountain formation Alcide d'Orbigny was promoting in a multi-volume account of the continent begun two years previously.

On Monday 27 February Darwin presented a talk to the Cambridge Philosophical Society on glassy tubes he had found amongst Maldonado sand dunes, explained by lightning having fused the sand.

To supervise his collections Darwin had to return to London, and on Lyell's advice he planned to arrive on Friday 3 March 1837, in time for one of Charles Babbage's Saturday parties, talking shops about the latest developments "brilliantly attended by fashionable ladies, as well as literary and scientific gents" and "a good mixture of pretty women", bankers and politicians, where Babbage promoted such projects as his mechanical computer.[74] At first Darwin stayed with Erasmus, in his journal written up later he put his date of moving as 6 March 1837. On the 13th he moved to nearby lodgings, joining Erasmus's circle of friends including Martineau and Hensleigh and enjoying his intimate dinner parties with guests such as Lyell, Babbage and Thomas Carlyle.[75]

In their first meeting to discuss his detailed findings, Gould told Darwin that the Galápagos mockingbirds from different islands were separate species, not just varieties, and the finch group included the "wrens". The two rheas were also distinct species, and on 14 March Gould's announcement of this finding to the Zoological Society of London was accompanied by Darwin, who presented a paper on how distribution of the two species of rheas changed going southwards.

Transmutation

Context

Darwin was concerned to make sure that his theorising, whether published or private, fully complied with the accepted scientific methodology of his peers. In the scientific societies and at informal dinners he discussed methods with two leading authorities on the topic, John Herschel and William Whewell.

Scientific circles were buzzing with ideas of natural theology. In a letter to Lyell, Herschel had written of "that mystery of mysteries, the replacement of extinct species by others". This was circulated and widely discussed, with scientists sharing Herschel's approach of looking for an answer through laws of nature and rejecting *ad hoc* miracles as an explanation. Charles Babbage expressed in his *Ninth Bridgewater Treatise* (1837) a view of "Nature's God" along the lines of a programmer of such laws. Darwin's freethinking brother Erasmus was part of this Whig circle and a close friend of the writer Harriet Martineau, who promoted the Malthusianism underlying the controversial Whig Poor Law reforms (1834) to stop welfare from causing overpopulation and more poverty, which were then being implemented piecemeal in the face of opposition to the new poorhouses. As a Unitarian, Martineau welcomed the radical implications of transmutation of species, which was promoted by Grant and some medical men but anathema to Darwin's Anglican friends who saw it as a threat to the social order. Transmutation threatened the essential distinction between man and beast, and implied progressive improvement with the implication that the lower orders could aspire to the privileges of their aristocratic overlords.

The medical establishment controlling the London teaching hospitals, including the Royal College of Surgeons, was restricted to Anglicans and dominated by the aristocracy who saw perfect animal design as proof of a natural theology supporting their ideas of God-given rank and privilege. Since the 1820s large numbers of private medical schools joined by the new London University had introduced the "philosophical anatomy" of Geoffroy Saint-Hilaire based on unity of plan compatible with the transmutation of species, implying ideas of progressive improvement and supporting radical demands for democracy. This anatomy had already spread from Paris to the medical schools of Edinburgh, and the new London schools attracted Scots, including Grant. Numerous journals now promoted these radical ideas, including Thomas Wakley's *The Lancet* (started in 1823 with support from William Cobbett and William Lawrence, whose 1819 publication of evolutionary ideas the Crown had prosecuted for blasphemy). In response, the medical establishment gave support to the idealist biology of Joseph Henry Green (1791–1863) and of his younger protégé Richard Owen (1804–1892), based on the vitalism of German *Naturphilosophie* and Platonic idealism, which saw anatomical forms as "archetypes" in the Divine mind, imposed through "descensive" powers of delegation of divine authority in accordance with traditional hierarchies.

Red Notebook

In 1836 Darwin used his *Red Notebook* to record field observations during the last stages of his *Beagle* voyage, from May to 25 September. Page 113 mentions a meeting with Richard Owen, after the ship's return to England in October. Later notes mention discussions with other experts, including the geographer Sir Woodbine Parish, geologists Charles Lyell and Roderick Murchison, and the conchologist James De Carle Sowerby. Darwin also took brief notes on what he was reading, reminders on planned publications including his Journal of the voyage, and his developing "theories", "conjectures", and "hypotheses". He continued using the notebook until May or June 1837.[76]

In his later "Journal", Darwin recalled having been "greatly struck from about month of previous March on character of S. American fossils – & species on Galapagos Archipelago. – These facts origin (especially latter) of all my views." His first reference to transmutation appears in the Red Notebook around early March 1837, after John Gould told him that the common Rhea was a different species to the Petisse. Darwin wrote "Speculate on neutral ground of 2 ostriches; bigger one encroaches on smaller. change not progressif<e>: produced at one blow. if one species altered", proposing a sudden change or saltation in contrast to Lamarck's idea that species graded imperceptibly into each other: later, Darwin referred to this jump as inosculation. He drew on the relationship Owen had shown between fossils of the extinct giant *Macrauchenia* and the modern guanacos that Darwin had hunted in Patagonia: "The same kind of relation that common ostrich bears to [Petisse]: extinct Guanaco to recent: in former case position, in latter time. .... – As in first cases distinct species inosculate, so must we believe ancient ones: not gradual change or degeneration. from circumstances: if one species does change into another it must be per saltum – or species may perish." Here, he related the geographical distribution of species to their replacement over time, and tentatively proposed that the Rheas had a shared ancestor.

He noted his thoughts on reproduction and extinction; "Tempted to believe animals created for a definite time: – not extinguished by change of circumstances", and various domesticated animals had "all run wild & bred. no doubt with perfect success. – showing non Creation does not bear upon solely adaptation of animals. – extinction in same manner may not depend. – There is no more wonder in extinction of species than of individual."

Darwin's notes mention several papers based on his geological writings during the voyage. At the Geographical Society meeting on 3 May 1837, Darwin read his paper on strata around Río de la Plata where he had found fossils including the *Toxodon*.[77] At the same meeting, announcements were made of the first discoveries of ancient fossil primates; finds by Proby Cautley and Hugh Falconer in Neogene strata of the Sivalik Hills, and by Édouard Lartet in Miocene beds at Sansan, Gers. Later, Lyell joked uncomfortably to his sister that "according to Lamarck's view, there may have been a great many thousand centuries for their tails to wear off, and the transformation to men to take place", but Darwin was beginning to look at these "wonderful" fossils in relation to transmutation.[78] Darwin's notes mentioned his "Coral Paper" which he had originally drafted in 1835; he presented this on 31 May 1837 at the Geological Society of London, and later used it as the basis for his book on *The Structure and Distribution of Coral Reefs*.

At their frequent meetings, Owen argued that intrinsic "organising energy" in the "embryonic germ" set the lifespan of the species and precluded transmutation. The botanist Robert Brown showed Darwin a different concept, of "swarming atoms" *inside* the germ, allowing nature's self-development. Embarrassed by his lack of labels for his finch specimens, he examined FitzRoy's in the British Museum and contacted seamen including Syms Covington for their collections. From this he was able to relate the finches to separate islands, with distinct species on each island. As well as pressing on with his *Journal*, he started an ambitious project to get the expert reports on his collection published as a multi-volume *Zoology of the Voyage of H.M.S. Beagle*. A search for sponsorship was answered when Henslow used his contacts with the Chancellor of the Exchequer Thomas Spring Rice to arrange a Treasury grant of £1,000, a sum equivalent to about £83,000 in present-day terms.[79]<templatestyles src="Module:Citation/CS1/styles.css"></templatestyles>

During the *Beagle* voyage Darwin had noted the distribution of the two species of Galápagos iguanas and suspected that "this genus, the species of which are so well adapted to their respective localities, is peculiar to this group of Isds". He had identified the sea iguanas from a book on board as having been named *Amblyrhyncus Cristatus* by Bell from a specimen which had arrived in Mexico, probably found on the Pacific shore. In June he gave this information to William Buckland. As the Victorian era began, Darwin pressed on with writing his *Journal*, and in August 1837 began correcting printer's proofs.

Transmutation notebooks

In mid-July 1837, as his *Red Notebook* filled up, Darwin reorganised his note-taking, and began two new notebooks: his *"A" notebook* on geology, and his *"B" notebook*, the first of a series on "transmutation of Species", in which he scribbled down a framework for his speculations, jotting down thoughts on evolution. In a phrase he used later, this became "mental rioting".

B notebook

The title page of the *"B" notebook* was headed *Zoönomia*, referring to his late grandfather's evolutionary ideas, and began with questions about the reasons for "generation" in which asexual reproduction resulted in copies of the original, while sexual reproduction produced variation in the offspring, and organisms had short lifespans. The world was known to have changed over time, and "the young of living beings, become permanently changed or subject to variety, according to circumstances". This included plants, animals,

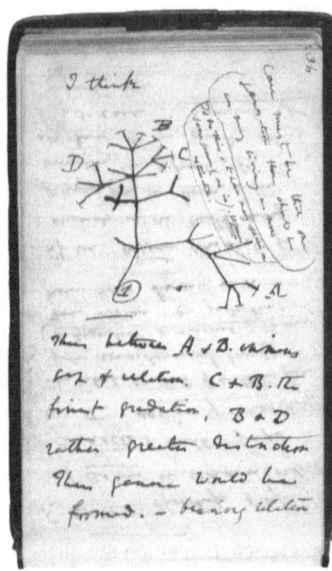

Figure 28: *In mid-July 1837 Darwin started his "B" notebook on Transmutation of Species, and quickly developed unique ideas of branching descent. On page 36 wrote "I think" above his first evolutionary tree diagram.*

and humanity: "in course of generations even mind and instinct become influenced. – child of savage not civilized man." Full-grown organisms might be unchangeable, but variability of their offspring would "adapt & alter the race to changing world." His ideas predated genetic concepts, and he continued to believe that variations arose through reproduction in a purposeful way responding to changes in the environment.[80] Not all would succeed: "The father being climatized, climatizes the child. Whether every animal produces in course of ages ten thousand varieties (influenced itself perhaps by circumstances) & those alone preserved which are well adapted."

In a large population, "intermarriages" (crossing) would even out these variations and explain why species appeared constant, but reproductive isolation of a small sub-group could lead to divergence and geographic speciation: "animals on separate islands ought to become different if kept long enough apart with slightly differing circumstances", as in the various species he had seen of Galápagos tortoises and mockingbirds, the Falkland Fox and the Chiloe fox, the "Inglish and Irish Hare". What Darwin called "inosculation" would abruptly introduce a clear distinction between even the most closely related species, explaining the rheas which remained distinct species with overlapping territories.

Uniquely for his time, he envisaged this diverging adaptation as genealogical branching from a common ancestor, an evolutionary tree: "Organized beings represent a tree irregularly branched some branches far more branched – Hence Genera. –) As many terminal buds dying as new ones generated". Refining the concept; "The tree of life should perhaps be called the coral of life, base of branches dead; so that passages cannot be seen". With the words "I think", he sketched a diagram of this branching pattern. This novel view contrasted with the ideas of transmutationists of the time (including Lamarck and Grant), who envisaged independent parallel lineages impelled by inner forces to make progress to higher forms. Darwin protested against these linear ideas of progress; "It is absurd to talk of one animal being higher than another. – We consider those, when the intellectual faculties [or] cerebral structure most developed, as highest. – A bee doubtless would when the instincts were". Later in the notebook, he set down a progressionist concept of human origins: "If all men were dead, then monkeys make men. – Men make angels".

Darwin thought that the possibility of a common ancestor of "mammalia & fish" could not be ruled out when such strange forms as the platypus existed. The unique plants and animals on the Galápagos islands sharing features with mainland American species, while wandering birds such as sandpipers were unchanged, showed the way "creative power acted at Galapagos", confirmed "if we believe the Creator created by any laws, which I think is shown by the very facts of the Zoological character of these islands". A similar relationship in time was shown by the extinct armoured giant Glyptodon resembling the modern South American armadillo. He considered that the way that astronomers once thought that God ordered the movement of individual planets was comparable to individual creation of species in particular countries, but divine powers were "much more simple & sublime" in creating the first animals so that species then arose by "the fixed laws of generation". A hypothesis of "fresh creations" he saw as "mere assumption, it explains nothing further". From Owen, he learnt of John Hunter's observations on "the production of monsters" (mutants) at birth, and he noted that this could "present an analogy to production of species". He jotted down thoughts on how organisms could reach new islands: could "Owls transport mice alive?". Seeds might be blown over, transported by floating trees or eaten by birds which flew to the islands. He noted a reminder to "Experimentise on land shells in salt water & lizards" ditto.

Under pressure with organising *Zoology* and correcting proofs of his *Journal* (which had to have the introduction revised when FitzRoy complained that he was "astonished at the total omission of any notice of the officers" for their help), Darwin's health suffered. On 20 September 1837 he suffered "an uncomfortable palpitation of the heart". His doctors advised him "*strongly* to knock off all work" and to leave for the country. Two days later he went to Maer Hall, the Wedgwoods' home, for a month of recuperation. His relations wore him out with questions about gaucho life. His invalid aunt was being cared for by the as-yet unmarried Emma, and his uncle Jos pointed out an area of ground where cinders had disappeared under loam which Jos though might have been the work of earthworms. Darwin returned to London on 21 October and on 1 November gave a talk on the role of earthworms in soil formation to the Geological Society, a mundane subject which to them may have seemedWikipedia:No original research eccentric. William Buckland subsequently recommended Darwin's paper for publication, praising it as "a new & important theory to explain Phenomena of universal occurrence on the surface of the Earth – in fact a new Geological Power", while rightly rejecting Darwin's suggestion that chalkland could have been formed in a similar way.

Darwin had avoided taking on official posts which would take valuable time, turning down William Whewell's request that he become Secretary of the Geological Society with excuses including "anything which flurries me completely knocks me up afterwards and brings on a bad palpitation of the heart",[81] but in January 1838 he accepted the post. On 7 March he read to the Society his longest paper yet, which explained the earthquake he had witnessed at Concepción, Chile, in terms of gradual crustal movements, to the delight of Lyell. Despite hours of practice, as he later recalled; "I was so nervous at first, I somehow could see nothing all around me, & felt as if my body was gone, & only my head left".[82]

At the same time, Darwin pondered likely opposition to his ideas. Sure that there must have been "a thousand intermediate forms" between the modern otter and its land-only ancestor, he thought "Opponent will say. show them me. I will answer yes, if you will show me every step between bull Dog & Greyhound".[83] He privately scorned Whewell's faith in a human-centred universe, perfectly adapted to man, and wrote that "My theory would give zest to recent & fossil Comparative Anatomy, it would lead to study of instincts, heredity & mind heredity, whole metaphysics". Contrary to the views of his Cambridge professors that humans were "godlike", around February 1838 Darwin wrote in his B notebook; "Animals whom we have made our slaves we do not like to consider our equals. – Do not slave holders wish to make the black man other kind – animals with affections, imitation, fear of death, pain, sorrow for the dead. – respect." The expectation of finding "the father of mankind" was comparable to finding *Macrauchenia*, and "if we choose to let conjecture run wild then our animals our fellow brethern in pain, disease, death & suffering, & famine, our slaves in the most laborious works, our companions in our amusements. they may partake from our origin in one common ancestor; we may be all netted together."

C notebook: animal observations

By February 1838 Darwin was on to a new pocketbook, the maroon *C notebook*, and was investigating the breeding of domestic animals. He found the newspaper wholesaler William Yarrell at the Zoological museum a fund of knowledge, and questioned if breeders weren't going against nature in "picking varieties". He was now writing of "Descent" rather than transmutation, and hinting at ideas of "adaptation" to climate.

At the zoo on 28 March he had his first sight of an ape, and was impressed at the orang-utan's antics "just like a naughty child" when the keeper held back an apple. In his notes he wrote "Let man visit Ourang-outang in domestication, hear expressive whine, see its intelligence.... let him look at savage...naked, artless, not improving yet improvable & let him dare to boast of his proud preeminence." Here Darwin was drawing on his experience of the natives of Tierra del Fuego and daring to think that there was little gulf between man and animals despite the theological doctrine that only humanity possessed a soul.

On 1 April Charles wrote to his older sister Susan that he had also seen the rhinoceros in the zoo let out for the first time that spring, "kicking & rearing" and galloping for joy. He then passed on the gossip that Miss Martineau had been "as frisky lately [as] the Rhinoceros. – Erasmus has been with her noon, morning, and night: – if her character was not as secure, as a mountain in the polar regions she certainly would loose it. – Lyell called there the other day & there was a beautiful rose on the table, & she coolly showed it to him & said "Erasmus Darwin" gave me that. – How fortunate it is, she is so very plain; otherwise I should be frightened: She is a wonderful woman". He began thinking about marriage himself, and on the back of an old letter (dated 7 April 1838) he listed the pros and cons of London, Cambridge or the countryside, noting that "I have so much more pleasure in direct observation, that I could not go on as Lyell does, correcting & adding up new information to old train & I do not see what line can be followed by man tied down to London. – In country, experiment & observations on lower animals. – more space – ".[84] In an 8 May letter to his Cambridge friend Charles Thomas Whitley, who had recently married, Darwin described himself as having "turned a complete scribbler", and said "Of the future I know nothing I never look further ahead than two or three Chapters – for my life is now measured by volume, chapters & sheets & has little to do with the sun – As for a wife, that most interesting specimen in the whole series of vertebrate animals, Providence only know whether I shall ever capture one or be able to feed her if caught."

Darwin found a pamphlet by Yarrell's friend Sir John Sebright, with a passage reading:

A severe winter, or a scarcity of food, by destroying the weak and the unhealthy, has all the good effects of the most skilful selection. In cold or barren countries no animals can live to the age of maturity, but those who have strong constitutions; the weak and the unhealthy do not live to propagate their infirmities.[85]

Sebright said females went to "the most vigorous males", and "the strongest individuals of both sexes, by driving away the weakest, will enjoy the best food, and the most favourable positions, for themselves and their offspring." After reading the pamphlet, Darwin commented "excellent observations of sickly offspring being cut off so that not propagated by nature. – Whole art of making varieties may be inferred from facts stated".[86]

Speculations

Darwin's speculations in his notebooks deepened as he wondered how instincts and mental traits were passed on to offspring; "Thought (or desires more properly) being hereditary it is difficult to imagine it anything but structure of brain hereditary, analogy points out to this. – love of the deity effect of organization, oh you materialist!", and reminded himself to read Barclay "on organization!!" He struggled on with the Beagle geology, overworked, worried and suffering stomach upsets and headaches which laid him up for days on end. Privately he thought of the social implications of evolution, writing "Educate all classes. avoid the contamination of castes, improve the women (double influence) & mankind must improve." This was similar to the position of the radical Lamarckians, but female education was already supported by the whole Wedgwood-Darwin family, and strongly advocated by Martineau.

Darwin wrote "Man in his arrogance thinks himself a great work worthy the interposition of a deity, more humble & I believe truer to consider him created from animals." In an early precursor of his work on *The Expression of the Emotions in Man and Animals*, Darwin turned round the theological idea of Charles Bell that humans were designed to expose their canine teeth when grinning, and explained the expression by shared descent: "no doubt a habit gained by formerly being a baboon with great canine teeth. – Blend this argument with his having canine teeth at all. – This way of viewing the subject important. Laughing modified barking, smiling modified laughing. Barking to tell other animals in associated kinds of good news, discovery of prey, arising no doubt from want of assistance. – crying is a puzzler. – Under this point of view expression of all animals becomes very curious – a dog snarling in play." Darwin had privately talked with his cousin "Hensleigh Wedgwood about the relationship of humans to animals; "Hensleigh says the love of the deity & thought of him or eternity only difference between the mind of man

& animals. – yet how faint in a Fuegian or Australian!" Darwin's own experience with "savages" he had met on the *Beagle* expedition showed that not all humans shared these religious beliefs.

As he worried at these ideas and the Beagle *Geology* his illness intensified, with stomach upsets, headaches and heart troubles, so that he became overworked and laid up for days on end.[87] In May he wrote to his sister Caroline Wedgwood hoping to visit his relatives in July or early August, "but I shall be cruelly hurried – as I have to go to Scotland for Geological work" and also had to be in London every second month for the publication of his *Zoology*. "I hope I may be able to work on right hard during the next three years, otherwise I shall never have finished, – but I find the noddle & the stomach are antagonist powers, and that it is a great deal more easy to think too much in a day, than to think too little – What thought has to do with digesting roast beef, – I cannot say, but they are brother faculties." Darwin's cousin William Darwin Fox gave helpful answers to his questions about crossing domestic breeds, and in his reply of 15 June, Darwin admitted for the first time that "It is my prime hobby & I really think some day, I shall be able to do something on that most intricate subject species & varieties."[83]

At the same time Darwin was gaining public position, and on 21 June 1838 was elected to the establishment Athenæum Club, along with Charles Dickens. From the start of August, Darwin began going there each day to "dine at the Athenæum like a gentleman, or rather like a Lord, for I am sure the first evening I sat in that great drawing room, all on a sofa by myself, I felt just like a duke. – I am full of admiration at the Athenæum; one meets so many people there, that one likes to see. ... I enjoy it the more, because I fully expected to detest it."[88]

Thoughts of marriage

The Hensleigh Wedgwoods were now living next door to Erasmus. In early June 1838 they were visited for a week by Catherine Darwin and Emma Wedgwood, returning from a family get-together in Paris. As Emma told her aunt a few weeks later, "Charles used to come from next door, so we were a very pleasant, merry party."

Illness prompted Darwin to take a break from the pressure of work: on 15 June he told his cousin William Darwin Fox; "I have not been very well of late, which has suddenly determined me to leave London earlier than I had anticipated. I go by the steam-packet to Edinburgh. – take a solitary walk on Salisbury crags & call up old thoughts of former times then go on to Glasgow & the great valley of Inverness, – near which I intend stopping a week to geologise the parallel roads of Glen Roy, – thence to Shrewsbury, Maer for one day, & London for smoke, ill health & hard work." On 23 June 1838 he took the steamboat to Edinburgh to go "geologising" in Scotland. After revisiting Edinburgh on 28 June (the day that Queen Victoria had her coronation in London) he went on to Fort William. At Glen Roy in glorious weather he was convinced that he had solved the riddle of the "parallel roads" around the glen, which he identified as raised beaches, though later geologists would support the ideas of Louis Agassiz that these had been formed by glaciation.

Fully recuperated and optimistic, he returned home to The Mount, Shrewsbury. He discussed his ideas with his father and asked for advice about Emma. Speaking from experience, Doctor Robert Waring Darwin told his son to conceal religious doubts which could cause "extreme misery... Things went on pretty well until the husband or wife became out of health, and then some women suffered miserably by doubting about the salvation of their husbands, thus making them likewise to suffer." Charles drew up a list with two columns on a scrap of paper. Under *Marry* he listed benefits, "Children–if it please God–Constant companion & friend in old age will feel interested in one,–object to be beloved and played with, better than a dog anyhow", while under *Not Marry* he put "Freedom to go where one liked ... Not forced to visit relatives ... to have the expense and anxiety of children ... fatness & idleness ... if many children forced to earn one's bread ...". He jotted down further thoughts, then concluded "My God, it is intolerable to think of spending ones whole life, like a neuter bee, working, working, & nothing after all. – No, no won't do. – Imagine living all one's day solitarily in smoky dirty London House. – Only picture to yourself a nice soft wife on a sofa with good fire, & books & music perhaps – Compare this vision with the dingy reality of Grt. Marlbro' St. Marry–Marry–Marry Q.E.D."[89]

Then he spent his fortnight being "Very idle at Shrewsbury" which meant starting his *"D" notebook* on the transmutation sequence and his *"M" notebook* on the evolutionary basis of moral and social behaviour, filling sixty pages with notes and anecdotes from his father about experiences with patients.

Having come down in favour, he went to visit his cousin Emma on 29 July. He did not get around to proposing, but failed to conceal his ideas on transmutation. Emma noted "he is the most open, transparent man I ever saw, and every word expresses his real thoughts." When she asked about ultimate origins he steered clear of the subject, aware that "it will become necessary to show how the first eye is formed" which he could not yet do.

Malthus and natural law

After returning to London on 1 August 1838 Darwin read a review of Auguste Comte's *Positive Philosophy* at the Athenaeum Club. It bolstered his pantheist ideas of natural laws, making him remark "What a magnificent view one can take of the world" with everything synchronised "by certain laws of harmony", a vision "far grander" than the Almighty individually creating "a long succession of vile Molluscous animals – How beneath the dignity of Him"! Only a "cramped imagination" saw God "warring against those very laws he established in all organic nature." His work on *Coral Reefs* and a paper theorising that Glen Roy had been an arm of the sea soldiered on. He visited the zoo to experiment, observing the reactions of the apes and seeing emotions like "revenge and anger", implying that "Our descent, then, [is the root] of our evil passions." He needed an ally, and hinted to Lyell that his work was "bearing on the question of species", amassing "facts, which begin to group themselves *clearly* under sub-laws."

Then in late September he began reading "for amusement" the 6th edition of Malthus's *An Essay on the Principle of Population* which reminded him of Malthus's statistical proof that human populations breed beyond their means and compete to survive, at a time when he was primed to apply these ideas to animal species. Malthus had softened from the bleakness of the earlier editions, now allowing that the population crush could be mitigated by education, celibacy and emigration. Already Radical crowds were demonstrating against the harsh imposition of Malthusian ideas in the Poor Laws, and a slump was resulting in mass emigration. Lyell was convinced that animals were also driven to spread their territory by overpopulation, but Darwin went further in applying the Whig social thinking of struggle for survival with no handouts. His views were secular, but not atheistic. He asked how God's laws had produced "so high a mind" as ours, with purpose shown by descent geared towards the "production of higher animals", suggesting that "we are [a] step towards some higher end".

Malthus's essay calculates from the birth rate that human population could double every 25 years, but in practice growth is kept in check by death, disease, wars and famine.[90,91] Darwin was well prepared to see at once that this related to de Candolle's concept of "nature's war" and also applies to the struggle for existence amongst wildlife, so that when there is more population than resources can maintain, favourable variations that allow the organism to better use the limited resources available tend to be preserved, and unfavourable ones destroyed by being unable to get the means for existence, resulting in the formation of new species. On 28 September 1838 he noted this insight, describing it as a kind of wedging, forcing adapted structures into gaps in the economy of nature formed as weaker ones were thrust out. He now had a theory by which to work.[92]

Proposal

Darwin's thoughts and work continued and he suffered repeated bouts of illness. On 11 November he returned to Maer Hall and proposed to Emma.

Again he discussed his ideas, and she subsequently wrote telling him of her "fear that our opinions on the most important subject should differ widely. My reason tells me that honest & conscientious doubts cannot be a sin, but I feel it would be a painful void between us. I thank you from my heart for your openness with me & I should dread the feeling that you were concealing your opinions from the fear of giving me pain." She continued; "my own dear Charley we now do belong to each other & I cannot help being open with you. Will you do me a favour? yes I am sure you will, it is to read our Saviours farewell discourse to his disciples which begins at the end of the 13th Chap of John. It is so full of love to them & devotion & every beautiful feeling." In the Farewell Discourse from the Gospel of St. John, Jesus instructs his disciples to "love one another", a central part of Christian doctrine which emphasises the need for belief. For Emma the importance of faith had been reinforced by the death of her sister Fanny in 1832, and her need to meet Fanny again in the afterlife. She clearly felt that Darwin would be able to overcome doubt and believe.[93] John 15 also says "If a man abide not in me...they are burned". Darwin's warm reply reassured her, and she replied that "To see you in earnest on the subject will be my greatest comfort & that I am sure you are. I believe I agree with every word you say, & it pleased me that you shd have felt inclined to enter a little more on the subject." However, this tension would remain.[94]

Emma's father promised a dowry of £5,000 plus £400 a year, while Doctor Darwin added £10,000 for Charles, to be invested. They decided to move to London until Charles had "wearied the geological public" with his itch to write, then they would "decide, whether the pleasures of retirement & country... are preferable to society."

Theory

Charles went house-hunting by day. At night he thought about "innumerable variations" (which he still thought were acquired in some way) with competitive nature selecting the best leading to step by step change, while vestigial organs like the human coccyx (tail) were not, as commonly thought, God "rounding out his original thought [to its] exhaustion", but ancestral remnants pointing to "the parent of man".

Darwin considered Malthus's argument, that human populations breed beyond their means and compete to survive, in relation to his findings about species relating to localities, earlier enquiries into animal breeding, and ideas of Natural "laws of harmony". Around late November 1838 he compared breeders selecting traits to a Malthusian Nature selecting from random variants, now thrown up by "chance", and in mid-December described this comparison as "a beautiful part of my theory, that domesticated races of organics are made by precisely same means as species – but latter far more perfectly & infinitely slower", so that in "species every part of newly acquired structure is fully practical & perfected."

The second edition of Charles Babbage's *The Ninth Bridgewater Treatise. A Fragment* published that year included a copy of a letter John Herschel had sent to Charles Lyell in 1836, not long before Darwin visited Herschel in Cape Town. On 2 December, Darwin wrote in his E Notebook "Babbage 2d Edit. p. 226 – Herschel calls the appearance of new species the mystery of mysteries, & has grand passage upon the problem.! Hurrah – 'intermediate causes' ". Herschel's letter advocated seeking natural causes, as opposed to miraculous causes, and gave philosophical justification to Darwin's project.

Stress

The *Zoology* ran into difficulties, with Richard Owen having to halt work on *Fossil Mammalia*, and John Gould sailing off for Tasmania leaving Darwin to complete the half finished *Birds*. "What can a man have to say, who works all morning in describing hawks & owls; & then rushes out , & walks in a bewildered manner up one street & down another, looking out for the word To Let'." Emma had arranged to come with the Hensleigh Wedgwoods to London for a week to help with the search for a house, and wrote telling him "It is very well I am coming to look after you my poor old man", before arriving on 6 December.

On 19 December 1838 as secretary of the Geological Society of London Darwin witnessed the vicious interrogation by Owen and his allies including Sedgwick and Buckland of Darwin's old tutor Robert Edmund Grant when they ridiculed Grant's Lamarckian heresy in a clear reminder of establishment hatred of evolutionism.

During her visit, Emma thought Darwin looked unwell and overtired. At the end of December she wrote urging him "to leave town at once & get some rest. You have looked so unwell for some time that I fear you will be laid up... nothing *could* make me so happy as to feel that I could be of any use or comfort to my own dear Charles when he is not well. So don't be ill any more my dear Charley till I can be with you to nurse you".

Marriage

On 29 December 1838, Darwin took the let of a furnished property at 12 Upper Gower Street. He wrote to Emma that "Gower St is ours, yellow curtains & all", and of his delight at being the "possessor of Macaw Cottage". which he long recalled for its gaudy coloured walls and furniture that "combined all the colours of the macaw in hideous discord",[95] Emma rejoiced at their getting a house she liked, while hoping that they had got rid of "that dead dog out of the garden". Darwin impatiently moved his "museum" in on 31 December, astounding himself, Erasmus and the porters with the weight of his luggage containing geological specimens.

On 24 January 1839 he was honoured by being elected as Fellow of the Royal Society and presented his paper on the Roads of Glen Roy. The next day he took the train home to Shrewsbury, then on the 28th travelled to Maer Hall.

On 29 January 1839, Charles married Emma at Maer, Staffordshire in an Anglican ceremony arranged to also suit the Unitarians, conducted by the vicar, their cousin John Allen Wedgwood. Emma's bedridden mother slept through the service, sparing Emma "the pain of parting". Immediately afterwards Charles and Emma rushed off to the railway station, raising their relative's eyebrows, and ate their sandwiches and toasted their future from a "bottle of water" on the train. Back at Macaw Cottage, Charles noted in his journal "Married at Maer & returned to London 30 years old", and in his *"E" notebook* recorded uncle John Wedgwood's views on turnips.

See the development of Darwin's theory for the ensuing developments, in the context of his life, work and outside influences at the time.

References

Note that this article is largely based on Desmond and Moore's book, with commentary summarised in other words and quotations (or extracts from quotations) repeated verbatim.

- Bowler, Peter J. (1996), *Charles Darwin : the man and his influence*, Cambridge [England] ; New York NY, USA: Cambridge University Press, ISBN 0-521-56668-1<templatestyles src="Module:Citation/CS1/styles.css"></templatestyles>
- Browne, E. Janet (1995), *Charles Darwin: vol. 1 Voyaging*, London: Jonathan Cape, ISBN 1-84413-314-1<templatestyles src="Module:Citation/CS1/styles.css"></templatestyles>
- Browne, E. Janet (2002), *Charles Darwin: vol. 2 The Power of Place*, London: Jonathan Cape, ISBN 0-7126-6837-3<templatestyles src="Module:Citation/CS1/styles.css"></templatestyles>

- Darwin, Charles (1835), *Extracts from letters to Professor Henslow*[96], Cambridge: [privately printed], retrieved 1 November 2008<templatestyles src="Module:Citation/CS1/styles.css"></templatestyles>
- Darwin, Charles (1837), *Notebook B: [Transmutation of species, 1837–1838]*[97], Darwin Online, CUL-DAR121, retrieved 20 December 2008<templatestyles src="Module:Citation/CS1/styles.css"></templatestyles>
- Darwin, C. R. (1837a), "Observations of proofs of recent elevation on the coast of Chili, made during the survey of His Majesty's Ship Beagle commanded by Capt. FitzRoy R.N. [Read 4 January]"[98], *Proceedings of the Geological Society of London* (2), pp. 446–49, retrieved 23 January 2008<templatestyles src="Module:Citation/CS1/styles.css"></templatestyles>
- Darwin, C. R. (1837b), "A sketch of the deposits containing extinct Mammalia in the neighbourhood of the Plata. [Read 3 May]"[99], *Proceedings of the Geological Society of London* (2), pp. 542–44, retrieved 23 January 2008<templatestyles src="Module:Citation/CS1/styles.css"></templatestyles>
- Darwin, C. R. (1837c), "On certain areas of elevation and subsidence in the Pacific and Indian oceans, as deduced from the study of coral formations. [Read 31 May]"[100], *Proceedings of the Geological Society of London* (2), pp. 552–54, retrieved 23 January 2008<templatestyles src="Module:Citation/CS1/styles.css"></templatestyles>
- Darwin, Charles (1838), *Notebook C: [Transmutation of species]*[101], Darwin Online, CUL-DAR122, retrieved 5 August 2016<templatestyles src="Module:Citation/CS1/styles.css"></templatestyles>
- Darwin, Charles (1838a), *Notebook D: [Transmutation of species]*[102], Darwin Online, CUL-DAR123, retrieved 5 August 2016<templatestyles src="Module:Citation/CS1/styles.css"></templatestyles>
- Darwin, Charles (1838b), *Notebook E: [Transmutation of species 1838–1839]*[103], Darwin Online, CUL-DAR124, retrieved 5 August 2016<templatestyles src="Module:Citation/CS1/styles.css"></templatestyles>
- Darwin, Charles (1838c), *Notebook M: Metaphysics on morals & expression*[104], Darwin Online, CUL-DAR125, retrieved 5 August 2016<templatestyles src="Module:Citation/CS1/styles.css"></templatestyles>
- Darwin, Charles (1838d), *Notebook N: Metaphysics & expression (1838–1839)*[105], Darwin Online, CUL-DAR126, retrieved 5 August 2016<templatestyles src="Module:Citation/CS1/styles.css"></templatestyles>
- Darwin, Charles (1839), *Narrative of the surveying voyages of His Majesty's Ships Adventure and Beagle between the years*

1826 and 1836, describing their examination of the southern shores of South America, and the Beagle's circumnavigation of the globe. Journal and remarks. 1832–1836.[106], **III**, London: Henry Colburn, retrieved 24 October 2008<templatestyles src="Module:Citation/CS1/styles.css"></templatestyles>
- Darwin, Charles (1859), *On the Origin of Species by Means of Natural Selection, or the Preservation of Favoured Races in the Struggle for Life*[107] (1st ed.), London: John Murray, retrieved 24 October 2008<templatestyles src="Module:Citation/CS1/styles.css"></templatestyles>
- Darwin, Charles (1887), Darwin, Francis, ed., *The life and letters of Charles Darwin, including an autobiographical chapter*[108], London: John Murray, retrieved 4 November 2008<templatestyles src="Module:Citation/CS1/styles.css"></templatestyles>
- Darwin, Charles (1958), Barlow, Nora, ed., *The Autobiography of Charles Darwin 1809–1882. With the original omissions restored. Edited and with appendix and notes by his granddaughter Nora Barlow*[108], London: Collins, retrieved 4 November 2008<templatestyles src="Module:Citation/CS1/styles.css"></templatestyles>
- Darwin, Charles (2006), "Journal"[109], in van Wyhe, John, [*Darwin's personal 'Journal' (1809–1881)*][110], Darwin Online, CUL-DAR158.1–76, retrieved 20 December 2008<templatestyles src="Module:Citation/CS1/styles.css"></templatestyles>
- Desmond, Adrian J. (1989), *The Politics of Evolution: Morphology, Medicine, and Reform in Radical London*, University of Chicago Press, ISBN 0-226-14374-0<templatestyles src="Module:Citation/CS1/styles.css"></templatestyles>
- Desmond, Adrian; Moore, James (1991), *Darwin*, London: Michael Joseph, Penguin Group, ISBN 0-7181-3430-3<templatestyles src="Module:Citation/CS1/styles.css"></templatestyles>
- Eldredge, Niles (2006), "Confessions of a Darwinist"[111], *The Virginia Quarterly Review*, The Virginia Quarterly Review (Spring 2006), pp. 32–53, retrieved 4 November 2008<templatestyles src="Module:Citation/CS1/styles.css"></templatestyles>
- FitzRoy, Robert (1839), *Voyages of the Adventure and Beagle, Volume II*[112], London: Henry Colburn, retrieved 4 November 2008<templatestyles src="Module:Citation/CS1/styles.css"></templatestyles>
- Herbert, Sandra (1980), "The red notebook of Charles Darwin"[113], *Bulletin of the British Museum (Natural History)*, Historical Series (7 (24 April)), pp. 1–164, retrieved 11 January 2009<templatestyles src="Module:Citation/CS1/styles.css"></templatestyles>
- Litchfield, Henrietta Emma (1915), *Emma Darwin, A century of family letters, 1792–1896, edited by her daughter Henrietta Litch-*

- *field*[114], London: John Murray, retrieved 15 June 2010<templatestyles src="Module:Citation/CS1/styles.css"></templatestyles>
- Moore, James (2005), *Darwin – A 'Devil's Chaplain'?*[115] (PDF), American Public Media, archived from the original[116] (PDF) on 27 February 2008, retrieved 22 November 2008<templatestyles src="Module:Citation/CS1/styles.css"></templatestyles>
- Moore, James (2006), *Evolution and Wonder – Understanding Charles Darwin*[117], Speaking of Faith (Radio Program), American Public Media, archived from the original[118] on 22 December 2008, retrieved 22 November 2008<templatestyles src="Module:Citation/CS1/styles.css"></templatestyles>
- Owen, Richard (1840), Darwin, C. R., ed., *Fossil Mammalia Part 1*, The zoology of the voyage of H.M.S. Beagle, London: Smith Elder and Co<templatestyles src="Module:Citation/CS1/styles.css"></templatestyles>
- Sulloway, Frank J. (1982), "Darwin and His Finches: The Evolution of a Legend"[119] (pdf), *Journal of the History of Biology*, **15** (1), pp. 1–53, doi: 10.1007/BF00132004[120], retrieved 9 December 2008<templatestyles src="Module:Citation/CS1/styles.css"></templatestyles>
- van Wyhe, John (27 March 2007), "Mind the gap: Did Darwin avoid publishing his theory for many years?"[121], *Notes and Records of the Royal Society*, **61** (2): 177–205, doi: 10.1098/rsnr.2006.0171[122], retrieved 7 February 2008<templatestyles src="Module:Citation/CS1/styles.css"></templatestyles>
- van Wyhe, John (2008), *Charles Darwin: gentleman naturalist: A biographical sketch*[123], Darwin Online, retrieved 17 November 2008<templatestyles src="Module:Citation/CS1/styles.css"></templatestyles>
- van Wyhe, John (2008b), *Darwin: The Story of the Man and His Theories of Evolution*, London: Andre Deutsch Ltd (published 1 September 2008), ISBN 0-233-00251-0<templatestyles src="Module:Citation/CS1/styles.css"></templatestyles>
- von Sydow, Momme (2005), "Darwin – A Christian Undermining Christianity? On Self-Undermining Dynamics of Ideas Between Belief and Science"[124] (PDF), in Knight, David M.; Eddy, Matthew D., *Science and Beliefs: From Natural Philosophy to Natural Science, 1700–1900*, Burlington: Ashgate, pp. 141–56, ISBN 0-7546-3996-7, retrieved 16 December 2008<templatestyles src="Module:Citation/CS1/styles.css"></templatestyles>

External links

- The Complete Works of Charles Darwin Online – Darwin Online[125]; Darwin's publications, private papers and bibliography, supplementary works including biographies, obituaries and reviews. Free to use, includes items not in public domain.
- Works by Charles Darwin[126] at Project Gutenberg; public domain
- Darwin Correspondence Project[127] Text and notes for most of his letters

Charles Darwin's health

Health of Charles Darwin

For much of his adult life, **Charles Darwin's health** was repeatedly compromised by an uncommon combination of symptoms, leaving him severely debilitated for long periods of time. However, in some ways this may have helped his work, and Charles Darwin wrote "Even ill-health, though it has annihilated several years of my life, has saved me from the distractions of society and amusement."

He consulted numerous doctors, but, with the medical science of the time, the cause remained undiagnosed. He tried all available treatments, but, at best, they had only temporary success. More recently, there has been much speculation as to the nature of his illness.

Development of illness and symptoms

As a medical student at Edinburgh University, Darwin found that he was too sensitive to the sight of blood and the brutality of surgery at the time, so he turned his attention to natural history, an extramural interest he developed when studying at the University of Cambridge to qualify as a clergyman.

On 10 December 1831, as he waited in Plymouth for the voyage on HMS *Beagle* to begin, he suffered from chest pain and heart palpitations, but told no one at the time in case it stopped him from going on the survey expedition. During the voyage, he suffered badly from sea-sickness during the eighteen months he was at sea, but he spent much of the three years and three months he was on land in strenuous exploration. In Argentina at the start of October 1833, he collapsed with a fever. He spent two days in bed, and then memories of a young shipmate who had died of the fever persuaded him to take a boat down river to Buenos Aires, lying ill in his cabin until the fever passed. On 20 September 1834, while returning from a horseback expedition in the Andes

Figure 29: *Charles Darwin (1809–1882)*

mountains, he fell ill and spent the month of October in bed in Valparaiso. In his journal for 25 March 1835, while to the east of the Andes near Mendoza, he noted "an attack (for it deserves no less a name) of the Benchuca, a species of Reduvius, the great black bug of the Pampas", which are associated with transmittal of Chagas' disease.

After the voyage ended on 2 October 1836, he quickly established himself as an eminent geologist, at the same time secretly beginning speculations on transmutation as he conceived of his theory. On 20 September 1837, he suffered "an uncomfortable palpitation of the heart" and as "*strongly*" advised by his doctors, left for a month of recuperation in the countryside. That October he wrote, "Of late anything which flurries me completely knocks me up afterwards, and brings on a violent palpitation of the heart."[128] In the spring of 1838 he was overworked, worried and suffering stomach upsets and headaches which caused him to be unable to work for days on end. These intensified and heart troubles returned, so in June he went "geologising" in Scotland and felt fully recuperated. Later that year however, bouts of illness returned—a pattern which would continue. He married Emma Wedgwood on 29 January 1839, and in December of that year as Emma's first pregnancy progressed, he fell ill and accomplished little during the following year.

For over forty years Darwin suffered intermittently from various combinations of symptoms such as: malaise, vertigo, dizziness, muscle spasms and tremors, vomiting, cramps and colics, bloating and nocturnal intestinal gas, headaches, alterations of vision, severe tiredness, nervous exhaustion, dyspnea, skin problems such as blisters all over the scalp and eczema, crying, anxiety, sensation of impending death and loss of consciousness, fainting, tachycardia, insomnia, tinnitus, and depression. These symptoms displayed by Darwin may have been diagnosed today as a form of dysautonomia known as hyperadrenergic postural orthostatic tachycardia syndrome, postural orthostatic tachycardia syndrome or orthostatic intolerance.

Water treatment

Darwin had no success with conventional treatments. In 1849, after about four months of incessant vomiting he took up the recommendation of his friend Captain Sulivan and cousin Fox to try the water therapy regimen at Dr James Gully's Water Cure Establishment at Malvern. He read Gully's book, which provided case histories and had a price list at the back. Darwin rented a villa at Malvern for his family and started a two-month trial of the treatment on 10 March. Gully agreed with Darwin's self-diagnosis of nervous dyspepsia and set him a routine including being heated by a spirit lamp until dripping with perspiration, then vigorous rubbing with cold wet towels and cold foot baths, a strict diet, and walks. Darwin enjoyed the attention and the demanding regime which left him no time to feel guilty about not working. His health improved rapidly, and he felt that the water cure was "no quackery".[129] He had no faith in the homeopathic medicines Gully gave him three times a day but took them obediently.[130] They stayed on until 30 June, and back home at Down House, he continued with the diet and with the water treatment aided by his butler. He followed the rules about rising early and rationing his working time and had the Sandwalk constructed in the grounds for his walking exercise, setting a routine which he continued.

In September, his sickness returned during the excitement of a British Association for the Advancement of Science meeting, and Darwin made a day visit to Malvern, then recuperated at home. In June 1850, after losing time to illness (without vomiting), he spent a week at Malvern. Later that year he wrote to Fox about the credulity of his "beloved Dr Gully" who when his daughter was ill, treated her with a clairvoyant girl to report on internal changes, a mesmerist to put her to sleep, John Chapman as homeopathist and himself as hydropathist, after which Gully's daughter recovered. Darwin explained to Fox his wrathful scepticism about clairvoyance and worse, homeopathy, thinking the infinitesimal doses were against all common sense and should be compared against the effects of no treatment at all. Gully had pestered Darwin to subject himself to clairvoyance, and when he saw the clairvoyant, he tried to test her by asking her to read the number on a banknote he had in an envelope, but she scornfully said this was something her maidservant did and proceeded to diagnose horrors in Darwin's insides, a tale he recounted for years afterwards.[131] When Darwin's own young daughter Annie had persistent indigestion, he confidently took her to Gully on 24 March 1851 and after a week, left her there to take the cure but a fortnight later was recalled by Dr. Gully as Annie had bilious fever. Dr. Gully was attentive and repeatedly reassured them that she was recovering, but after a series of crises, Annie died on 23 April. Darwin was heartbroken at this tragic loss, but surprisingly stayed well in the aftermath, busy with organising the funeral arrangements.

Darwin kept records of the effects of the continuing water treatment at home and in 1852 stopped the regime, having found that it was of some help with relaxation but overall had no significant effect, indicating that it served only to decrease his psychosomatic symptomatology.

With the memories of Annie's death, Darwin did not want to return to Malvern. In 1856, he began writing for publication of his theory, and he pressed on, overworking, until by March 1857 illness was cutting his working day "ridiculously short". He found a new hydrotherapist, Dr. Edward Wickstead Lane, whose Moor Park hydropathic establishment near Farnham in Surrey was only 40 miles from Darwin's home. His condition was much as when Darwin had first seen Gully, and Dr. Lane later wrote, "I cannot recall any [case] where the pain was as poignant as his. When the worst attacks were on, he seemed crushed with agony." Darwin arrived on 22 April and wrote to Fox that "it is really quite astonishing & utterly unaccountable the good this one week has done me", deciding to stay on to 5 May. He enjoyed the more relaxed regime, which did not include clairvoyance, mesmerism or homeopathy, as Lane did "not believe in all the rubbish which Dr G. does." Darwin became a complete convert, "well convinced that the only thing for Chronic cases is the water-cure", and wrote, "I really think I shall make a point of coming here for a fortnight occasionally, as the country is very pleasant for walking." He told Hooker he had "already received an amount of good, which is quite incredible to myself & quite unaccountable.—I can walk & eat like a hearty Christian; & even my nights are good.—I cannot in the least understand how hydropathy can act as it certainly does on me. It dulls one's brain splendidly, I have not thought about a single species of any kind, since leaving home." He then contradicted himself by asking about alpine species.

He returned to Moor Park from 16–29 June and 5–12 November 1857 and from 20 April to 3 May 1858, but this retreat was unavailable when he was shocked by receipt of Wallace's paper on 18 June, as Dr. Lane was put on trial accused of adultery with a lady patient. Darwin was able to resume treatment at Moor Park from 25–31 October 1858, as he struggled on to write *On the*

Origin of Species despite repeated health problems. He was able to keep writing thanks to visits to the spa on 5–18 February, 21–28 May and 19–26 July 1859.

With the proofs of the book returned to the printers, he was worn out. On 2 October, he left for Ilkley and had treatment at Ilkley Wells hydropathic establishment operated by Dr. Edmund Smith, a surgeon and hydropathic doctor. Emma brought their children on 17 October, and the family including Darwin stayed in North House, Wells Terrace, which he rented. Reading the first adverse reviews there, his health worsened with a sprained ankle followed by a swollen leg and face, boils and a rash. He had an "odious time", and wrote of Smith that "he constantly gives me impression, as if he cared very much for the Fee & very little for the patient". By 6 November, he felt worse than when he came. Emma and the children went home on 24 November. Darwin stayed on in the establishment, and for the last ten days of the stay, he felt much better. He returned home on 7 December, and under pressure of work, his health slipped back a bit.

As arguments continued, Darwin had more stomach upsets, and on 28 June 1860, two days before the famous 1860 Oxford evolution debate, he fled to Lane's new hydropathic establishment at Sudbrooke Park, Petersham, near Richmond in Surrey and recuperated as well as reading reports of the debate.

Darwin avoided further hydropathy, perhaps recalling his time at Ilkley, and Lane left the business for a while after selling Sudbrooke Park. In 1863, Darwin's illness worsened seriously, and Emma Darwin persuaded her husband to return to Malvern. His cousin Fox had earlier told him that Gully had suffered a mental breakdown and was unavailable. They arrived on 2 September, but Darwin felt that he was being fobbed off with the supervising physician, Dr. Ayerst. Emma arranged for Dr. Gully to attend and endorse Ayerst's treatment, but by then Darwin's eczema was too raw to bear any water. Darwin had a complete breakdown and on 13 October, left the spa worse than when he arrived. His ill health was the worst he had ever experienced and continued until the start of 1866.

Continuing illness

Darwin desperately tried many different therapies, within the limitations of medical science of his time. He took all kinds of medicines, including bismuth compounds and laudanum, and even tried quack therapies, such as electrical stimulation of the abdomen with a shocking belt. On 16 May 1865, he wrote to John Chapman, who was now a qualified specialist in dyspepsia, sickness and psychological medicine. Chapman had sent Darwin a book about a therapy for seasickness of applying ice bags to the small of the back, and Darwin invited him to Down House to try out this therapy. In a manuscript dated 20 May 1865, thought to have been for Chapman, Darwin described his symptoms:

> *Age 56–57. – For 25 years extreme spasmodic daily & nightly flatulence: occasional vomiting, on two occasions prolonged during months. Vomiting preceded by shivering, hysterical crying, dying sensations or half-faint. & copious very palid urine. Now vomiting & every paroxys[m] of flatulence preceded by singing of ears, rocking, treading on air & vision. focus & black dots – All fatigues, specially reading, brings on these Head symptoms ?? nervousness when E[mma] leaves me ..." [the list continues]*[132]

In his autobiography of 1876, Darwin wrote of his illness, emphasising that it had been brought on by "the excitement" of socialising:

> *Few persons can have lived a more retired life than we have done. Besides short visits to the houses of relations, and occasionally to the seaside or elsewhere, we have gone nowhere. During the first part of our residence we went a little into society, and received a few friends here; but my health almost always suffered from the excitement, violent shivering and vomiting attacks being thus brought on. I have therefore been compelled for many years to give up all dinner-parties; and this has been somewhat of a deprivation to me, as such parties always put me into high spirits. From the same cause I have been able to invite here very few scientific acquaintances.*

> *My chief enjoyment and sole employment throughout life has been scientific work; and the excitement from such work makes me for the time forget, or drives quite away, my daily discomfort. I have therefore nothing to record during the rest of my life, except the publication of my several books. ...*

Possible causes

Medical science has tried repeatedly to pinpoint the etiology, and many hypotheses were made, such as:

- Asperger's syndrome or other Pervasive developmental disorder
- Chagas disease
- Chronic fatigue syndrome[133]
- Crohn's disease
- Cyclic vomiting syndrome
- Lactose intolerance
- Lupus erythematosus
- Ménière's disease
- Tick-borne disease
- Panic disorder with agoraphobia

- Obsessive–compulsive disorder[134]
- Psychosomatic disease
- Postural Orthostatic Tachycardia Syndrome
- Orthostatic intolerance

Psychic causation

Darwin found that his illness often followed stressful situations, such as the excitement of attending a meeting. Having escaped "smoky dirty London" to his country retreat of the former parsonage of Down House at Downe, he became increasingly reclusive, actually fitting a mirror outside the house, so that he could withdraw when visitors were coming around the corner. When he left, it was mostly to visit friends or relatives, though he did endeavour to meet his obligations to attend scientific meetings.

Diagnosis of panic disorder and agoraphobia

Barloon and Noyes[1] report that as a young man, Darwin had "episodes of abdominal distress, especially in stressful situations". He had a "premorbid vulnerability" which in his youth was referred to as "sensitivity to stress of criticism in his youth". They contend that "variable intensity of symptoms and chronic, prolonged course without physical deterioration also indicate that his illness was psychiatric." Panic disorder usually appears in the teens or in early adulthood with an association with potentially stressful life transitions.[2] The histories of panic disorder patients often include some type of separation from a person who is emotionally important to them, which may be significant as Darwin's mother died in 1817 when he was eight, though apparently Darwin had a happy childhood overall and was encouraged by his siblings. Bowlby suggested that separation anxiety may help cause the development of panic disorder in adulthood and that agoraphobic patients frequently describe parents as dominant, controlling, critical, frightening, rejecting, or overprotective, which matches (disputed) descriptions of Darwin's father as tyrannical (see below).

A study by Chambless and Mason[3] says that regardless of gender, the less masculine in trait a person afflicted with panic disorder is, the more likely they are to use avoidance (social withdrawal) as a coping mechanism. Individuals who have more masculine traits often turn to external coping strategies (for example, alcohol). Dr. Bean[4] wrote that while Darwin had great confidence, at the same time he was neurotic, became nervous when his routine was altered, and was upset by a holiday, trip, or unexpected visitor.

Colp[5] disputes a diagnosis of agoraphobia, because Darwin dutifully attended 16 meetings of the Council of the Royal Society and was away from home about 2,000 days between 1842 and his death in 1882, but Barloon and Noyes[1] state that Darwin only left home infrequently, usually accompanied by his wife. They cite Darwin declining an invitation: "I have long found it impossible to visit anywhere; the novelty and excitement would annihilate me."

Relationship with father

Rempf[6] imputes a psychic cause based on the theory of Oedipal complex, proposing that Darwin's illness was "an expression of repressed anger toward his father" (the physician Robert Darwin). Rempf believed that Darwin's "complete submission" to a tyrannical father prevented Darwin from expressing anger towards his father and then subsequently toward others. In a similar diagnosis, English psychiatrist Dr. Rankine Good stated, "Thus, if Darwin did not slay his father in the flesh, then he certainly slew the Heavenly Father in the realm of natural history," suffering for his "unconscious patricide" which accounted for "almost forty years of severe and crippling neurotic suffering." Sir Gavin de Beer disputed this explanation, claiming a physical causation.[8]

Darwin's autobiography says of his father, "... [he] was a little unjust to me when I was young, but afterwards I am thankful to think that I became a prime favourite with him." Bradbury[7] quotes J. Huxley and H.B.D. Kettlew: "The predisposing cause of any psychoneurosis which Charles Darwin displayed seems to have been the conflict and emotional tension springing from his ambivalent relations with his father ... whom he both revered and subconsciously resented." Bradbury also quotes John Chancellor's analysis: "... [Darwin's] obsessive desire to work and achieve something was prompted by hatred and resentment of his father, who had called him an idler and good-for-nothing during his youth."

Such psychoanalysis remains controversial, particularly when based only on writings.

Relationship with wife, nervousness about being left alone

Peter Brent writes in his biography of Darwin, *Darwin: A Man of Enlarged Curiosity*, that Charles and Emma Darwin's "ties to each other were linked to childhood and the very beginnings of memory. They had a common history, a joint tradition. It is hard to think their relationship a passionate one, but it was happy, and the happiness had deep roots." Bradbury[7]—himself a social psychologist—draws on this biography to argue that in Darwin's letters, Emma was "always the mother, never the child, Darwin always the child, never the father." Darwin gave his wife the nickname "mammy", writing, "My dearest old Mammy ... Without you, when sick I feel most desolate ... Oh Mammy, I do long to be with you and under your protection for then I feel safe." Brent states that it is difficult to see that this is a thirty-nine-year-old man writing to his wife and not a young child writing to his mother. Barloon and Noyes[1] quote Darwin's admission to Dr. Chapman of "nervousness when Emma leaves me", which they interpret as a fear of being alone associated with his panic disorder.

Like his mother, Darwin's wife Emma was devoutly Unitarian. His father, speaking from experience, warned Charles before he proposed to Emma that "some women suffered miserably by doubting about the salvation of their husbands, thus making them likewise to suffer." Darwin did tell Emma of his ideas at that stage, and, while she was deeply concerned about the danger to his afterlife expressed in the Gospel, "If a man abide not in me...they are burned", she married him and remained fully supportive of his work throughout their marriage. She read and helped with his "Essay" setting out his theory in 1844, long before he showed his theory to anyone else. She went through the pages, making notes in the margins pointing out unclear passages and showing where she disagreed. As his illness progressed, she nursed him, restraining him from overworking and making him take holiday breaks, always helping him to continue with his work.

Religious tension

Darwin had a complex relationship to religion. The Darwin–Wedgwood family were of the Unitarian church, with his grandfather Erasmus Darwin and father taking this to the extent of Freethought, but, in the repressive climate of the early 19th century, his father complied with the Anglican Church of England.

Charles Darwin's education at school was Anglican, then after in Edinburgh, he joined student societies where his tutors espoused Lamarckian materialism. He liked the thought of becoming a country clergyman, and before studying at the University of Cambridge, "as I did not then in the least doubt the strict and literal truth of every word in the Bible, I soon persuaded myself that our Creed must be fully accepted." The clergyman naturalist professors there who became his lifelong friends fully accepted an ancient earth but opposed evolutionism which they felt would undermine the social order. He did well at theology and, in his finals, came 10th out of a pass list of 178. At both universities, he saw how evolution was associated with radicals and democrats seeking to overthrow society and how publicly supporting such ideas could lead to destruction of reputation, loss of position and even imprisonment for blasphemy.

At Cambridge, he was convinced by William Paley's writings of design by a Creator, but, on the *Beagle* expedition, his findings contradicted Paley's beneficent view. On his return, his deepening speculations led to the inception of Darwin's theory, and he increasingly disbelieved in the Bible, gradually becoming what was later termed an agnostic.

Darwin was clearly worried by the implications of his ideas and desperate to avoid distress to his naturalist friends and to his wife. When first telling his friends, he wrote "it is like confessing a murder", and his writings at the time of the publication of Darwin's theory suggest emotional turmoil. What is unclear is whether this was anxiety about disgrace and damage to his friends, or about his loss of faith in Christianity, or indeed a rational fear of the harsh treatment he had seen meted out to radicals and proponents of evolutionism.

The Chagas hypothesis

Advanced for the first in time in 1959 by eminent Israeli specialist in tropical medicine Dr. Saul Adler from Hebrew University, the hypothesis of Chagas disease was based partly on the fact that during the *Beagle* expedition, Darwin was bitten by the insect vector of this disease near Mendoza to the east of the Argentinian Andes while on one of his land exploration trips. He noted in his journal for 26 March 1835:

> At night I experienced an attack, & it deserves no less a name, of the Benchuca, the great black bug of the Pampas. It is most disgusting to feel soft wingless insects, about an inch long, crawling over ones body; before sucking they are quite thin, but afterwards round & bloated with blood, & in this state they are easily squashed.

The great black bug of the Pampas is identified by Richard Keynes as *Triatoma infestans*, commonly called *winchuka (vinchuca)*, the vector for *Trypanosoma cruzi* which leads to Chagas disease. It is unlikely that Darwin was infected on this occasion as he did not mention having a fever in the days following the incident, but it is possible that he could have been infected in September 1834 when he recorded being ill but made no note about being bitten by a *Benchuca* at that time.

Arguments for the Chagas hypothesis were mainly his gastric symptoms and some of his nervous signs and symptoms (caused in Chagas by an imbalance of the autonomic nervous system), malaise and fatigue, as well as his ultimate cause of death, which seems to have been chronic cardiac failure (present in ca. 20% of Chagas patients, with cardiomegaly and ventricular tip aneurysm) accompanied by lung edema.

Evidences against the Chagas hypothesis are numerous, however:

- Darwin died at a relatively old age for his time (73 years old);
- The symptoms abated as he aged, which is not typical for the disease, where age exacerbates the symptoms;
- He did not seem to have several of the pathological damages present at chronic Chagas disease, such as megacolon and megaesophagus;

- Some of the symptoms, such as tachycardia, fatigue and tremors, were already present before the *Beagle* voyage;
- The numerous partial exacerbations and remissions are unusual in Chagas disease;
- The incidence of trypanosome-infested benchucas in Mendoza, Argentina (which has a colder climate), where Darwin reported the bite, is very low;
- No other members of *Beagle*'s crew who accompanied Darwin in his land trip showed signs of a similar disease;

Recently, unsuccessful requests were made to test Darwin's remains for *T. cruzi* DNA at the Westminster Abbey by using modern PCR techniques but were met with a refusal by the Abbey's curator. The attempt was the subject of a recent documentary of Discovery Health Channel.

Ménière's disease

The hypothesis of Ménière's disease has gained some popularity. A diagnosis of Ménière's disease is based on a series of symptoms, some of which were present in Darwin's case, such as tinnitus, vertigo, dizziness, nausea, motion sickness, vomiting, continual malaise and fatigue. The fact that Darwin did not suffer from hearing loss and that "fullness" of the ears is never mentioned practically excludes Ménière's disease. The definition of this disease is, however, not very solid, and some form of "atypical Ménière's disease" remains a remote possibility. Motion sickness was present throughout his life and became apparent very early, when he suffered horribly of seasickness during the whole *Beagle* voyage. Darwin himself had the opinion that most of his health problems had an origin in his four-year bout with seasickness. Later, he could not stand traveling by carriage, and only horse riding would not affect his health. Psychic alteration often accompanies Ménière's and many other chronic diseases. An argument put forward for a diagnosis of Ménière's is that Darwin hunted a lot when he was young and could have damaged his inner ear with the repeated noise of shooting. While it is not unlikely that the noise damaged the inner ear and caused tinnitus, it could not have caused Ménière's disease. While Ménière's disease patients suffer during vertigo attacks from sickness and vomiting, the dyspepsia problems of Darwin have nothing to do with it. One of the diagnoses that he received from his physicians at the time was that of "suppressed gout"; the idea that this was an early name for Ménière's lacks any ground.

Cyclic vomiting syndrome

The pathologist John A. Hayman of the University of Melbourne has presented a case that Darwin's symptoms indicate that he suffered from cyclic vomiting syndrome (CVS), an illness associated with mitochondrial DNA abnormalities.[135] His paper on the topic was accepted by the *BMJ* and the *Medical Journal of Australia*, and was published in December 2009. In a supplement published in February 2012, he proposed that stroke-like episodes of memory loss and partial paralysis which do not occur with CVS are characteristic of the MELAS syndrome. An A3243G mtDNA mutation has been found in 80% of patients with this syndrome, and has also been described in those with CVS. This mutation in mitochondria is associated with symptoms of intestinal problems, seasickness and Ménière's disease as well as CVS and MELAS syndrome, thus giving a shared source of the various problems that affected Darwin. Any mitochondrial disease would have been inherited from his mother Susannah Darwin, whose own mother had 8 other children. Some of them had illnesses which could have been related to the same mutation.

CVS was also proposed as part of the cause in a 2011 analysis by gastroenterologist Sidney Cohen of the medical college of Thomas Jefferson University in Philadelphia. His study explained the illness as being due to a combination of cyclic vomiting syndrome, Chagas disease, and *Helicobacter pylori*.

Other possible causes

Evidence for familial systemic lactose intolerance syndrome was that vomiting and gastrointestinal symptoms usually appeared two to three hours after meals and that, apparently, Darwin got better when he stopped taking milk or cream.

Food intolerance and lactase deficiency may also be confused with food allergies. Symptoms include difficulty swallowing and breathing, nausea, vomiting, diarrhea, and abdominal pain. Upon reaching several other organs in the body, allergens can cause hives, eczema, lightheadedness, weakness, hypotension, etc. This has been proposed as the source of Darwin's illness, but the hypothesis is improbable, because, as with lactose intolerance, its temporal and causal relationship with food is easily established, and this was not always the case.

Chronic arsenic poisoning (arsenicosis) has been considered too. This hypothesis has been advanced by John H. Winslow, who published a book arguing that Darwin took arsenic at low dosages as a remedy and that there was "a very close match" between his symptoms and those of arsenicosis. However, it is highly improbable too, due to the long duration of the illness (40 years), the abruptness of symptoms, the cause of his death, and the absence of many symptoms and signs of this kind of poisoning (persistent weight loss and diarrhea, the appearance of dark brown calluses on the palms and the soles of the feet and of skin, known as hyperpigmentation).

Barry Marshall proposed in February 2009 that the cause of Darwin's illness was the ulcer-causing bacterium *Helicobacter pylori*. Marshall, who together with Robin Warren won the Nobel Prize in 2005 for discovery of the bacterium, states that this was a very common gastric infection of the time which causes ulcers in 10% of infected persons and causes dyspepsia in another 10% or so. He had yet to have a short paper on this accepted for publication.

Combined causes

From a clinical point of view, perhaps Darwin suffered from more than one disease, and had many psychosomatic complications and phobias arising from his debilitating condition. This is known to happen with many patients today, such as in severe cases of panic disorder, usually accompanied by hypochondria and depression.

Dr. Peter Medawar has supported the diagnosis that Darwin's health problems were part organic, part psychological. Colp[5] concluded that Darwin's illness consisted most probably of panic disorder without agoraphobia, psychosomatic skin disorder, and possibly Chagas disease of the stomach, which he suggested "was first active and then became inactive, permanently injuring the parasympathetic nerves of his stomach and making it more sensitive to sympathetic stimulation and hence more sensitive to the psychosomatic impact of his anxieties. An organic impairment best explains the lifelong chronicity of many of his abdominal complaints." Thus, the psychological aspects of Darwin's illness might be both a cause and an effect of Darwin's illness. D.A.B. Young wrote in a Royal Society journal in 1997 that the psychogenic view of Darwin's sickness "holds the field". The proponent of Chagas disease, Dr. Saul Adler, stated that Darwin may have suffered both from Chagas disease and from "an innate or acquired neurosis".

At a conference hosted by the University of Maryland, Baltimore, School of Medicine on the topic of Darwin's ailments, gastroenterologist Dr. Sidney Cohen of Thomas Jefferson University concluded that in his early years Darwin had suffered cyclic vomiting syndrome, but as he had brought up secretions such as stomach acid rather than food, this had not affected his weight and nutrition. He believed that Chagas disease contracted during the *Beagle* voyage was consistent with Darwin's account of his fever at that time and his later gastrointestinal complaints, as well as the heart disease later in life that led to Darwin's death. In addition, *Helicobacter pylori* which often occurs with Chagas would have caused Darwin to have peptic ulcer disease.

Hereditary disease

Many of Darwin's children suffered from similarly vague illnesses for much of their early lives. Darwin himself—concerned with heredity—wondered if he had passed on his generally infirm condition to his children, and was especially interested if their mother Emma Wedgwood, his cousin, was also responsible. His concerns later in life with the effects of inbreeding were potentially motivated by this personal aspect as well.

Contribution to Darwin's work

Darwin's illness may have contributed to his long and fruitful career in science. George Pickering, in his book *Creative Malady* (1974), wrote that Darwin—isolated from social life and obligations of a "normal" scientist, such as administrative and teaching work—had ample time and material comforts for research, thought, and writing extensively, which he did. Despite long periods of unproductivity due to ill health, he produced much research. Darwin often complained that his malady robbed him of half a lifetime, but even so, many believe that his scientific contributions can be compared favorably to those of such figures as Isaac Newton and Albert Einstein Wikipedia:Avoid weasel words.

Darwin himself wrote about this, in his autobiographical "Recollections of the Development of my Mind and Character" (1876):

<templatestyles src="Template:Quote/styles.css"/>

> Lastly, I have had ample leisure from not having to earn my own bread. Even ill-health, though it has annihilated several years of my life, has saved me from the distractions of society and amusement.

References

- ^2 American Psychology Association Answers to Your Questions About Panic Disorder[136]
- ^3 Chambless DL, Mason J (1986). "Sex, sex-role stereotyping and agoraphobia"[137]. *Behav Res Ther*. **24** (2): 231–35. doi: 10.1016/0005-7967(86)90098-7[138]. PMID 3964189[139].<templatestyles src="Module:Citation/CS1/styles.css"></templatestyles>
- ^4 Bean WB (Oct 1978). "The illness of Charles Darwin"[140]. *Am J Med*. **65** (4): 572–74. doi: 10.1016/0002-9343(78)90843-4[141]. PMID 360834[142].<templatestyles src="Module:Citation/CS1/styles.css"></templatestyles>

- ^5 Colp, Ralph (1977). *To be an invalid: the illness of Charles Darwin*. Chicago: University of Chicago Press. ISBN 0-226-11401-5.<templatestyles src="Module:Citation/CS1/styles.css"></templatestyles>
  - Colp R (Jun 2000). "More on Darwin's illness". *Hist Sci*. **38** (120 Pt 2): 219–36. PMID 14674422[143].<templatestyles src="Module:Citation/CS1/styles.css"></templatestyles>
  - Colp R (1997). "The dueling diagnoses of Darwin". *JAMA*. **277** (16): 1275–76, author reply 1276–77. doi:10.1001/jama.277.16.1275b[144]. PMID 9109457[145].<templatestyles src="Module:Citation/CS1/styles.css"></templatestyles>
- ^6 Rempf, Edward J (1918). "Charles Darwin — The Affective Sources of His Inspiration and Anxiety-Neurosis". *Psychoanalytic Review*. **5**: 151–92.<templatestyles src="Module:Citation/CS1/styles.css"></templatestyles>
- ^7 Bradbury, Andrew, J - Charles Darwin - The Truth? - Father to the Man - Of Father Figures - In Sickness and In Ill Health[146]
- ^8 Carolyn Douglas - Changing Theories of Darwin's Illness[147]
- ^9 Jerry Bergman - Was Charles Darwin Psychotic? A Study of His Mental Health (#367)[148]
- AboutDarwin.com[149]
- Adler (Oct 1959). "Darwin's illness". *Nature*. **184** (4693): 1102–04. doi:10.1038/1841102a0[150]. PMID 13791916[151].<templatestyles src="Module:Citation/CS1/styles.css"></templatestyles>
- Browne, Janet (1990). "Spas and sensibilities: Darwin at Malvern"[152] (PDF). *Medical History* (Suppl. #10): 102–113. doi:10.1017/s0025727300071027[153]. PMC 2557456[154].<templatestyles src="Module:Citation/CS1/styles.css"></templatestyles>
- Browne, E. Janet (1995). *Charles Darwin: vol. 1 Voyaging*. London: Jonathan Cape. ISBN 1-84413-314-1.<templatestyles src="Module:Citation/CS1/styles.css"></templatestyles>
- Browne, E. Janet (2002). *Charles Darwin: vol. 2 The Power of Place*. London: Jonathan Cape. ISBN 0-7126-6837-3.<templatestyles src="Module:Citation/CS1/styles.css"></templatestyles>
- Darwin, Charles (1887). Darwin, Francis, ed. *The life and letters of Charles Darwin, including an autobiographical chapter*[155]. **1**. London: John Murray. ISBN 0-404-08417-6.<templatestyles src="Module:Citation/CS1/styles.css"></templatestyles> (*The Autobiography of Charles Darwin*)
- Desmond, Adrian; Moore, James (1991). *Darwin*. London: Michael Joseph, Penguin Group. ISBN 0-7181-3430-3.<templatestyles src="Module:Citation/CS1/styles.css"></templatestyles>

- Desmond, A. and Moore, J. *Darwin: The Life of a Tormented Evolutionist*. NY: Warner Books, 1991.
- Goldstein JH (1989). "Darwin, Chagas', mind, and body". *Perspect Biol Med*. **32** (4): 586–601. PMID 2506517[156].<templatestyles src="Module:Citation/CS1/styles.css"></templatestyles>
- Circumnavigating Darwin - A paper by Dr Robert Gordon and Deborah Thomas[157]
- Keynes, Richard (2001). *Charles Darwin's Beagle Diary*[158]. Cambridge University Press. Retrieved 23 August 2011.<templatestyles src="Module:Citation/CS1/styles.css"></templatestyles>
- Medawar, Peter (1967). "Darwin's Illness". *The Art of the Soluble*. London: Methuen.<templatestyles src="Module:Citation/CS1/styles.css"></templatestyles>
- Pickering, George White (1974). *Creative malady: illness in the lives and minds of Charles Darwin, Florence Nightingale, Mary Baker Eddy, Sigmund Freud, Marcel Proust, Elizabeth Barrett Browningh*. Oxford [Oxfordshire]: Oxford University Press. ISBN 0-04-920040-2.<templatestyles src="Module:Citation/CS1/styles.css"></templatestyles>
- Pickover, Clifford A. (1998). *Strange brains and genius: the secret lives of eccentric scientists and madmen*. New York: Plenum Trade. ISBN 0-306-45784-9.<templatestyles src="Module:Citation/CS1/styles.css"></templatestyles>
- Queendom.com : Mental Health Articles: Panic Disorder and Agoraphobia - Etiology of panic disorder[159]
- Woodruff, AW (Mar 1990). "Darwin's illness". *Isr J Med Sci*. **26** (3): 163–64. PMID 2109737[160].<templatestyles src="Module:Citation/CS1/styles.css"></templatestyles>
- Woodruff, AW (June 1968). "The impact of Darwin's voyage to South America on his work and health"[161]. *Bull N Y Acad Med*. **44** (6): 661–72. PMC 1750247[161]. PMID 4870694[162].<templatestyles src="Module:Citation/CS1/styles.css"></templatestyles>
- Woodruff, AW (Mar 1965). "Darwin's health in relation to his voyage to South America"[163]. *Br Med J*. **1** (5437): 745–50. doi: 10.1136/bmj.1.5437.745[164]. PMC 2166138[163]. PMID 14248443[165].<templatestyles src="Module:Citation/CS1/styles.css"></templatestyles>

External links

- Milnter R (Oct 2002). "Putting Darwin in His Place"[166]. *Scientific American*.<templatestyles src="Module:Citation/CS1/styles.css"></templatestyles>
- Douglas, C. Changing Theories of Darwin's Illness[147], Purdue University.
- The Origin of Darwin's Anxiety[167]. *ScienceNow*, January 8, 1997.
- Darwin Illness[168]. The Talk.Origins Archive. Refutation to Claim no. CA131 of creationists that Darwin's illness was caused by feeling guilt of his "sins".
- Chagas Disease Claimed an Eminent Victim[169]. *The New York Times*, June 15, 1989.

Development of Darwin's theory

Development of Darwin's theory

Following the inception of Charles Darwin's theory of natural selection in 1838, the **development of Darwin's theory** to explain the "mystery of mysteries" of how new species originated was his "prime hobby" in the background to his main occupation of publishing the scientific results of the *Beagle* voyage. He was settling into married life, but suffered from bouts of illness and after his first child was born the family moved to rural Down House as a family home away from the pressures of London.

The publication in 1839 of his *Journal and Remarks* (now known as *The Voyage of the Beagle*) brought him success as an author, and in 1842 he published his first major scientific book, *The Structure and Distribution of Coral Reefs*, setting out his theory of the formation of coral atolls. He wrote out a sketch setting out his basic ideas on transmutation of species, which he expanded into an "essay" in 1844, and discussed his theory with friends as well as continuing with experiments and wide investigations. In the same year the anonymous *Vestiges of the Natural History of Creation* brought wide public interest in evolutionary ideas, but also showed the need for sound evidence to gain scientific acceptance of evolution.

In 1846 he completed his third geological book, and turned from supervising the publication of expert reports on the findings from the voyage to examining barnacle specimens himself. This grew into an eight-year study, making use of his theory to find hitherto unknown relationships between the many species of barnacle, and establishing his expertise as a biologist. His faith in Christianity dwindled and he stopped going to church. In 1851 his treasured daughter suffered a long illness and died. In 1854 he resumed his work on the species question which led on to the publication of Darwin's theory.

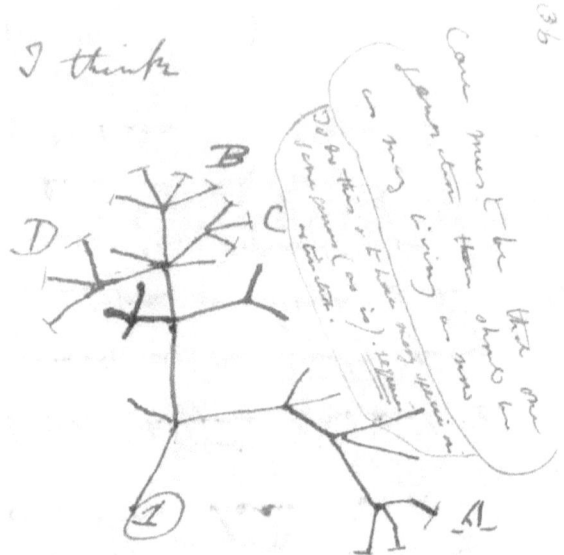

Figure 30: *Darwin's first sketch of an evolutionary tree from his First Notebook on Transmutation of Species (1837)*

Background

Charles Darwin became a naturalist at a point in the history of evolutionary thought when theories of Transmutation were being developed to explain discrepancies in the established faith based explanations of species. He considered these problems at first hand during the *Beagle* survey. On its return in 1836 his ideas developed rapidly. His collections and writings established him as an eminent geologist and collector.

Darwin read Malthus's *Essay on the Principle of Population* in the context of his findings about species relating to localities, enquiries into animal breeding, and ideas of Natural "laws of harmony". Around late November 1838 he compared breeders selecting traits with a Malthusian Nature selecting from variants thrown up by "chance" so that "every part of newly acquired structure is fully practical & perfected", thinking this "a beautiful part of my theory" of how species originated.

His theory of how species originated had now come together in principle, but he was vividly aware of the difficulties he would face in getting it accepted by his friends and colleagues in the scientific establishment. On 19 December 1838 as secretary of the Geological Society of London Darwin witnessed the vicious interrogation by Richard Owen and his allies of Darwin's old tutor Robert Edmund Grant in which they ridiculed Grant's Lamarckian heresy, showing establishment intolerance of materialist theories.

Married life

In 1839, now married to Emma and settled in London, Darwin continued to look to the countryside for information and began a *Questions & Experiments* notebook with ideas that would have seemed bizarrely mundane to the "philosophical" scientists of the time. He printed *Questions about the Breeding of Animals* and sent them out to gentlemen farmers, asking for information on animal husbandry from their nurserymen and gamekeepers on how they crossed varieties or selected offspring. Of only three who responded one simply found the questions too overwhelming to answer. He found agreement with the visiting Swiss botanist Alphonse de Candolle whose father Augustin had used the idea of "nature's war".[170] However, when he tried explaining his theory to Hensleigh Wedgwood, his cousin "seemed to think it absurd... that [a] tiger springing an inch further would determine his preservation".

The publication in May of Darwin's *Journal and Remarks* (The Voyage of the Beagle) brought reviews accusing him of theorising rather than letting the facts speak for themselves. He turned his attention to expanding his investigations and theory of the formation of coral atolls as the first part of his planned book on geology.

In December as Emma's first pregnancy progressed, Charles fell ill and accomplished little during the following year. He did accept a position on the Council of the Geographical Society in May 1840. In 1841 he became able to work for short periods a couple of days a week, and produced a paper on stones and debris being carried by ice floes, but his condition did not improve. Having consulted his father he began looking for a house in the countryside to escape a city suffering from economic depression and civil unrest. Owen was one of the few scientific friends to visit Darwin at this time, but Owen's opposition to any hint of Transmutation made Darwin keep quiet about his theories.

First writings on the theory

In January 1842 Darwin sent a tentative description of his ideas in a letter to Lyell, who was then touring America. Lyell, dismayed that his erstwhile ally had become a Transmutationist, noted that Darwin "denies seeing a beginning to each crop of species".

Darwin's book *The Structure and Distribution of Coral Reefs* on his theory of atoll formation was published in May after more than three years of work, with *Part 4: Fish* of *Zoology of the Voyage of H.M.S. Beagle* also going to print. Illness was a continuing problem, and he and Emma left London on 18 May, visiting her parents at Maer Hall before moving on to Shrewsbury on 15 June for rest and quiet. Now Darwin "first allowed myself the satisfaction of writing a very brief abstract of my theory in pencil in 35 pages", the "'Pencil Sketch'" of his theory. This discussed farmers breeding animals, gave the analogy of overpopulation and competition leading to "Natural Selection" through the "war of nature" and the mechanism of *descent*. Every living thing was related in a branching pedigree, not ascending a Lamarckian ladder, and this pedigree was the proper basis for classification. He thought it "derogatory" to argue that God had made every kind of parasite and worm on an individual whim. Already, a rough form of the phrasing and ideas which he went on to publish 17 years later in the closing paragraph of *On the Origin of Species* can be seen in his conclusion in this first draft: <templatestyles src="Template:Quote/styles.css"/>

> *From death, famine, rapine, and the concealed war of nature we can see that the highest good, which we can conceive, the creation of the higher animals has directly come. Doubtless it at first transcends our humble powers, to conceive laws capable of creating individual organisms, each characterised by the most exquisite workmanship and widely-extended adaptations. It accords better with [our modesty] the lowness of our faculties to suppose each must require the fiat of a creator, but in the same proportion the existence of such laws should exalt our notion of the power of the omniscient Creator. There is a simple grandeur in the view of life with its powers of growth, assimilation and reproduction, being originally breathed into matter under one or a few forms, and that whilst this our planet has gone circling on according to fixed laws, and land and water, in a cycle of change, have gone on replacing each other, that from so simple an origin, through the process of gradual selection of infinitesimal changes, endless forms most beautiful and most wonderful have been evolved.*

Essay

They returned on 18 July to a London seething with Chartist unrest, and Darwin copied and scribbled changes to his "Sketch" until it was almost illegible. He returned to house hunting and found a former parsonage in the rural hamlet of Downe at a good price. A general strike led to huge demonstrations all over London, but was crushed by troops by the time Darwin moved. On 17 September 1842 the family moved into Down House (around 1850 the village

Development of Darwin's theory

Figure 31: *The Darwins lived in Gower Street in London.*

Figure 32: *In 1842 they moved to Down House in rural Kent.*

changed its name to Downe to avoid confusion with County Down in Ireland, but the house kept the old spelling). After a series of alterations Darwin settled in, and in 1843 returned to writing his *Volcanic Islands*. In May he began a (mostly geological) country diary he called *The General Aspect*.

In response to a request from George Robert Waterhouse for advice on classification, Darwin replied that it properly "consists in grouping beings according to their actual *relationship*, ie their consanguinity, or descent from common stocks". He followed this up with another letter expressing belief that "all the orders, families & genera amongst the Mammals are merely artificial terms highly useful to show the relationship of those members of the series, *which have not become extinct*", before cautiously asking for the letter to be returned. Waterhouse was influenced by Owen and in a paper attacked such heresies, setting his species in the symbolic circles of the Quinarian system, not hereditary trees.[171] Darwin sent a sharp response about these "vicious circles".

Darwin became a close friend of the botanist Joseph Dalton Hooker, and on 11 January 1844 wrote to with melodramatic humour that he was "almost convinced (quite contrary to opinion I started with) that species are not (it is like confessing a murder) immutable. Heaven forfend me from Lamarck nonsense of a "tendency to progression" "adaptations from the slow willing of animals" &c,—but the conclusions I am led to are not widely different from his—though the means of change are wholly so— I think I have found out (here's presumption!) the simple way by which species become exquisitely adapted to various ends." Hooker's reply was cautious but friendly, saying that "There may in my opinion have been a series of productions on different spots, & also a gradual change of species. I shall be delighted to hear how you think that this change may have taken place, as no presently conceived opinions satisfy me on the subject."

Darwin worked up his "Sketch" into a 189-page '"Essay"' and in July entrusted the manuscript to the local schoolmaster to copy. He then wrote a difficult letter to be opened by his wife in the event of his death requesting that the essay be published posthumously. He started his *Geological Observations on South America*, and corresponded with Hooker about this, feeding in questions related to his "Essay". The copied "Essay", now 231 pages, was returned to him for corrections in September. Then one day he brought it to Emma and asked her to read it. She went through the pages, making notes in the margins pointing out unclear passages and showing where she disagreed.

The Reverend Leonard Jenyns, a naturalist Darwin had known since his time at the University of Cambridge, had at Darwin's request contributed the volume on *Fish* in *Zoology of the Voyage of H.M.S. Beagle*, and was now working on a book of notes on observations of plants and animals. On 12 October Darwin wrote to tell him that "work on the species question has impressed me very forcibly with the importance of all such works, as your intended one, containing what people are pleased generally to call trifling facts. These are the facts, which make one understand the working or œconomy of nature .... namely what are the checks & what the periods of life, by which the increase of any given species is limited." He told Jenyns that he had "continued steadily reading & collecting facts on variation of domestic animals & plants & on the question of what are species; I have a grand body of facts & I think I can draw some sound conclusions. The general conclusion at which I have slowly been driven from a directly opposite conviction is that species are mutable & that allied species are co-descendants of common stocks. I know how much I open myself, to reproach, for such a conclusion, but I have at least honestly & deliberately come to it. I shall not publish on this subject for several years." In November he thanked Jenyns for sending a detailed note, and told him "With respect to my far-distant work on species, I must have expressed myself with singular inaccuracy, if I led you to suppose that I meant to say that my conclusions were inevitable. They have become so, after years of weighing puzzles, to myself alone;; but in my wildest day-dream, I never expect more than to be able to show that there are two sides to the question of the immutability of species, ie whether species are directly created, or by intermediate laws, (as with the life & death of individuals)." He outlined the events that had led him to these ideas, and while cautious about "numerous immense difficulties on my notions" told him that he had "drawn up a sketch & had it copied (in 200 pages) of my conclusions; & if I thought at some future time, that you would think it worth reading, I shd. of course be most thankful to have the criticism of so competent a critic." Jenyns never took up this offer to read the "Essay", but did advise Darwin on possible issues with the term "mutation". Darwin replied "it will be years before I publish, so that I shall have plenty of time to think of better words".

Vestiges published

In October 1844 Transmutation became a middle class talking point with the anonymous publication of *Vestiges of the Natural History of Creation* by Robert Chambers presenting Lamarckian views. It brought the notion of transmutation out into the public arena and was a sensation, quickly becoming a best-seller in fashionable society circles and going into new editions. Darwin read it in November,[172] and when questioned by Hooker in January he admired its prose, but wrote that the "geology strikes me as bad, & his zoology far worse". The book was liked by many Quakers and Unitarians. Darwin's friend the Unitarian physiologist William Carpenter called it "a very beautiful and a very interesting book", and helped Chambers with correcting later editions. Critics thanked God that the author began "in ignorance and presumption", for the revised versions "would have been much more dangerous".

Vestiges paved the way for discussion, but emphasised the need for secure mastery of awkward facts.

Hooker became Darwin's mainstay in the search to find and explain anomalous facts, though Darwin was greatly disappointed in February 1845 when Hooker was invited to teach botany at Edinburgh. Others helping included Captain Beaufort of the Admiralty who invited Darwin to list any facts he wanted checking, for investigation by ship's surgeons (naturalists) when their ship was in the appropriate part of the world. In March Darwin followed his father's investment advice and became owner of a farmhouse and estate in Lincolnshire, where the Reverend Samuel Wilberforce advised local squires to take education in hand lest the countryfolk learn "a smattering of science" and forget their God-given duties.

The publisher John Murray made an offer of payment for a revised second edition of *Journal and Remarks*, diverting Darwin's attention from *South America*. On 25 April Darwin began extensive revisions incorporating his latest information and interpretations, including several hints about his species speculation. He now saw the Galápagos Archipelago as "a little world within itself, or rather a satellite attached to America, whence it has derived a few stray colonists," where we were "astonished at the number of their aboriginal beings, and at their confined range", and "seem to be brought somewhat near to that great fact – that mystery of mysteries – the first appearance of new beings on this earth." On 5 August Darwin began reading Lyell's *Travels in North America*, and was horrified that it saw no harm in slavery. He added two new paragraphs to his *Journal*, cataloguing atrocities after stating "I thank God, I shall never again visit a slave-country", and finished his revisions on 26 August.

Anglican clergymen / naturalists had been slow to respond to *Vestiges*, not wanting to give its vile ideas of transmutation publicity, but it sold increasing numbers to polite society. In the July *Edinburgh Review* a lengthy and scathing attack by Adam Sedgwick, who had taught Darwin geology at university, predicted "ruin and confusion in such a creed" which if taken up by the populace would "undermine the whole moral and social fabric" bringing "discord and deadly mischief in its train." On 8 October Darwin wrote telling Lyell that the review was "far from popular with non-scientific readers. I think some few passages savour of the dogmatism of the pulpit, rather than of the philosophy of the Professor chair". Nevertheless, it was "a grand piece of argument against mutability of species; & I read it with fear & trembling, but was well pleased to find, that I had not overlooked any of the arguments, though I had put them to myself as feebly as milk & water."

In correspondence Darwin continued to discuss his species work with Hooker, and he took it personally when Hooker remarked of another naturalist "that no

Figure 33: *In 1846 Darwin rented land from his neighbour John Lubbock to plant woodland and lay out the "sandwalk" at Down House which became his usual "Thinking Path".*

one has hardly a right to examine the question of species who has not minutely described many." However, even Richard Owen who was opposed to any mutability in species had told him it was "a very fair subject" with a mass of facts to be investigated, "& though I shall get more kicks than half-pennies, I will, life serving, attempt my work." Early in November Darwin, hinting that "geographical distrib: will be the key which will unlock the mystery of species", invited Hooker to "look over a rough sketch (well copied) on this subject" while fearing this was "too impudent a request".

Darwin's researches led to a meeting on 23 November with Charles James Fox Bunbury, in which he discussed the geographical distribution of plants and animals, particularly in the Galapagos islands where they strikingly showed "a South American character as it were stamped on them all, while nearly all the species are peculiar." As Bunbury recalled, "He avowed himself to some extent a believer in the transmutation of species, though not, he said, exactly according to the doctrine either of Lamarck or of the *Vestiges*. But he admitted that all the leading botanists and zoologists, of this country at least, are on the other side."[173] Darwin was familiarising the "most rising naturalists" with the idea, and on 6 December enjoyed having Hooker, Edward Forbes, Hugh

Figure 34: *Barnacles from Darwin's collection, sent as a gift to Japetus Steenstrup and Johan Georg Forchhammer in 1854, Zoological Museum of Copenhagen*

Falconer, and George Robert Waterhouse visit Down for dinner and "raging discussions".

In the following year potato blight brought famine which impinged on the Darwins' servants and workmen, and led to overthrow of the Corn Laws. Darwin welcomed this, but as a landowner now found that it affected his income from rent and he wrote to his agent that "Although I am on principle a free-trader, of course I am not willing to make a larger reduction than necessary to retain a good tenant." Despite his own illness recurring, Darwin pressed on with *South America*, having to jointly subsidise it with the publisher when the Treasury grant ran out, and it was completed by October 1846.

Barnacles

A single barnacle species was left to describe, and on 1 October 1846 Darwin began a paper on it, working on dissecting with the assistance of Hooker who was now at Kew. To compare this with other species he borrowed specimens, and soon became involved in a much needed comprehensive study of these peculiar creatures that had recently been found to be crustaceans rather than molluscs. To Hooker such an exhaustive study might dampen Darwin's tendency to speculative theorising, and to Darwin it would establish his credentials.

Hooker reads the "Essay"

Hooker paid frequent visits, and in January 1847 when Darwin was particularly ill Hooker took away a copy of the "Essay". After some delays he sent a page of notes, giving the calm critical feedback that Darwin needed. He did not go along with Darwin's rejection of continuing Creation, arguing "All allusions to superintending providence unnecessary – The Creator able to make first [organisms] able also to go on directing & [it's] a matter of moonshine to [the] argument whether he does or no." Their debates continued, sometimes argumentatively, and Darwin felt devastated by Hooker's intention to set off on a survey voyage.

British Association: *Vestiges* and Wilberforce

Darwin overcame illness to attend the British Association for the Advancement of Science meeting at Oxford in May 1847, to discuss the "Sketch" with Hooker. Darwin attended the geological section which featured a talk by Robert Chambers on ancient beaches. An observer at the meeting reported that Chambers "pushed his conclusions to a most unwarrantable length and got roughly handled on account of it by Buckland, De la Beche, Sedgwick, Murchison, and Lyell. The last told me afterwards that he did so purposely that [Chambers] might see that reasonings in the style of the author of the Vestiges would not be tolerated among scientific men." This was a clear warning from Darwin's Cambridge friends.

On the Sunday Samuel Wilberforce, now the Bishop of Oxford, used his sermon at St. Mary's Church on "the wrong way of doing science" to deliver a stinging attack obviously aimed at Chambers. The church "crowded to suffocation" with geologists, astronomers and zoologists heard jibes about the "half-learned" seduced by the "foul temptation" of speculation looking for a self-sustaining universe in a "mocking spirit of unbelief", showing a failure to understand the "modes of the Creator's acting" or to meet the responsibilities of a gentleman. Chambers denounced this as an attempt to stifle progressive opinion, but others thought he must have gone home "with the feeling of a martyr". Darwin was not present, but in the following week at the Association dissociated himself from the error-ridden *Vestiges* in Lyell's presence, attacking the author's "poverty of intellect" and dismissing it as a "literary curiosity."

Health problems

For the rest of the year Darwin suffered increasing health problems, with fiercely inflamed boils, and in November Hooker left for India. Darwin returned his attention to family life and dissecting barnacles. In February 1848 the leader of British science Sir John Herschel wrote recruiting Darwin to a project drawing up instructions for sailors on scientific field work, at the request of the First Sea Lord. Darwin spent five weeks writing a section for the manual explaining how any gentleman could "geologize".

That summer Communist revolution in France was followed by a massive Chartist demonstration in London, with the wealthy and the Queen fleeing to safety. Darwin's friends were mustered to defend the scientific institutions against the possibility of attacks by rioters who would have welcomed his secret theory. Continuing with the barnacles he found that what seemed like minute parasites were in some cases the minute males "& half embedded in the flesh of their wives they spend their whole lives", a "wonder of nature" not flattering to the Creation idea that God appointed the social system.

Darwin visited The Mount, Shrewsbury for the 82nd birthday of his father who was now seriously ill. He became desperately ill himself and returned home to be nursed by Emma who gave birth to their third son in August, then in November was devastated when his father died. Emma sustained him, and they read religious books together. In February 1849 he drew some comfort from Harriet Martineau's new *Eastern Life, Past and Present*, a travelogue of tombs with the message that Christian beliefs in reward and punishment were founded in heathen superstitions.

Water Cure

His illness had long baffled doctors. Reluctantly and sceptically he took friend's advice and the whole family and household set out on 8 March 1849 for Malvern so that he could try Dr James Gully's *Water Cure Establishment* for a two-month cold water treatment. They rented "The Lodge" in a quiet location nearby, and he embarked on a course including drinking spa water and being scrubbed in cold water, walks for exercise, a strict diet and mesmerism and homoeopathic medicines.

The family enjoyed the spring weather and liked Dr Gully, and it developed into a delightful holiday in the festive atmosphere around the spa. His stomach trouble was diagnosed as nervous in origin, and he was soon free of sickness and walking seven miles (11 km) a day. Despite his suspicions of quackery, the cure worked, and after staying 16 weeks they returned home, arriving on 30 June with Darwin eager to resume work on his barnacles.

He continued a slightly relaxed version of the treatment, having a hut built with a cold water douche and getting up at seven a.m. to get heated up with a spirit lamp then take a cold plunge bath and get scrubbed by his butler. In September his duties as Vice-President of the British Association and interest in a paper on barnacles led him to attend their meeting at Birmingham, but he found it unpleasant and the excitement brought back the sickness. Even after a quick visit to Dr Gully and rest at home he took weeks to recover.

Homologies in barnacles

His investigation of barnacles now found how their segmentation related to other crustaceans, showing how they had diverged from their relatives. To Owen such "homologies" in comparative anatomy showed "archetypes" in the Divine mind, but to Darwin this was evidence of Descent, showing dramatically how organs could have changed functions to meet new conditions. Darwin was "cock-a-hoop", writing to Louis Agassiz of this odd metamorphosis and getting him and others around the world to send more barnacle specimens. His cascade of letters made Hooker tire of barnacle details, and write from the Himalayas that on reflection he really did prefer to hear the evolutionary speculation after all. Darwin responded that "this is too bad" as "your decided approval of my Barnacle work" had "led me...to defer my species-paper" in the first place.

As his work progressed on to fossil barnacles, pressures brought on illness again and in June 1850 he went to Malvern for a week of treatment. Hooker was helping search for evidence, now trying to test evolutionary ideas and writing that "they have possessed me, without however converting me". While Hooker was not finding gradations of varieties, Darwin's barnacles were showing this to the extent that defining species was extremely difficult.

Annie falls ill

Darwin returned from Malvern at the end of June 1850 to a reawakening of his fears that his illness might be hereditary. His bright nine-year-old daughter Anne who had become a particular favourite and comfort to him fell sick. She was miserable for weeks on end, then became feverish. Their doctor could do nothing and thought it might be inherited. She had recovered to some extent by March 1851, but then she and her father were both laid low by influenza. Darwin recovered but Annie was still ill, and on 24 March he took her to Malvern, leaving her there for the best treatment he knew of, and returning to Downe where Emma had stayed as she was pregnant. With his first paper on barnacles printed and Hooker safely returned to Britain laden with specimens, things were looking up, but then on 15 April Annie suffered a serious relapse and Darwin had to rush to her side.

An agonised Darwin stayed at Annie's bedside as the crisis deepened. Dr Gully attended through the night thinking her unlikely to last, but at 6 a.m. she vomited and her condition stabilised. She seemed to recover slightly and a series of ups and downs followed with Darwin and Fanny Wedgwood anxiously watching and writing home, but she deteriorated and died on 23 April 1851.

Darwin's faith in Christianity had already dwindled away and from around 1849 he had stopped going to church. During Annie's long illness Darwin had read books by Francis William Newman, a Unitarian evolutionist who called for a new post-Christian synthesis and wrote that "the fretfulness of a child is an infinite evil". For three years Darwin had deliberated about the Christian meaning of mortality, opening a vision of tragically circumstantial nature. On 30 April he wrote a brief and intensely emotional memoir of Annie for himself and Emma.

Family life

Darwin was on good terms with the local curate. He contributed to the church, helped with parish assistance and proposed a benefit society which became the *Down Friendly Society* with Darwin as guardian and treasurer. On Sundays Emma took the children to church. Darwin sometimes went with them as far as the lychgate to the churchyard, and then he would go for a walk. During the service, Emma continued to face forward when the congregation turned to face the altar for the Creed, sticking to her Unitarian faith.

The Darwins went up to the Great Exhibition in 1851, staying with "Uncle Ras", but while the children enjoyed their several visits, Darwin's ailments returned with the excitement. The slog of describing barnacles continued. Family life was rewarding but also brought pressures. The worst of his bugbears was a fear of inherited weaknesses. His oldest son William was a slow learner, and after much agonising Darwin sent him to Rugby School. While they had inherited wealth, it had to be wisely invested. A large proportion was cautiously put in railway stock, then in a boom but subject to fluctuations. He had kept records of the effects of the continuing water treatment, and finding that it was of some help with relaxation but had no significant effect he stopped it in 1852 and proceeded to try various experimental therapies without any confidence in their effects.

Progressive reforms

The Great Exhibition heralded the success of free trade and modern science in improving prosperity. There was a new appetite for liberal, progressive reforms. An alliance of thinkers began recasting nature as a competitive market-place. *The Westminster Review* recently acquired by John Chapman became their focus, and an early article by Herbert Spencer set out a Malthusian view that people who multiply beyond their means take "the high road to extinction", while "the select of their generation" remained to ensure progress. Spencer became a close friend and ally of Thomas Huxley, an ambitious naturalist who had returned from a long survey trip but lacked the family wealth or contacts to find a career. Huxley had sent papers to Darwin which began a correspondence, and Darwin sent him a copy of the first volume of *Barnacles* when it was printed. Huxley called it an exemplary work, all the more remarkable for coming from a distinguished geologist rather than an anatomist.[174]

In recognition of his work on South American geology, invertebrate research and particularly his work on Barnacles, Darwin was awarded the Royal Medal of the Royal Society and received it at their meeting on 30 November 1853. The excitement brought back illness and he resumed the water treatment. This time it was successful and his health improved. He finished the second volume of *Barnacles*, completing almost eight years of work which had made him the world's foremost authority on the subject.[175]

In the spring of 1854 he joined the Royal Society's Philosophical Club, and he also became a Fellow of the Linnean Society of London, gaining postal access to its library. To his surprise his stomach was not troubled and he greatly enjoyed visiting London regularly and meeting with the new generation of scientists, in particular John Tyndall, Hooker and Huxley. Darwin supported them in gaining gold medals from the Society, saying that they would become "scientific giants" and he thought it only right that they should get the accolades to spur them on. Tyndall had taken the chair of natural philosophy at the Royal Institution in 1853 and was now helping Huxley run the science section of *The Westminster Review*. Huxley began teaching at the Royal School of Mines in November, then "sick of the dilettante middle class" began his working men's lectures a year later, and Hooker settled into his post at Kew Gardens.[176,177]

Biology was becoming liberalised, even among some churchmen. The Reverend Baden Powell, a mathematics professor at the University of Oxford, applied the theological argument that God is a lawgiver, miracles break the lawful edicts issued at Creation, therefore belief in miracles is atheistic.[178]

Renewal of work on Species

By September 1854 his second volume of *Barnacles* had been printed and dispatched, and he turned his attention to Species, telling his cousin William Darwin Fox that he planned to "view all facts that I can master..to see how far they favour or are opposed to the notion that wild species are mutable or immutable". All available information was examined for "hostile facts" and discussed with Hooker, who had resisted what he called Darwin's "Elastic theory" but who was now developing an "utter disbelief of my own Genera and species".

In the Spring of 1855, as the Crimean war developed, Darwin was pondering the war of nature, taking the then current analogy with an industrial economy further than others, and wondering how species spread. He was dismissive of the ideas that others had put forward of sunken continents like Atlantis, and began experimenting in his house with soaking seeds in brine then seeing if they could germinate. He reported his results in *Gardeners' Chronicle* and roped in his curate friends including Henslow. The consul in Norway sent seed pods which had washed ashore. Hooker was able to identify them as coming from the Caribbean and get them to germinate at Kew. Investigation of variation brought him back to animal husbandry. He now began dissecting domestic animals and breeding pigeons, joining a pigeon fancier's club: very unorthodox behaviour for naturalists at that time.

Huxley had obtained a position and his friends had been having an impact on the establishment. In particular Huxley had strongly dismissed the transmutationist thesis of Chambers' *Vestiges*. He also argued vociferously against the dominant Owen who had demonstrated fossil evidence of an evolutionary sequence of horses as supporting his idea of development from archetypes in "ordained continuous becoming", and who had in 1854 given a British Association talk on the impossibility of bestial apes such as the recently discovered gorilla standing erect and being transmuted into men. Darwin tried at a gathering at Downe on 22 April 1856 to amiably argue Huxley and Hooker round towards accepting evolution as a process, without going into the mechanism.

Darwin intended to write human beings into *Natural Selection* through mid-1857. But his work required a tremendous amount of evidence and facts. He left humans out in part because "mutiny in India" had stopped his correspondence with Edward Blyth in Calcutta. Had he included sexual selection, at that time it would have been only the male competition element and not female choice.

Towards publication

It was at this stage that Alfred Russel Wallace became involved and Darwin's work took on a new urgency. While Darwin continued to amass knowledge and carry out experiments, he now became committed to publication.

See the publication of Darwin's theory for the resulting developments, in the context of his life, work and outside influences at the time.

References

- Bowler, Peter J. (11 April 1996), *Charles Darwin: The Man and His Influence*[179], Cambridge University Press, ISBN 978-0-521-56668-1<templatestyles src="Module:Citation/CS1/styles.css"></templatestyles>
- Browne, E. Janet (1995), *Charles Darwin: vol. 1 Voyaging*, London: Jonathan Cape, ISBN 1-84413-314-1<templatestyles src="Module:Citation/CS1/styles.css"></templatestyles>
- Darwin, Charles (2006), "Journal"[180], in van Wyhe, John, *[Darwin's personal 'Journal' (1809–1881)]*[181], Darwin Online, CUL-DAR158.1–76, retrieved 20 December 2008<templatestyles src="Module:Citation/CS1/styles.css"></templatestyles>
- Desmond, Adrian; Moore, James (1991), *Darwin*, London: Michael Joseph, Penguin Group, ISBN 0-7181-3430-3<templatestyles src="Module:Citation/CS1/styles.css"></templatestyles>
- Desmond, Adrian; Moore, James (2004), *"Introduction" to The Descent of Man, and Selection in Relation to Sex*, London: Penguin Group, ISBN 978-0-14-043631-0<templatestyles src="Module:Citation/CS1/styles.css"></templatestyles>
- von Sydow, Momme (2005), "Darwin – A Christian Undermining Christianity? On Self-Undermining Dynamics of Ideas Between Belief and Science"[182] (PDF), in Knight, David M.; Eddy, Matthew D., *Science and Beliefs: From Natural Philosophy to Natural Science, 1700–1900*, Burlington: Ashgate, pp. 141–156, ISBN 0-7546-3996-7, retrieved 16 December 2008<templatestyles src="Module:Citation/CS1/styles.css"></templatestyles>
- van Wyhe, John (2008), *Darwin: The Story of the Man and His Theories of Evolution*, London: Andre Deutsch Ltd (published 1 September 2008), ISBN 0-233-00251-0<templatestyles src="Module:Citation/CS1/styles.css"></templatestyles>

Further reading

- Ospovat, Dov (1981), *The Development of Darwin's Theory : Natural History, Natural Theology, and Natural Selection, 1838–1859*, Cambridge ; New York : Cambridge University Press, ISBN 0-521-23818-8<templatestyles src="Module:Citation/CS1/styles.css"></templatestyles>
- The Complete Works of Charles Darwin Online – Darwin Online[183]; Darwin's publications, private papers and bibliography, supplementary works including biographies, obituaries and reviews. Free to use, includes items not in public domain.
- Works by Charles Darwin[184] at Project Gutenberg; public domain

- Darwin Correspondence Project[185] Text and notes for most of his letters

Publication of the theory of natural selection

Publication of Darwin's theory

The **publication of Darwin's theory** brought into the open Charles Darwin's theory of evolution through natural selection, the culmination of more than twenty years of work.

Thoughts on the possibility of transmutation of species which he recorded in 1836 towards the end of his five-year voyage on the *Beagle* were followed on his return by findings and work which led him to conceive of his theory in September 1838. He gave priority to his career as a geologist whose observations and theories supported Charles Lyell's uniformitarian ideas, and to publication of the findings from the voyage as well as his journal of the voyage, but he discussed his evolutionary ideas with several naturalists and carried out extensive research on his "hobby" of evolutionary work.

He was writing up his theory in 1858 when he received an essay from Alfred Russel Wallace who was in Borneo, describing Wallace's own theory of natural selection, prompting immediate joint publication of extracts from Darwin's 1844 essay together with Wallace's paper as *On the Tendency of Species to form Varieties; and on the Perpetuation of Varieties and Species by Natural Means of Selection* in a presentation to the Linnaean Society on 1 July 1858. This attracted little notice, but spurred Darwin to write an "abstract" of his work which was published in 1859 as his book *On the Origin of Species*.

Figure 35: *Darwin, as photographed in 1860, was still clean shaven at this time.*

Background

Darwin's ideas developed rapidly from the return in 1836 of the *Beagle* survey expedition. By December 1838 he had developed the principles of his theory. At that time similar ideas brought others disgrace and association with the revolutionary mob. He was conscious of the need to answer all likely objections before publishing. While he continued with research as his "prime hobby", his priority was an immense amount of work on geology and analysing and publishing findings from the *Beagle* expedition. This was repeatedly delayed by illness.

Natural history at that time was dominated by clerical naturalists whose income came from the Established Church of England and who saw the science of the day as revealing God's plan. Darwin found three close allies: Charles Lyell, Joseph Dalton Hooker and Thomas Huxley. Books by the eminent geologist Charles Lyell had influenced the young Darwin during the voyage, and he then befriended Darwin who he saw as a supporter of his ideas of gradual geological processes with continuing divine Creation of species. By the 1840s Darwin became friends with the young botanist Joseph Dalton Hooker, who had followed his father into that science, and after going on a survey voyage used his contacts to eventually find a position. In the 1850s Darwin met Thomas Huxley, an ambitious naturalist who had returned from a long survey trip but lacked the family wealth or contacts to find a career and who joined the progressive group around Herbert Spencer fighting to make science a profession, freed from the clerics.

Darwin made attempts to open discussions about his theory with his close scientific colleagues. In January 1842 Darwin sent a tentative description of his ideas in a letter to Lyell, then prepared a "Pencil Sketch" of his theory. He worked up his "Sketch" into an "Essay" in 1844, and eventually persuaded Hooker to read a copy in January 1847. His geology books and publication of *Beagle* findings were completed in 1846, when he began what became eight years of research into classification of barnacle species, exploring the immense amount of variation in nature.

In September 1854 Darwin had the last of his barnacle monographs ready for publication, and he turned his attention fully to questions about how species originated. He freely discussed his intention to write a book on the subject, and planned avenues of research with other scientists. He went over his previous notes and writings on the topic, and drew up proposals for investigations and research into the implications of his theory. One topic was explaining geographical distribution of organisms; he got information from international correspondence, and experimented on the viability of methods of dispersal. He widened his investigations into variability in nature, and experimented on plant hybridisation and cross-fertilisation.

Variation under domestication became a major topic of research: in 1855 he began to develop a web of contacts, both in the UK and worldwide, to get information on the origins and variation of domesticated animals, particularly poultry, ducks, rabbits, and pigeons. He got extensive information, specimens and ideas from Edward Blyth in India, who put him in contact with Edgar Leopold Layard in South Africa. At the suggestion of William Yarrell, Darwin began pigeon breeding at Down House to investigate varieties of domestic pigeons, and gained access to the expertise of William Bernhard Tegetmeier who was glad to research aspects of interest to Darwin. From March, he also got information and specimens from his relative William Darwin Fox who bred poultry and ducks at his rectory in the parish of Delamere, Cheshire.

In 1856 he was gradually bringing his friends round towards accepting evolution as a process, but was far from convincing them about the mechanism, when Wallace's entry into the discussion brought a new urgency to publication.

Wallace

Alfred Russel Wallace, a naturalist working as a specimen collector in Borneo, spent Christmas 1854 visiting Sir James Brooke, the White Rajah of Sarawak, then during the ensuing rainy season lived alone in a little Dayak house, with only one Malay servant as cook. He recalled, "during the evening and wet days, I had nothing to do but look over my books". He had already read Lyell's *Principles of Geology* which opposed Lamarck by arguing that the fossil record showed no progress, and the 1845 second edition of Darwin's *Journal of Researches* which hinted at evolution by describing the "wonderful relationship in the same continent" between fossil and extant species, which would "throw more light on the appearance of organic beings on our earth, and their disappearance from it, than any other class of facts", and how species unique to the Galápagos Islands "all show a marked relationship with those of America" despite its distance.[186,187]

Wallace had also been impressed by Pictet's studies of palaeontology, and was now annoyed by a recent article by Edward Forbes which dismissed evolutionary ideas and instead proposed that species were created in a pattern showing a divine plan of polarity. In February, Wallace completed his paper "On the Law which has Regulated the Introduction of New Species" which was published in September 1855 in the *Annals and Magazine of Natural History*.[186]

This "Sarawak paper" countered Forbes, and showed Wallace's opinions. He incorporated points from Lyell, Darwin, Pictet and others, including *Vestiges of the Natural History of Creation*, combined with Wallace's own observations to support his conclusion that "Every species has come into existence coincident both in space and time with a closely allied species". This was a theory of a succession of species, but referred to "creation" rather than explicitly citing an evolutionary mechanism [in 1905 Wallace recalled that he left descent to be inferred]. Brooke read it as either a series of creations or one species growing into another, and in 1856 told Wallace he had no objection to the latter. Wallace had told him that the paper was to "feel the pulse of scientific men" about the hypothesis, and Brooke was indignant at the suggestion that "bigotry & intolerance" would be aroused by novel views: this would explain Wallace's ambiguity.[188,189] Lyell's resistance to Darwin's evolutionary ideas was shaken by the paper; in November 1855 Lyell began writing species notebooks, starting with a note about Wallace.[190] On 8 December Edward Blyth wrote from Calcutta to ask Darwin for his views on the paper. Blyth thought it "Good! Upon the whole!" and said "according to his theory, the various domestic races of animals have been fairly developed into species." It is not known when Darwin read this letter.

During December 1855, Darwin extended his research into variation under domestication with letters to nearly 30 people around the world,[191] requesting their help in obtaining specimens of "Any domestic breed or race, of Poultry, Pigeons, Rabbits, Cats, & even dogs, if not too large, which has been bred for many generations in any little visited region." As Blyth had suggested earlier, Darwin wrote on 9 December to Edgar Leopold Layard in South Africa, and said that he was "collecting all the facts & reasoning which I could, in regard to the variation & origin of species", particularly pigeons. On 24 December Darwin wrote to the diplomat Sir Charles Murray in Persia, similarly saying he had "for many years been working on the perplexed subject of the origin of varieties & species, & for this purpose I am endeavouring to study the effects of domestication". Letters also went to Brooke, and to Wallace via his agent Samuel Stevens. In August 1856 Wallace told Stevens that specimens for Darwin were included in a shipment. In November Darwin wrote to tell William Bernhardt Tegetmeier that a box of Persian poultry specimens from Murray had arrived, and "Mr Wallace is collecting in the Malay Archipelago".[191]

Wallace's "Sarawak paper" was included in the July–December 1855 volume of the *Annals and Magazine of Natural History*. Darwin jotted comments in his copy of this volume: "Laws of Geograph. Distrib. nothing very new", and "Uses my simile of tree— It seems all creation with him", but "he puts the facts in striking point of view". He noted Wallace's point that geological knowledge was imperfect, and commented "put generation for creation & I quite agree". In December 1857 Darwin still thought Wallace was proposing creation as an explanation, and told him "I believe I go much further than you".[192]

"Natural Selection"

When Lyell and his wife visited the Darwins at Downe from 13 to 16 April 1856, Darwin explained his theory to Lyell, who then wrote up notes headed "With Darwin: On the Formation of Species by Natural Selection", with pigeons as one example. At another Down House party on 26–27 April, Darwin had long discussions with his guests Joseph Dalton Hooker, Thomas Henry Huxley, and Thomas Vernon Wollaston. Lyell subsequently heard that they "ran a tilt against species farther I believe than they are deliberately prepared to go. ... I cannot easily see how they can go so far, and not embrace the whole Lamarckian doctrine."[193]

On 1 May Lyell wrote to urge Darwin to establish priority: "I wish you would publish some small fragment of your data *pigeons* if you please & so out with the theory & let it take date—& be cited—& understood." Darwin replied on 3 May: "With respect to your suggestion of a sketch of my view; I hardly know what to think, but will reflect on it; but it goes against my prejudices. To give a fair sketch would be absolutely impossible, for every proposition requires such an array of facts. If I were to do anything it could only refer to the main agency of change, selection,—& perhaps point out a very few of the leading features which countenance such a view, & some few of the main difficulties. But I do not know what to think: I rather hate the idea of writing for priority, yet I certainly sh^d be vexed if any one were to publish my doctrines before me."

On Thursday 8 May, while in London for meetings, Darwin visited Lyell. In a letter to Hooker the next day, Darwin said he "had good talk with Lyell about my species work, & he urges me strongly to publish something. I am fixed against any periodical or Journal, as I positively will not expose myself to an Editor or Council allowing a publication for which they might be abused". If he published, it could only be "a very thin & little volume, giving a sketch of my views & difficulties; but it is really dreadfully unphilosophical to give a resumé, without exact references, of an unpublished work". Lyell appeared to think it could be done "at the suggestion of friends" as Darwin had "been at work for 18 years, & yet could not publish for several years". Hooker's response encouraging publication was welcomed by Darwin, who thought his suggestion "that the Essay might supersede & take away all novelty & value from my future larger Book, is very true; & that would grieve me beyond everything. On the other hand, (again from Lyell's urgent advice) I published a preliminary sketch of Coral Theory & this did neither good nor harm.— I begin most heartily to wish that Lyell had never put this idea of an Essay into my head." On 14 May 1856 Darwin noted in his journal that he had begun his "species sketch".

By July, Darwin had decided to produce *Natural Selection* as a full technical treatise on species. Lyell seemed to be coming round to Darwin's ideas, but in private was agonising over the social implications if humans had animal ancestry, particularly now that race was becoming an issue, with Robert Knox describing races as different species and warning of racial wars. Hooker's verdict on the growing manuscript was "incomparably more favourable" than Darwin had anticipated, while Darwin tried to put over the point that "external conditions do extremely little", it was the selection of "chance" variations that produced new species.

Darwin's experiments on how species spread were now extended to considering how animals such as snails could be carried on birds' feet, and seeds in birds' droppings. His tenth child, Charles Waring Darwin was born on 6 December apparently without his full share of intelligence, renewing fears of inbreeding and hereditary defects, a topic that he covered in principle in his book.

Darwin's cousin William Darwin Fox continued to give hims strong support, warning him against overworking on his huge book and recommending a holiday, but Darwin was immersed in his experiments and his writing.[194] "I am got most deeply interested in my subject; though I wish I could set less value on the bauble fame, either present or posthumous, than I do, but not, I think, to any extreme degree; yet, if I know myself, I would work just as hard, though with less gusto, if I knew that my Book w^d be published for ever anonymously".

On 23 February 1857 the Darwins were visited for lunch by Robert FitzRoy, who had been the captain of HMS *Beagle* during Darwin's voyage, together with his second wife, his first wife and his only daughter having died.[194]

Struggle for existence

Alfred Tennyson wrote his great poem "In Memoriam A.H.H." which introduced the phrase "Nature, red in tooth and claw", and Darwin worked on *The Struggle for Existence*. A discussion with Thomas Huxley on how jellyfish might cross-fertilise got the witty response that "the indecency of the process is to a certain extent in favour of its probability".[195] In July 1856 Darwin passed Huxley's remark on to Hooker with the comment, "What a book a Devil's chaplain might write on the clumsy, wasteful, blundering low & horridly cruel works of nature!", apparently a reference to the nickname given to the Radical Revd. Robert Taylor who had visited Cambridge on an "infidel home missionary tour" when Darwin was a student there (though the term goes back to Chaucer's *Parson's Tale*).

Darwin pressed on with writing his "big book" on *Natural Selection*, overworking, until in March 1857 illness began cutting his working day "ridiculously short". Eventually, he took a fortnight's water treatment at the nearby Moor Park spa run by Edward Lane, and this revived him.[196]

Wallace had been working for Darwin, sending domestic fowl specimens from Indonesia,[196] and a letter he had written in October reached Darwin at the spa. On 1 May Darwin replied, agreeing with Wallace's 1855 paper "On the Law which has Regulated the Introduction of New Species": "I can see that we have thought much alike & to a certain extent have come to similar conclusions. ... This summer will make the 20th year (!) since I opened my first-note-book, on the question how & in what way do species & varieties differ from each other.— I am now preparing my work for publication, but I find the subject so very large, that though I have written many chapters, I do not suppose I shall go to press for two years." He agreed with Wallace that "climatal conditions" had little effect, and wrote "It is really *impossible* to explain my views in the compass of a letter on the causes & means of variation in a state of nature; but I have slowly adopted a distinct & tangible idea.— Whether true or false others must judge".

Darwin returned home in early May, but a cold and social pressure set him back. He had to return to the spa, finishing "variation" in July and posting pages to Huxley for checking.[197]

Working class militants were seizing on the popularity of gorillas (which were now appearing in travelling menageries) to trumpet man's monkey origins. To crush these ideas, Richard Owen as President-elect of the Royal Association announced his authoritative anatomical studies of primate brains showing that humans were not just a separate species, but a separate sub-class.[198] In July 1857, Darwin commented to Hooker, "Owen's is a grand Paper; but I cannot swallow Man making a division as distinct from a Chimpanzee, as an ornithorhynchus from a Horse: I wonder what a Chimpanzee wd. say to this?".

Asa Gray and the young guard

Others helped with providing information, including Asa Gray on American plants. Darwin wrote to Gray on 20 July 1857 saying that after 19 years of work on the question of whether species "have descended from other species, like varieties from one species" and "that species arise like our domestic varieties with *much* extinction", he had "come to the heteredox conclusion that there are no such things as independently created species – that species are only strongly defined varieties. I know that this will make you despise me. – I do not much underrate the many huge difficulties on this view, but yet it seems to me to explain too much, otherwise inexplicable, to be false." An intrigued Gray admitted to his own notion that there was some law or power inherent in plants making varieties appear, and asked if Darwin was finding this law. Realising that Gray had not grasped what he was suggesting, Darwin sent him a letter on 5 September outlining the difficulties involved. He enclosed a brief but detailed abstract of his ideas on natural selection and divergence, copied out by the schoolmaster to make it more legible.

Gray responded, questioning his use of the term "natural selection" as an agent. In his reply Darwin said that he had to use this shorthand to save incessantly having to expand it into a formula such as "the tendency to the preservation (owing to the severe struggle for life to which all organic beings at some time or generation are exposed) of any the slightest variation in any part, which is of the slightest use or favourable to the life of the individual which has thus varied; together with the tendency to its inheritance". He asked Gray to maintain secrecy. The young guard of naturalists were now putting the "mode of creation" openly on the agenda, even in addresses to the Geological Society, but Darwin wanted his case to be fully prepared.

Joseph Dalton Hooker, John Tyndall and Thomas Huxley now formed a group of young naturalists holding Darwin in high regard, basing themselves in the Linnean Society of London which had just moved to Burlington House, Piccadilly, London, near the Royal Society. Huxley had not yet understood natural selection despite Darwin's hints about pedigree and genealogical trees. Huxley's attention was focussed on defeating the dominant orthodoxy of the arrogant Owen.

The country squire

Darwin's attention turned from pigeons to seedlings, experimenting with subjecting plants to conditions which might produce variation. His family helped with this and with tracking bees, experimenting (unsuccessfully) to try to find out what would influence their flight path.

His wife Emma Darwin was now known throughout the parish for helping in the way a parson's wife might be expected to, and as well as providing nursing care for her own family's frequent illnesses, she gave out bread tokens to the hungry and "small pensions for the old, dainties for the ailing, and medical comforts and simple medicine" based on Robert Darwin's old prescription book. Charles Darwin also took on local duties, increasing his social standing by becoming a Justice of the Peace and a magistrate. To accommodate the needs of his large family and accommodate visiting cousins further house extensions got under way. In November 1857 he escaped the worries for a week's recuperation at Lane's Moor Park spa.

Human origins, Wallace encouraged

During his research in 1856, Darwin noted his intention to publish his views on human racial ancestry: by early September of that year while drafting his book on *Natural Selection* he began collecting notes for Chapter 6 on the topic of sexual selection. This would cover humans as well as birds and fishes. By 31 March 1857 he had drafted five chapters with the sixth under way, and he wrote out a table of contents. In the following months he completed ten pages of Chapter 6, some 2,500 words, and pencilled in the heading "Theory applied to Races of Man". At this stage he regarded sexual selection as due to a "struggle for supremacy" between males, and did not yet think of female choice as significant. He then apparently dropped the whole topic for some reason, possibly Charles Lyell's caution: the brief abstract Darwin sent to Asa Gray on 5 September made no mention of sexual selection or human evolution.[199]

Wallace, responding to Darwin's 1 May letter, discussed his own theorising. Darwin replied on 22 December that he was "extremely glad to hear that you are attending to distribution in accordance with theoretical ideas. I am a firm believer, that without speculation there is no good & original observation", and added that "I believe I go much further than you; but it is too long a subject to enter on my speculative notions." He also said "You ask whether I shall discuss 'man';—I think I shall avoid whole subject, as so surrounded with prejudices, though I fully admit that it is the highest & most interesting problem for the naturalist."

Huxley used his March 1858 Royal Institution lecture to claim that structurally gorillas are as close to humans as they are to baboons. He added "Nay more I believe that the mental & moral faculties are essentially & fundamentally the same kind in animals & ourselves". This was a clear challenge to Owen's lecture claiming human uniqueness, given at the same venue. In a subsequent lecture Huxley stated that if there was a solution to the problem of species, it "must come from the side of indefinite modifiability", an indication that he was moving towards Darwin's position. In June he used his lecture at the Royal Society to attack Owen's "etherial archetype". Having gained a foothold in science with the aid of the *Westminster Review* group led by John Chapman and Herbert Spencer, Huxley was out to dislodge the domination of science by wealthy clergymen– led by Owen– instead wanting to create a professional salaried scientific civil service. To Spencer, animal species had developed by "adaptions upon adaptions". Huxley was using arguments on origins to split science from theology, arguing that "it is as respectable to be modified monkey as modified dirt".

Forestalled

Darwin was throwing himself into his work and his "big book" on *Natural Selection* was well under way, when on 18 June 1858 he received a parcel from Wallace. It enclosed about twenty pages describing an evolutionary mechanism, an unexpected response to Darwin's recent encouragement, with a request to send it on to Lyell. Shocked that he had been "forestalled", Darwin sent it on that day to Lyell, as requested by Wallace,[200,201] with a letter: <templatestyles src="Template:Quote/styles.css"/>

> Some year or so ago you recommended me to read a paper by Wallace in the 'Annals,' which had interested you, and, as I was writing to him, I knew this would please him much, so I told him. He has to-day sent me the enclosed, and asked me to forward it to you. It seems to me well worth reading. Your words have come true with a vengeance–that I should be forestalled. You said this, when I explained to you here very briefly my views of 'Natural Selection' depending on the struggle for existence. I never saw a more striking coincidence; if Wallace had my MS. sketch written out in 1842, he could not have made a better short abstract! Even his terms now stand as heads of my chapters. Please return me the MS., which he does not say he wishes me to publish, but I shall, of course, at once write and offer to send to any journal. So all my originality, whatever it may amount to, will be smashed, though my book, if it will ever have any value, will not be deteriorated; as all the labour consists in the application of the theory.

I hope you will approve of Wallace's sketch, that I may tell him what you say.

There were differences, though these were not evident to Darwin on reading the paper. Wallace's idea of selection was the environment eliminating the unfit rather than cut-throat competition among individuals, and he took an egalitarian view of the Dayak natives he was among, while Darwin had seen the Fuegians as backwards savages, albeit capable of improvement.

It had come at a bad time, as his favourite retreat at Moor Spa was threatened by Lane being put on trial accused of adultery, and five days later Darwin's baby Charles Waring came down with scarlet fever. Darwin's first impression had been that though it meant losing priority, it would be dishonourable for him to be "induced to publish from privately knowing that Wallace is in the field", but Lyell quickly responded strongly urging him to reconsider. Darwin's reply of 25 June was a plea for advice, noting that the points in Wallace's sketch had been fully covered in his own *Essay* of 1844 which Hooker had read in 1847, and that he had also set out his ideas in a letter to Asa Gray in 1857, "so that I could most truly say and prove that I take nothing from Wallace. I should be extremely glad now to publish a sketch of my general views in about a dozen pages or so. But I cannot persuade myself that I can do so honourably... I would far rather burn my whole book than that he or any man should think that I had behaved in a paltry spirit". He added a request that Hooker be informed to give a second opinion.

Darwin was overwrought when baby Charles Waring Darwin died on 28 June, and the next day acknowledged Hooker's letters saying "I cannot think now on the subject, but soon will." That night he read the letters, and to meet Hooker's request, though "quite prostrated", got his servant to deliver Wallace's essay, the letter to Asa Gray and "my sketch of 1844 solely that you may see by your own handwriting that you did read it". He left matters in the hands of Lyell and Hooker, writing "Do not waste much time. It is miserable in me to care at all about priority."

Publication of joint paper

Lyell and Hooker agreed on a joint paper to be presented at the Linnean Society – Lyell, Hooker and Darwin were all fellows of the society and council members, and Hooker had been closely involved in reviving the fortunes of the society and running its journal. Other venues were either inappropriate, or in the case of the Zoological Society of London, potentially hostile under the leadership of Richard Owen. It was now time for the summer break but, as they knew, its meeting had been postponed due to the death of former president Robert Brown on 10 June 1858, and the Council had arranged an extra meeting on 1 July.

At the last minute, late in the evening of 30 June, Lyell and Hooker forwarded the Wallace and Darwin papers to the Secretary John Joseph Bennett, to be read at the meeting the next day. Mrs. Hooker had spent the afternoon copying out extracts from the handwritten documents Darwin had sent with his letter of the previous night, presumably chosen by Hooker to suit the verbal presentation, and Lyell and Hooker wrote a short introductory letter. The papers entitled respectively *On the Tendency of Species to form Varieties; and on the Perpetuation of Varieties and Species by Natural Means of Selection*, incorporated Wallace's pages; and extracts from Darwin's 1844 *Essay* and his 1857 letter to Gray. At the meeting the Secretary read the papers out, before going on to six other papers, and there was no discussion of them at the end of the meeting, perhaps because of the amount of business that had been dealt with including an obituary notice for Robert Brown given by Lyell, or possibly due to reluctance to speak out against a theory supported by the eminent Lyell and Hooker. Thomas Bell, who had written up the description of Darwin's reptile specimens from the *Beagle* expedition, presided over the meeting. He apparently disapproved, and in his annual presidential report presented in May 1859 wrote that "The year which has passed has not, indeed, been marked by any of those striking discoveries which at once revolutionize, so to speak, the department of science on which they bear". However, the Vice-President promptly removed all references to immutability from his own paper which was awaiting publication.

As might be expected, the joint paper alerted those subscribers who met the argument for the first time in print, and whose minds were prepared by prior struggles with the species question. Alfred Newton, who held the chair in Zoology and Comparative Anatomy at Cambridge from 1866 to 1907, wrote this: "I sat up late that night to read it [the Linnean Society paper]; and never shall I forget the impression it made upon me. Herein was contained a perfectly simple solution of all the difficulties which had been troubling me for months past. I hardly know whether I at first felt more vexed at the solution not having occurred to me than pleased that it had been found at all" (he was not alone in *that* thought!—see T.H. Huxley). Newton remained a Darwinian for the rest of his life. (Wollaston 1921 p112; see also Newton 1888)

While the meeting took place, Darwin was attending his son's funeral. His family moved to his sister-in-law's in Sussex to escape the fever, which eventually killed six children in the village of Downe. It had been a frightening and miserable fortnight, but he was "more than satisfied" with the outcome of the meeting. He then took his children to the seaside at the Isle of Wight and pushed ahead with an "abstract" of *Natural Selection* which again began growing to book size. He returned to the Moor Park spa with stomach ailments.

Wallace's reaction, delivered in January 1859, was that he was gratified to have spurred Darwin into making the announcement and that it would have caused him "much pain & regret" if his papers had been published on their own, without Darwin's papers. Darwin was still sensitive on the point, and assured Wallace that he "had absolutely nothing whatever to do with leading Lyell and Hooker to what they thought was a fair course of action". He responded to Wallace's enquiry about what Lyell thought of the theory by saying that "I think he is somewhat staggered, but does not give in and speaks with horror [of] what a job it would be for the next edition of "The Principles" [of Geology] if he were "perverted". But he is most candid and honest, and I think he will end up by being "perverted"." Lyell was still struggling to come to terms with the idea of mankind, with immortal soul, originating from animals, but "Considering his age, his former views and position in society, I think his conduct has been heroic on the subject."

Publication of the "Origin of Species"

Darwin was now working hard on an "abstract" trimmed from his *Natural Selection*, writing much of it from memory. The chapters were sent to Hooker for correcting as they were completed, which led to a minor disaster when a large bundle was put by accident into the drawer Hooker's wife used to keep paper for the children to draw on. Lyell made arrangements with the publisher John Murray, who had brought out the second edition of *The Voyage of the Beagle*. Darwin fretted, asking "Does he know all the subject of the book?", and saying that to avoid being more "*un*-orthodox than the subject makes inevitable" he did not discuss the origin of man, or bring in any discussion about Genesis. Unusually, Murray agreed to publish the manuscript sight unseen, and to pay Darwin two-thirds of the net proceeds. He anticipated printing 500 copies.

Darwin had decided to call his book *An Abstract of an Essay on the Origin of Species and Varieties through Natural Selection*, but with Murray's persuasion it was eventually reduced to the snappier *On the Origin of Species through Natural Selection*. The full title reads **On the Origin of Species** *by Means of Natural Selection, or the Preservation of Favoured Races in the Struggle for Life*, with races referring to varieties of domestic and wild organisms and not to human groups.

By the end of May, Darwin's health had failed again, but after a week's hydrotherapy he was able to start correcting the proofs. He struggled on despite

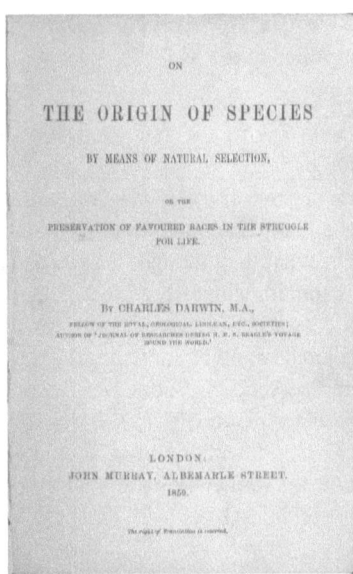

Figure 36: *Title page of the first edition of On the Origin of Species*

rarely being able to write free of stomach pains for more than twenty minutes at a stretch, and made drastic revisions which left Murray with a huge £72 bill for corrections. Murray upped the print run to 1,250 copies, with a publication date in November. A copy was sent to Lyell, with a "foolishly anxious" Darwin hoping that he would "come round". An eager Lyell gave Darwin "very great *kudos*", though he was still concerned that "the dignity of man is at stake". One of Lyell's relatives commented that it was "sure to be very curious and important... however mortifying it may be to think that our remote ancestors were jelly fishes". Darwin was "sorry to say that I have no 'consolatory view' on the dignity of man. I am content that man will probably advance, and care not much whether we are looked at as mere savages in a remotely distant future."

On 1 October Darwin finished the proofs, suffering from fits of vomiting. He then went off for a two-month stay at Ilkley Wells House, a spa in the town of Ilkley. He was joined by his family for a time of "frozen misery" in the unusually early winter. Darwin wrote "I have been very bad lately, having had an awful 'crisis' one leg swelled like elephantiasis – eyes almost closed up – covered with a rash & fiery Boils; but they tell me it will surely do me much good – it was like living in Hell." On 2 November he was pleased to receive from Murray a specimen copy bound in royal green cloth, priced at fifteen shillings.

Presentation copies were sent out by Murray, and on 11 and 12 November, still at the spa, Darwin wrote notes to go with these complimentary copies. He disarmingly anticipated their reactions: to Asa Gray "there are very many serious difficulties", to the Revd. John Stevens Henslow "I fear you will not approve of your pupil", to Louis Agassiz "[not sent in] a spirit of defiance or bravado" and to Richard Owen "it will seem 'an abomination'.", amongst others. For Wallace's copy he wrote "God knows what the public will think".

Origin of Species goes on sale

On the Origin of Species was first published on 24 November 1859, priced at fifteen shillings. The book had been offered to booksellers at Murray's autumn sale on 22 November, and all available copies had been taken up immediately. In total, 1,250 copies were printed but after deducting presentation and review copies, and five for Stationers' Hall copyright, 1,192 copies were available for sale. Significantly, 500 were taken by Mudie's Library, ensuring that the book would be widely circulated.

By then the novelist Charles Kingsley, a Christian socialist country rector, had sent Darwin a letter of praise (dated 18 November) regarding the presentation copy he had received: it was "just as noble a conception of Deity, to believe that He created primal forms capable of self development...as to believe that He required a fresh act of intervention to supply the lacunas which He Himself had made." In the second edition Darwin added these lines to the last chapter, with attribution to "a celebrated author and divine".

See the Reactions to On the Origin of Species for developments following publication, in the context of his life, work and outside influences at the time.

References

Note that this article is largely based on Desmond and Moore's book, with commentary summarised in other words and quotations (or extracts from quotations) repeated verbatim. <templatestyles src="Template:Refbegin/styles.css" />

- Browne, E. Janet (1995), *Charles Darwin: vol. 1 Voyaging*, London: Jonathan Cape, ISBN 1-84413-314-1<templatestyles src="Module:Citation/CS1/styles.css"></templatestyles>
- Browne, E. Janet (2002), *Charles Darwin: vol. 2 The Power of Place*, London: Jonathan Cape, ISBN 0-7126-6837-3<templatestyles src="Module:Citation/CS1/styles.css"></templatestyles>

- Darwin, Charles (1842), "Pencil Sketch of 1842", in Darwin, Francis, *The foundations of The origin of species: Two essays written in 1842 and 1844.*[202], Cambridge: Cambridge University Press, retrieved 2006-12-15, <q>(published 1909)</q><templatestyles src="Module:Citation/CS1/styles.css"></templatestyles>
- Darwin, Charles (1845), *Journal of Researches (The Voyage of the Beagle)*[203] (Second ed.), London: John Murray<templatestyles src="Module:Citation/CS1/styles.css"></templatestyles> Retrieved on 2006-12-15
- Darwin, Charles; Bennett, Alfred W. (1859), "On the Origin of Species by Means of Natural Selection, or the Preservation of Favoured Races in the Struggle for Life"[204], *Nature*, London: John Murray, **5** (121): 318, Bibcode: 1872Natur...5..318B[205], doi: 10.1038/005318a0[206]<templatestyles src="Module:Citation/CS1/styles.css"></templatestyles> (The Origin of Species) Retrieved on 2006-12-15
- Darwin, Charles (1887), Darwin, F, ed., *The life and letters of Charles Darwin, including an autobiographical chapter*[207], London: John Murray<templatestyles src="Module:Citation/CS1/styles.css"></templatestyles> (The Autobiography of Charles Darwin) Retrieved on 2006-12-15
- Darwin, Charles (1958), Barlow, N, ed., *The autobiography of Charles Darwin 1809–1882. With the original omissions restored. Edited and with appendix and notes by his granddaughter Nora Barlow*[208], London: Collins<templatestyles src="Module:Citation/CS1/styles.css"></templatestyles> (The Autobiography of Charles Darwin) Retrieved on 2006-12-15
- Desmond, Adrian; Moore, James (1991), *Darwin*, London: Michael Joseph, Penguin Group, ISBN 0-7181-3430-3<templatestyles src="Module:Citation/CS1/styles.css"></templatestyles>
- Freeman, Richard B. (1977), "On the Origin of Species"[209], *The Works of Charles Darwin: An Annotated Bibliographical Handlist* (2nd ed.), Folkestone, England: Dawson, ISBN 0-7129-0740-8, retrieved 15 August 2009<templatestyles src="Module:Citation/CS1/styles.css"></templatestyles>
- Keynes, Richard (ed.) (2000), " June – August 1836[210]", *Charles Darwin's zoology notes & specimen lists from H.M.S. Beagle*, Cambridge: Cambridge University Press External link in | chapter= (help)<templatestyles src="Module:Citation/CS1/styles.css"></templatestyles> Retrieved on 2006-12-15
- Moore, James; Desmond, Adrian (2004), *"Introduction",*

in The Descent of Man, and Selection in Relation to Sex,
Penguin Group, ISBN 978-0-14-043631-0<templatestyles src="Module:Citation/CS1/styles.css"></templatestyles>
- Moore, James (2006), "Evolution and Wonder – Understanding Charles Darwin", *Speaking of Faith (Radio Program)*[211], American Public Media, archived from the original[212] on 22 December 2008<templatestyles src="Module:Citation/CS1/styles.css"></templatestyles> Retrieved on 2006-12-15
- Newton, Alfred. Early days of Darwinism. *Macmillan's Magazine* No. 340, 1888.
- van Wyhe, John (2006), *Charles Darwin: gentleman naturalist: A biographical sketch*[213]<templatestyles src="Module:Citation/CS1/styles.css"></templatestyles> Retrieved on 2006-12-15
- van Wyhe, John (27 March 2007), "Mind the gap: Did Darwin avoid publishing his theory for many years?"[214] (PDF), *Notes and Records of the Royal Society*, **61** (2): 177–205, doi:10.1098/rsnr.2006.0171[215], retrieved 7 February 2008<templatestyles src="Module:Citation/CS1/styles.css"></templatestyles>.
- van Wyhe, John (2013), *Dispelling the Darkness: Voyage in the Malay Archipelago and the Discovery of Evolution by Wallace and Darwin*[216], World Scientific, ISBN 978-981-4458-81-8<templatestyles src="Module:Citation/CS1/styles.css"></templatestyles>.
- Wollaston, A.F.R. (1921), *Life of Alfred Newton*, N.Y.: Dutton<templatestyles src="Module:Citation/CS1/styles.css"></templatestyles>

Further reading

- The Complete Works of Charles Darwin Online – Darwin Online[217]; Darwin's publications, private papers and bibliography, supplementary works including biographies, obituaries and reviews. Free to use, includes items not in public domain.
- Works by Charles Darwin[218] at Project Gutenberg; public domain
- Darwin Correspondence Project[219] Text and notes for most of his letters

Responses to publication

Reactions to On the Origin of Species

This article covers the time period from November 1859 to April 1861.

The immediate **reactions to** *On the Origin of Species*, the book in which Charles Darwin described evolution by natural selection, included international debate, though the heat of controversy was less than that over earlier works such as *Vestiges of Creation*. Darwin monitored the debate closely, cheering on Thomas Henry Huxley's battles with Richard Owen to remove clerical domination of the scientific establishment. While Darwin's illness kept him away from the public debates, he read eagerly about them and mustered support through correspondence.

Religious views were mixed, with the Church of England's scientific establishment reacting against the book, while liberal Anglicans strongly supported Darwin's natural selection as an instrument of God's design. Religious controversy was soon diverted by the publication of *Essays and Reviews* and debate over the higher criticism.

The most famous confrontation took place at the public 1860 Oxford evolution debate during a meeting of the British Association for the Advancement of Science, when the Bishop of Oxford Samuel Wilberforce argued against Darwin's explanation. In the ensuing debate Joseph Hooker argued strongly in favor of Darwinian evolution. Thomas Huxley's support of evolution was so intense that the media and public nicknamed him "Darwin's bulldog". Huxley became the fiercest defender of the evolutionary theory on the Victorian stage. Both sides came away feeling victorious, but Huxley went on to depict the debate as pivotal in a struggle between religion and science and used *Darwinism* to campaign against the authority of the clergy in education, as well as daringly advocating the "Ape Origin of Man".

Background

Darwin's ideas developed rapidly after returning from the Voyage of the Beagle in 1836. By December 1838, he had developed the basic principles of his theory. At that time, similar ideas brought others disgrace and association with the revolutionary mob.Wikipedia:Vagueness He was conscious of the need to answer all likely objections before publishing. While he continued with research, he had an immense amount of work in hand analyzing and publishing findings from the Beagle expedition, and was repeatedly delayed by illness.

Natural history at that time was dominated by clerical naturalists who saw their science as revealing God's plan, and whose income came from the Established Church of England.Wikipedia:Citation needed Darwin found three close allies. The eminent geologist Charles Lyell, whose books had influenced the young Darwin during the Voyage of the Beagle, befriended Darwin who he saw as a supporter of his ideas of gradual geological processes with continuing divine Creation of species. By the 1840s Darwin became friends with the young botanist Joseph Dalton Hooker who had followed his father into the science, and after going on a survey voyage used his contacts to eventually find a position. In the 1850s Darwin met Thomas Huxley, an ambitious naturalist who had returned from a long survey trip but lacked the family wealth or contacts to find a career and who joined the progressive group around Herbert Spencer looking to make science a profession, freed from the clerics.

This was also a time of intense conflict over religious morality in England, where evangelicalism led to increasing professionalism of clerics who had previously been expected to act as country gentlemen with wide interests, but now were seriously focussed on expanded religious duties. A new orthodoxy proclaimed the virtues of truth but also inculcated beliefs that the Bible should be read literally and that religious doubt was in itself sinful so should not be discussed. Science was also becoming professional and a series of discoveries cast doubt on literal interpretations of the Bible and the honesty of those denying the findings. A series of crises erupted with fierce debate and criticism over issues such as George Combe's *The Constitution of Man* and the anonymous *Vestiges of the Natural History of Creation* which converted vast popular audiences to the belief that natural laws controlled the development of nature and society. German higher criticism questioned the Bible as a historical document in contrast to the evangelical creed that every word was divinely inspired. Dissident clergymen even began questioning accepted premises of Christian morality, and Benjamin Jowett's 1855 commentary on St. Paul brought a storm of controversy.

By September 1854 Darwin's other books reached a stage where he was able to turn his attention fully to *Species*, and from this point he was working to publish

Figure 37: *Darwin, as photographed in 1860*

his theory. On 18 June 1858 he received a parcel from Alfred Russel Wallace enclosing about twenty pages describing an evolutionary mechanism that was similar to Darwin's own theory. Darwin put matters in the hands of his friends Lyell and Hooker, who agreed on a joint presentation to the Linnean Society on 1 July 1858. Their papers were entitled, collectively, *On the Tendency of Species to form Varieties; and on the Perpetuation of Varieties and Species by Natural Means of Selection.*

Publication of *The Origin of Species*

Darwin now worked on an "abstract" trimmed from his *Natural Selection* manuscript. The publisher John Murray agreed the title as *On the Origin of Species through Natural Selection* and the book went on sale to the trade on 22 November 1859. The stock of 1,250 copies was oversubscribed, and Darwin, still at Ilkley spa town, began corrections for a second edition. The novelist Charles Kingsley, a Christian socialist country rector, sent him a letter of praise: "It awes me...if you be right I must give up much that I have believed", it was "just as noble a conception of Deity, to believe that He created primal forms capable of self development... as to believe that He required a fresh act of intervention to supply the lacunas which he himself had made." Darwin added these lines to the last chapter, with attribution to "a celebrated author and divine".

First reviews

The reviewers were less encouraging. Four days before publication, a review in the authoritative *Athenaeum* (by John Leifchild, published anonymously, as was the custom at that time) was quick to pick out the unstated implications of "men from monkeys" already controversial from *Vestiges*, saw snubs to theologians, summing up Darwin's "creed" as man "was born yesterday – he will perish tomorrow" and concluded that "The work deserves attention, and will, we have no doubt, meet with it. Scientific naturalists will take up the author upon his own peculiar ground; and there will we imagine be a severe struggle for at least theoretical existence. Theologians will say—and they have a right to be heard—Why construct another elaborate theory to exclude Deity from renewed acts of creation? Why not at once admit that new species were introduced by the Creative energy of the Omnipotent? Why not accept direct interference, rather than evolutions of law, and needlessly indirect or remote action? Having introduced the author and his work, we must leave them to the mercies of the Divinity Hall, the College, the Lecture Room, and the Museum." At Ilkley, Darwin raged "But the manner in which he drags in immortality, & sets the Priests at me, & leaves me to their mercies, is base. He would on no account burn me; but he will get the wood ready and tell the black beasts how to catch me." Darwin sprained an ankle and his health worsened, as he wrote to friends it was "odious".

By 9 December when Darwin left Ilkley to come home, he had been told that Murray was organising a second run of 3,000 copies. Hooker had been "converted", Lyell was "absolutely gloating" and Huxley wrote "with such tremendous praise", advising that he was sharpening his "beak and claws" to disembowel "the curs who will bark and yelp".

First response

Richard Owen had been the first to respond to the complimentary copies, courteously claiming that he had long believed that "existing influences" were responsible for the "ordained" birth of species. Darwin now had long talks with him, and told Lyell that "Under garb of great civility, he was inclined to be most bitter & sneering against me. Yet I infer from several expressions, that *at bottom* he goes immense way with us." Owen was furious at being included among those defending immutability of species, and in effect said that the book offered the best explanation "ever published of the manner of formation of species", though he did not agree with it in all respects. He still had the gravest doubts that transmutation would bestialise man. It appears that Darwin had assured Owen that he was looking at everything as resulting from designed laws, which Owen interpreted as showing a shared belief in "Creative Power".

Darwin had already made his views clearer to others, telling Lyell that if each step in evolution was providentially planned, the whole procedure would be a miracle and natural selection superfluous. He had also sent a copy to John Herschel, and on 10 December he told Lyell of having "heard by round about channel that Herschel says my Book "is the law of higgledy-piggledy".– What this exactly means I do not know, but it is evidently very contemptuous.– If true this is great blow & discouragement." Darwin subsequently corresponded with Herschel, and in January 1861 Herschel added a footnote to the draft of his *Physical Geography* which, while disparaging "the principle of arbitrary and casual variation and natural selection" as insufficient without "intelligent direction", said that "with some demur as to the genesis of man, we are far from disposed to repudiate the view taken of this mysterious subject in Mr. Darwin's book."

Geological time

It was known that the geologic time scale was "incomprehensibly vast", if unquantifiable. From 1848 Darwin discussed data with Andrew Ramsay, who had said "it is vain to attempt to measure the duration of even small portions of geological epochs." A chapter of Lyell's *Principles of Geology* described the enormous amount of erosion involved in forming the Weald.[220] To demonstrate the time available for natural selection to operate, Darwin drew on Lyell's example and Ramsay's data in chapter 9 of *On the Origin of Species* to estimate that erosion of the Weald's layered dome of Lower Cretaceous rocks "must have required 306,662,400 years; or say three hundred million years".[221]

The "necessary corrections" Darwin made to his drafts for the second edition of the *Origin* were based on comments from others, particularly Lyell, and added a caveat suggesting a faster rate of erosion of the Weald:[222] "perhaps it would be safer to allow two or three inches per century, and this would reduce the number of years to one hundred and fifty or one hundred million years."[223,224] Copies of the second edition were advertised as ready on 24 December, in advance of official publication on 7 January 1860.[225]

The *Saturday Review* of 24 December 1859 strongly criticised the methodology of Darwin's calculations.[226] On 3 January 1860, Darwin wrote to Hooker about it: "Some of the remarks about the lapse of years are very good, & the Reviewer gives me some good & well deserved raps,—confound it I am sorry to confess the truth. But it does not at all concern main argument." A day later, he said to Lyell "You saw I suppose Saturday Review: argument confined to Geology, but has given me some perfectly just & severe raps on knuckles."

In the third edition published on 30 April 1861, Darwin cited the *Saturday Review* article as reason to remove his calculation altogether.

Friendly reviews

The December 1859 review in the British Unitarian *National Review* was written by Darwin's old friend William Carpenter, who was clear that only a world of "order, continuity, and progress" befitted an Omnipotent Deity and that "any theological objection" to a species of slug or a breed of dog deriving from a previous one was "simply absurd" dogma. He touched on human evolution, satisfied that the struggle for existence tended "inevitably... towards the progressive exaltation of the races engaged in it".

On Boxing Day (26 December) *The Times* carried an anonymous review. The staff reviewer, "as innocent of any knowledge of science as a babe", gave the task to Huxley, leading Darwin to ask his friend how "did you influence Jupiter Olympus and make him give three and a half columns to pure science? The old fogies will think the world will come to an end." Darwin treasured the piece more than "a dozen reviews in common periodicals", but noted "Upon my life I am sorry for Owen... he will be so d—d savage, for credit given to any other man, I strongly suspect, is in his eyes so much credit robbed from him. Science is so narrow a field, it is clear there ought to be only one cock of the walk!".

Hooker also wrote a favourable review, which appeared at the end of December in the *Gardener's Chronicle* and treated the theory as an extension of horticultural lore.

Clerical concern, atheist enthusiasm

In his lofty position at the head of Science, Owen received numerous complaints about the book. The Revd. Adam Sedgwick, geologist at the University of Cambridge who had taken Darwin on his first geology field trip, could not see the point in a world without providence. The missionary David Livingstone could see no struggle for existence on the African plains. Jeffries Wyman at Harvard saw no truth in chance variations.

The most enthusiastic response came from atheists, with Hewett Watson hailing Darwin as the "greatest revolutionist in natural history of this century". The 68-year-old Robert Edmund Grant, who had shown him the study of invertebrates when Darwin was a student at the University of Edinburgh and who was still teaching Lamarckian evolution weekly at University College London, brought out a small book on classification dedicated to Darwin: "With one fell-sweep of the wand of truth, you have now scattered to the winds the pestilential vapours accumulated by 'species-mongers'."

Widespread interest

In January 1860, Darwin told Lyell of a reported incident at Waterloo Bridge Station: "I never till to day realised that it was getting widely distributed; for in a letter from a lady today to Emma, she says she heard a man enquiring for it at Railway Station!!! at Waterloo Bridge; & the Bookseller said that he had none till new Edit. was out.— The Bookseller said he had not read it but had heard it was a very remarkable book!!!"

Asa Gray in the United States

In December 1859 the botanist Asa Gray negotiated with a Boston publisher for publication of an authorised American version, however, he learnt that two New York publishing firms were already planning to exploit the absence of international copyright to print *Origin*. Darwin wrote in January, "I never dreamed of my Book being so successful with general readers: I believe I should have laughed at the idea of sending the sheets to America." and asked Gray to keep any profits. Gray managed to negotiate a 5 per cent royalty with Appleton's of New York, who got their edition out in mid January, and the other two withdrew. In a May letter Darwin mentioned a print run of 2,500 copies, but it is not clear if this was the first printing alone as there were four that year.

When sending his *Historical preface* and corrections for the American edition in February, Darwin thanked Asa Gray for his comments, as "a Review from a man, who is not an entire convert, if fair & moderately favourable, is in all respects the best kind of Review. About weak points I agree. The eye to this day gives me a cold shudder, but when I think of the fine known gradations, my reason tells me I ought to conquer the cold shudder." In April he continued, "It is curious that I remember well time when the thought of the eye made me cold all over, but I have got over this stage of the complaint, & now small trifling particulars of structure often make me very uncomfortable. The sight of a feather in a peacock's tail, whenever I gaze at it, makes me sick!" A month later Darwin emphasised that he was bewildered by the theological aspects and "had no intention to write atheistically, *but could not* see, as plainly as others do, & as I sh^d wish to do, evidence of design & beneficence on all sides of us. There seems to me too much misery in the world. I cannot persuade myself that a beneficent and omnipotent God would have designedly created the Ichneumonidae with the express intention of their feeding within the living bodies of caterpillars" – expressing his particular revulsion at the Ichneumonidae family of parasitic wasps that lay their eggs in the larvae and pupae of other insects so that their parasitoid young have a ready source of food. He therefore could not believe in the necessity of design, but rather than attributing the wonders of the universe to brute force was "inclined to look at everything as resulting from designed laws, with the details, whether good or bad, left to the working out of what we may call chance. Not that this notion at all satisfies me. I feel most deeply that the whole subject is too profound for the human intellect. A dog might as well speculate on the mind of Newton" – referring to Isaac Newton.

Erasmus and Martineau

Darwin's brother Erasmus reported on 23 November that their cousin Henry Holland was reading the book and in "a dreadful state of indecision", sure that explaining the eye would be "utterly impossible", but after reading it "he hummed & hawed & perhaps it was partly conceivable". Erasmus himself thought it "the most interesting book I ever read", and sent a copy to his old flame Miss Harriet Martineau who, at 58, was still reviewing from her home in the Lake District. Martineau sent her thanks, adding that she had previously praised "the quality & conduct of your brother's mind, but it is an unspeakable satisfaction to see here the full manifestation of its earnestness & simplicity, its sagacity, its industry, & the patient power by w^h. it has collected such a mass of facts, to transmute them by such sagacious treatment into such portentious knowledge. I sh^d. much like to know how large a proportion of our scientific men believe he has found a sound road."[227]

Writing to her fellow Malthusian (and atheist) George Holyoake she enthused, "What a book it is! – overthrowing (if true) revealed Religion on the one hand, & Natural (as far as Final Causes & Design are concerned) on the other. The range & mass of knowledge take away one's breath." To Fanny Wedgwood she wrote, "I rather regret that C.D. went out of his way two or three times to speak of "The Creator" in the popular sense of the First Cause.... His subject is the 'Origin of Species' & not the origin of Organisation; & it seems a needless mischief to have opened the latter speculation at all – There now! I have delivered my mind."

Clerical reaction

The Revd. Adam Sedgwick had received his copy "with more pain than pleasure." Without Creation showing divine love, "humanity, to my mind, would suffer a damage that might brutalise it, and sink the human race..." He indicated that unless Darwin accepted God's revelation in nature and scripture, Sedgwick would not meet Darwin in heaven, a sentiment that upset Emma. The Revd. John Stevens Henslow, the botany professor whose natural history course Charles had joined thirty years earlier, gave faint praise to the *Origin* as "a stumble in the right direction" but distanced himself from its conclusions, "a question past our finding out..."

The Anglican establishment predominantly opposed Darwin. Palmerston, who became Prime Minister in June 1859, mooted Darwin's name to Queen Victoria as a candidate for the Honours List with the prospect of a knighthood. While Prince Albert supported the idea, after the publication of the *Origin* Queen Victoria's ecclesiastical advisers, including the Bishop of Oxford Samuel Wilberforce, dissented and the request was denied. Some Anglicans were more in favour, and Huxley reported of Kingsley that "He is an excellent Darwinian to begin with, and told me a capital story of his reply to Lady Aylesbury who expressed astonishment at his favouring such a heresy – 'What can be more delightful to me Lady Aylesbury, than to know that your Ladyship & myself sprang from the same toad stool.' Whereby the frivolous old woman shut up, in doubt whether she was being chaffed or adored for her remark."

There was no official comment from the Vatican for several decades, but in 1860 a council of the German Catholic bishops pronounced that the belief that "man as regards his body, emerged finally from the spontaneous continuous change of imperfect nature to the more perfect, is clearly opposed to Sacred Scripture and to the Faith." This defined the range of official Catholic discussion of evolution, which has remained almost exclusively concerned with human evolution.[228]

Huxley and Owen

On 10 February 1860 Huxley gave a lecture titled *On Species and Races, and their Origin* at the Royal Institution, reviewing Darwin's theory with fancy pigeons on hand to demonstrate artificial selection, as well as using the occasion to confront the clergy with his aim of wresting science from ecclesiastical control. He referred to Galileo's persecution by the church, "the little Canutes of the hour enthroned in solemn state, bidding that great wave to stay, and threatening to check its beneficent progress." He hailed the *Origin* as heralding a "new Reformation" in a battle against "those who would silence and crush" science, and called on the public to cherish Science and "follow her methods faithfully and implicitly in their application to all branches of human thought," for the future of England. To Darwin such rhetoric was "time wasted" and on reflection he thought the lecture "an entire failure *which* gave no just idea of *natural* selection," but by March he was listing those on "our side" as against the "outsiders." His close allies were Hooker and Huxley, and in August he called Huxley his "good and kind agent for the propagation of the Gospel – i.e. the devil's gospel."

The position of Richard Owen was unknown: when emphasising to a Parliamentary committee the need for a new Natural History museum, he pointed out that "The whole intellectual world this year has been excited by a book on the origin of species; and what is the consequence? Visitors come to the

Figure 38: *The combative Thomas Huxley demanded a fair hearing for Darwin's ideas.*

British Museum, and they say, 'Let us see all these varieties of pigeons: where is the tumbler, where is the pouter?' and I am obliged with shame to say, I can show you none of them..." As to showing you the varieties of those species, or of any of those phenomena that would aid one in getting at that mystery of mysteries, the origin of species, our space does not permit; but surely there ought to be a space somewhere, and, if not in the British Museum, where is it to be obtained?"

Huxley's April review in the *Westminster Review* included the first mention of the term "Darwinism" in the question, "What if the orbit of Darwinism should be a little too circular?" Darwin thought it a "brilliant review."

> *Overflowing the narrow bounds of purely scientific circles, the "species question" divides with Italy and the Volunteers the attention of general society. Everybody has read Mr. Darwin's book, or, at least, has given an opinion upon its merits or demerits; pietists, whether lay or ecclesiastic, decry it with the mild railing which sounds so charitable; bigots denounce it with ignorant invective; old ladies of both sexes consider it a decidedly dangerous book, and even savants, who have no better mud to throw, quote antiquated writers to show that its author is no better than an ape himself; while every philosophical thinker hails it as a veritable*

Figure 39: *Thomas Henry Huxley applied Darwins ideas to humans. This showed humans and apes had a common ancestor.*

Whitworth gun in the armoury of liberalism; and all competent naturalists and physiologists, whatever their opinions as to the ultimate fate of the doctrines put forth, acknowledge that the work in which they are embodied is a solid contribution to knowledge and inaugurates a new epoch in natural history. – Thomas Huxley, 1860

When Owen's own anonymous review of the *Origin* appeared in the April *Edinburgh Review* he praised himself and his own *axiom of the continuous operation of the ordained becoming of living things*, and showed his anger at what he saw as Darwin's caricature of the creationist position and ignoring Owen's pre-eminence. To him, new species appeared at birth, not through natural selection. As well as attacking Darwin's "disciples" Hooker and Huxley, he thought that the book symbolised the sort of "abuse of science to which a neighbouring nation, some seventy years since, owed its temporary degradation." Darwin had Huxley and Hooker staying with him when he read it, and he wrote telling Lyell that it was "extremely malignant, clever & I fear will be very damaging. He is atrociously severe on Huxley's lecture, & very bitter against Hooker. So we three enjoyed it together: not that I really enjoyed it, for it made me uncomfortable for one night; but I have got quite over it today. It requires much study to appreciate all the bitter spite of many of the remarks against me; indeed I did not discover all myself.– It scandalously misrepresents many parts. ..... It is painful to be hated in the intense degree with which Owen hates me." He commented to Henslow that "Owen is indeed very spiteful. He misrepresents & alters what I say very unfairly. .... The Londoners says he is mad with envy because my book has been talked about: what a strange man to be envious of a naturalist like myself, immeasurably his inferior!"

Geological time and Phillips

Darwin's had estimated that erosion of the Weald would take 300 million years, but in the second edition of *On the Origin of Species* published on 7 January 1860 he accepted that it would be safer to allow 150 million to 200 million years.[229]

Geologists knew the earth was ancient, but had felt unable to put realistic figures on the duration of past geological changes. Darwin's book provided a new impetus to quantifying geological time. His most prominent critic, John Phillips, had investigated how temperatures increased with depth in the 1830s, and was convinced that, contrary to Lyell and Darwin's uniformitarianism, the Earth was cooling over the long term. Between 1838 and 1855 he tried various ways of quantifying the timing of stratified deposits, without success.[230] On 17 February 1860, Phillips used his presidential address to the Geological Society of London to accuse Darwin of "abuse of arithmetic". He said 300 million years was an "inconceivable number" and that, depending on assumptions, erosion of the Weald could have taken anything from 12,000 years to at most 1,332,000 years, well below Darwin's estimate. When giving the May 1860 Rede Lecture, Phillips produced his own first published estimates of the duration of the whole stratigraphic record,[220] using rates of sedimentation to calculate it at around 96 million years.[231]

Natural persecution

Most reviewers wrote with great respect, deferring to Darwin's eminent position in science though finding it hard to understand how natural selection could work without a divine selector. There were hostile comments, at the start of May he commented to Lyell that he had "received in a Manchester Newspaper a rather a good squib, showing that I have proved 'might is right', & therefore that Napoleon is right & every cheating Tradesman is also right". The *Saturday Review* reported that "The controversy excited by the appearance of Darwin's remarkable work on the *Origin of Species* has passed beyond the bounds of the study and lecture-room into the drawing-room and the public street."[232]

The older generation of Darwin's tutors were rather negative, and later in May he told his cousin Fox that "the attacks have been falling thick & heavy on my now case-hardened hide.— Sedgwick & Clarke opened regular battery on me lately at Cambridge Phil. Soc^y. & dear old Henslow defended me in grand style, saying that my investigations were perfectly legitimate." While defending Darwin's honest motives and belief that "he was exalting & not debasing our views of a Creator, in attributing to him a power of imposing laws on the Organic World by which to do his work, as effectually as his laws imposed upon the inorganic had done it in the Mineral Kingdom", Henslow had not disguised his own opinion that "Darwin has pressed his hypothesis too far".

In June, Karl Marx saw the book as a "bitter satire" that showed "a basis in natural science for class struggle in history", in which "Darwin recognizes among beasts and plants his English society".[233]

Darwin remarked to Lyell, "I must be a very bad explainer... Several Reviews, & several letters have shown me too clearly how little I am understood. I suppose *natural selection* was bad term; but to change it now, I think, would make confusion worse confounded. Nor can I think of better; *Natural preservation* would not imply a preservation of particular varieties & would seem a truism; & would not bring man's & nature's selection under one point of view. I can only hope by reiterated explanations finally to make matter clearer." It was too illegible for Lyell, and Darwin later apologised "I am utterly ashamed & groan over my hand-writing. It was *Natural Preservation*. Natural persecution is what the author ought to suffer."

Debate

Essays and Reviews

Around February 1860 liberal theologians entered the fray, when seven produced a manifesto titled *Essays and Reviews*. These Anglicans included Oxford professors, country clergymen, the headmaster of Rugby school and a layman. Their declaration that miracles were irrational stirred up unprecedented anger, drawing much of the fire away from Darwin. *Essays* sold 22,000 copies in two years, more than the *Origin* sold in twenty years, and sparked five years of increasingly polarised debate with books and pamphlets furiously contesting the issues.

The most scientific of the seven was the Reverend Baden Powell, who held the Savilian chair of geometry at the University of Oxford. Referring to "Mr Darwin's masterly volume" and restating his argument that God is a lawgiver, miracles break the lawful edicts issued at Creation, therefore belief in miracles is atheistic, he wrote that the book "must soon bring about an entire revolution in opinion in favour of the grand principle of the self-evolving powers of nature." He drew attacks, with Sedgwick accusing him of "greedily" adopting nonsense and Tory reviews saying he was joining "the infidel party". He would have been on the platform at the British Association debate, facing the bishop, but died of a heart attack on 11 June.

The British Association debate

The most famous confrontation took place at a meeting of the British Association for the Advancement of Science in Oxford on Saturday 30 June 1860. While there was no formal debate organised on the issue, Professor John William Draper of New York University was to talk on Darwin and social progress at a routine "Botany and Zoology" meeting. The new museum hall was crowded with clergy, undergraduates, Oxford dons and gentlewomen anticipating that Samuel Wilberforce, the Bishop of Oxford, would speak to repeat the savage trouncing he had given in 1847 to the *Vestiges* published anonymously by Robert Chambers. Owen lodged with Wilberforce the night before, but Wilberforce would have been well prepared as he had just reviewed the *Origin* for the Tory *Quarterly* for a fee of £60. Huxley was not going to wait for the meeting, but met Chambers who accused him of "deserting them" and changed his mind. Darwin was taking treatment at Dr. Lane's new hydropathic establishment at Sudbrooke Park, Petersham, near Richmond in Surrey.

From Hooker's account, Draper "droned on for an hour", then for half an hour "Soapy Sam" Wilberforce replied with the eloquence that had earned him his nickname. This time the climate of opinion had changed and the ensuing debate was more evenly matched, with Hooker being particularly successful in defence of Darwin's ideas. In response to what Huxley took as a jibe from Wilberforce as to whether it was on Huxley's grandfather's or grandmother's side that he was descended from an ape, Huxley made a reply which he later recalled as being that "[if asked] would I rather have a miserable ape for a grandfather or a man highly endowed by nature and possessed of great means and influence and yet who employs these faculties and that influence for the mere purpose of introducing ridicule into a grave scientific discussion I unhesitatingly affirm my preference for the ape". No verbatim record was taken: eyewitness accounts exist, and vary somewhat.[234]

Robert FitzRoy, who had been the captain of HMS *Beagle* during Darwin's voyage, was there to present a paper on storms. During the debate FitzRoy, seen by Hooker as "a grey haired Roman nosed elderly gentleman", stood in the centre of the audience and "lifting an immense Bible first with both and afterwards with one hand over his head, solemnly implored the audience to believe God rather than man". As he admitted that the *Origin of Species* had given him "acutest pain" the crowd shouted him down.

Figure 40: *The debate was held in the Oxford University Museum of Natural History*

Hooker's "blood boiled, I felt myself a dastard; now I saw my advantage–I swore to myself I would smite that Amalekite Sam hip and thigh", (he was invited up to the platform and) "there and then I smacked him amid rounds of applause... proceeded to demonstrate... that he could never have read your book... wound up with a very few observations on the...old and new hypotheses... Sam was shut up... and the meeting was dissolved forthwith leaving you [Darwin] master of the field after 4 hours battle."

Both sides came away claiming victory, with Hooker and Huxley each sending Darwin rather contradictory triumphant accounts. Supporters of Darwinism seized on this meeting as a sign that the idea of evolution could not be suppressed by authority, and would be defended vigorously by its advocates. Liberal clerics were also satisfied that literal belief in all aspects of the Bible was now questioned by science; they were sympathetic to some of the ideas in *Essays and Reviews*.[235,236] William Whewell wrote to his friend James David Forbes that "Perhaps the Bishop was not prudent to venture into a field where no eloquence can supersede the need for precise knowledge. The young naturalists declared themselves in favour of Darwin's views which tendency I saw already at Leeds two years ago. I am sorry for it, for I reckon Darwin's book to be an utterly unphilosophical one."[237]

Figure 41: *1869 Caricature of Wilberforce. His hand washing gesture helped earn the Bishop of Oxford his nickname*

Wilberforce's *Quarterly* review

In late July Darwin read Wilberforce's review in the *Quarterly*. It used a 60-year-old parody from the *Anti-Jacobin* of the prose of Darwin's grandfather Erasmus, implying old revolutionary sympathies. It argued that if "transmutations were actually occurring" this would be seen in rapidly reproducing invertebrates, and since it isn't, why think that "the favourite varieties of turnips are tending to become men". Darwin pencilled "rubbish" in the margin. To the statement about classification that "all creation is the transcript in matter of ideas eternally existing in the mind of the Most High!!", Darwin scribbled "mere words". At the same time, Darwin was willing to grant that Wilberforce's review was clever: he wrote to Hooker that "it picks out with skill all the most conjectural parts, and brings forward well all the difficulties. It quizzes me quite splendidly by quoting the 'Anti-Jacobin' against my Grandfather."

Wilberforce also attacked *Essays and Reviews* in the *Quarterly Review*, and in a letter to *The Times*, signed by the Archbishop of Canterbury and 25 bishops, which threatened the theologians with the ecclesiastical courts. Darwin quoted a proverb: "A bench of bishops is the devil's flower garden", and joined others including Lyell, though not Hooker and Huxley, in signing a counter-letter supporting *Essays and Reviews* for trying to "establish religious teachings on a firmer and broader foundation". Despite this alignment of pro-evolution scientists and Unitarians with liberal churchmen, two of the authors were indicted for heresy and lost their jobs by 1862.

Geological time, Phillips and third edition

In October 1860, John Phillips published *Life on the Earth, its origin and succession*, reiterating points from his Rede Lecture and disputing Darwin's arguments. He sent a copy to Darwin, who thanked him, though "sorry, but not surprised, to see that you are dead against me".

On 20 November, Darwin told Lyell of his revisions for a third edition of the *Origin*, including removing his estimate of the time it took for the Weald to erode: "The confounded Wealden calculation, to be struck out. & a note to be inserted to effect that I am convinced of its inaccuracy from Review in Saturday R. & from Phillips, as I see in Table of Contents that he attacks it." He later told Lyell that "Having burnt my own fingers so consumedly with the Wealden, I am fearful for you", and advised caution: "for Heaven-sake take care of your fingers; to burn them severely, as I have done, is very unpleasant." The third edition, as published on 30 April 1861, stated "The computation of time required for the denudation of the Weald omitted. I have been convinced of its inaccuracy in several respects by an excellent article in the 'Saturday Review,' Dec. 24, 1859."

Natural History Review

The *Natural History Review* was bought and refurbished by Huxley, Lubbock, Busk and other "plastically minded young men" – supporters of Darwin. The first issue in January 1861 carried Huxley's paper on man's relationship to apes, "showing up" Owen. Huxley cheekily sent a copy to Wilberforce.

Darwin at home

As the battles raged, Darwin returned home from the spa to proceed with experiments on chloroforming carnivorous sundew plants, looking over his *Natural Selection* manuscript and drafting two chapters on pigeon breeding that would eventually form part of *The Variation of Animals and Plants under Domestication*. He wrote to Asa Gray and used the example of fantail pigeons to argue against Gray's belief "that variation has been led along certain beneficial lines", with the implication of Creationism rather than Natural Selection.

Over the winter he organised a third edition of the *Origin*, adding an introductory historical sketch. Asa Gray had published three supportive articles in the *Atlantic Monthly*. Darwin persuaded Gray to publish them as a pamphlet, and was delighted when Gray came up with the title of *Natural Selection Not Inconsistent with Natural Theology*. Darwin paid half the cost, imported 250 copies into Britain and as well as advertising it in periodicals and sending 100 copies out to scientists, reviewers, and theologians (including Wilberforce), he included in the *Origin* a recommendation for it, available to be purchased for 1s. 6d. from Trübner's in Paternoster Row.

The Huxleys became close family friends, frequently visiting Down House. When their 3-year-old son died of scarlet fever they were badly affected. Henrietta Huxley brought their three infants to Down in March 1861 where Emma helped to console her, while Huxley continued with his working-men's lectures at the Royal School of Mines, writing that "My working men stick with me wonderfully, the house fuller than ever, By next Friday evening they will all be convinced that they are monkeys."[238]

Arguments with Owen

Huxley's arguments with Owen continued in the *Athenaeum* so that each Saturday Darwin could read the latest ripostes. Owen tried to smear Huxley by portraying him as an "advocate of man's origins from a transmuted ape", and one of his contributions was titled "Ape-Origin of Man as Tested by the Brain". This backfired, as Huxley had already delighted Darwin by speculating on "pithecoid man" – ape-like man, and was glad of the invitation to publicly turn the anatomy of brain structure into a question of human ancestry. He was determined to indict Owen for perjury, promising "before I have done with that mendacious humbug I will nail him out, like a kite to a barn door, an example to all evil doers." Darwin egged him on from Down, writing "Oh Lord what a thorn you must be in the poor dear man's side".

Their campaign ran over two years and was devastatingly successful, with each "slaying" being followed by a recruiting drive for the Darwinian cause. The spite lingered. When Huxley joined the Zoological Society Council in 1861, Owen left, and in the following year Huxley moved to stop Owen from being elected to the Royal Society Council as "no body of gentlemen" should admit a member "guilty of wilful & deliberate falsehood."

Lyell was troubled both by Huxley's belligerence and by the question of ape ancestry, but got little sympathy from Darwin who teased him that "*Our* ancestor was an animal which breathed water, had a swim bladder, a great swimming tail, an imperfect skull, and undoubtedly was a hermaphrodite! Here is a pleasant genealogy for mankind." Lyell began work on a book examining human origins.

Geological time: William Thomson (Lord Kelvin)

Like the geologist John Phillips, the physicist William Thomson (later ennobled as Lord Kelvin) had considered since the 1840s that the physics of thermodynamics required that the Earth was cooling from an initial molten state. This contradicted Lyell's uniformitarian concept of unchanging processes over deep geological time, which Darwin shared and had assumed would allow ample time for the slow process of natural selection.[230]

In June 1861 Thomson asked Phillips how geologists felt about Darwin's "prodigious durations for geological epochs". and mentioned his own preliminary calculation that the Sun was 20 million years old, with the Earth at most 200 to 1,000 million years old. Phillips discussed his own published view that stratified rocks went back 96 million years, and dismissed Darwin's original estimate that the Weald had taken 300 million years to erode. In September 1861 Thomson produced a paper "On the age of the Sun's heat" which estimated that the Sun was between 100 and 500 million years old,[239] and in 1862 he used assumptions on the rate of cooling from a molten condition to estimate the age of the Earth at 98 million years. The dispute continued for the rest of Darwin's life.[240]

Continued debate

The reception of Darwin's ideas continued to arouse scientific and religious debates, and wide public interest. Satirical cartoonists seized on animal ancestry in relation to other topical issues, drawing on a long tradition of identifying animal traits in humans. In Britain mass circulation magazines were droll rather than cruel, and thus presented Darwin's theory in an unthreatening way. Due to illness, Darwin began growing a beard in 1862, and when he reappeared in public in 1866 with a bushy beard, caricatures centred on Darwin and his new look contributed to a trend in which all forms of evolutionism were identified with Darwinism.

Bibliography

Note: this article uses Desmond and Moore, *Darwin*, as a general reference. Other references used for specific points or quotations.

- Altholz, Josef L. (1976), "The warfare of conscience with theology"[241], in Altholz, Josef L., *The Mind and Art of Victorian England*, University of Minnesota Press, pp. 58–77, ISBN 0-8166-5693-2<templatestyles src="Module:Citation/CS1/styles.css"></templatestyles>

Figure 42: *A French caricature around 1878 shows a bearded Darwin breaking through hoops of "gullibility, superstitions, errors, and ignorance" held up by Émile Littré.*

- Browne, E. Janet (2002), *Charles Darwin: vol. 2 The Power of Place*[242], London: Jonathan Cape, ISBN 0-7126-6837-3<templatestyles src="Module:Citation/CS1/styles.css"></templatestyles>
- Burchfield, Joe D. (1974). "Darwin and the Dilemma of Geological Time"[243]. *Isis*. University of Chicago Press. **65** (3): 301–321. doi: 10.1086/351300[244]. Retrieved 28 April 2017.<templatestyles src="Module:Citation/CS1/styles.css"></templatestyles> pdf[245]
- Carpenter, William Benjamin (1859), "Darwin on the Origin of Species"[246], *National Review*, vol. 10 no. December 1859, pp. 188–214<templatestyles src="Module:Citation/CS1/styles.css"></templatestyles>. Published anonymously.
- Darwin, Charles; Costa, James T. (2009). *The Annotated Origin: A Facsimile of the First Edition of On the Origin of Species*[247]. Harvard University Press. ISBN 978-0-674-03281-1.<templatestyles src="Module:Citation/CS1/styles.css"></templatestyles>
- Darwin, Charles (1859), "On the Origin of Species by Means of Natural Selection, or the Preservation of Favoured Races in the Struggle for Life"[248], *Nature* (Full image view[249] 1st ed.), Lon-

- don: John Murray, **5** (121): 502, Bibcode: 1872Natur...5..318B[250], doi: 10.1038/005318a0[251], retrieved 1 March 2011<templatestyles src="Module:Citation/CS1/styles.css"></templatestyles>
- Darwin, Charles (1860), "On the Origin of Species by Means of Natural Selection, or the Preservation of Favoured Races in the Struggle for Life"[252], *Nature* (2nd ed.), London: John Murray, **5** (121): 318, Bibcode: 1872Natur...5..318B[250], doi: 10.1038/005318a0[251], retrieved 9 January 2009<templatestyles src="Module:Citation/CS1/styles.css"></templatestyles>
- Darwin, Charles (1861), "On the Origin of Species by Means of Natural Selection, or the Preservation of Favoured Races in the Struggle for Life"[253], *Nature* (3rd ed.), London: John Murray, **5** (121): 318, Bibcode: 1872Natur...5..318B[250], doi: 10.1038/005318a0[251], retrieved 9 January 2009<templatestyles src="Module:Citation/CS1/styles.css"></templatestyles>
- Darwin, Francis (1887), *The Life and Letters of Charles Darwin, including an autobiographical chapter (3 Volumes)*[254], London: John Murray, retrieved 7 March 2008<templatestyles src="Module:Citation/CS1/styles.css"></templatestyles>
- Darwin, Francis; Seward, A. C (1903), *More letters of Charles Darwin (2 Volumes)*[255], London: John Murray, retrieved 28 January 2016<templatestyles src="Module:Citation/CS1/styles.css"></templatestyles>
- Desmond, Adrian; Moore, James (1991), *Darwin*[256], London: Michael Joseph, Penguin Group, ISBN 0-7181-3430-3<templatestyles src="Module:Citation/CS1/styles.css"></templatestyles>
- Freeman, R.B. (2007), *Charles Darwin: A companion*[257] (2d online edition, compiled by Sue Asscher and edited by John van Wyhe ed.), The Complete Works of Charles Darwin Online, retrieved 26 November 2010<templatestyles src="Module:Citation/CS1/styles.css"></templatestyles>
- Freeman, Richard B. (1977a), "On the Origin of Species"[258], *The Works of Charles Darwin: An Annotated Bibliographical Handlist* (2nd ed.), Folkestone, England: Dawson, ISBN 0-7129-0740-8<templatestyles src="Module:Citation/CS1/styles.css"></templatestyles>
- Henslow, John Stevens (1861), "Letter from Professor Henslow"[259], *Macmillan's Magazine*, **3**: 336<templatestyles src="Module:Citation/CS1/styles.css"></templatestyles>. Letter dated January 1861.
- Herbert, Sandra (January 2005). *Charles Darwin, Geologist*[260]. Cornell University Press. ISBN 0-8014-4348-2.<templatestyles src="Module:Citation/CS1/styles.css"></templatestyles>
- Hooker, Joseph D. (1859), "(Review of) On the origin of species"[261],

- *The Gardeners' Chronicle* (1052: 31 December 1859)<templatestyles src="Module:Citation/CS1/styles.css"></templatestyles>
- Huxley, Leonard (1903), *Life and letters of Thomas Henry Huxley (2 Volumes)*[262] (2nd ed.), London: Macmillan<templatestyles src="Module:Citation/CS1/styles.css"></templatestyles>. The first edition was published in 1900.
- Huxley, Thomas H. (1859), "Darwin on the Origin of Species"[263], *The Times* (26 December 1859): 8–9<templatestyles src="Module:Citation/CS1/styles.css"></templatestyles>. Published anonymously.
- Huxley, Thomas H. (1860), "Darwin on the Origin of Species"[264], *Westminster Review*, **17** (April 1860): 541–570<templatestyles src="Module:Citation/CS1/styles.css"></templatestyles>. Published anonymously.
- Leifchild, John R. (1859), "Review of 'Origin'"[265], *Athenaeum* (No. 1673, 19 November 1859), retrieved 22 November 2008<templatestyles src="Module:Citation/CS1/styles.css"></templatestyles>
- Lucas, J. R. (1979), "Wilberforce and Huxley: A Legendary Encounter"[266], *The Historical Journal*, **22** (2), pp. 313–330, doi: 10.1017/S0018246X00016848[267], PMID 11617072[268], retrieved 22 November 2008<templatestyles src="Module:Citation/CS1/styles.css"></templatestyles>
- Morrell, Jack (2001). "Genesis and geochronology: the case of John Phillips (1800–1874)"[269]. *Geological Society, London, Special Publications*. Geological Society of London. **190** (1): 85–90. Bibcode: 2001GSLSP.190...85M[270]. doi: 10.1144/gsl.sp.2001.190.01.07[271]. Retrieved 27 April 2017.<templatestyles src="Module:Citation/CS1/styles.css"></templatestyles> (pdf[272])
- Owen, Richard (1860), "Review of Darwin's Origin of Species"[273], *Edinburgh Review*, **3** (April 1860): 487–532<templatestyles src="Module:Citation/CS1/styles.css"></templatestyles>. Published anonymously.
- Wilberforce, Samuel (1860), "(Review of) On the Origin of Species"[274], *Quarterly Review*, **108** (215: July 1860): 225–264<templatestyles src="Module:Citation/CS1/styles.css"></templatestyles>. Published anonymously.
- Wilberforce, Samuel (1861), "(Review of) Essays and Reviews"[275], *Quarterly Review*, **109**: 248–301<templatestyles src="Module:Citation/CS1/styles.css"></templatestyles>. Published anonymously.
- Wollaston, A.F.R. (1921), *Life of Alfred Newton: late Professor of Comparative Anatomy, Cambridge University 1866–1907, with a*

Preface by Sir Archibald Geikie[276], New York: Dutton<templatestyles src="Module:Citation/CS1/styles.css"></templatestyles>.

Further reading

- Darwin, Charles (1837–1838), *Notebook B:* [*Transmutation of species*][277], Darwin Online, CUL-DAR121, retrieved 20 December 2008<templatestyles src="Module:Citation/CS1/styles.css"></templatestyles>
- Darwin, Charles (1859), *On the Origin of Species by Means of Natural Selection, or the Preservation of Favoured Races in the Struggle for Life*[248] (1st ed.), London: John Murray, retrieved 24 October 2008<templatestyles src="Module:Citation/CS1/styles.css"></templatestyles>
- Darwin, Charles (1958), Barlow, Nora, ed., *The Autobiography of Charles Darwin 1809–1882. With the original omissions restored. Edited and with appendix and notes by his granddaughter Nora Barlow*[254], London: Collins, retrieved 4 November 2008<templatestyles src="Module:Citation/CS1/styles.css"></templatestyles>
- Darwin, Charles (2006), "Journal"[278], in van Wyhe, John, [*Darwin's personal 'Journal' (1809–1881)*][279], Darwin Online, CUL-DAR158.1–76, retrieved 20 December 2008<templatestyles src="Module:Citation/CS1/styles.css"></templatestyles>
- Freeman, R.B. (1977), *The Works of Charles Darwin: An Annotated Bibliographical Handlist*[280] (2nd ed.), Folkestone, Kent, England: Wm Dawson & Sons, retrieved 15 December 2006<templatestyles src="Module:Citation/CS1/styles.css"></templatestyles>
- Huxley, Thomas H. (1863), *Six Lectures to Working Men "On Our Knowledge of the Causes of the Phenomena of Organic Nature" (Republished in Volume II of his Collected Essays, Darwiniana)*[281], retrieved 15 December 2006<templatestyles src="Module:Citation/CS1/styles.css"></templatestyles>

External links

- The Complete Works of Charles Darwin Online – Darwin Online[282]; Darwin's publications, private papers and bibliography, supplementary works including biographies, obituaries and reviews. For a comprehensive set of reviews of *On the Origin of Species* see Reviews & Responses to Darwin[283].
- Works by Charles Darwin[284] at Project Gutenberg
- Darwin Correspondence Project[285] Text and notes for most of his letters.

Descent of Man, sexual selection, and botany

Darwin from Orchids to Variation

Between 1860 and 1868, the life and work of Charles **Darwin from** *Orchids* **to** *Variation* continued with research and experimentation on evolution, carrying out tedious work to provide evidence of the extent of natural variation enabling artificial selection. He was repeatedly held up by his illness, and continued to find relaxation and interest in the study of plants. His studies of insect pollination led to publication of his book *Fertilisation of Orchids* as his first detailed demonstration of the power of natural selection, explaining the complex ecological relationships and making testable predictions. As his health declined, he lay on his sickbed in a room filled with inventive experiments to trace the movements of climbing plants.

Darwinism became a movement covering a wide range of evolutionary ideas. In 1863 Lyell's *Geological Evidences of the Antiquity of Man* popularised prehistory, though his caution on evolution disappointed Darwin. Weeks later Huxley's *Evidence as to Man's Place in Nature* showed that anatomically, humans are apes, then *The Naturalist on the River Amazons* by Henry Walter Bates provided empirical evidence of natural selection. Lobbying brought Darwin Britain's highest scientific honour, the Royal Society's Copley Medal, awarded on 3 November 1864. That day, Huxley held the first meeting of what became the influential *X Club* devoted to "science, pure and free, untrammelled by religious dogmas".

Admiring visitors included Ernst Haeckel, a zealous follower of *Darwinismus* in a translation favouring progressive evolution over natural selection.[286] Wallace remained supportive, though he increasingly turned to Spiritualism.

The first part of Darwin's planned "big book", *The Variation of Animals and Plants under Domestication*, grew to two huge volumes, forcing him to leave out human evolution and sexual selection. It sold briskly in 1868 despite its size, and was translated into many languages. Darwin's work on the *Descent of Man* and *Emotions* followed after this publication.

Background

Darwin's ideas developed rapidly from the return in 1836 of *The Voyage of the Beagle*. By December 1838 he had developed the principles of his theory, but was conscious of the need to answer all likely objections before publishing. While he continued with research, he had an immense amount of work in hand analysing and publishing findings from the *Beagle* expedition, and was repeatedly delayed by illness.

Natural history at that time was dominated by clerical naturalists, whose income came from the Established Church of England, and who saw their science as revealing God's plan. Darwin found two close allies: the young botanist Joseph Dalton Hooker and the ambitious naturalist Thomas Huxley who lacked the family wealth or contacts to find a career and joined a progressive group looking to make science a profession, freed from the clerics. Darwin's correspondent Wallace arrived independently at his own version of the theory, which brought an early announcement of the theory and the publication of *On the Origin of Species through Natural Selection* in 1859.

This brought a storm of argument. Many naturalists attacked what they saw as an assault on established beliefs about the natural world, and perhaps the ideological foundations of the British social order, while liberal theologians and a new generation of scientists welcomed the theory. Charles Lyell and Hooker, as well as Asa Gray in America, gave support despite difficulty in coming to terms with natural selection and man's descent from animals. Huxley's interest in aggressively attacking the scientific establishment earned him the moniker "Darwin's bulldog" in a ferocious dispute with the leading anatomist Richard Owen as to whether the anatomy of brain structure was consistent with humans and apes having shared ancestry. The campaign was devastatingly successful for the Darwinian cause and brought new recruits.

Ape-men

Lyell was troubled both by Huxley's belligerence and by the question of ape ancestry, but got little sympathy from Darwin who teased him in January 1860: "*Our* ancestor was an animal which breathed water, had a swim-bladder, a great swimming tail, an imperfect skull & undoubtedly was an hermaphrodite! Here is a pleasant genealogy for mankind." In April Lyell noted thoughts on humanity, and Darwin commented that "to me it would be an infinite satisfaction to believe that mankind will progress to such a pitch, that we shd. be looked back at as mere Barbarians." Huxley was busy attacking the old theory of divine providence as "anthropomorphism" and promoting the new Darwinian orthodoxy of "the passionless impersonality of the unknown and unknowable". He told Lyell that the range of brain sizes between people was greater than the difference between small-brained people and gorillas, and "Under these circumstances it would certainly be well to let go the head (as a way of distinguishing species) though I am afraid it does not mend matters much to lay hold of the foot."

Lyell began work on a book examining human origins. He toured archaeological sites in Britain and France, examining such evidence as the pre-glacial stone scrapers Falconer had found in a cave at Brixham in Devon in 1858 and flint tools in a Bedford, Bedfordshire, gravel pit. After touring the Abbeville flint site in France in 1859, Lyell announced that he had overcome thirty years of denial of such antiquity and accepted that ancient man pre-dated the ice age. A delighted Darwin responded in April 1861 "It is grand. What a fine long pedigree you have given the Human Race!" Lyell questioned Huxley about the Neanderthal fossil found near Düsseldorf and described by Hermann Schaaffhausen in 1858 which Huxley examined at the College of Surgeons in London. Lyell still, however, remained deeply critical of Darwin's idea of natural selection.

In the spring of 1861 John Stevens Henslow, the botany professor whose natural history course Charles had joined thirty years earlier who was also Hooker's father-in-law, lay dying of heart disease. Darwin's own health was precarious, and he had recently suffered 24 hours of vomiting after the excitement of a few minutes of speaking at the Linnean Society. He agonised about visiting the man who had made the Beagle trip possible and had given him much support since, and on 23 April told Hooker that "the agitation would cause me probably to arrive utterly prostrated." He had "never felt my weakness a greater evil." Henslow died on 18 May.

Darwin was well into his work on domestication, obtaining skeletons of fowl and animals, borrowing specimens or stewing pigeons he had bred and rabbits he had requested, "I want it dead for the skeleton, not knocked on the head". This would eventually lead to his book *The Variation of Animals and Plants under Domestication.*

He continued to suffer from illness and worries about the health of his children, and felt "incessant anxiety" about his daughter Henrietta. She had suffered a typhoid infection the previous month, and was an invalid at only 18, close to death and needing three attendants round the clock. Emma Darwin was used to nursing, but was at her wit's end: "I have succeeded pretty well in teaching myself not to give way to despondency, [but can] only live from day to day." She wrote another touching letter to Charles, saying the "only relief [was to take] affliction as from God's hand [and] try to believe that all suffering & illness is meant to help us to exalt our minds & look forward with hope to a future state... When I see your patience, deep compassion for others, self command & above all gratitude for the smallest thing done to help you I cannot help longing that these precious feelings should be offered to Heaven for the sake of your daily happiness... It is feeling & not reasoning that drives one to prayer." Charles wrote "God Bless you" at the bottom of the note.

Lyell attended Huxley's continuing working-men's lectures, and was "astonished at the attentiveness and magnitude of the audience...[who would] devour any amount of your anthropoid ape questions". Human origins had been taboo to the scientific élite, but had long been featured in the radical press and the secularist *Reasoner* was currently running a series about evolution to combat "Theological Theories of the Origin of Man" with information about human fossils and Darwin's book. Huxley was tailoring his lectures to bring Darwinism to this wider constituency, saying that "Brought face to face [with chimpanzees or apes] these blurred copies of himself, the least thoughtful of men is conscious of a certain shock... It is as if Nature herself has foreseen the arrogance of man, and with Roman severity had provided that his intellect by its very triumphs, should call into prominence the slaves, admonishing the conqueror that he is but dust." Man might have come from the brutes, but "he is assuredly not of them... [man is not] degraded from his high estate [by descent from a] bestial savage,... [but] once escaped from the blinding influences of traditional prejudice, will find in the lowly stock whence Man has sprung, the best evidence of the splendour of his capacities; and will discern in his long progress through the Past, a reasonable ground of faith in his attainment of a nobler future." This was Darwinism supporting the creed of working class self-improvement.

Orchids

For July and August 1861 they took their daughter Henrietta to the seaside village of Torquay. Darwin was diverted by spending hours considering the variety of wild orchids to be found along the shore, continuing an interest in insect pollination dating back to the late 1830s when on the recommendation of Robert Brown he had read Christian Konrad Sprengel on the subject. He wrote a brief paper on the topic. On returning home he looked for these plants near Downe, and found a beautiful spot teeming with orchids which his family named "Orchid Bank". His requests to the wealthy enthusiasts who had taken up growing rare orchids brought large numbers of specimens. These would be a test of his theory: Huxley had once asked "Who has ever dreamed of finding an utilitarian purpose in the forms and colours of flowers?"

He explored the intricacies of how the petals guided specific bees or moths, and found that what had been thought to be three different genera of flowers growing on the same plant (a mysteriously monstrous specimen that puzzled the Linnean Society) were actually the male, female and hermaphrodite forms of the orchid *Catasetum*. This unusual plant, Darwin discovered, fired arrows with a sticky pollen head as the insects brushed past – to which Hooker responded "Do you really think I can believe all that!" In this, Darwin followed his grandfather Erasmus Darwin in exploring the sex life of plants, he analysed how parts of the plants were "homologous", having evolved from an original structure to meet different functions in different species. He persuaded John Murray that this would be a fashionable book to publish, but his illness returned, causing delay.

Huxley's argument, that natural selection was unproven until evolving varieties could be shown to form species which could not interbreed, turned Darwin's attention to experimenting, pollinating plants and sifting seeds. By collating his results in January 1862 he showed that primroses and cowslips, thought to be varieties, produced sterile hybrids. He convinced Huxley with letters sent to Edinburgh where Huxley was "preaching Darwinism pure & simple as applied to man.... [and] I made 'em listen.. I told them in so many words that I entertained no doubt of the origin of man from the same stock as the apes. Everyone prophesied I should be stoned and cast out of the city gate, but I met with unmitigated applause!"' Darwin was impressed that he had "attacked Bigotry in its strong-hold". Huxley published his lectures as a slim book on *Man's Place in Nature*.

Darwin persevered with his orchids, and the book, *On the various contrivances by which British and foreign orchids are fertilised by insects and the good effects of intercrossing*, was published on 15 May 1862, just in time to give Wallace a copy on his return from the far East. While demonstrating that orchids evolve mechanisms that allow for cross-fertilisation, and offering strong evidence for Darwin's larger arguments about variation, the volume also countered natural theology in what Darwin himself admitted was a "flank movement against the enemy." By showing that the "wonderful contrivances" of the orchid have discoverable evolutionary histories, he countered claims by natural theologians that the organisms were examples of the perfect work of the Creator. His interest in orchids continued and he had a hot-house built at Down House, as well as experimenting with other seedlings and "slaving on bones of ducks and pigeon" and variations in other farmyard animals. His illness led to his skin becoming inflamed and shedding, taking "the epidermis a dozen times clean off".

Because of the problems with eczema, Emma told him to grow a beard, and in December his friend Mary Butler commented on the idea of this "long beard".

In January 1863 he got word from Hugh Falconer of a "mis-begotten-bird-creature" fossil, the archaeopteryx, which Owen bought for the British Museum. It fulfilled Darwin's prediction that a proto-bird with unfused wing fingers would be found. Though Owen described it unequivocally as a bird, the subsequent finding that it had teeth left no doubt of its relevance to the *Origin of Species*. This sudden finding showed just how patchy the known fossil record was.

Huxley continued with his lectures to the working men, and a member of the audience took notes and published six fourpenny pamphlets which were brought together into a book which Darwin thought "capitally written... I may as well shut up shop altogether." On 4 February Lyell published his *Geological Evidences of the Antiquity of Man*. To Darwin's disappointment Lyell had still not brought himself to clearly endorse Darwin's theory on species or on man, though he had "spoken out... even beyond my state of feeling as to man's unbroken descent from the brutes". Darwin's disappointment brought on ten days of vomiting, faintness and stomach distress. He was much better pleased to then receive Huxley's *Man's Place in Nature*, printed with a frontispiece showing a line of skeletons, with a gibbon at the end, stooping apes in the middle and upright man at the head, exclaiming "Hurrah, the Monkey Book has come". It included a jibe at Owen's ambiguous "ordained continuous becoming", and though some were horrified at this line of "gibbering, grovelling apes" the 1,000 copies sold quickly, requiring a reprint within weeks.

Tendrils and loosestrife

The sickness grew worse, and Darwin could only lie on his couch watching the growing tendrils of plants. This interest started with wild cucumber seeds sent by Asa Gray, and he found it "just the sort of niggling work which suits me". After some delays Emma managed to get him to Dr. Gully's spa at Malvern in September 1863, but the prescribed six months rest meant only six months sickness. He was too ill to write, so Emma took dictation.

He began to recover in April 1864, sitting in his greenhouse at home and becoming fascinated by the purple loosestrife (*Lythrum*) he had been breeding for years. This has three kinds of flowers and Darwin explored the eighteen possible sexual combinations, counting the resulting seeds and testing their fertility. Only six "marriages" proved "legitimate", showing that this was another mechanism for cross-pollination. He tabulated the results of his experiments on seeds and wrote them up for the Linnean Society of London. Around this time a Mrs. Becker wrote requesting something edifying for her ladies' literary society, so he sent her *On the Sexual Relations of the Three Forms of Lythrum salicaria*.

His bedroom, study and greenhouses became filled with climbers, creepers and coiling tendrils, and in May he began a short paper on these plants. He marked their tips to time their movements, and brought Hops indoors, using weights to try to slow their ascent as he sat ill in bed. By 13 September his paper had grown to a 118-page monograph, published by the Linnean Society.

Changing times

Meanwhile, as Darwin worked from his sickbed his friends continued with debates. Asa Gray sent news of the American Civil War, but to Darwin "the destruction of slavery would be well worth a dozen year's war".

Wallace, stirred by the *Origin* and by Herbert Spencer's *Social Statics*, had presented his first paper to the racist pro-slavery Anthropological Society of London. He, along with Darwin and the others, supported the abolitionist Ethnological Society of London, but Wallace tried to reach a truce by proposing that races had long been separate, but had emerged from a single stock after the ape stage. His view was that competition was between groups, leading "to the inevitable extinction of all those low and mentally undeveloped populations with which the Europeans come into contact", Darwin's experience supported this and he wrote on his copy *"natural selection is now acting on the inferior races when put into competition"*, giving the example of Māoris in New Zealand "dying out like their own native rat".

Where they differed was that Wallace saw mankind evolving mentally but not physically, and this would bring a utopia where everyone would "work out his own happiness" free from policing "since the well balanced moral faculties will never permit any one to transgress on the equal freedom of others... every man will know how to govern himself" and so government would be "replaced by voluntary associations for all beneficial public purposes". Darwin responded that the mental / physical distinction was "grand and most eloquently done" but physical selection continued, through "constant battles" of savages, and unimpeded competition was vital to English society. Wallace replied that wars tended to kill the most fit at the battlefront, and he demurred from "sexual selection". He disputed Darwin's idea that the aristocracy was handsomer than the middle classes by saying that mere manner and refinement were being confused with beauty.

Wallace also thought that the caves of Borneo might reveal "our progenitors" and Lyell tried to organise an expedition hoping to find "extinct ourangs, if not the missing link itself"', but in the absence of funding the consul agreed to have a look.

The scandal of the liberal Anglican theologians' acceptance of evolution and rejection of miracles in *Essays and Reviews* continued. The two essayists convicted of heresy had the judgement overturned on appeal. Samuel Wilberforce, the High Church and evangelicals organised petitions and a mass backlash against evolution. At the Anglican convocation they tried to make a declaration reaffirming their faith in the harmony of God's word and his works a "Fortieth Article" of the Church of England, and at the British Association moved to overthrow Huxley's "dangerous clique".

The X Club

Darwin's friends energetically lobbied for his recognition, and after failed attempts in 1862 and 1863 to have him awarded the Royal Society's highest honour, the Copley Medal, their careful preparations and lobbying succeeded in voting their nomination through despite furious politicking in opposition. Darwin was awarded the medal at the Council meeting on the evening of 3 November 1864.

Huxley had made arrangements for a dining club of close friends as select supporters of the evolutionary "new reformation" in naturalism, united by a "devotion to science, pure and free, untrammelled by religious dogmas", and it held its first meeting that same day. Those present were all Fellows of the Royal Society: Huxley, Hooker, John Tyndall, George Busk, Edward Frankland, Herbert Spencer, John Lubbock, and Thomas Archer Hirst. At the December meeting they were joined by William Spottiswoode, and while the club had no agreed name at first, it subsequently became known as the "X Club".

The medal was formally presented at a full meeting on 30 November, which Darwin was unable to attend due to illness. The President, Edward Sabine, used his address to give the *Origin* faint praise and claim that "Speaking generally and collectively, we have expressly omitted it from the grounds of our award." After the address Huxley called for the Council minutes to prove this false. The minutes made no reference to such an exclusion, or to the *Origin*, to which Sabine argued that no allusion equalled express exclusion. The row continued afterwards, and the offending passages were altered in the official record of the address. Lyell used his after-dinner speech at the meeting to give guarded support to Darwin's theory in which he gave a "confession of faith as to the *Origin*", and said that he "had been forced to give up my old faith without thoroughly seeing my way to a new one." Darwin subsequently said that his friend's congratulations "are the real medal to me, and not the round bit of gold".

Early in 1865 Darwin's sickness worsened and he was overcome for almost eight months, lying in bed for weeks at a time, with Emma reading aloud to him. In May he heard of the suicide of Robert FitzRoy, who had been captain of HMS *Beagle*, and commented that "I never knew in my life so mixed a character. Always much to love & I once loved him sincerely; but so bad a temper & so given to take offence, that I gradually quite lost my love & wished only to keep out of contact with him. Twice he quarrelled bitterly with me, without any just provocation on my part. But certainly there was much noble & exalted in his character."

The *Westminster* magazine publisher John Chapman was now a qualified specialist in sickness and psychological medicine, and Darwin invited Dr. Chapman to Downe and gave him a long list of the symptoms he had suffered from for 25 years. A spinal freezing treatment seemed to help, and Darwin pressed on with his *Variation Under Domestication*.

Pangenesis

He now tackled the chapter of *Variation* setting out his hypothesis about heredity, that "pangenesis" brought "gemmules" from every cell of the body to the reproductive organs, where they formed the "true ovule or bud" that could pass on traits to the next generation. Huxley was dubious, cautiously writing "Somebody rummaging among your papers half a century hence will find Pangenesis and say, 'See this wonderful anticipation of our modern theories, and that stupid ass Huxley prevented his publishing them."

Times were changing. Lyell became embroiled in a row for having incorporated into *Antiquity of Man* whole paragraphs of a paper by Lubbock. The "X Club" continued to gain power in the British Association. Huxley's lectures were drawing huge crowds. Darwin had relapsed, but found a new doctor who put him on a crash diet. It seemed to work, but the photographic calling cards popular at the time recorded his deteriorating appearance.

His beard grew bushy and he had to reintroduce himself to friends when he emerged into society at a Royal Society reception on 28 April 1866. Emma recalled that "He was obliged to name himself to almost all of them, as his beard alters him so." This image was made famous by Julia Margaret Cameron's iconic portraits taken during the Darwin family's 1868 holiday in her Isle of Wight cottage. Spencer, in his *Principles of Biology*, had coined the phrase "survival of the fittest", and though Darwin had struggled with the "detestable style" of the turgid tome, he now agreed with Wallace that it avoided the troublesome anthropomorphism of "selecting", though it "lost the analogy between nature's selection and the fanciers'."

Figure 43: *Iconic 1868 portrait by Julia Margaret Cameron showing the bushy beard Darwin had grown by April 1866.*

British Association

In 1866 at the British Association meeting at Nottingham the *Guardian* reported that Darwin's theory "was everywhere in the ascendant... it was impossible to pass from Section to Section without seeing how deeply these views have leavened the scientific minds of the day."' The President, W.R.Grove, said it should be seen "in the history of our own race... the product of slow adaptions, resulting from continuous struggles. Happily in this country, practical experience has taught us to improve rather than remodel; we follow the law of nature and avoid cataclysms." Darwinism was now justifying British society rather than destroying it.

Hooker's speech ended by satirising their opponents of evolution at the 1860 meeting as an uncivilised tribe who saw "every new moon as a new creation of their gods" and ate "the missionaries of the most enlightened nation" for explaining the truth. "The priests first attacked the new doctrine and with fury... the medicine men, however, sided with the missionaries – many from spite to the priests, but a few, i could see, from conviction." Now after six years, the elders were baptised in the new faith and applauded their president for leading them out of the wilderness. Darwin was told of the stunned silence at first, followed by roars of laughter.

The religious press was "surprised and grieved" at this, but now the radical audience splintered into different directions. Following popular interest in Modern Spiritualism, winning over Robert Chambers and Wallace, they printed a pamphlet *The Scientific Aspect of the Supernatural*.

Haeckel

Darwin was visited in October 1866 by the zoologist Ernst Haeckel, who over the years had built support for Darwin in Germany, now getting huge classes at Jena for his lectures on *Darwinismus*. He had gone further, extending selection and struggle to society where it would "drive the peoples onward... to higher cultural stages." He had set out to rearrange all biological knowledge along Darwinian lines in his *Generelle Morphologie*. He was taken "by storm" when they met and, overawed, began speaking quickly in broken English, then found he could not understand Darwin's reply. They stared at each other for a moment, then burst into laughter and managed to communicate more slowly. When the two volumes of *Morphologie* arrived later Darwin struggled for weeks with the number of new words like "phylogeny" and "ecology" as well as with the German, before giving up. His only hope was a translation, but the anti-clerical comments would prevent this. He gathered glimpses of Haeckel's ambition to achieve a universal Theory of Development embracing all human knowledge, if not his ideas of German *Volk* and support for Bismarck's unification of Germany.

Spencer roped Darwin into giving a donation and adding his name, along with Huxley, Wallace and Lyell, to the "Jamaica Committee" seeking to bring to justice Governor Eyre whose troops had brutally crushed a peasant revolt, with over 400 blacks being executed. Some of his other friends supported the opposing "Eyre Defence and Aid Committee", outraging Darwin's feelings against slavery and oppression. When Darwin's son William, now a banker in Southampton, had his name published "by accident" as having attended a banquet in Eyre's honour, Darwin wrote to the Lord Chancellor to rectify the error. Then the family got together at the house of Erasmus Alvey Darwin, where William made a disparaging remark about the "Jamaica Committee". A furious Charles shouted that if he felt that way, he "had better go back to Southampton". The next morning Charles entered his son's bedroom and told him that he hadn't slept a wink, his anger had been cruel and he was sorry.

Variation under Domestication

Before Christmas 1866 *Variation* was sent to the printers, save for the last chapter. In this, Darwin wanted to overcome the persistent argument of divinely guided variation. He used the analogy of an architect using rocks which had broken off naturally and fallen to the foot of a cliff, asking "Can it be reasonably maintained that the Creator intentionally ordered... that certain fragments should assume certain shapes so that the builder might erect his edifice?" In the same way, breeders or natural selection picked those that *happened* to be useful from variations arising by "general laws", to improve plants and animals, "man included". Darwin was now openly including man in his theory, and wanted to add a chapter on this but the book was already too "horridly, disgustingly big" and he shortly decided to write a separate "short essay" on ape ancestry, sexual selection and human expression.

Murray had to make two volumes of it, and being advised that it was hard going planned only 750 copies, though he later doubled that. Translators were eager to get to work: Carus into German, and Vladimir Kovalevsky into Russian – he was sent Murray's proofs, and successfully beat his publication date so that the earliest edition of *Variation* was in Russian.

During the Spring Darwin tried to find explanations in Sexual Selection for variations in that "eminently domesticated animal", mankind, and for the plumage of birds. As well as drawing on information, he experimented with dying pigeons red and trimming the feathers of game-cocks to see if this affected their desirability as a mate. The Duke of Argyll had thrown down a challenge with his book *The Reign of Law*, which collected criticisms of the *Origin* and put forward theories of divine design and providential law in a way that struck Darwin as "very well written, very interesting, honest, & clever & very arrogant". It made a particular point of the iridescent colours of hummingbirds, claiming that this was beauty for God's sake without any earthly reason, not explicable by struggle. Wallace gave *Reign of Law* a withering review, pointing to the existence of stink bugs as well as beauty, and then became entangled in an exchange of detailed arguments with the Duke. To Darwin's despair, Wallace refused to accept a rôle for Sexual Selection.

Further damage to the *Origin* came from professor Sir William Thomson (later Lord Kelvin) used calculations of heat loss to estimate a much younger age for the earth than Darwin had been assuming. Thomson's partner in a submarine cable business, the engineer Fleeming Jenkin, then argued convincingly that any single variation would be blended back into the population, so that to form a new species numerous variations would have to be created simultaneously, reintroducing the need for divine intervention.

By June Lyell was struggling to revise his *Principles of Geology*, though Darwin still hoped that he would at last "speak out plainly about species". Lyell found Darwin's proofs of *Variation* "most persuasive", but Darwin was struggling to sort out the changes and corrections he wanted. Encouragement came from the Reverend professor Charles Kingsley who sent the previously unthinkable news that "the best and strongest men" at the University of Cambridge were "coming over [to] what the world calls Darwinism... The younger M.A.'s are not only willing, but greedy, to hear what you have to say, and... the elder... are facing the whole question in quite a different tone from that they did three years ago... I have been surprised at the change since last winter."

The proofs were finished on 15 November, and *The Variation of Animals and Plants Under Domestication* went on sale on 30 January 1868, thirteen years after Darwin had begun his experiments on breeding and stewing the bones of pigeons. He was feeling deflated, and concerned about how these large volumes would be received, writing "if I try to read a few pages I feel fairly nauseated... The devil take the whole book". The public were undeterred, and the 1,500 copies went within a week with a second printing at eleven days. The *Pall Mall Gazette* praised its "noble calmness... undisturbed by the heats of polemical agitation" which made the far from calm Darwin laugh, and left him "cock-a-hoop".

Darwin continued his work with the *Descent of Man* and *Emotions*.

References

- Adrian Desmond and James Moore, *Darwin* (London: Michael Joseph, the Penguin Group, 1991). <templatestyles src="Module:Citation/CS1/styles.css" />ISBN 0-7181-3430-3
- The Correspondence of Charles Darwin[287]
- On the various contrivances by which British and foreign orchids are fertilised by insects[288]
- The variation of animals and plants under domestication[289]
- Orchids and Evolution[290]
- Freeman, R.B. (2007), *Charles Darwin: A companion*[291] (2d online edition, compiled by Sue Asscher and edited by John van Wyhe ed.), The Complete Works of Charles Darwin Online, retrieved 26 November 2010<templatestyles src="Module:Citation/CS1/styles.css"></templatestyles>

Further reading

- The Complete Works of Charles Darwin Online – Darwin Online[292]; Darwin's publications, private papers and bibliography, supplementary works including biographies, obituaries and reviews. Free to use, includes items not in public domain.
- Works by Charles Darwin[293] at Project Gutenberg; public domain

- Darwin Correspondence Project[294] Text and notes for most of his letters
- Armstrong, Nancy (December 2016). "Do Wasps Just Want to Have Fun? Darwin and the Question of Variation"[295]. *differences: A Journal of Feminist Cultural Studies*. Duke University Press. **27** (3): 1&ndash, 19. doi: 10.1215/10407391-3696607[296].<templatestyles src="Module:Citation/CS1/styles.css"></templatestyles>

Darwin from Descent of Man to Emotions

Between 1868 and 1872, the life and work of Charles **Darwin from *Descent of Man* to *Emotions*** continued with aspects of his intended "Big Book" on evolution through natural selection. He had by then hurriedly published an "abstract" of this work as *On the Origin of Species* in 1859, and following the immediate reaction to Darwin's theory his earlier work included demonstrating the utility of the flowers of Orchids in directing insect pollination to achieve cross fertilisation, and a summing up of thirteen years of experiments in *The Variation of Animals and Plants under Domestication* which went on sale on 30 January 1868. He now published his ideas on human evolution and on how beautiful but apparently impractical features could have evolved in *The Descent of Man, and Selection in Relation to Sex*. After revising *The Origin of Species* as the definitive 6th edition, his major works on species culminated in *The Expression of the Emotions in Man and Animals*. This period was followed by extensive work on insectivorous plants and research into worms.

Family and research

Despite Darwin's concerns that his children were weakened as his wife Emma Darwin was his cousin or had inherited his own illness, around early 1868 his sons had successes with William Darwin doing well as a bank manager, Leonard Darwin coming second in the entrance exam for the Royal Military Academy and George coming runner-up in his mathematics degree class at the University of Cambridge, getting offered a science mastership at Eton College but choosing to make his career in law.

Sexual selection

Darwin turned his attention to sexual selection, writing to scientist friends for information. He got commercial breeders to experiment with altering the appearance of their stock and recording the subject's sexual prowess. He thought that exotic creatures like hummingbirds and peacocks owed their appearance, not to divine design to please man, but to the cumulative effect of the female preferring minute differences in choosing a mate, writing that "A girl sees a handsome man, and without observing whether his nose or whiskers are the tenth or an inch longer or shorter than in some other man, admires his appearance and says she will marry him. So, I suppose, with the pea-hen."

To meet a lack of books supporting the *Origin* on natural selection, Darwin arranged with John Murray to publish a translation of *Für Darwin*, written by Fritz Müller exiled in Brazil. Darwin provided £100 subsidy and arranged the translator, and *Facts and Arguments for Darwin*. sold well.

In the spring of 1868 Darwin got information on newts from St George Mivart, a brilliant anatomist and one of Huxley's protégés who had dropped law for zoology after hearing Owen lecture. He assured Darwin that "As to "natural selection" I accepted it completely" but added that he had "doubts & difficulties.. first excited by attending Prof. Huxley's lectures".

Descent of Man

The book *The Reign of Law* by the Duke of Argyll argued that beauty with no obvious utility, such as exotic birds' plumage, proved divine design. Darwin had to show how this was explained by his theory of sexual selection, and was now working to include this with ape ancestry and evolution of morality and religion in a new book which he now decided to call *The Descent of Man*.

Sources

Darwin found many ideas in the quality magazines. Wallace argued that group co-operation increased fitness for survival. Darwin's cousin Francis Galton wrote *Hereditary Talent and Character* for *Macmillan's Magazine* emphasising the inheritance of traits, and their extension to races and classes, and calling for better breeding to ensure that the "nobler varieties of mankind" prevailed, with civilisation being saved from "intellectual anarchy" by scientific "master minds" rising to power. These views were shared by Darwin's old friend W. R. Greg whose *Fraser's Magazine* article about natural selection in society raised fears of the "unfit" and of the prudent middle classes being out-bred by the idle rich and the feckless poor.

These ideas raised a dilemma, of evolution working against progress. Darwin found help in Walter Bagehot's essays on *Physics and Politics* in the *Fortnightly Review* which argued that progress depended on the command structure of society. Civilisation came from obedience, respect for law and a "military bond". Through tribal and imperial battles new racial and national types would emerge, selected as "The characters which do win in war are the characters which we should wish to win in war". Darwin added his comment "nations which wander & cross would be most likely to vary" in the face of wider competition, and commended to Hooker Bagehot's analysis of "prehistoric politics".

Figure 44: *Julia Margaret Cameron's 1868 portrait shows the beard Darwin began growing during illness in July 1862, which became so bushy that he had to reintroduce himself to friends in April 1866.*

British Association

Hooker became the first Darwinian to become president of the British Association for the Advancement of Science. While Hooker was working on his initial address, Darwin with his wife Emma and daughter Henrietta went on holiday to the Isle of Wight on 16 July 1868, and rented a cottage from the photographer Julia Margaret Cameron who took Darwin's portrait. Hooker joined them and the Irish poet William Allingham described "Dr. Hooker in lower room writing away at his Address... Upstairs Mrs. Darwin, Miss D. and Mr. Charles Darwin himself–, yellow, sickly, very quiet. He has his meals at his own times, sees people or not as he chooses, has invalid's privileges in full, a great help to a studious man."

Hooker's address to the Norwich British Association was a great success for the X Club (a dining club formed in November 1864 to support the evolutionary "new reformation" in naturalism, including Huxley, Hooker, John Tyndall, Busk, Spencer, and Spottiswoode). Darwin arrived home on 21 August with a clutch of the day's newspapers carrying the address and editorial comments. *The Guardian* said Darwinism's "reign was triumphant", and it was generally said that the disciples were "ready to push their consequences more fearlessly than the master himself". Darwin enjoyed John Tyndall's lecture in which the physicist widened the application of his theory.

Ernst Haeckel's *Darwinismus* was even more universal, incorporating life, mind, society, politics and knowledge itself, though Darwin had struggled with reading his book and his efforts to get it translated were thwarted as the book proved too controversial. Haeckel, the "indomitable worker", quickly produced his *History of Creation*. An impressed Huxley adopted Haeckel's approach, and did what he had told Darwin was impossible and wrong, drawing up a genealogical tree for the ancestry of partridges and pigeons which traced them back to the dinosaurs. Huxley also arranged audiences for Germans arriving to pay their "devotions at the shrine of Mr. Darwin".

That autumn, the botanist Asa Gray came to England with his wife for a long rest from "drudgery" at Harvard. He spent the time with Hooker at Kew, visiting the Darwins at weekends. There were many other visitors at this time, including Gray's friend Charles Eliot Norton who brought his wife and her sister Sara Sedgwick, who caught William Darwin's eye. Gray was theologically uncomfortable with the implications of *Variation*, and returned home wanting to avoid further "Darwinian discussions" or become "mixed up" with the Huxley set.Wikipedia:Citation needed

Parish affairs

Ever since moving to Downe, Darwin had supported the parish church's work and had been a friend of the Revd. John Innes since he had taken over in 1846. Darwin continued to help, though he stopped attending church after his daughter Annie died in 1851. By 1864 Innes had retired to a property he had inherited in the Scottish Highlands, changing his name to Brodie Innes and leaving the parish in the dubious hands of his curate, the Revd. Stevens, while still remaining the patron. The meagre "living" and lack of a vicarage made it hard to attract a priest of quality. Innes made Darwin treasurer of Downe village school and they continued to correspond, with Innes seeking help and advice on parish matters. The Revd. Stevens proved lax, and departed in 1867. His successors were worse, one absconding with the school's funds after Darwin mistakenly shared the treasurer's duties with him. The next was rumoured to have disgraced himself by "walking with girls at night". Darwin now became involved in helping Innes with detective work, subsequently advising him that the gossip that had reached Innes was not backed up by any reliable evidence.

Thomson and Mivart

Concerned about Thomson's calculations giving a young age for the earth, Darwin asked his mathematical son George to check the figures, disbelieving the "brevity of the world... else my views would be wrong, which is impossible – Q.E.D.". Darwin modified the 5th edition of the *Origin*, speeding up the process of variation and reviving the Lamarckian "useful inheritance" notion. In February 1869 Huxley at the Geological Society argued that '" Biology takes her time from geology...[even] if the geological clock is wrong, all the naturalist will have to do is to modify his notions of the rapidity of change accordingly".

Huxley was charged with heresy after giving a Sunday "lay sermon" in Edinburgh "on the physical basis of life". In April the "Metaphysical Society", a group of liberal churchmen of all denominations and even atheists, attempted to reach a consensus and Huxley coined a new label for his position – agnostic. Wallace was now arguing that human brains were an over-endowment created by "spiritual forces" rather than natural selection, leading Darwin to write "I differ grievously from you, and I am very sorry for it".

Mivart gained his Fellowship of the Royal Society on 3 June with Huxley's help, then surprised him by announcing that he was going to publish his objections to Darwinian views of human nature and morality. Mivart placed anonymous articles criticising natural selection in the Catholic *Month*. The Duke of Argyll published his *Primeval Man* arguing that man could not rise unaided from "utter barbarism", and that "savages" were degenerates forced out by fitter races. Argyll claimed that "Man must have had the human proportions of mind before he could afford to lose bestial proportions of body", contrasting a gorilla with an elder of the British Association, but Darwin noted that without remains of ancestors there was no evidence for this, and that man's vulnerability would have encouraged social cohesion and moral sense.

Holiday in Wales

On 10 June "his ladies" took Darwin away on holiday to Caerdon in the Barmouth valley, but he was depressed to be barely able to walk half a mile. On one walk the feminist Frances Power Cobbe caught up with him and tried to persuade him that John Stuart Mill's book *The Subjection of Women* was an ideal source for his study of man's origins and sexual selection. When Darwin, who had read Cobbe's review of Mill, answered that Mill '"could learn some things" from biology, and that the "struggle for existence" produced man's special "vigour and courage" from battling "for the possession of women", she offered him a copy of Kant on the "moral sense" to sort out his ethical problems, but he declined. He did ask his son William to read Mill and tell him

Figure 45: *Darwin sought to trump Frances Power Cobbe by writing in the Descent of Man that though women tended to be more intuitive, this was shared by less advanced peoples.*

what to think. On 16 July, Darwin started to work out a strategy to "trump" Cobbe, and wrote down his notes that men were superior to women because they had been "defending the tribe & hunting" for many generations and that Mill didn't think of sexual selection. When he returned home, Darwin added his notes to *Descent*, commenting that women seemed to show "greater tenderness and less selfishness", suggesting that this came from maternal instincts in contrast to male competitiveness. He wrote that "It is generally admitted that with woman the powers of intuition, of rapid perception, and perhaps of imitation, are more strongly marked than in man; but some, at least, of these faculties are characteristic of the lower races, and therefore of a past and lower state of civilisation." His views supported Victorian stereotypes.

In November the founding of *Nature* gave the X Club an outlet for their views. As well as Hooker and Huxley, it featured Darwin's cousin Francis Galton.

Editing and translation

Darwin continued to slog away at the *Descent of Man*, feeling "as dull as a duck". He dreaded publication, telling Mivart that "I can see that I shall meet with universal disapprobation, if not execution". As he wrote, he posted chapters to his daughter Henrietta at Cannes, for editing to ensure that damaging inferences could not be drawn. He thought he was getting rather evangelical, writing "Who would ever have thought I should turn parson!"

Emma also advised, writing that the treatment of morals and religion might be "very interesting", but she would still "dislike it very much as again putting God further off". They took a break in mid May 1870 along with Henrietta and Bessy to visit Cambridge where Horace had started and Frank was graduating with a good mathematics degree. Charles was haunted by the absence of "Dear Henslow", but on the last day met Sedgwick who was overjoyed to see him with his "dear family party". They had a long chat, with Sedgwick not mentioning the *Origin*, possibly from tact though Darwin thought his brain "enfeebled". Late in the day Sedgwick insisted on showing Charles round his new geological museum, by the end of which Darwin was "utterly prostrated". As Darwin on struggled to get to the train the next day he remarked on the humiliation of being "thus killed by a man of eighty-six, who evidently never dreamed that he was thus killing me?".

The South American Missionary Society had converted and clothed the natives of Tierra del Fuego that Darwin thought were untameable, and after Bartholomew Sulivan sent a photograph of Jemmy Button's son as evidence, Darwin made donations for several years. Darwin was proud to become an honorary member, but warned Sulivan that he would shortly publish "another book partly on man, which I dare say many will decry as very wicked".

Darwin's neighbour Lubbock had been elected Member of Parliament for Maidstone in February 1870 and Darwin lobbied him to get a question added to the census to find if married cousins had as many surviving children as unrelated parents, but when it came up in July, Lubbock's amendment caused furious debate and was heavily defeated. As the Franco-Prussian war got under way, Darwin pressed on to finish the manuscript while worrying about how it would affect his German allies. When the French surrendered at Sedan in November he wrote that "I have not met a soul in England who does not rejoice in the splendid triumph of Germany over France... It is a most just retribution against that vainglorious, war-liking nation." An "ailing and grumbling" Darwin worked on with his corrections, and the proofs were sent off on 15 January 1871 with him doubting that the book was "worth publishing". He promptly started on his next book, using left over material on emotional expressions.

Figure 46: *A caricature in The Hornet satirical magazine dated 22 March 1871 was typical of many portraying Darwin with an ape body, identifying him in popular culture as the leading author of evolutionary theory and helping to identify all forms of evolutionism with Darwinism.*

Mivart's *Genesis*

Within a week Mivart had published *On the Genesis of Species*, the cleverest and most devastating critique of natural selection in Darwin's lifetime. Mivart wrote expressing "sympathy and esteem" for Darwin, blaming "irreligious deductions" on overzealous supporters and adding "God grant that we in England may not be approaching a religious decay at all similar to that of the middle of the 18th century in France which Frenchmen are now paying for in blood & tears!" As Paris suffered under siege, Darwin sent out review copies of his book, expecting a backlash.

Just at this point parish affairs intruded. The Revd. Henry Powell had now taken over, but the two previous curates got together to sue Darwin for defamatory remarks about the first absconding with the school's cash. Darwin wrote to Brodie Innes that "being examined in court could half-kill me, but was assured that the case would never come to court."

Publication

The two 450-page volumes of *The Descent of Man, and Selection in Relation to Sex* went on sale at twenty-four shillings, with a publication date of 24 February 1871. Within three weeks a reprint had been ordered, and 4,500 copies were in print by the end of March 1871, netting Darwin almost £1,500. Darwin's name created demand for the book, but the ideas were old news. "Everybody is talking about it without being shocked" which he found "proof of the increasing liberality of England". To critics, the book was "raising a storm of mingled wrath, wonder and admiration", though they denied that "spiritual powers" had evolved from brutes in case earnest men gave up "those motives by which they have attempted to live noble and virtuous lives".

The Prussians had been defeated, but 26 March an insurrection led by socialists and republicans took over Paris and set up the Paris Commune, which was then besieged by French troops. *The Times* condemned the Communards, and accused Darwin of undermining authority and principles of morality, opening the way to "the most murderous revolutions". A "man incurs a grave responsibility when, with the authority of a well-earned reputation, he advances at such a time the disintegrating speculations of this book." Darwin was able to shrug this off as from a "windbag full of metaphysics and classics". When his Tory friend Brodie Innes taunted him that God's scheme, before being thwarted by interfering radicals, was that "Man was made a man..[split] into niggers who must be made to work [and] better men able to make them", Darwin responded that "I consider myself a good way ahead of you, as far as this goes."

He dismissed the objections raised in Wallace's review in the *Academy* as "almost stereotyped", but to his brother Erasmus Alvey Darwin the generous and polite exchanges formed a "perfectly beautiful" controversy, and thought that "In future histories of science the Wallace-Darwin episode will form one of the few bright points."

6th Edition of the *Origin*

Mivart wrote wishing "with all my heart that we did not differ so widely", but challenging Darwin to debate the basic metaphysics underlying science, from his Roman Catholic position writing that "while combatting (as duty compels me to do) positions you adopt, I am not so much combatting you as others to whose view your scientific labours give additional currency." Darwin took this personally, feeling that Mivart's *Genesis of Species* was "producing a great effect against Natural Selection, and more especially against me." After completing a rough draft of *Expressions* in April 1871 he set it aside and turned to revising the *Origin* to meet Mivart's arguments and counter the claim that some divine inner force was driving evolution. Darwin told Murray of working men in Lancashire clubbing together to buy the 5th edition at fifteen shillings, and he wanted a new cheap edition to make it more widely available.

In June Edward L. Youmans, over from the United States to seek authors for his *International Scientific Series*, told Darwin about lecturing on the *Descent of Man* to a "clerical club" in Brooklyn. Darwin burst out "What! Clergymen of different denominations all together? How they would fight if you should get them together here!" He was cheered by a damning analysis of Mivart's *Genesis of Species* by Chauncey Wright (one of Gray's students) for the *North American Review*, and thought of importing it, but Wallace thought it too heavy and obscure.

Next Mivart's anonymous *Quarterly Review* article claimed that the *Descent of Man* would unsettle "our half educated classes" and talked of people doing as they pleased, breaking laws and customs. The author was obvious to a furious Darwin who thought "I shall soon be viewed as the most despicable of men". He wrote to ask Wright for permission to reprint his article as a pamphlet, then feeling "giddy and bad" was taken by Emma to recuperate at the nearby hamlet of Albury. His head remained "rocky and wretched" and for two months he suffered giddiness and inability to work. They returned for Henrietta's marriage after a whirlwind courtship to Richard Litchfield. She departed, leaving behind her fox terrier "Polly" who now became Darwin's dog.

Murray sent out copies of Wright's pamphlet in September 1871. Only fourteen sold, but by then Huxley had already written a cutting review of Mivart's book and article. A relieved Darwin told him "How you do smash Mivart's theology... He may write his worst & he will never mortify me again". Hooker thought he surely would not be the happier for Mivart's humiliation, but an unrepentant Darwin responded that "'I am not so good a Christian as you think me, for I did enjoy my revenge".

In December Darwin completed extensive revisions of the *Origin*, using the word "evolution" for the first time and adding a new chapter to refute Mivart's guided jumps, tackling the argument of uselessness of part-evolved organs with myriad examples of gradual development or organs changing function. As 1872 began, Mivart politely inflamed the argument again, writing "wishing you very sincerely a happy new year" while wanting a disclaimer of the "fundamental intellectual errors" in the *Descent of Man*. This time Darwin ended the correspondence.

The Index

Darwin reacted positively to a tract by the American Francis Abbott proposing "the extinction of faith in the Christian Confession" and a new humanist "Free Religion" for the "spiritual perfection of the individual and the spiritual unity of the race". He subscribed to Abbott's weekly *The Index* and allowed it to print his endorsement of the tract's "truths", "I admire them from my inmost heart & I agree to almost every word".

Publication

Darwin told Haeckel "I doubt whether my strength will last for much more serious work. I shall continue to work for as long as I can, but it does not much signify when I stop, as there are so many good men fully as capable, perhaps more capable than myself, of carrying on our work; and of these you rank as the first." With "the little strength left in me" he reopened his enquiries into earthworms, requesting information from correspondents.

The 6th edition of *Origin of Species* was published by Murray on 19 February 1872 at a price kept down to 7s. 6d. by using minute print, and sales increased from 60 to 250 a month.

Emotions

Through the spring Darwin pressed on with *The Expression of the Emotions in Man and Animals*, pointing to shared evolution in contrast to Charles Bell's *Anatomy and Physiology of Expression* which claimed divinely created muscles to express man's exquisite feelings. Darwin drew on worldwide responses to his questionnaires, hundreds of photographs of actors, babies and "imbeciles" in an asylum, as well as his own observations, with particular empathy for the grief following a family death. The proofs, tackled by Henrietta and Leo, needed major revision which made him "sick of the subject, and myself, and the world". It was to be one of the first books with photographs, with seven heliotype plates, and Murray warned that this "would poke a terrible hole in the profits".

In May 1872 Darwin became a foreign member of the Royal Netherlands Academy of Arts and Sciences.

Wallace wrote in August, enthusing about H. Charlton Bastian's *The Beginnings of Life* claiming the spontaneous generation of life, but Darwin told him that "I have taken up old botanical work, and have given up all theories". By the end of September he was again near collapse, but Emma arranged three weeks away to rest, which worked well though he was still "growing old and weak".

Hooker's collections at Kew were threatened with government cuts under Acton Smee Ayrton. The X Club petitioned Gladstone. When Richard Owen was found to be involved, possibly trying to bring Kew under his British Museum, Darwin commented that "I used to be ashamed of hating him so much, but now I will carefully cherish my hatred & contempt to the last days of my life". In October Hooker sent sun-dews and Venus fly-traps for Darwin's experiments, then was devastated when his bedridden mother died. In his hot-house Darwin experimented, giving such plants from around the world a variety of foods and poisons, and began writing *insectivorous Plants*.

The Expression of the Emotions in Man and Animals proved very popular, selling over 5,000 copies, but an exhausted Darwin became a "confirmed invalid" and at his brother Eramus's over Christmas 1872 sat drawing up his will.

New edition of *The Descent of Man*

Darwin recovered and pressed on with several projects. He subsequently tackled a new edition of the *Descent of Man*, incorporating ideas from Galton and new anecdotes. The manuscript was completed in April 1874, and the new edition was published on 13 November.

Darwin continued his work following this period.

References

- Darwin, Charles (1871). *The Descent of Man, and Selection in Relation to Sex*[297] (1st ed.). London: John Murray. ISBN 0-8014-2085-7. Retrieved 18 June 2009.<templatestyles src="Module:Citation/CS1/styles.css"></templatestyles>
- Desmond, Adrian; Moore, James (1991), *Darwin*, London: Michael Joseph, Penguin Group, ISBN 0-7181-3430-3<templatestyles src="Module:Citation/CS1/styles.css"></templatestyles>
- James Moore and Adrian Desmond, "Introduction", in *The Descent of Man, and Selection in Relation to Sex*, 2nd edn. (London: Penguin Classics, 2004). <templatestyles src="Module:Citation/CS1/styles.css" />ISBN 978-0-14-043631-0
- Janet Browne, *Charles Darwin: The Power of Place* (Alfred A. Knopf, 2002). <templatestyles src="Module:Citation/CS1/styles.css" />ISBN 0-679-42932-8

Further reading

- The Complete Works of Charles Darwin Online – Darwin Online[298]; Darwin's publications, private papers and bibliography, supplementary works including biographies, obituaries and reviews. Free to use, includes items not in public domain.
- Works by Charles Darwin[299] at Project Gutenberg; public domain
- Darwin Correspondence Project[300] Text and notes for most of his letters

Darwin from Insectivorous Plants to Worms

Darwin from Insectivorous Plants to Worms

Between 1873 and 1882, the life and work of Charles **Darwin from *Insectivorous Plants* to *Worms*** continued with investigations into carnivorous and climbing plants that had begun with his previous work. Worries about family illnesses contributed to his interest in Galton's ideas of "hereditary improvement" (which would later be called Eugenics). He continued to help with the work of Downe parish church and associated village amenities, despite problems with control being seized by a new High Church vicar, and he remained on good terms with the Church's patron, the Revd. John Brodie Innes. There was continuing interest in Charles Darwin's views on religion, but he remained reticent.

Despite repeated problems and delays caused by Charles Darwin's illness, his work on evolution-related experiments and investigations continued, with the production of books on the movement of climbing plants, insectivorous plants, the effects of cross and self fertilisation of plants, different forms of flowers on plants of the same species, and *The Power of Movement in Plants*. His ideas on evolution were increasingly accepted in scientific circles despite some bitter disputes, and he received numerous honours. As well as writing out his own autobiography for his family, he wrote an introduction to a biography of his grandfather Erasmus Darwin. In his last book, he returned to the effect earthworms have on soil formation.

He died in Downe, Kent, England, on 19 April 1882. He had expected to be buried in St Mary's churchyard at Downe, but at the request of Darwin's colleagues, William Spottiswoode (President of the Royal Society) arranged for Darwin to be given a major ceremonial funeral and buried in Westminster Abbey, close to John Herschel and Isaac Newton.

Background

In the aftermath of the publication of *On the Origin of Species through Natural Selection* in 1859, Charles Darwin's allies Charles Lyell, Joseph Dalton Hooker, Thomas Huxley, Alfred Russel Wallace and Asa Gray in America worked to spread acceptance of its ideas despite difficulty in coming to terms with natural selection and man's descent from animals.

Darwin's research and experiments on plants and animals continued, and his extensive writings countered the arguments against evolution, particularly those put by the Duke of Argyll and St George Mivart.

Family matters, eugenics

Darwin's sons George and Horace were ill and arrived home at Christmas 1872 for nursing. Darwin turned from his insectivorous plants to a more leisurely update of his monograph on climbing plants.

He was intrigued by Galton's latest "hereditary improvement" ideas (which would be called Eugenics after 1883), proposing that society should breed out mental and physical disability and improve the nation's stock by introducing "a sentiment of caste among those who are naturally gifted". Families would be registered and incentives offered so that the best children chosen from each "superior family" would marry and reproduce. Darwin, aware that of his brood only William had good health, had already dismissed the aims as too "utopian" in *the Descent of Man*. He thought these new proposals impractical if voluntary and politically horrifying if enforced by compulsory registration, even were they the "sole feasible" way of "improving the human race". He felt it better simply to publicise the "all-important principle of inheritance" and let people pursue the "grand" objective for themselves. In any case it was too late for his own infirm offspring.

Huxley was also ill, needing a rest and harried by a neighbour suing over a damp basement. The X Club (a dining club formed in November 1864 to support the evolutionary "new reformation" in naturalism, including Huxley, Hooker, John Tyndall, Busk, Spencer, and Spottiswoode) raised a £2,000 collection for him, primed by Darwin with £300. Darwin's spirits were again downcast when Lyell's wife died.

In June 1873 Darwin resumed work on his insectivorous plants, with some distractions as his wife Emma took care of the seven Huxley children while Huxley and Hooker went on holiday to the continent. Having young children in the house was like the 1850s again.

Parish conflict

A new reforming High Church vicar, the Revd. George Sketchley Ffinden, had been imposing his ideas since taking over the parish in November 1871. Darwin had to write to the patron, John Brodie Innes, explaining what had upset the parishioners. Ffinden now usurped control of the village school which had been run for years by a committee of Darwin, Lubbock and the incumbent priest, with a "conscience clause" which protected the children from Anglican indoctrination. Ffinden began lessons on the *Thirty-nine Articles of the Anglican faith*, an unwelcome move from the point of view of the Baptists in the village. Darwin withdrew from the committee and cut his annual donation to the church, but continued with the Friendly Society work.

Hensleigh Wedgwood's daughter Effie had married Thomas "Theta" Farrer in May, and on 5 August 1873 the Darwins went to visit them for a few days. They arrived to hear that a fortnight previously the Farrer's servants had been called to an accident. Earl Granville's riding companion Samuel Wilberforce had been killed in a fall from his horse, and was subsequently laid out in state for two days in the Farrer's drawing room. Although an opponent of the *Origin*, Wilberforce had always thought Darwin a "capital fellow".

Pause

At home, a heated discussion with Hooker ended with Darwin lying in bed with his memory gone and "a severe shock continually passing through my brain". Emma feared an epileptic fit, but the doctor put him on a diet and in September he returned to work on insectivorous plants. His correspondence continued, funding worthy projects and acknowledging countless gifts including *Das Kapital* from "a sincere admirer", Karl Marx, which Darwin had difficulty in following, but hoped that both their efforts towards "the extension of knowledge... [would] add to the happiness of mankind".

Frank struggled with his medical studies, and after finishing his thesis on animal tissues he was to assist with plant tissues at Downe. George's legal career had been ended by stomach illness and he had spent two years going to spas. He began writing topical essays, the first in the *Contemporary Review* on Galton. His latest essay boldly dismissed prayer, divine morals and "future rewards & punishments". Darwin urged him not to publish it for some months, and "to pause, pause, pause."

Fiske

During a visit in November 1873 the Harvard philosopher John Fiske amused the X Club with his story of a cockney in New York warning him "What, that 'orrid hold hinfidel 'Uxley? Why, we don't think hanythink of 'im in Hingland! We think 'e's 'orrid!", himself writing that "I am quite wild over Huxley... what a pleasure to meet such a clean-cut mind! It is like Saladin's sword which cut through the cushion." and "Old Darwin is the dearest, sweetest, loveliest old grandpa that ever was. And on the whole he impresses me with his strength more than any man I have seen yet. There is a charming kind of quiet strength about him and about everything he does. He isn't burning and eager like Huxley. He has a mild blue eye, and is the gentlest of gentle old fellows. [His] long white hair and enormous white beard [made him] very picturesque... guileless simplicity... I am afraid I shall never see him again, for his health is very bad. Of all my days in England I prize today the most."

New edition of *The Descent of Man*

Darwin tackled a new edition of the *Descent of Man*, and offered the self-financing Wallace the work of assisting him. Wallace quoted seven shillings an hour, mentioning that he was "dipping into politics" proposing nationalisation of coal mining. Emma found out and had the task given to their son George, so Darwin had to write apologetically to Wallace, adding "I hope to Heaven that politics will not replace natural science."

Parish reading room

For two years, Emma had organised a winter reading room in the local school for local labourers, who subscribed a penny a week to smoke and play games, with "Respectable newspapers & a few books... & a respectable housekeeper..there every evening to maintain decorum." This was a common facility to save men from "resorting to the public house". In 1873 the Revd. Ffinden opposed it, as "Coffee drinking, bagatelle & other games" had been allowed and "the effects of tobacco smoke & spitting" were seen when the children returned in the morning. Emma got Darwin to get the approval of the education inspectorate in London, and just before Christmas 1873 the Darwins and Lubbocks got the agreement of the school committee, offering to pay for any repairs needed "to afford every possible opportunity to the working class for self improvement & amusement". A furious Ffinden huffed that it was "quite out of order" for the Darwins to have gone to the inspectorate behind his back. In the autumn of 1874 Darwin let off steam at Ffinden and formally resigned from the school committee on health grounds.

Spiritualism

Francis Galton was attracted to the recent spiritualism movement. On a visit to London in January 1874 Darwin attended a séance at Erasmus's house with relatives including Hensleigh Wedgwood, as well as Huxley. George had hired the medium Charles Williams, and they sat round the table in the dark, but as the room grew stuffy Darwin went upstairs to lie down, missing the show, with sparks, sounds and the table rising above their heads. While Galton thought it a "good séance", Darwin later wrote "The Lord have mercy on us all, if we have to believe such rubbish" and told Emma that it was "all imposture" and "it would take an enormous weight of evidence" to convince him otherwise. At a second séance Huxley and George found that Williams was nothing but a cheat, to Darwin's relief. Emma told Hensleigh's daughter Snow that Charles "won't believe it, he dislikes the thought of it so much". Snow remembered that her uncle "used to look upon it as a great weakness if one allowed wish to influence belief" and when Emma said that "he does not always act up to his principles" Snow thought that was "what one means by bigotry", to which Emma said "Oh yes, he is a regular bigot".

New edition of *Descent*

Darwin continued painfully rewriting his books with the help of Henrietta and George, incorporating ideas from Galton and new anecdotes. He bought from Lubbock the Sandwalk he had been renting for years, but the price seemed excessive and affected their friendship. News of a dispute involving the removal of George Bentham from presidency of the Linnean Society, allegedly spurred on by Owen, led Darwin to write "What a demon on earth Owen is. I do hate him". With Huxley's assistance he updated the *Descent* on ape-brain inheritance, which Huxley thought "pounds the enemy into a jelly... though none but anatomists" would know it.

The manuscript was completed in April 1874, and the publisher John Murray planned a 12 shilling half-price edition to replicate the success of the cheap revision of the *Origin*. Darwin left the proofs to George, and turned again to Plants. The new edition was published on 13 November with the price cut to the bone at 9 shillings.

Insectivorous plants

During 1874 Darwin contacted many of his old friends to assist with experimentation on insectivorous or carnivorous plants. Helpers included Hooker and his assistant William Thiselton-Dyer at Kew, John Burdon-Sanderson at University College London running lab tests on the plant's digestion, and Asa

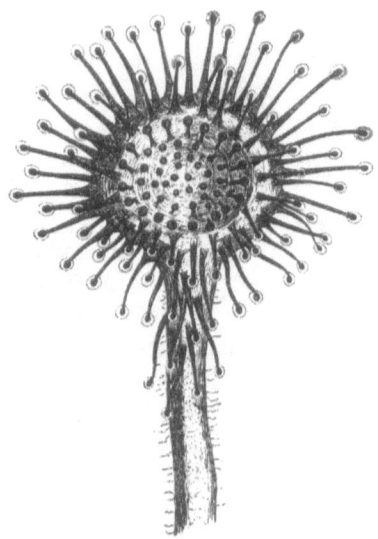

Figure 47: *Figure 1 from Insectivorous Plants.*

Gray at Harvard. Enquiries to *Nature* magazine brought in sacks of mail to be dealt with by Frank, who settled into Brodie Innes's old house in the village and married Amy Ruck on 23 July. At this time the family was joined by George Romanes who had been a student with Frank at Cambridge. Plants experimented on were members of the genera *Drosera* and *Pinguicula*, including *D. rotundifolia* and *P. vulgaris*.

Controversy with Mivart

As well as working on the proofs, George Darwin made a statistical analysis of first cousin marriages (three times more frequent in "our rank" than in the lower) and, influenced by Galton, published an article on "beneficial restrictions in marriage". Mivart attacked this anonymously in the *Quarterly Review*, misinterpreting advocacy of divorce in cases of criminality or advice as " the most oppressive laws, and the encouragement of vice in order to check population", talking of "hideous sexual criminality". A furious Darwin told George to take legal advice while he contacted the publisher of his books and the *Quarterly*, John Murray, threatening to "take his business elsewhere".

Darwin's holiday at Southampton with William was overshadowed as he drafted George's response. John Tyndall's address to the British Association later that month laid claim to "wrest from theology the entire domain of cosmological theory" and led to calls for his prosecution for blasphemy. Lyell, now nearly blind and in deteriorating health, wrote to Darwin applauding the boost to "you and your theory of evolution" despite his qualms about the hereafter. Darwin was sympathetic, but did "not feel any innate conviction" of life after death. The October issue of the *Quarterly* carried George's response and an "apology" from Mivart which still maintained "that the doctrines... are most dangerous and pernicious" and infuriated Darwin.

On 13 November Hooker's wife Fanny died suddenly, and a devastated Hooker felt unable to return home after the funeral and brought his family to Downe. Emma looked after the children, and when Hooker returned to Kew, Darwin urged "hard work" to overcome his "utter desolation". Later, Darwin mentioned the Mivart argument and Hooker rallied the X Club (a dining club formed in November 1864 to support the evolutionary "new reformation" in naturalism, including Huxley, Hooker, John Tyndall, Busk, Spencer, and Spottiswoode). Huxley eagerly used a review to attack "anonymous slander", telling Darwin that he "ought to be like one of the blessed gods of Elysium, and let the inferior deities do battle with the infernal powers." Mivart confidentially pleaded to make amends, but Huxley told Darwin that the "most effectual punishment" was to "give him the cold shoulder". Darwin was itching to speak his mind, and when no apology had come by 12 January 1875 he wrote vowing never to communicate with Mivart again.

Insectivorous Plants, parish and vivisection

Darwin struggled on, by February 1875 telling George that "I know full well the feeling of life being objectless & all being vanity of vanities", and Hooker that he was even "ready to commit suicide". The death of Lyell on 22 February had him feeling "as if we were all soon to go". Their friendship had cooled after Lyell declined to back natural selection, and Darwin pleaded illness rather than take part as a pall-bearer at the funeral in Westminster Abbey. In March Darwin took the proofs of *Insectivorous Plants* to Murray.

For a year the vicar had refused to speak to any of the Darwins, and when two evening lectures were proposed for the village, Lubbock had to act as an intermediary in requesting use of the schoolroom. The committee agreed, but Ffinden refused to co-operate, writing that "I had long been aware of the harmful tendencies to revealed religion of Mr. Darwin's views, but.. I had fully determined.. not to let my difference of opinion interfere with a friendly feeling as neighbours, trusting that God's grace might in time bring one so highly gifted intellectually and morally to a better mind." Darwin was equally haughty in return, condescending that "If Mr. F bows to Mrs D. and myself, we will return it". He found that dealing with Mivart and Ffinden was increasing his private hostility to Christianity.

Darwin's daughter Henrietta at first supported a petition drawn up by Frances Power Cobbe demanding anti-vivisection legislation. Though Darwin was an animal lover and had never carried out vivisection, he persuaded her that "Physiology can only progress by experiments on living animals". During his spring break in London he took the matter up with his contacts, at first thinking of a counter-petition, then on Huxley's advice seeking support lobbying for a pre-emptive bill to provide for regulated vivisection with what he called a "more humanitarian aspect". The hint to the fox-hunting houses of parliament that a ban could lead to further restrictions helped, and though Cobbe's bill reached the House of Lords on 4 May 1875 a week before the scientist's bill reached the House of Commons, the Home Secretary announced a Royal Commission of inquiry to resolve the arguments, with Huxley co-opted on to the Commission.

The demand for Darwin as an author was shown when *Insectivorous Plants*, a 450-page catalogue of plant experiments, sold out quickly and in July a 1,000 copy reprint sold out within a fortnight.

Variation revised

Now Darwin turned to work on a new edition of *The Variation of Animals and Plants under Domestication* incorporating additions from the hundreds of letters and scores of monographs that had been sent to Darwin in the seven years since it had been published. Parts were altered or discarded, and George Romanes set aside work on jellyfish to graft vegetable plants in experiments aimed at finding out about the "gemmules" which Darwin thought formed the mechanism of inheritance of characteristics. Investigations into "pangenesis" by Galton had tried blood transfusions between different breeds of rabbits without success. Darwin continued to look for proof of inheritance of acquired characteristics, amassing evidence of blacksmith's children being muscular and babies born with scars matching those of their parents. He would not follow Huxley in discarding these ideas, and *Descent* had presented such inheritance as a significant factor in human evolution.

Darwin had long been concerned that his children could have inherited his weaknesses. He was proud that Frank seemed to have inherited his interest in natural history, coming to Down House from the village to carry out plant experiments, and put his son up for a Fellowship of the Linnean Society.

Cross and Self Fertilisation

With *Variation* at the printers and with his old essay on *The Movements and Habits of Climbing Plants* due out in November 1875 with "illustrations... drawn by my son, George", Darwin wrote *The Effects of Cross and Self Fertilisation in the Vegetable Kingdom*. This drew on a painstaking series of experiments, protecting the plants from insects and controlling the pollination of flowers, counting the seeds and checking them for fertility, repeated for up to ten generations with detailed records kept at every stage.

Darwin tabulated the results, Galton checked his statistics, and they found the crossed plants significantly superior to self-fertilised ones in height, weight, vigour and fertility. The same principle would apply to people, and though the attempt to get a question on the census had failed, George analysed data from lunatic asylums and the *Pall Mall Gazette* which Darwin cited as showing a small effect produced by first-cousin marriages.

While Emma ensured that he took short breaks, Darwin pressed on with work as "my sole pleasure in life" and finished the first draft of *Fertilisation* in May 1876, promptly going on to a revision of *Orchids*.

Recollections

They visited Hensleigh and Fanny to celebrate the announcement that Frank's wife Amy was five months pregnant, and Charles and Emma would shortly become grandparents. Darwin decided to leave a posthumous memoir for his family, and on Sunday 28 May 1876 he began *Recollections of the Development of my mind and character*. He found this candid private memoir easy going, covering his childhood, university, life on the Beagle and developing work in science. A section headed "Religious Belief" opened just before his marriage, and frankly discussed his long disagreement with Emma. (*see Charles Darwin's views on religion*) He recalled Annie and thought of how, but for her untimely death, she would now "have grown into a delightful woman... Tears still come into my eyes, when I think of her sweet ways". He completed his memoir on 3 August, concluding that after his book on fertilisation was published, "my strength... will probably be exhausted".

On 7 September the baby, named Bernard, was born at Down House, but his mother suffered a fever and convulsions, and died four days later at the age of 26. Darwin thought it the "most dreadful thing", and Frank in a state of shock and grief moved into Down House with the baby. The contractors were brought in to extend the house for him, and Frank carried on with mechanical chores for his father, making a fair copy of the memoir and correcting proofs of *Orchids*.

Liberalism

Despite Ffinden's continuing opposition, Emma's project of a parish reading room for labourers was restarted and opened before Christmas. Darwin saw *Orchids* and *Cross and Self Fertilisation* published as he wrote his next book on flowers. In February 1877 he attended the *George and Dragon* in his position as treasurer and persuaded the village labourers, who were suffering from wage cuts and a threat to their jobs in a farm slump, not to disband the *Friendly Society* and take the proceeds, but to keep some protection for their longer term security by keeping the books open while distributing their surplus funds. His old Whig principles fitted well with the *Self-Help* philosophy of another Murray author, Samuel Smiles, who had impressed Darwin.

As a "thorough Liberal", Darwin supported Gladstone, the "Grand Old Man" of British politics. Three months earlier Darwin had backed the outcry against the "Bulgarian horrors" when 15,000 (Christian) Bulgarian rebels were massacred by Muslim "Turkish" troops of the Ottoman Empire, and supported Gladstone's calls for Russian intervention in opposition to the Tory government's support for the Turks. Marx thought this a hypocritical preference for a Christian oppressor, and complained about Darwin's support for the "piggish demonstration". On 10 March Gladstone, while doing the rounds of his backbenchers and visiting Lubbock, turned up with his entourage at Down House and for two hours regaled a silent Darwin with comments from his latest pamphlet on "Turkish terrorism", and "launched forth his thunderbolts with unexhausted zest". Before leaving he asked Darwin if evolution meant that the future belonged to America as the Eastern civilisations decayed; after thinking it over, Darwin responded "Yes." Watching Gladstone's "erect alert figure" walking away, he said "What an honour that such a great man should come to visit me!"

A fortnight after Gladstone's visit, the leading secularist, militant atheist and unofficial Liberal candidate Charles Bradlaugh with co-publisher Annie Besant caused public outrage by publishing do-it-yourself contraceptive advice from an American doctor, Charles Knowlton, in a sixpenny pamphlet *Fruits of Philosophy*.[301] Bradlaugh and Besant were accused of obscenity and committed for trial on 18 June 1877. A fortnight beforehand they subpoenaed Darwin for their defence, expecting his support. Appalled, he wrote protesting the "great suffering" this would put him to, and advised that he would have to denounce the defendants as he had "long held an opposite opinion" on birth control, as evidenced by an extract from the *Descent of Man* stating that "our natural rate of increase, though leading to many and obvious evils, must not be greatly diminished by any means." The practice of contraception would "spread to unmarried women & would destroy chastity on which the family bond depends; & the weakening of this bond would be the greatest of all evils to mankind."

Holidays

The subpoena was dropped, and Darwin was not held back from holidaying at Leith Hill and Southampton for his much needed "rest" which, as usual, meant working furiously away from home. He visited Stonehenge for the first time, examining how worm castings had buried the megaliths over time. Emma feared that the day-trip involving two hours train journey and a 24-mile drive would "half kill" him, but he was in wonderful form even after digging in the hot sun.

In mid July 1877 his work on the sex life of plants culminated in the publication of *The Different Forms of Flowers on Plants of the Same Species*, dedicated to Asa Gray. He could not "endure being idle" and turned to his next book, on plant movement. Emma got him away for his autumn break to Abinger on the North Downs, and though Wallace now lived only a few miles away, Darwin avoided him, diplomatically writing that he "wished to come over to see you, but driving tires me so much that my courage failed."

Honorary Doctorate

The University of Cambridge had come round to Darwinism, and on Saturday 17 November the family attended the Senate House for a ceremony in which Darwin was awarded an honorary Doctorate of Laws in front of crowds of students, who strung a cord across the chamber with a monkey-marionette which was removed by a Proctor then replaced by a "missing link", a beribboned ring which hung over the crowd through the ceremony.

Darwin entered to a roar of approval. The Public Orator gave his panegyric describing Darwin's work with purple Latin prose, to some good humoured heckling from the students, and distanced the dignitaries from "the unlovely tribe of apes" saying "'Mores in utroques dispares' – the moral nature of the two races is different".

Emma had a headache, so she and Darwin let their boys to stand in for them at a dinner in his honour at which Huxley chided the university for failing to honour Darwin twenty years earlier. On the Sunday, after a "brilliant luncheon" with George at Trinity College, they were given guided tours. The engineering professor James Stuart showed Emma and Darwin round his workshop and later wrote of "A strong.. looking man with iron grey hair..[as though] rough hewn from a rock with a heavy..hammer,... A man of genius.. indeed one of 'the few'."

Romanes

Into the spring of 1878 Darwin and Frank again filled the house with experiments on the movement of plants. To Frank it was "as if an outside force were compelling him", and in March the strain brought back his old sickness of attacks of dizziness. Dr. Clark in London prescribed a "dry diet" which helped, and refused to charge his patient so Darwin sent £100 towards the development of a fungus-proof potato by a "highly respectable" Belfast breeder. He also responded to an appeal asking the HMS Beagle's officers for help in supporting an orphan – the grandson of Jemmy Button.

George Romanes had become Darwin's leading protégé, but a conflict between his reasoned scepticism and earlier longing for faith came to a head when his sister died. His attempt to get solace from a leading spiritualist came to nothing. Darwin invited Romanes to Downe to help him recover. Romanes had earlier written a refutation of theism, and had taken Darwin's advice to pause, but now wanted to publish. Darwin counselled anonymity, and suggested study of the evolution of religious reasoning, giving him unused notes on instinct from his work on *Natural Selection*. Romanes launched on the study of comparative psychology, and in August was given a standing ovation for his talk at the British Association. In November the Darwins were staying with the Litchfields, and Romanes drove there to introduce his fiancé and present his new book, *A Candid Examination of Theism* by "Physicus". Darwin read it with "very great interest", but was unconvinced.

Biography of Erasmus Darwin

The German scientific periodical *Kosmos* featured, as a 70th birthday tribute to Charles Darwin, an essay by Ernst Krause on his grandfather Erasmus Darwin. In March 1879 he arranged for it to be translated as a book to which he would add a biographical preface. This would counter Samuel Butler's *Evolution Old and New* in which the previously supportive, though unscientific, author of *Erewhon* had turned against Darwinism, and he sent a copy of it to Krause. In the summer he became bogged down with the proofs of his preface about Erasmus, and Henrietta edited out controversial points. The publisher John Murray was satisfied, but Darwin vowed "never again" to be "tempted out of my proper work".

Abominable mystery

The origin and swift diversification of flowering plants in the Early Cretaceous appeared to go against Darwin's view of gradual evolution, and in a July 1879 letter to Joseph Dalton Hooker he called this an "abominable mystery". He sought explanations such as a long earlier development having taken place in an area where the fossil record had been lost, possibly a sunken continent, or relatively rapid development having been spurred by coevolution between insects and plants.

Although he tired more quickly now, Darwin still worked for several hours a day. Emma ensured he took holidays, in autumn 1879 joining the Litchfields for a month in the Lake District where he met with John Ruskin, though this was not a meeting of minds. On return the Darwins were visited by Ernst Haeckel whose "roaring" about the freedom of science had Darwin retreating to his plants.

Darwin unsuccessfully tried to get government support for the Belfast potato breeder from the Permanent Secretary, Thomas "Theta" Farrer (Effie Wedgwood's husband). Farrer was more concerned that his daughter by his first marriage wanted to marry the unsuitable sickly Horace Darwin. Despite her father's opposition the young couple prevailed, with Darwin giving his son £5,000 of railway stock and assuring Farrer that Horace would have a suitable inheritance. The wedding took place on 3 January 1880, with the families not on speaking terms.

Samuel Butler

In *Evolution Old and New* Samuel Butler claimed that earlier evolutionists had correctly seen the mind as controlling evolution, and Mivart told Richard Owen that he thought the book would "help to burst the bubble of 'Natural Selection'." Ernst Krause's *Erasmus Darwin* countered this, and Butler took affront at Darwin's preface which said that Krause's essay predated Butler's book, when it clearly had passages written later. Darwin had to admit that Krause had revised his essay, and spent a week in February 1880 drafting responses, then was persuaded to ignore the dispute, writing to Huxley "I feel like a man condemned to be hung who has just got a reprieve". Butler took the silence as a tacit admission of guilt.

Coming of Age

Huxley titled his Royal Institution talk *The Coming of Age of the Origin of Species*, celebrating its 21st anniversary, though wrongly claiming that before its publication only catastrophism was accepted. While Darwin (on holiday with the Farrers, now on good terms) was delighted by the press coverage, he was disappointed to find no mention in its text of natural selection – even "Darwin's Bulldog" was still not committed to the central plank of his theory.

In April, Gladstone defeated the Tories at the general election, delighting Charles and Emma Darwin though not all their relatives, and a buoyant Charles

Figure 48: *Darwin as photographed by Elliott & Fry at Down House, 1879*

sent a large subscription to Abbot's *The Index* with hearty wishes for success in the "good cause of truth" and 'free religion'. The Liberal success even got the militant atheist Charles Bradlaugh elected as MP for Northampton, and public controversy about atheism erupted. He was prevented from taking his seat in the House of Commons by procedural requirements of the oath of allegiance, and secularists such as Edward Aveling toured the country leading protests. Aveling had been writing a series on *Darwin and his Works* in Bradlaugh's paper *The National Reformer*, and Darwin had sent written thanks which he now feared would be published to his shame.

In June, after sending *Movement in Plants* to his publisher John Murray, Darwin visited William and Sarah at Southampton, and he got William to write to Abbot withdrawing the endorsement that had been printed as advertising copy in the magazine: even association with free thought in distant America could damage his respectability.

Worms

Darwin again took up his work on worms. As ever, he corresponded widely, encouraging and helping fund research and collecting anecdotes. Emma supported his commitment, saying that "if it was a condition of his living, that he sh[oul]d do now work, she was willing for him to die". For their autumn break they visited Horace and Ida in Cambridge, and to spare him the stress of getting between London stations and changing trains Emma arranged a private railway carriage. At Cambridge he showed Emma around the "scenes of my early life".

In September 1880 he completed the proofs of *Movement in Plants*, his largest botany book at 600 pages with 196 wood-cuts, sighing "I am turned into a sort of machine for observing facts & grinding out conclusions." When on 13 October he got the request he had feared from Aveling, for permission to dedicate the *Darwin and his Works* articles to Darwin in book format, he declined in a four-page letter marked PRIVATE emphasising that he confined his writing to science and avoided aiding attacks on religion.

Attacks on Darwin's theory continued, and when the official report of a scientific voyage slighted "the theory which refers the evolution of species to extreme variation guided only by natural selection" he responded in *Nature*, "Can Sir Wyville Thomson name any one who has said that the evolution of species depends only on natural selection?" and set out multiple causes, including "use and disuse of parts". He called Thomson's criticism appropriate to "theologians and metaphysicians", and was only stopped by Huxley from using "irreverent language".

Help for Wallace

Wallace was suffering "ever-increasing anxiety" over funds, and Arabella Buckley, Lyell's old secretary, pleaded with Darwin to help him find "some modest work". Hooker persuaded Darwin it was hopeless, noting that Wallace had "lost caste" over spiritualism and a £500 bet he had won by proving the world was a globe to a rich flat-earth fanatic who then started litigation which cost Wallace more than the bet had won. When Wallace's "best book" to date, *Island Life*, came out in November 1880 Darwin devoted all his attention to getting his friends to sign a testimonial he wrote, then rushed it to Gladstone before the re-opening of Parliament at the start of January and was overjoyed when Gladstone agreed to recommend a civil list pension of £200 a year, backdated six months. As Darwin passed on the good news to Wallace, Emma organised the family accounts so that Charles could distribute the surplus from the year's £8,000 investment income to the children.

Work on worms

Downe was snowed in, and an outbreak of swine fever involved Darwin as magistrate signing orders daily to allow movement of stock. He wrote to Kovalevsky "I make sure, but wo[e]fully slow progress, with my new book" on worms. In late February he visited London, and called on Duke of Argyll, his old opponent. They had a long and "awfully friendly" discussion, and when Argyll asked if it was not "impossible to look at [the design of orchids] without seeing that they were the effect and the expression of Mind?", Darwin looked at him "very hard" before replying that he could see the "overwhelming force" this argument might have, but he could no longer accept it.

The billiard room at Down House was now devoted to worm experiments which included Darwin shining different colours of lights at them at night, his sons playing different musical instruments to them, different scents and kinds of food. Other stimuli were ignored, but a bright white light or a touch of breath would make them bolt "like rabbits" into their burrows. They appeared to "enjoy the pleasure of eating" showing "eagerness for certain kinds of food", sexual passion was "strong enough to overcome... their dread of light", and he saw "a trace of social feeling" in their way of "crawling over each other's bodies". Experiments showed that they dragged leaves into their burrows narrow end first, having somehow got a "notion, however rude, of the shape of an object", maybe by "touching it in many places" with a sense like "a man... born blind and deaf" and a rudimentary intelligence.

By mid march he was writing the final chapters of what he told Victor Carus would be "a small book of little moment. I have little strength & feel very old." He wrote to *The Times* about the anti-vivisection cause, accusing it of committing "a crime against humanity" by holding back the "progress of physiology", then commented that we "ought to be grateful" to worms, which reached a depth of "five or six feet" even "here at Down" where he expected to be buried shortly.

No heart or strength

Before Easter he sent off his manuscript for *The Formation of Vegetable Mould through the Action of Worms*, and found he had no "heart or strength... to begin any investigation lasting for years". "Never happy except when at work", he was at a loose end until he remembered his autobiography. On 22 April 1881, exactly 30 years after Annie's burial, he re-read the passages about her and Emma's letter of that time, and added a note under his daguerreotype of Annie, "When I am dead, know that many times, I have kissed & cryed over this." [sic].

He left the proofs of *Worms* to Frank and, despondent, turned down Gladstone's invitation to become a Trustee of the British Museum. Early in June 1881 Emma and the Litchfields took him to the Lake District, together with William and young Bernard. The sky was "like lead" and an attempt at climbing brought spots before his eyes and a doctor's diagnosis that his heart condition was "precarious". He wrote to Hooker that "Illness is downright misery to me... I cannot forget my discomfort for an hour [and] must look forward to Down graveyard as the sweetest place on earth."

The Creed of Science

Then he was perked up by the 400-page *The Creed of Science* by the Irish philosopher William Graham arguing the validity of traditional beliefs in the face of materialism. Darwin wrote to Graham expressing doubts about the conclusions – "The chief one is that the existence of so-called natural laws implies purpose. I cannot see this." He was swayed by one – "You have expressed my inward conviction.. that the Universe is not the result of chance", but then qualified this by his "horrid doubt" that such beliefs might have arisen as the human mind evolved, and were no more to be trusted than "the convictions of a monkey's mind, if there are any convictions in such a mind". He still supported natural selection as the engine of social progress, pointing out that "The more civilised so-called Caucasian races have beaten the Turkish hollow in the struggle for existence" and telling Graham that elimination of "lower races" by "higher civilised races" was inevitable in the progress of Malthusian struggle.

Back at Downe, a letter from Wallace promoted the socialist ideas of Henry George's *Progress and Poverty* proposing to "make land common property" as morally just. The landowner Darwin responded that such books had "a disastrous effect" on his mind, he hoped that Wallace would not "turn renegade to natural history" while adding that "I have everything to make me happy and contented".

Pleasant memories

To Hooker he wrote of "Pleasant memories of long past days... many a discussion and... a good fight". Hooker valued their arguments "as iron sharpeneth iron" and, longing to "throw off the trammels of official life" and retire from Kew, found it "difficult to resist the pessimist view of creation", but "when I look back... to the days I have spent in intercourse with you and yours, that view takes wings to itself and flies away." That summer Darwin was in his "happiest spirits", chatting "deliciously" for hours and in the evenings asking for Bach and Handel to be played repeatedly. Romanes, visiting with his wife and baby, thought the old man as "grand and good and bright as ever".

Darwin stayed with Erasmus while his portrait was painted by John Collier and on 3 August dined by special invitation with the Prince of Wales, the Crown Prince of Germany and eminent physicians at the start of the Seventh International Medical Congress. Later, Erasmus became gravely ill and died on 26 August, and at the funeral at Downe on 1 September Charles, looking "old and ill", was a picture of "sad reverie". Subsequently Darwin inherited half Erasmus's estate. William announced that this made Darwin's wealth over a quarter of a million pounds, "*without* mother's fortune", and Darwin redrafted his will. He sent a note to his sister Caroline about her half of Erasmus's estate, enclosing a miniature of their mother and commenting that he could not remember her face, though he did recall her "black velvet gown" and the "death scene".

A requested visit from the eminent but atheist German Doctor Ludwig Büchner in company with the notorious Edward Aveling went amiably on Thursday 28 September with Darwin introducing his old friend the Revd. Brodie Innes, and defending agnosticism *(see Charles Darwin's views on religion)*.

Worms was published in October 1881 and within weeks thousands had been sold. It brought a flood of letters, with many "idiotic" enquiries, and a "worn out" Darwin escaped with Emma to visit Horace and Ida in Cambridge.

Roots and illness

Darwin, "quite set up", returned to his experiments on plant roots standing in an ammonia solution, preparing sections and looking for "physiological division of labour" through his microscope.

In London he made an unannounced visit to the house of Romanes on 15 December. Romanes was absent, and Darwin declined the concerned butler's invitation to come in. He crossed the street, stumbled and clutched the railings before getting a cab. The next morning Dr. Clark pronounced him fine, but Emma kept him indoors and he was visited by eminent scientists. He seemed bright and animated, but told the geologist John Judd that he had "received his warning".

Once home, this did not hold him back from working hard at his root cells, as well as still doing his walks round the Sandwalk, receiving visitors and dealing with letters. In one he argued with an American feminist that women are "inferior intellectually". In February he was "miserable to a strange degree" with a cough. On 7 March 1882 he had a seizure while on the Sandwalk 400 yards from the house and struggled back to collapse in Emma's arms. Dr. Clark diagnosed angina and prescribed morphine pills for the pain. Darwin lay prostrate in despair, then a younger doctor, Dr. Norman Moore, assured him that his heart was only weak and within days Darwin was back at work, writing to *Nature* about beetles.

Having company helped. Henrietta brought her friend Laura Forster (aunt of E. M. Forster), herself making a rapid recovery from illness. Darwin daily told Laura of his symptoms and feelings. One day he came out into the garden and, putting his arms round Emma, said "Oh Laura, what a miserable man I should be without this dear woman." Another afternoon he joined her in the drawing-room and said "The clocks go dreadfully slowly, I have come in here to see if this one gets over the hours any quicker than the study one does."

Emma wanted a quiet Easter, so Laura and Henrietta left on 4 April, but on the 4th and 5th Darwin suffered attacks, noting "much pain". He recorded his own symptoms, and continued to note sporadic attacks. He took capsules of amyl nitrite, an antispasmodic, and was attended by Dr. Moore and a local physician, Dr. Allfrey.

On the 10th, George arrived back from the West Indies, and though Darwin was not up to talking for very long, he enjoyed George's news. Emma remembered how Darwin was "gracious & tender" when being attended for his illness, and would say "It is almost worth while to be so to be nursed by you".

George helped Frank and Jackson (the butler) to carry Darwin to and from his bed. On the nights of 11 and 12 April, Darwin had excruciating attacks of pain. On Saturday 15 April they were visited by the Lichfield family. Darwin joined them for dinner but had a giddy attack and fell down, and had to retire early. He did better on the Sunday, and on Monday was well enough to walk, supported on both sides, as far as the orchard.

Death

Darwin seemed "fully up to the average, so on Tuesday 18 April the Lichfields left and George went to Cambridge. Darwin stayed up late later than usual in the evening, chatting to Bessy. Just before midnight he again had agonising pain, and woke a flustered Emma to ask for the amyl nitrite. She had difficulties finding it at first, and with the assistance of Bessy gave him brandy.

Emma later noted that he had woken her saying "I have got the pain & I shall feel better or bear it better if you are awake". He had taken the antispasmodic twice, and afterwards said "I am not the least afraid of death- Remember what a good wife you have been to me – Tell all my children to remember how good they have been to me".

Dr Allfrey attended and gave some relief, then after he left at 8 a.m. Charles began violent vomiting, after two hours gasping "If I could but die" repeatedly. Frank and Henrietta returned to join Bessy, who persuaded a worn out Emma to take an opium pill and rest. Charles woke in a daze, recognised his children and embraced them with tears. Emma's notes state that after the worse of the distress he said "I was so sorry for you – but I could not help you... there never were such good nurses as you [Francis] & Henrietta – Where is Mammy", and when told she was lying down, "I am glad of it... Don't call her I don't want her", and often "It's almost worth while to be sick to be nursed by you".

He suffered more bouts of nausea and pain, then at 3.25 p.m. groaned "I feel as if I should faint". Emma was called and held him as he suffered excruciating pain, then lost consciousness and died at 4 p.m. on Wednesday 19 April 1882. Dr Allfrey signed the death certificate which gave "Angina pectoris Syncope" as the cause of death.

Frank brought Bernard from the nursery to the garden. As they walked past the drawing-room window Bernard noticed his aunts and said "Why are Bessy and Etty crying? because Grandpa is so ill?" Grief-stricken, Frank eventually said "Grandpa has been so ill that he won't be ill any more." They reached the Sandwalk and Bernard gathered a bouquet of wild lilies.

Funeral

Arrangements were made for burial in St. Mary's churchyard at Downe, with Brodie Innes offering to perform the rites, and the customary black edged letters were sent out to friends, relatives and colleagues.

In London Galton got William Spottiswoode as President of the Royal Society to telegraph the Darwins asking if they would consent to burial in Westminster Abbey, an honour that Darwin had been glad to see given to Lyle in 1875. They told Hooker, Lubbock and Huxley who with Spottiswoode met the Revd. Frederic Farrar, Canon of Westminster. Farrar suggested a petition to overcome any objections to an agnostic being buried in the Abbey, and approached the Revd. George Granville Bradley, Dean of Westminster. Lubbock took up a petition in the House of Commons stating that "it would be acceptable to a very large number of our countrymen of all classes and opinions that our illustrious countryman Mr. Darwin should be buried in Westminster Abbey." It was "very influentially signed". Newspapers took the request up, sending a public plea to Emma and the children to consent, as foreign tributes poured in. *The Standard* maintained that "true Christians can accept the main scientific facts of Evolution just as they do of Astronomy and Geology", *The Times* declared the 1860 debate was "ancient history" and the *Daily News* said that Darwin's doctrine was consistent "with strong religious faith and hope".

Hurried arrangements were made, and Emma saw it "nearly settled. It gave us all a pang not to have him rest quietly by Eras – ; but William felt strongly, and on reflection I did also, that his gracious & grateful nature would have wished to accept the acknowledgement of what he had done". While her children and relatives attended the funeral, she stayed at Downe.

The Downe tradesmen were disappointed, the publican pointing out that it "would have helped the place so much, for it would have brought hosts of people down to see his grave". The joiner had "made his coffin just the way he wanted it, all rough, just as it left the bench, no polish, no nothin", but this was returned and replaced by one "you could see to shave in". He added that "They buried him in Westminster Abbey, but he always wanted to lie here, and I don't think he'd have liked it."

That Sunday, Church sermons praised Darwin, saying Natural Selection was "by no means alien to the Christian tradition" (if interpreted correctly) and seeking a "reconciliation between Faith and Science". On Tuesday there was a massive demand for admission cards to the funeral.

All day on Tuesday the hearse was drawn by four horses the 16 miles from Downe to Westminster in cold drizzling rain. Next morning the Abbey filled with mourners including international dignitaries and scientists. At mid day on Wednesday 26 April 1882 the full pomp of a state occasion began.

The service included a specially commissioned anthem setting words from the Book of Proverbs to music composed for the occasion by Frederick Bridge, "Happy is the man that findeth wisdom, and getteth understanding".[302] As the Darwin family later recalled, William "was sitting in the front seat as eldest son and chief mourner, and he felt a draught on his already bald head; so he put his black gloves to balance on the top of his skull, and sat like that all through the service with the eyes of the nation upon him." Darwin was buried beneath the monument to Isaac Newton, next to Sir John Herschel, and as the coffin was lowered, the choir sang an anthem from Ecclesiasticus to music by Handel, "His body is buried in peace, but his name liveth evermore".

Pallbearers at the funeral included: William Cavendish, 7th Duke of Devonshire; George John Douglas Campbell, 8th Duke of Argyll; Edward Henry Stanley, 15th Earl of Derby; James Russell Lowell; William Spottiswoode; Joseph Dalton Hooker; Alfred Russel Wallace; Thomas Henry Huxley; John Lubbock, 1st Baron Avebury; and last but by no means least Rev. Frederic Farrar;[303] Stanley and Farrar were both Cambridge Apostles as Erasmus Alvey 'Ras' Darwin had been; Charles Darwin himself had not been a member of the Cambridge Apostles.

The service was conducted by Canon George Prothero (1818-1894) and the other Westminster Abbey staff present were minor canon Rev. John Henry Cheadle (? - ?); minor canon Rev. John Troutbeck (1832-1899); Canon Thomas James Rowsell (1816-1894); Canon Alfred Barry (1826-1910); Canon Robinson Duckworth (1834-1911); Rev. Samuel Flood Jones, precentor, (1826-1895); the Chapter Clerk, Mr. Charles St. Clare Bedford (1810-1900); Frederick Bridge, organist 1844-1924 (according to The Times, he composed an anthem for the funeral). The Dean, George Granville Bradley, was not in the country at the time of the funeral hence Canon Prothero was in charge.

Commemoration

Galton proposed a commemorative stained glass window in the Abbey, with panels symbolising the works of nature, each contributed by a different country. The evolution pane did not proceed, but the Royal Society formed a committee which decided on a bronze plaque in the Abbey, and a statue for the new Natural History Museum at South Kensington. Richard Owen remained opposed, and unveiling of the statue had to wait till 1885, after his retirement. The pomp and ceremony was attended by the Prince of Wales, scientists and the family, though not Emma, and led by Huxley.

Darwin's Westminster Abbey funeral expressed a public feeling of national pride, with the *Pall Mall Gazette* proclaiming that Great Britain had "lost a man whose name is a glory to his country". Religious writers of all persuasions praised his "noble character and his ardent pursuit of truth", calling him a "true Christian gentleman". In particular the Unitarians and free religionists, proud of his Dissenting upbringing, supported his naturalistic views. William Benjamin Carpenter carried a resolution praising Darwin's unravelling of "the immutable laws of the Divine Government", shedding light on "the progress of humanity". The Unitarian preacher John Chadwick from New York wrote that "The nation's grandest temple of religion opened its gates and lifted up its everlasting doors and bade the King of Science come in."[304]

References

- Browne, E. Janet (2002). "Charles Darwin: vol. 2 The Power of Place". London: Jonathan Cape. ISBN 0-7126-6837-3.<templatestyles src="Module:Citation/CS1/styles.css"></templatestyles>
- Desmond, Adrian; Moore, James (1991). "Darwin". London: Michael Joseph, Penguin Group. ISBN 0-7181-3430-3.<templatestyles src="Module:Citation/CS1/styles.css"></templatestyles>

Further reading

- The Complete Works of Charles Darwin Online – Darwin Online[305]; Darwin's publications, private papers and bibliography, supplementary works including biographies, obituaries and reviews. Free to use, includes items not in public domain.
- Works by Charles Darwin[306] at Project Gutenberg; public domain
- Darwin Correspondence Project[307] Text and notes for most of his letters

Commemoration

Commemoration of Charles Darwin

Commemoration of Charles Darwin began with geographical features named after Darwin while he was still on the *Beagle* survey voyage, continued after his return with the naming of species he had collected, and extended further with his increasing fame. Many geographical features, species and institutions bear his name. Interest in his work has led to scholarship and publications, nicknamed the *Darwin Industry*, and his life is remembered in fiction, film and TV productions as well as in numerous biographies. Darwin Day has become an annual event, and in 2009 there were worldwide celebrations to mark the bicentenary of Darwin's birth and the 150th anniversary of the publication of *On the Origin of Species*.

Geographical features

During Darwin's lifetime, many geographical features were given his name. An expanse of water adjoining the Beagle Channel was named Darwin Sound by *HMS Beagle* captain Robert FitzRoy after Darwin's prompt action, along with two or three of the men, saved them from being marooned on a nearby shore when a collapsing glacier caused a large wave that would have swept away their boats, and the nearby Mount Darwin in the Andes was named in celebration of Darwin's 25th birthday. Another Darwin Sound in British Columbia's Queen Charlotte Islands, between Moresby Island and Lyell Island, was named in 1878 by Canada's then-chief geographer George M. Dawson for Darwin. When the *Beagle* was surveying Australia in 1839, Darwin's friend John Lort Stokes sighted a natural harbour which the ship's captain Wickham named Port Darwin. The settlement of Palmerston founded there in 1869 was officially renamed Darwin in 1911. It became the capital city of Australia's Northern Territory.

Figure 49: *In 1881 Darwin was an eminent figure, still working on his contributions to evolutionary thought that had had an enormous effect on many fields of science.*

Species

More than 250 species nine genera, and some higher taxa have been named after Darwin. In 1837, the ornithologist John Gould named a specimen Darwin had collected in Patagonia *Rhea darwinii*, it is now known as Darwin's rhea (*Rhea pennata*). Similarly, Darwin's frog, *Rhinoderma darwinii*, was so named because Darwin discovered the species in Chile, and the Rhinodermatidae family are commonly known as Darwin's frogs.

In 2009, a remarkably complete fossil primate from 47 million years ago was announced as a significant transitional fossil, and named *Darwinius* to celebrate Darwin's bicentenary.

Although related to American Emberizidae or Tanagers rather than finches, the group of species related to those Darwin found in the Galápagos Islands became popularly known as "Darwin's finches" following publication of David Lack's book of that name in 1947, fostering inaccurate legends about their significance to his work.

Figure 50: *The holotype of Darwinilus sedarisi, published on Darwin's 205th birthday*

Scientific names

Genera

- *Darwinilus*, a genus of staphylinid beetles
- *Darwiniothamnus*, a genus of flowering plant
- *Darwinius*, a genus of Eocene primates
- *Darwinopterus*, a genus of long-tailed pterosaurs from China
- *Darwinula*, a genus of seed shrimp in the eponymous suborder Darwinulocopina, superfamily Darwinuloidea, family Darwinulidae.

Species Numerous species are named *darwinii* or *darwini*. Examples include:

- *Caerostris darwini*, Darwin's bark spider, an orb-weaver spider discovered in Madagascar
- *Demandasaurus darwini*, a rebbachisaurid sauropod dinosaur from Spain.

Other honorary epithets include *Ingerana charlesdarwini*, an endangered frog of Southeast Asia

Figure 51: *Statue of Charles Darwin at the Natural History Museum in London*

Institutions

Darwin in Australia features Charles Darwin University and Charles Darwin National Park.[308] However, Darwin College, Cambridge, founded in 1964, was named in honour of the Darwin family, in part because they owned some of the site.[309]

The Linnean Society of London has commemorated Darwin's achievements by the award of the Darwin-Wallace Medal since 1908.

In the Galápagos Islands, the Charles Darwin Foundation based at the Charles Darwin Research Station does research and conservation. To mark 2009 they are helping to reintroduce to Floreana Island (Charles Island) the specific mockingbird which first alerted Darwin to species being unique to islands. It was eradicated from the main island by European species, mainly rats and goats, but survived on two small islands nearby.

Darwin came fourth in the *100 Greatest Britons* poll sponsored by the BBC and voted for by the public.[310] In 2000 Darwin's image appeared on the Bank of England ten pound note, replacing Charles Dickens. His impressive, luxuriant beard (which was reportedly difficult to forge) was said to be a contributory factor to the bank's choice.[311]

As a humorous celebration of evolution, the annual Darwin Award is bestowed on individuals who "improve our gene pool by removing themselves from it."[312]

Darwin day, and 2009 commemorations

Darwin Day has become an annual celebration, and in 2009 the bicentenary of Darwin's birth and the 150th anniversary of the publication of *On the Origin of Species* were celebrated by events and publications around the world. The Darwin exhibition, after opening at the American Museum of Natural History in New York City in 2006, was shown at the Museum of Science, Boston, the Field Museum in Chicago, the Royal Ontario Museum in Toronto, then from 14 November 2008 to 19 April 2009 in the Natural History Museum, London, as part of the *Darwin200* programme of events across the United Kingdom. It also appears at the Palazzo delle Esposizioni in Rome from 12 February to 3 May 2009. The University of Cambridge featured a festival in July 2009. His birthplace, Shrewsbury, celebrated with "Darwin's Shrewsbury 2009 Festival" events during the year. An abstract sculpture, *The Quantum Leap*, was erected for the celebrations, and unveiled on 8 October 2009 by Randal Keynes, a great-great-grandson of Darwin. A 'geological garden' was created on its site to mark the interest which Darwin had in the field during his childhood.

In the United Kingdom a special commemorative issue of the two pound coin shows a portrait of Darwin facing a chimpanzee surrounded by the inscription 1809 DARWIN 2009, with the edge inscription ON THE ORIGIN OF SPECIES 1859. Collector versions of the coin have been released at a premium, and during the year the coins will be available from banks and post offices at face value. To celebrate Darwin's life and achievements, the BBC has commissioned numerous television and radio programmes known collectively as the BBC Darwin Season.

In September 2008, the Church of England issued an article saying that the 200th anniversary of his birth was a fitting time to apologise to Darwin "for misunderstanding you and, by getting our first reaction wrong, encouraging others to misunderstand you still".[313]

Since 2004, Universidad Francisco Marroquín (UFM)[314] in Guatemala, has celebrated Darwin Day with a series of conferences that includes international speakers. To watch the UFM's Darwin Day video collection click here.[315]

On 22 January 2013, a resolution was introduced to the United States Congress designating 12 February 2013 (Charles Darwin's 204th birthday) as "Darwin Day" to recognise "the importance of sciences in the betterment of humanity".

Darwin's alma mater, Christ's College, commemorated the bicentenary with the unveiling of a life-sized bronze statue of the young Darwin (aged 22). The

Figure 52: *The Quantum Leap, an abstract sculpture erected in 2009 in Darwin's birthplace, Shrewsbury, for the bi-centennial of his birth*

statue was created by Anthony Smith and unveiled by Prince Philip on 12 February 2009. It now forms the centrepiece of the college's *Darwin Garden*.

Books and films

Numerous biographies of Darwin have been written, and the 1980 biographical novel *The Origin* by Irving Stone gives a closely researched fictional account of Darwin's life from the age of 22 onwards.

A dramatic motion picture entitled *Creation* was released in 2009, joining a short list of film dramas about Darwin, including *The Darwin Adventure*, released in 1972.

External links

 Wikimedia Commons has media related to *Things named after Charles Darwin*.

- The Complete Works of Charles Darwin Online – Darwin Online[316]; Darwin's publications, private papers and bibliography, supplementary works including biographies, obituaries and reviews.
- Darwin Correspondence Project[317] Full text and notes for complete correspondence to 1867, with summaries of all the rest
- Darwin 200: Celebrating Charles Darwin's bicentenary[318], Natural History Museum
- Listing of the significant places in Shrewsbury relevant to Darwin's early life.[319]
- *The life and times of Charles Darwin*, an audio slideshow[320], *The Guardian*, Thursday 12 February 2009, (3 min 20 sec).
- CBC Digital Archives: Charles Darwin and the Origins of Evolution[321]
- Darwin's Volcano[322] – a short video discussing Darwin and Agassiz' coral reef formation debate
- Darwin's Brave New World[323] – A 3-part drama-documentary exploring Charles Darwin and the significant contributions of his colleagues Joseph Hooker, Thomas Huxley and Alfred Russel Wallace also featuring interviews with Richard Dawkins, David Suzuki, Jared Diamond and Iain McCalman.
- A naturalists voyage around the world[324] Account of the *Beagle* voyage using animation, in English from Centre national de la recherche scientifique, Paris.

List of things named after Charles Darwin

Several places, concepts, institutions, and things are namesakes of the English biologist Charles Darwin:

Places

- Charles Darwin National Park
- Charles Darwin Foundation
- Charles Darwin Research Station
- Charles Darwin University
- Darwin College, Cambridge
- Darwin, Falkland Islands
- Darwin, Northern Territory

- Darwin Glacier (California)
- Darwin Island, Galapagos Islands
- Darwin Island (Antarctica)
- Darwin Sound (Canada)
- Mount Darwin (California)
- Mount Darwin (Tasmania)

Things named after Darwin in relation to his *Beagle* voyage

- Cordillera Darwin
- Darwin's finches
- Darwin's frog
- Darwin Sound
- Mount Darwin (Andes)

Scientific names of organisms

Some 250 species and several higher groups bear Darwin's name; most are insects.

- *Darwinilus*, a rove beetle
- *Darwinius*, an extinct primate
- *Darwinopterus*, a genus of pterosaur
- *Darwinula*, a genus of seed shrimp
- *Darwinivelia*, a water treader genus
- *Darwinysius*, a seed bug
- *Darwinomya*, a genus of flies
- *Darwinella*, a sponge genus
- *Darwinsaurus*, a dinosaur
- *Darwinhydrus*, a diving beetle
- *darwini* (multiple species)
- *darwinii* (multiple species)
- *Ingerana charlesdarwini*, a frog

Philosophies

- Darwinism
- Social Darwinism

Other

- Darwin, a unit of evolutionary change
- Darwin, an operating system
- Darwin (ESA) (a proposed satellite system)
- Darwin Awards
- Darwin Medal
- Darwin fish
- Division of Darwin, a former electoral division in Australia

- 1991 Darwin, a stony Florian asteroid
- Darwin (lunar crater) a lunar crater
- Darwin (Martian crater) a martian crater

List of taxa described by Charles Darwin

This is a list of **taxa described by Charles Darwin**. Many of them are barnacles from his study of that group.[325,326]

- *Balanus improvisus*, bay barnacle
- *Colorhamphus parvirostris*, Patagonian tyrant
- *Acasta cyathus*, sponge barnacle
- *Balanus nubilus*, giant barnacle
- *Balanus glandula*, acorn barnacle
- *Amphibalanus amphitrite*, striped barnacle
- *Elminius modestus*, New Zealand barnacle
- *Notomegabalanus decorus*
- *Megabalanus occator*
- *Lepas australis*
- *Tetraclita rubescens*
- *Coronula reginae*
- *Anelasma squalicola*
- *Heteralepas cornuta*
- *Tetraclita serrata*
- *Nobia conjugatum*
- *Rostratoverruca nexa*
- *Fistulobalanus pallidus*
- *Wanella milleporae*
- *Balanus trigonus*
- *Nesochthamalus intertextus*
- *Temnaspis fissum*
- *Balanus vestitus*
- *Balanus decorus*
- *Balanus* (genus), barnacles
- *Megabalanus stultus*
- *Octolasmis lowei*
- *Acasta fenestrata*
- *Balanus venustus*
- *Membranobalanus declivis*
- *Chthamalus fragilis*
- *Poecilasma kaempferi*
- *Megabalanus coccopoma*, titan acorn barnacle

Figure 53: *A plate from Charles Darwin's Monograph on the Cirripedia, 1854, engraved by George Brettingham Sowerby, Jr.*

Figure 54: *The bay barnacle, Balanus improvisus, described by Charles Darwin, on a shell of the sand gaper clam Mya arenaria*

List of taxa described by Charles Darwin

- *Megabalanus decorus*
- *Megabalanus crispatus*
- *Acasta purpurata*
- *Euraphia intertexta*
- *Amphibalanus cirratus*
- *Euacasta sporillus*
- *Megabalanus vinaceus*
- *Megabalanus vesiculosus*
- *Epopella eosimplex*
- *Balanus poecilus*
- *Armatobalanus allium*
- *Centrostomum incisum* (Platyhelminth)
- *Savignium dentatum*
- *Coronula barbara*
- *Leptoplana notabilis*
- *Leptoplana formosa*
- *Pachylasma auranticacum*

Religious views

Religious views of Charles Darwin

Charles Darwin's views on religion have been the subject of much interest. His pivotal work in the development of modern biology and evolution theory played a prominent part in debates about religion and science at the time, then, in the early 20th century became a focus of the creation-evolution controversy in the United States.

Charles Darwin had a non-conformist Unitarian background, but attended a Church of England school. With the aim of becoming a clergyman he went to the University of Cambridge for the required BA degree, which included studies of Anglican theology. He took great interest in natural history and became filled with zeal for science as defined by John Herschel, based on the natural theology of William Paley which presented the argument from divine design in nature to explain adaptation as God acting through laws of nature. On the voyage of the *Beagle* he remained orthodox and looked for "centres of creation" to explain distribution, but towards the end of the voyage began to doubt that species were fixed. By this time he was critical of the Bible as history, and wondered why all religions should not be equally valid. Following his return in October 1836, he developed his novel ideas of geology while speculating about transmutation of species and thinking about religion.

Following Darwin's marriage to Emma Wedgwood in January 1839, they shared discussions about Christianity for several years, Emma's views being Unitarian like much of her family. The theodicy of Paley and Thomas Malthus vindicated evils such as starvation as a result of a benevolent creator's laws which had an overall good effect. To Darwin, natural selection produced the good of adaptation but removed the need for design, and he could not see the work of an omnipotent deity in all the pain and suffering such as the ichneumon wasp paralysing caterpillars as live food for its eggs. Until 1844 he followed Paley in viewing organisms as perfectly adapted with only a few imperfections,

Figure 55: *Charles Darwin (1809–1882), who proposed the theory of evolution by means of natural selection.*

and only partly modified that view by 1859. *On the Origin of Species* reflects theological views.Wikipedia:Citation needed Though he thought of religion as a tribal survival strategy, Darwin still believed that God was the ultimate lawgiver, and later recollected that at the time he was convinced of the existence of God as a First Cause and deserved to be called a theist. This view subsequently fluctuated, and he continued to explore conscientious doubts, without forming fixed opinions on certain religious matters.

Darwin continued to play a leading part in the parish work of the local church, but from around 1849 would go for a walk on Sundays while his family attended church. Though reticent about his religious views, in 1879 he responded that he had never been an atheist in the sense of denying the existence of a god, and that generally "an Agnostic would be the more correct description of my state of mind." He went as far as saying that "Science has nothing to do with Christ, except insofar as the habit of scientific research makes a man cautious in admitting evidence. For myself, I do not believe that there ever has been any revelation. As for a future life, every man must judge for himself between conflicting vague probabilities."

Figure 56: *As a child, Darwin attended Shrewsbury Unitarian Church*

Darwin's religious background

Charles Darwin was born during the Napoleonic Wars and grew up in their aftermath, a conservative time when Tory-dominated government closely associated with the established Anglican Church of England repressed Radicalism, but when family memories recalled the 18th-century Enlightenment and a multitude of Non-conformist churches held differing interpretations of Christianity. His Whig supporting extended family of Darwins and Wedgwoods was strongly Unitarian, though one of his grandfathers, Erasmus Darwin, was a freethinker, and his father was quietly a freethinker but as a physician avoided any social conflict with his wealthy Anglican patrons. While Darwin's parents were open enough to changing social pressures to have Charles baptised in the Church of England, his pious mother took the children to the Unitarian chapel. After her death when he was only eight he became a boarder at the *Shrewsbury School*, an Anglican public school.

Edinburgh – medical studies and Lamarckian evolution theory

The two universities in England namely Oxford and Cambridge, were under the Church of England and required students to sign the *Thirty-nine Articles of the Anglican faith*, so many English Non-conformists sent their children to the Scottish universities which had a better reputation in fields like medicine. Charles initially attended the University of Edinburgh, and while he was put off medicine he took an active interest in natural history at the Plinian Society. One of his proposers for the society was the radical William A. F. Browne, and on 27 March 1827 Browne argued that mind and consciousness were simply aspects of brain activity, not "souls" or spiritual entities separate from the body. A furious debate ensued, and later someone struck out all mention of this materialist heresy from the minutes. This was the first time that Darwin was exposed to militant freethought and the arguments it aroused. On one occasion Robert Edmund Grant discussed Lamarck's evolutionary ideas. Darwin was astonished, but had recently read the similar ideas of his grandfather Erasmus and remained indifferent.

Natural history had grown from the idea that the different kinds of plants and animals showed the wonder of God's creation, making their study and cataloguing into species worthwhile. In Darwin's day it was common for clergymen to be naturalists, though scientific findings had already opened up ideas on creation. The established churches (of England and Scotland) and the English universities remained insistent that species were divinely created and man was distinct from the "lower orders", but the Unitarian church rejected this teaching and even proclaimed that the human mind was subject to physical law. Erasmus Darwin went further and his *Zoönomia* asks *..would it be too bold to imagine that all warm-blooded animals have arisen from one living filament, which the great First Cause endued with animality.... possessing the faculty of continuing to improve by its own inherent activity, and of delivering down these improvements by generation to its posterity, world without end!*, anticipating Lamarckism.

Cambridge – theology and geology

When Darwin proved unable to persevere at medical studies, his father sent him to Christ's College, Cambridge, for a Bachelor of Arts degree as the first step towards becoming an Anglican parson. Darwin was at first uncertain, he later wrote: "from what little I had heard and thought on the subject I had scruples about declaring my belief in all the dogmas of the Church of England; though otherwise I liked the thought of being a country clergyman. Accordingly I read with care 'Pearson on the Creed' and a few other books on divinity; and as I did not then in the least doubt the strict and literal truth of every word in the Bible, I soon persuaded myself that our Creed must be fully accepted. It never struck me how illogical it was to say that I believed in what I could not understand and what is in fact unintelligible. I might have said with entire truth that I had no wish to dispute any dogma; but I never was such a fool as to feel and say 'credo quia incredibile'. He was particularly convinced by the reasoning of the Revd. John Bird Sumner's *Evidences of Christianity* which set out the logic that the unbelief of sceptics gave them the dilemma that if Christianity were untrue, then either "Jesus did not live, or he actually lived, but was not the Son of God, hence an imposter." The Gospels made this highly improbable, as his miracles had convinced unbelievers, hence we had "no right to deny" that such events were probable. Jesus's religion was "wonderfully suitable... to our ideas of happiness in this & the next world" and there was "no other way... of explaining the series of evidence & probability."

The university was essentially tied into the Church of England, with virtually all of the college heads and most of the professors and fellows having been ordained. About half of the undergraduates were destined for the church, like Darwin hoping for a comfortable parish. During Darwin's second year, the harmony was disturbed when Cambridge was briefly visited by the Radicals Richard Carlile and the Revd Robert Taylor on an "infidel home missionary tour", causing a stir before being banned. Taylor would be remembered by Darwin as "the Devil's Chaplain", a warning example of an outcast from society who had challenged Christianity and had been imprisoned for blasphemy.

In his third year, he joined John Stevens Henslow's natural history course and was introduced to the Cambridge version of natural theology, part of the liberal Christianity of colleagues such as Adam Sedgwick, George Peacock and William Whewell who all had strong views about science as the search for the laws of nature. Study of nature was study of the work of the Lord, and scientists who were ordained clerics of the Church of England, such as themselves, could follow their enquiries without theological difficulties. Sedgwick gave a talk to the Geological Society of London in 1831 which declared that "No opinion can be heretical, but that which is not true.... Conflicting falsehoods we can comprehend; but truths can never war against each other. I affirm, therefore, that we have nothing to fear from the results of our enquiries, provided they be followed in the laborious but secure road of honest induction. In this way we may rest assured that we shall never arrive at conclusions opposed to any truth, either physical or moral, from whatever source that truth may be derived." For these men, science could not be out of harmony with religion, and in a sense it was religion.

Under pressure in the fourth year, Darwin worked hard at his studies, getting tuition in theology by Henslow. Darwin became particularly interested in the Revd William Paley's *Evidences of Christianity* and *Principles of Moral and Political Philosophy*, which were set texts. The latter was becoming outdated. It opposed arguments for increased democracy, but saw no divine right of rule for the sovereign or the state, only "expediency". Government could be opposed if grievances outweighed the danger and expense to society. The judgement was "Every man for himself". These ideas had suited the conditions of reasonable rule prevailing when the text was published in 1785, but in 1830 they were dangerous ideas at a time when the French king was deposed by middle class republicans and given refuge in England by the Tory government, and resulting radical street protests demanded suffrage, equality and freedom of religion. Paley's text even supported abolition of the *Thirty-nine Articles* of the Anglican faith which every student at Cambridge (and Oxford University) was required to sign. Henslow insisted that "he should be grieved if a single word of the Thirty-nine Articles were altered" and emphasised the need to respect authority. Darwin later wrote that he was convinced that he "could have written out the whole of the *Evidences* with perfect correctness, but not of course in the clear language of Paley. The logic of this book and as I may add of his *Natural Theology* gave me as much delight as did Euclid."

After doing particularly well in his final exam questions on Paleys' books, Darwin read Paley's *Natural Theology* which set out to refute David Hume's argument that the teleological argument for "design" by a Creator was merely a human projection onto the forces of nature. Paley saw a rational proof of God's existence in the complexity and perfect adaptation to needs of living beings exquisitely fitted to their places in a happy world, while attacking the evolutionary ideas of Erasmus Darwin as coinciding with atheistic schemes and lacking evidence. Paley's benevolent God acted in nature through uniform and universal laws, not arbitrary miracles or changes of laws, and this use of secondary laws provided a theodicy explaining the problem of evil by separating nature from direct divine action, drawing directly on the ideas of Thomas Malthus. For Paley, a Malthusian "system of natural hostilities" of animals living on prey was strictly connected to the surplus of births keeping the world appropriately stocked as circumstances changed, and poverty showed that the world was in a "state of probation... calculated for the production, exercise, and improvement of moral qualities, with a view to a future state", even where such divine purpose was not obvious. This convinced Charles and encouraged his interest in science. He later wrote "I do not think I hardly ever admired a book more than Paley's *Natural Theology*: I could almost formerly have said it by heart."

He read John Herschel's new *Preliminary Discourse on the Study of Natural Philosophy*, learning that nature was governed by laws, and the highest aim of natural philosophy was to understand them through an orderly process of induction, balancing observation and theorising. This exemplified the natural theology that Darwin had learnt in previous years. He also read Alexander von Humboldt's *Personal Narrative*, and the two books were immensely influential, stirring up in him "a burning zeal to add even the most humble contribution to the noble structure of Natural Science."

Voyage of the *Beagle*

Darwin planned a visit to the tropics before settling down as a clergyman, and on Henslow's advice studied geology with Adam Sedgwick, finding about the ancient age of the Earth, then went with him for two weeks surveying strata in Wales. He returned to find that his arrangements had fallen through, but was given the opportunity to join the *Beagle* survey expedition as a gentleman naturalist and companion to captain Robert FitzRoy. Before they left England FitzRoy gave Darwin a copy of the first volume of Charles Lyell's *Principles of Geology*, the subject which would be his primary work.

Darwin was questioning from the outset, and in his first zoology notes he wondered why deep-ocean plankton had been created with so much beauty for little purpose as no one could see them. He saw landforms as supporting Lyell's Uniformitarianism which explained features as the outcome of a gradual process over huge periods of time, and quickly showed a gift for theorising about the geology he was examining. He concluded that the land had indeed risen, and referred to loose rock deposits as "part of the long disputed Diluvium". Around 1825 both Lyell and Sedgwick had supported William Buckland's Catastrophism which postulated diluvialism to reconcile findings with the Biblical account of Noah's ark, but by 1830 evidence had shown them that the "diluvium" had come from a series of local processes. They still distinguished between diluvial and alluvial deposits, but Sedgwick no longer thought these deposits were connected with Noah's flood by the time he taught Darwin, though the debate continued. Darwin's notes show him increasingly discounting "debacles" to account for such formations. It was only later that glaciation was accepted as the source of these deposits.

Lyell's second volume explained extinctions as a "succession of deaths" due to changed circumstances with new species then being created, but Darwin found giant fossils of extinct mammals with no geological signs of a "diluvial debacle" or environmental change, and so rejected Lyell's explanation in favour of Giovanni Battista Brocchi's idea that species had somehow aged and died out. On the Galápagos Islands he remained convinced by Lyell's idea of species spreading from "centres of creation", and assumed that species had spread from the mainland rather than originating on these geologically recent volcanic islands. He failed to note locations of most of his finds, but fortunately recorded mockingbirds and plant life with more care. In Australia, reflecting on the marsupial kangaroos and potoroos, he thought them so strange that an unbeliever "might exclaim 'Surely two distinct Creators must have been [at] work; their object however has been the same & certainly the end in each case is complete'", yet an antlion he was watching was very similar to its European counterpart. "Now what would the Disbeliever say to this? Would any two workmen ever hit on so beautiful, so simple & yet so artificial a contrivance?

It cannot be thought so. – The one hand has surely worked throughout the universe. A Geologist perhaps would suggest, that the periods of Creation have been distinct & remote the one from the other; that the Creator rested in his labor." Darwin was struggling with inconsistencies in these ideas. As they neared the end of the voyage his thoughts about the mockingbirds shook his confidence that species were fixed and that variation was limited.

In Cape Town, South Africa, Darwin and FitzRoy visited John Herschel. On 20 February 1836, Herschel had written to Lyell praising his *Principles of Geology* as opening a way for bold speculation on "that mystery of mysteries, the replacement of extinct species by others." Herschel thought catastrophic extinction and renewal "an inadequate conception of the Creator", and by analogy with other intermediate causes "the origination of fresh species, could it ever come under our cognizance, would be found to be a natural in contradistinction to a miraculous process". The letter was widely circulated in London, and Darwin remembered the phrase "that mystery of mysteries". Missionaries were being accused of causing racial tension and profiteering, and after the *Beagle* set to sea on 18 June FitzRoy wrote an open letter to the evangelical *South African Christian Recorder* on the *Moral State of Tahiti* incorporating extracts from both his and Darwin's diaries to defend the reputation of missionaries. This was given to a passing ship which took it to Cape Town to become FitzRoy's (and Darwin's) first published work.

FitzRoy too had seen geological features as supporting Lyell's timescale, and on his return to England extracts from his diary stressing the immense age of the Patagonian raised beaches were read to the Royal Geographical Society,[327] but he married a very religious lady and in his *Narrative* of the voyage added a supplement regretting having "remarked to a friend" that these vast plains "could never have been effected by a forty days' flood", remarks he ascribed to his own "turn of mind and ignorance of scripture" during the voyage.

Darwin's loss of faith

In his later private autobiography, Darwin wrote of the period from October 1836 to January 1839:

> "During these two years I was led to think much about religion. Whilst on board the *Beagle* I was quite orthodox, & I remember being heartily laughed at by several of the officers (though themselves orthodox) for quoting the Bible as an unanswerable authority on some point of morality. I suppose it was the novelty of the argument that amused them. But I had gradually come, by this time, to see that the Old Testament from its manifestly false history of the world, with the Tower of Babel, rainbow as a sign, etc., etc., and from its attributing to God the feelings of a revengeful

tyrant, was no more to be trusted than the sacred books of the Hindoos, or the beliefs of any barbarian."

In seeking to explain his observations, by early 1837 Darwin was speculating in his notebooks on transmutation of species and writing of "my theory". His journal for 1838 records "All September read a good deal on many subject: thought much upon religion. Beginning of October ditto." At this time he outlined ideas of comparative anthropology, from his knowledge of different religious beliefs around the world as well as at various times in history, and came to the view that scriptures were unreliable and contradictory.

Discussions with Emma

Having decided to marry, Darwin visited his cousin Emma on 29 July 1838 and told her of his ideas on transmutation. On 11 November he returned and proposed to Emma. Again he discussed his ideas, and about ten days later she wrote,

> "When I am with you I think all melancholy thoughts keep out of my head but since you are gone some sad ones have forced themselves in, of fear that our opinions on the most important subject should differ widely. My reason tells me that honest & conscientious doubts cannot be a sin, but I feel it would be a painful void between us. I thank you from my heart for your openness with me & I should dread the feeling that you were concealing your opinions from the fear of giving me pain. It is perhaps foolish of me to say this much but my own dear Charley we now do belong to each other & I cannot help being open with you. Will you do me a favour? yes I am sure you will, it is to read our Saviours farewell discourse to his disciples which begins at the end of the 13th Chap of John. It is so full of love to them & devotion & every beautiful feeling. It is the part of the New Testament I love best. This is a whim of mine it would give me great pleasure, though I can hardly tell why I don't wish you to give me your opinion about it."

Darwin had already wondered about the materialism implied by his ideas, noting in his transmutation notebook "Thought (or desires more properly) being hereditary it is difficult to imagine it anything but structure of brain hereditary, analogy points out to this. – love of the deity effect of organization, oh you materialist!" The letter shows Emma's tension between her fears that differences of belief would separate them, and her desire to be close and openly share ideas. Emma cherished a belief in the afterlife, and was concerned that they should "belong to each other" for eternity. The Gospel of John says "Love one another" (13:34), then describes Jesus as the Word Incarnate saying "I am the way, the truth and the life: no man comes to the Father, except through me."

(14:6). Desmond and Moore note that the section continues "Whoever does not abide in me is thrown away like a branch and withers; such branches are gathered, thrown into the fire and burned"(15:6). As disbelief later gradually crept over Darwin, he could "hardly see how anyone ought to wish Christianity to be true; for if so the plain language of the text seems to show that the men who do not believe, and this would include my Father, Brother and almost all my best friends, will be everlastingly punished. And this is a damnable doctrine."

Following Darwin's marriage to Emma in January 1839, they shared discussions about Christianity for many years. Unitarianism emphasised inner feeling which overrode the authority of religious texts or doctrine, and her beliefs resulted from intensive study and questioning. They socialised with the Unitarian clergymen James Martineau and John James Tayler, and read their works as well as those of other Unitarian and liberal Anglican authors such as Francis William Newman whose *Phases of faith* described a spiritual journey from Calvinism to theism, all part of widespread and heated debate on the authority of Anglicanism. In Downe Emma attended the Anglican village church, but as a Unitarian had the family turn round in silence when the Trinitarian Nicene Creed was recited.

Soon after their marriage, Emma felt that "while you are acting conscientiously & sincerely wishing, & trying to learn the truth, you cannot be wrong", and though concerned at the threat to faith of the "habit in scientific pursuits of believing nothing till it is proved", her hope that he did not "consider his opinion as formed" proved correct. Methodical conscientious doubt as a state of inquiry rather than disbelief made him open to nature and revelation, and they remained open with each other.

Theorising

Darwin was interested in ideas of Natural "laws of harmony", and made enquiries into animal breeding. Having read the new 6th edition of the Revd. Thomas Malthus's *Essay on the Principle of Population*, around late November 1838 he compared breeders selecting traits to a Malthusian Nature selecting from variants thrown up by *chance* so that "every part of newly acquired structure is fully practical & perfected", thinking this "a beautiful part of my theory". The theodicy of Paley and Thomas Malthus vindicated evils such as starvation as a result of a benevolent creator's laws which had an overall good effect. To Darwin, Natural selection produced the good of adaptation but removed the need for design, and he could not see the work of an omnipotent deity in all the pain and suffering such as the ichneumon wasp paralysing caterpillars as live food for its eggs.

Early in 1842, Darwin wrote about his ideas to Lyell, who noted that his ally "denies seeing a beginning to each crop of species". On 11 January 1844 Darwin mentioned his theorising to the botanist Joseph Dalton Hooker, writing with melodramatic humour "I am almost convinced (quite contrary to opinion I started with) that species are not (it is like confessing a murder) immutable. Heaven forfend me from Lamarck nonsense of a 'tendency to progression' 'adaptations from the slow willing of animals' &c,—but the conclusions I am led to are not widely different from his—though the means of change are wholly so—I think I have found out (here's presumption!) the simple way by which species become exquisitely adapted to various ends." Hooker replied "There may in my opinion have been a series of productions on different spots, & also a gradual change of species. I shall be delighted to hear how you think that this change may have taken place, as no presently conceived opinions satisfy me on the subject."

In November 1844 public controversy erupted over ideas of evolutionary progress in the anonymously published *Vestiges of the Natural History of Creation*, a well written best-seller which widened public interest in transmutation. Darwin scorned its amateurish geology and zoology, but carefully reviewed his own arguments.

From around 1849 Darwin stopped attending church, but Emma and the children continued to attend services. On Sundays Darwin sometimes went with them as far as the lych gate to the churchyard, and then he would go for a walk. During the service, Emma continued to face forward when the congregation turned to face the altar for the Creed, sticking to her Unitarian faith.

Death of Annie

At the end of June 1850 his bright nine-year-old daughter Annie who had become a particular favourite and comfort to him fell sick and, after a painful illness, died on 23 April 1851. During Annie's long illness Darwin had read books by Francis William Newman, a Unitarian evolutionist who called for a new post-Christian synthesis and wrote that "the fretfulness of a child is an infinite evil". Darwin wrote at the time, "Our only consolation is that she passed a short, though joyous life." For three years he had deliberated about the Christian meaning of mortality. This opened a new vision of tragically circumstantial nature. His faith in Christianity had already dwindled away and he had stopped going to church. He wrote out his memories of Annie, but no longer believed in an afterlife or in salvation. Emma believed that Annie had gone to heaven and told this to the children, with the unfortunate result that Henrietta wondered, if all the angels were men, did women go to heaven?, and worried for months that her naughtiness while Annie was alive would mean that she would go to hell unless God forgave her.

On the Origin of Species

Darwin continued to avoid public controversy and to accumulate evidence supporting his theory against the anticipated arguments. In 1858 the information that Alfred Russel Wallace now had a similar theory forced an early joint publication of Darwin's theory. The reaction to Darwin's theory, even after publication of *On the Origin of Species* in 1859, was more muted than he had feared. One of the first responses to review copies came from Charles Kingsley, a Christian socialist country rector and novelist, who wrote that it was "just as noble a conception of Deity, to believe that He created primal forms capable of self development... as to believe that He required a fresh act of intervention to supply the lacunas which He Himself had made." For the second edition, Darwin added these lines to the last chapter, with attribution to "a celebrated author and divine".

In 1860 seven liberal Anglican theologians caused a much greater furore by publishing a manifesto titled *Essays and Reviews* in which they sought to make textual criticism of the Bible available to the ordinary reader, as well as supporting Darwin. Their new "higher criticism" represented "the triumph of the rational discourse of logos over myth." It argued that the Bible should not be read in an entirely literal manner, thus and would in the future become "a bogey of Christian fundamentalists ... but this was only because Western people had lost the original sense of the mythical." The traditional Christians were just as vocal.

There was close correspondence between Darwin and his American collaborator Asa Gray, a devout Presbyterian who discussed with him the relationship of natural selection to natural theology and published several reviews arguing in detail that they were fully compatible. Darwin financed a pamphlet publishing a collection of these reviews for distribution in Britain. In one 1860 letter to Gray, Darwin expressed his doubts about the teleological argument which claimed nature as evidence of god, though he was still inclined to vaguely believe in an impersonal God as first cause: <templatestyles src="Template:Quote/styles.css"/>

> With respect to the theological view of the question; this is always painful to me.— I am bewildered.— I had no intention to write atheistically. But I own that I cannot see, as plainly as others do, & as I [should] wish to do, evidence of design & beneficence on all sides of us. There seems to me too much misery in the world. I cannot persuade myself that a beneficent & omnipotent God would have designedly created the Ichneumonidæ with the express intention of their feeding within the living bodies of caterpillars, or that a cat should play with mice. Not believing this, I see no necessity in the belief that the eye was expressly designed. On the other hand I

cannot anyhow be contented to view this wonderful universe & especially the nature of man, & to conclude that everything is the result of brute force. I am inclined to look at everything as resulting from designed laws, with the details, whether good or bad, left to the working out of what we may call chance. Not that this notion at all satisfies me. I feel most deeply that the whole subject is too profound for the human intellect. A dog might as well speculate on the mind of Newton.—Let each man hope & believe what he can.

Autobiography on gradually increasing disbelief

In his autobiography written in 1876 Darwin reviewed questions about Christianity in relation to other religions and how "the more we know of the fixed laws of nature the more incredible do miracles become". Though "very unwilling to give up my belief", he found that "disbelief crept over me at a very slow rate, but was at last complete. The rate was so slow that I felt no distress, and have never since doubted even for a single second that my conclusion was correct." He noted how "The old argument of design in nature, as given by Paley, which formerly seemed to me so conclusive, fails, now that the law of natural selection has been discovered", and how Paley's teleological argument had difficulties with the problem of evil.

Even when writing *On the Origin of Species* in the 1850s he was still inclined to theism, but his views gradually changed to agnosticism: <templatestyles src="Template:Quote/styles.css"/>

> *Another source of conviction in the existence of God, connected with the reason and not with the feelings, impresses me as having much more weight. This follows from the extreme difficulty or rather impossibility of conceiving this immense and wonderful universe, including man with his capacity of looking far backwards and far into futurity, as the result of blind chance or necessity. When thus reflecting I feel compelled to look to a First Cause having an intelligent mind in some degree analogous to that of man; and I deserve to be called a Theist.*
> *This conclusion was strong in my mind about the time, as far as I can remember, when I wrote the Origin of Species; and it is since that time that it has very gradually with many fluctuations become weaker. But then arises the doubt–can the mind of man, which has, as I fully believe, been developed from a mind as low as that possessed by the lowest animal, be trusted when it draws such grand conclusions? May not these be the result of the connection between cause and effect which strikes us as a necessary one, but probably depends merely on inherited experience? Nor must we overlook the probability of the constant inculcation in a belief in God on*

the minds of children producing so strong and perhaps an inherited effect on their brains not yet fully developed, that it would be as difficult for them to throw off their belief in God, as for a monkey to throw off its instinctive fear and hatred of a snake.

I cannot pretend to throw the least light on such abstruse problems. The mystery of the beginning of all things is insoluble by us; and I for one must be content to remain an Agnostic.

Downe parish

Although he is commonly portrayed as being in conflict with the Church of England, Darwin was supportive of the local parish church.

On moving to Downe, Kent in 1842, Darwin supported the parish church's work, and became a good friend of the Revd. John Innes who took over in 1846. Darwin contributed to the church, helped with parish assistance and proposed a benefit society which became the *Down Friendly Society* with Darwin as guardian and treasurer. His wife Emma Darwin became known throughout the parish for helping in the way a parson's wife might be expected to, and as well as providing nursing care for her own family's frequent illnesses she gave out bread tokens to the hungry and "small pensions for the old, dainties for the ailing, and medical comforts and simple medicine".[328]

Innes inherited his family home of Milton Brodie, in the Scottish Highlands near Forres. In 1862 he retired there and changed his name to Brodie Innes,[329] leaving the parish in the dubious hands of his curate, the Revd. Stevens, while still remaining the patron. The meagre "living" and lack of a vicarage made it hard to attract a priest of quality. Innes made Darwin treasurer of Downe village school and they continued to correspond, with Innes seeking help and advice on parish matters. The Revd. Stevens proved lax, and departed in 1867. His successors were worse, one absconding with the school's funds and the church organ fund after Darwin mistakenly shared the treasurer's duties with him: Brodie Innes offered to sell Darwin the advowson, or right to appoint the parish priest, but Darwin declined. The next was rumoured to have disgraced himself by "walking with girls at night". Darwin now became involved in helping Innes with detective work, subsequently advising him that the gossip that had reached Innes was not backed up by any reliable evidence.[330]

A new reforming High Church vicar, the Revd. George Sketchley Ffinden, took over the parish in November 1871 and began imposing his ideas. Darwin had to write to Brodie Innes, explaining what had upset the parishioners. Ffinden now usurped control of the village school which had been run for years by a committee of Darwin, Lubbock and the incumbent priest, with a "conscience clause" which protected the children from Anglican indoctrination.

Ffinden began lessons on the *Thirty-nine Articles of the Anglican faith*, an unwelcome move from the point of view of the Baptists who had a chapel in the village. Darwin withdrew from the committee and cut his annual donation to the church, but continued with the Friendly Society work.[331]

For two years Emma organised a winter reading room in the local school for local labourers, who subscribed a penny a week to smoke and play games, with "Respectable newspapers & a few books... & a respectable housekeeper..there every evening to maintain decorum." This was a common facility to save men from "resorting to the public house". In 1873 the Revd. Ffinden opposed it, as "Coffee drinking, bagatelle & other games" had been allowed and "the effects of tobacco smoke & spitting" were seen when the children returned in the morning. Emma got Darwin to get the approval of the education inspectorate in London, and just before Christmas 1873 the Darwins and their neighbours the Lubbocks got the agreement of the school committee, offering to pay for any repairs needed "to afford every possible opportunity to the working class for self improvement & amusement". A furious Ffinden huffed that it was "quite out of order" for the Darwins to have gone to the inspectorate behind his back. Darwin's health suffered as he argued over natural selection with St. George Jackson Mivart, and in the autumn of 1874 Darwin expressed his exasperation at Ffinden when putting in his resignation from the school committee due to ill health.[332]

Ffinden then refused to speak to any of the Darwins, and when two evening lectures were proposed for the village in 1875, Lubbock had to act as an intermediary in requesting use of the schoolroom. The committee agreed, but Ffinden refused to co-operate, writing that "I had long been aware of the harmful tendencies to revealed religion of Mr. Darwin's views, but.. I had fully determined.. not to let my difference of opinion interfere with a friendly feeling as neighbours, trusting that God's grace might in time bring one so highly gifted intellectually and morally to a better mind." Darwin was equally haughty in return, condescending that "If Mr. F bows to Mrs D. and myself, we will return it".[333]

The dispute with Ffinden reflected the Church of England narrowing its social provision to its own adherents as secular provision of education became more widespread. Though Darwin no longer attended church, he was willing to give patronage to Non-conformism, and the family welcomed and supported the work of the Non-conformist evangelist J. W. C. Fegan in the village of Downe.

Religion as an evolved social characteristic

In his 1871 book *The Descent of Man* Darwin clearly saw religion and "moral qualities" as being important evolved human social characteristics. Darwin's frequent pairing of "Belief in God" and religion with topics on superstitions and fetishism throughout the book can also be interpreted as indicating how much truth he assigned to the former.

In the introduction Darwin wrote:

> "Ignorance more frequently begets confidence than does knowledge: it is those who know little, and not those who know much, who so positively assert that this or that problem will never be solved by science."[334]

Later on in the book he dismisses an argument for religion being innate:

> "Belief in God — Religion. — There is no evidence that man was aboriginally endowed with the ennobling belief in the existence of an Omnipotent God. On the contrary there is ample evidence, derived not from hasty travellers, but from men who have long resided with savages, that numerous races have existed, and still exist, who have no idea of one or more gods, and who have no words in their languages to express such an idea. The question is of course wholly distinct from that higher one, whether there exists a Creator and Ruler of the universe; and this has been answered in the affirmative by some of the highest intellects that have ever existed."[335]

> "The belief in God has often been advanced as not only the greatest, but the most complete of all the distinctions between man and the lower animals. It is however impossible, as we have seen, to maintain that this belief is innate or instinctive in man. On the other hand a belief in all-pervading spiritual agencies seems to be universal; and apparently follows from a considerable advance in man's reason, and from a still greater advance in his faculties of imagination, curiosity and wonder. I am aware that the assumed instinctive belief in God has been used by many persons as an argument for His existence. But this is a rash argument, as we should thus be compelled to believe in the existence of many cruel and malignant spirits, only a little more powerful than man; for the belief in them is far more general than in a beneficent Deity. The idea of a universal and beneficent Creator does not seem to arise in the mind of man, until he has been elevated by long-continued culture."[336]

Figure 57: *The classic image of Darwin as an old man*

Enquiries about religious views

Fame and honours brought a stream of enquiries about Darwin's religious views, leading him to comment "Half the fools throughout Europe write to ask me the stupidest questions." He sometimes retorted sharply, "I am sorry to have to inform you that I do not believe in the Bible as a divine revelation, & therefore not in Jesus Christ as the Son of God", and at other times was more guarded, telling a young count studying with Ernst Haeckel that "Science has nothing to do with Christ; except in so far as the habit of scientific research makes a man cautious in admitting evidence. For myself I do not believe that there ever has been any Revelation. As for a future life, every man must judge for himself between conflicting vague probabilities." He declined a request by the Archbishop of Canterbury to join a 'Private Conference' of devout scientists to harmonise science and religion, for he saw "no prospect of any benefit arising" from it.

When Brodie Innes sent on a sermon by E. B. Pusey, Darwin responded that he could "hardly see how religion & science can be kept as distinct as he desires, as geology has to treat of the history of the Earth & Biology that of man.— But I most wholly agree with you that there is no reason why the disciples of either school should attack each other with bitterness, though each upholding strictly their beliefs. You, I am sure, have always practically acted in this manner in your conduct towards me & I do not doubt to all others. Nor can I remember that I have ever published a word directly against religion or the clergy." In response to an enquiry about the same sermon from the botanist Henry Nicholas Ridley, Darwin stated that "Dr Pusey was mistaken in imagining that I wrote the *Origin* with any relation whatever to Theology", and added that "many years ago when I was collecting facts for the Origin, my belief in what is called a personal God was as firm as that of Dr Pusey himself, & as to the eternity of matter I have never troubled myself about such insoluble questions.— Dr Pusey's attack will be as powerless to retard by a day the belief in evolution as were the virulent attacks made by divines fifty years ago against Geology, & the still older ones of the Catholic church against Galileo". Brodie Innes deplored "unwise and violent" theological attacks on his old friend, for while they had disagreements, "How nicely things would go if other folk were like Darwin and Brodie Innes."

In a letter to a correspondent at the University of Utrecht in 1873, Darwin expressed agnosticism: <templatestyles src="Template:Quote/styles.css"/>

> *I may say that the impossibility of conceiving that this grand and wondrous universe, with our conscious selves, arose through chance, seems to me the chief argument for the existence of God; but whether this is an argument of real value, I have never been able to decide. I am aware that if we admit a first cause, the mind still craves to know whence it came from and how it arose. Nor can I overlook the difficulty from the immense amount of suffering through the world. I am, also, induced to defer to a certain extent to the judgment of many able men who have fully believed in God; but here again I see how poor an argument this is. The safest conclusion seems to me to be that the whole subject is beyond the scope of man's intellect; but man can do his duty.*

Caution about publication, spiritualism

In 1873 Darwin's son George wrote an essay which boldly dismissed prayer, divine morals and "future rewards & punishments". Darwin wrote "I would urge you not to publish it for some months, at the soonest, & then consider whether you think it new & important enough to counterbalance the evils; remembering the cart-loads which have been published on this subject. – The evils on giving pain to others, & injuring your own power & usefulness... It is an old doctrine of mine that it is of foremost importance for a young author to publish.. only what is very good & new... remember that an enemy might ask who is this man... that he should give to the world his opinions on the deepest subjects?... but my advice is to pause, pause, pause."

During the public interest in Modern Spiritualism, Darwin attended a séance at Erasmus's house in January 1874, but as the room grew stuffy Darwin went upstairs to lie down, missing the show, with sparks, sounds and the table rising above their heads. While Galton thought it a "good séance", Darwin later wrote "The Lord have mercy on us all, if we have to believe such rubbish" and told Emma that it was "all imposture" and "it would take an enormous weight of evidence" to convince him otherwise. At a second séance Huxley and George found that Williams was nothing but a cheat, to Darwin's relief.

In 1876 Darwin wrote the following regarding his publicly stated position of agnosticism: "Formerly I was led... to the firm conviction of the existence of God and the immortality of the soul. In my Journal I wrote that whilst standing in the midst of the grandeur of a Brazilian forest, 'it is not possible to give an adequate idea of the higher feelings of wonder, admiration, and devotion, which fill and elevate the mind.' I well remember my conviction that there is more in man than the mere breath of his body. But now the grandest scenes would not cause any such convictions and feelings to rise in my mind."[337]

In November 1878 when George Romanes presented his new book refuting theism, *A Candid Examination of Theism* by "Physicus", Darwin read it with "very great interest", but found it unconvincing; the arguments it put forward left open the possibility that God had initially created matter and energy with the potential of evolving to become organised.

Agnosticism

In 1879 John Fordyce wrote asking if Darwin believed in God, and if theism and evolution were compatible. Darwin replied that "a man may be an ardent Theist and an evolutionist", citing Charles Kingsley and Asa Gray as examples, and for himself, "In my most extreme fluctuations I have never been an atheist in the sense of denying the existence of a God.— I think that generally (& more and more so as I grow older) but not always, that an agnostic would be the most correct description of my state of mind."

Those opposing religion often took Darwin as their inspiration and expected his support for their cause, a role he firmly refused. In 1880 there was a huge controversy when the atheist Charles Bradlaugh was elected as a member of parliament and then prevented from taking his seat in the House of Commons. In response, the secularist Edward Aveling toured the country leading protests. In October of that year Aveling wanted to dedicate his book on *Darwin and his Works* to Darwin and asked him for permission. Darwin declined, writing that "though I am a strong advocate for free thought on all subjects, yet it appears to me (whether rightly or wrongly) that direct arguments against Christianity & theism produce hardly any effect on the public; & freedom of thought is best promoted by the gradual illumination of men's minds, which follows from the advance of science. It has, therefore, been always my object to avoid writing on religion, & I have confined myself to science. I may, however, have been unduly biased by the pain which it would give some members of my family, if I aided in any way direct attacks on religion."

Aveling and Büchner

In Germany militant *Darwinismus* elevated Darwin to heroic status. When the eminent Freethinker Doctor Ludwig Büchner requested an audience he thought he was greeting a noble ally. To Darwin this was a grotesque misunderstanding, but he felt unable to refuse. Darwin's wife Emma Darwin expressed her expectation that their guest "will refrain from airing his very strong religious opinions" and invited their old friend the Revd. John Brodie Innes. On Thursday 28 September 1881 Büchner arrived with Edward Aveling. Darwin's son Frank was also present. Darwin wittily explained that "[Brodie] & I have been fast friends for 30 years. We never thoroughly agreed on any subject but once and then we looked at each other and thought one of us must be very ill".

In uncharacteristically bold discussions after dinner Darwin asked his guests "Why do you call yourselves Atheists?" When they responded that they "did not commit the folly of god-denial, [and] avoided with equal care the folly of god-assertion", Darwin gave a thoughtful response, concluding that "I am with you in thought, but I should prefer the word Agnostic to the word Atheist." Aveling replied that, "after all, 'Agnostic' was but 'Atheist' writ respectable, and 'Atheist' was only 'Agnostic' writ aggressive." Darwin smiled and responded "Why should you be so aggressive? Is anything gained by trying to force these new ideas upon the mass of mankind? It is all very well for educated, cultured, thoughtful people; but are the masses yet ripe for it?" Aveling and Büchner questioned what would have happened if Darwin had been given that advice before publication of the *Origin*, and had confined "the revolutionary truths of Natural and Sexual Selection to the judicious few", where would the world be? Many feared danger if new ideas were "proclaimed abroad on the house-tops, and discussed in market-place and home. But he, happily for humanity, had by the gentle, irresistible power of reason, forced his new ideas upon the mass of the people. And the masses had been found ripe for it. Had he kept silence, the tremendous strides taken by human thought during the last twenty-one years would have been shorn of their fair proportions, perhaps had hardly been made at all. His own illustrious example was encouragement, was for a command to every thinker to make known to all his fellows that which he believed to be the truth."

Their talk turned to religion, and Darwin said "I never gave up Christianity until I was forty years of age." He agreed that Christianity was "not supported by the evidence", but he had reached this conclusion only slowly. Aveling recorded this discussion, and published it in 1883 as a penny pamphlet. Francis Darwin thought it gave "quite fairly his impressions of my father's views, but took issue with any suggestion of similar religious views, saying "My father's replies implied his preference for the unaggressive attitude of an Agnostic. Dr. Aveling seems to regard the absence of aggressiveness in my father's views as distinguishing them in an unessential manner from his own. But, in my judgment, it is precisely differences of this kind which distinguish him so completely from the class of thinkers to which Dr. Aveling belongs."

Funeral

Darwin's Westminster Abbey funeral expressed a public feeling of national pride, and religious writers of all persuasions praised his "noble character and his ardent pursuit of truth", calling him a "true Christian gentleman". In particular the Unitarians and free religionists, proud of his Dissenting upbringing, supported his naturalistic views. The Unitarian William Carpenter carried a resolution praising Darwin's unravelling of "the immutable laws of the Divine Government", shedding light on "the progress of humanity", and the Unitarian preacher John White Chadwick from New York wrote that "The nation's grandest temple of religion opened its gates and lifted up its everlasting doors and bade the King of Science come in."

Posthumous *Autobiography*

Darwin decided to leave a posthumous memoir for his family, and on Sunday 28 May 1876 he began *Recollections of the Development of my mind and character*. He found this candid private memoir easy going, covering his childhood, university, life on the *Beagle* expedition and developing work in science. A section headed "Religious Belief" opened just before his marriage, and frankly discussed his long disagreement with Emma. At first he had been unwilling to give up his faith, and had tried to "invent evidence" supporting the Gospels, but just as his clerical career had died a slow "natural death", so too did his belief in "Christianity as a divine revelation". "Inward convictions and feelings" had arisen from natural selection, as had survival instincts, and could not be relied on. He was quick to show Emma's side of the story and pay tribute to "your mother, ... so infinitely my superior in every moral quality ... my wise adviser and cheerful comforter".[338]

The Autobiography of Charles Darwin was published posthumously, and quotes about Christianity were omitted by Darwin's wife Emma and his son Francis because they were deemed dangerous for Charles Darwin's reputation. Only in 1958 did Darwin's granddaughter Nora Barlow publish a revised version which contained the omissions. This included statements discussed above in Autobiography on gradually increasing disbelief, and others such as the following:

> "By further reflecting that the clearest evidence would be requisite to make any sane man believe in the miracles by which Christianity is supported, — that the more we know of the fixed laws of nature the more incredible, do miracles become, — that the men at that time were ignorant and credulous to a degree almost incomprehensible by us, — that the Gospels cannot be proved to have been written simultaneously with the events, – that they differ in many important details, far too important as it seemed to me to be admitted as the usual inaccuracies of eyewitness; – by such reflections as these, which I give not as having the least novelty or value, but as they influenced me, I gradually came to disbelieve in Christianity as a divine revelation. The fact that many false religions have spread over large portions of the earth like wild-fire had some weight with me. Beautiful as is the morality of the New Testament, it can hardly be denied that its perfection depends in part on the interpretation which we now put on metaphors and allegories." (p.86)

> "I can indeed hardly see how anyone ought to wish Christianity to be true; for if so the plain language of the text seems to show that the men who do not believe, and this would include my Father, Brother and almost all my best friends, will be everlastingly punished. And this is a damnable doctrine." (p. 87)

> "The old argument of design in nature, as given by Paley, which formerly seemed to me so conclusive, fails, now that the law of natural selection had been discovered. We can no longer argue that, for instance, the beautiful hinge of a bivalve shell must have been made by an intelligent being, like the hinge of a door by man. There seems to be no more design in the variability of organic beings and in the action of natural selection, than in the course which the wind blows. Everything in nature is the result of fixed laws." (p.87)

> "At the present day (ca. 1872) the most usual argument for the existence of an intelligent God is drawn from the deep inward conviction and feelings which are experienced by most persons. But it cannot be doubted that Hindoos, Mahomadans and others might argue in the same manner and with equal force in favor of the existence of one God, or of many Gods, or as with the Buddhists of no God...This argument would be a valid one if all men of all races had the same inward conviction of the existence of one God: but we know that this is very far from being the case. Therefore I cannot see that such inward convictions and feelings are of any weight as evidence of what really exists." (p.91)

The Lady Hope Story

The "Lady Hope Story", first published in 1915, claimed that Darwin had reverted to Christianity on his sickbed. The claims were rejected by Darwin's children and have been dismissed as false by historians.

Bibliography

- Aveling, E. B. (1883), *The religious views of Charles Darwin*, London: Freethought Publishing Company |access-date= requires |url= (help)<templatestyles src="Module:Citation/CS1/styles.css"></templatestyles>
- Babbage, Charles (1838), *The Ninth Bridgewater Treatise*[339] (2nd ed.), London: John Murray<templatestyles src="Module:Citation/CS1/styles.css"></templatestyles>
- Browne, E. Janet (1995), *Charles Darwin: vol. 1 Voyaging*, London: Jonathan Cape, ISBN 1-84413-314-1<templatestyles src="Module:Citation/CS1/styles.css"></templatestyles>
- Darwin, Charles (1871), *The Descent of Man, and Selection in Relation to Sex*[340] (1st ed.), London: John Murray<templatestyles src="Module:Citation/CS1/styles.css"></templatestyles>
- Darwin, Charles (1887), Darwin, Francis, ed., *The life and letters of Charles Darwin, including an autobiographical chapter*[341], London: John Murray, retrieved 4 November 2008<templatestyles src="Module:Citation/CS1/styles.css"></templatestyles>
- Darwin, Charles (1958), Barlow, Nora, ed., *The Autobiography of Charles Darwin 1809–1882. With the original omissions restored. Edited and with appendix and notes by his granddaughter Nora Barlow*[341], London: Collins, retrieved 4 November 2008<templatestyles src="Module:Citation/CS1/styles.css"></templatestyles>
- Desmond, Adrian; Moore, James (1991), *Darwin*, London: Michael Joseph, Penguin Group, ISBN 0-7181-3430-3<templatestyles src="Module:Citation/CS1/styles.css"></templatestyles>
- FitzRoy, Robert (1839), *Voyages of the Adventure and Beagle, Volume II*[342], London: Henry Colburn, retrieved 4 November 2008<templatestyles src="Module:Citation/CS1/styles.css"></templatestyles>
- Freeman, R. B. (2007), *Charles Darwin: A companion*[343] (2d online ed.), The Complete Works of Charles Darwin Online, retrieved 16 August 2014<templatestyles src="Module:Citation/CS1/styles.css"></templatestyles>
- Herbert, Sandra (1991), "Charles Darwin as a prospective geological author"[344], *British Journal for the History of Science*

- (24), pp. 159–192, retrieved 24 October 2008<templatestyles src="Module:Citation/CS1/styles.css"></templatestyles>
- Keynes, Richard (2001), *Charles Darwin's Beagle Diary*[345], Cambridge University Press, ISBN 0-521-23503-0, retrieved 24 October 2008<templatestyles src="Module:Citation/CS1/styles.css"></templatestyles>
- Miles, Sara Joan (2001), "Charles Darwin and Asa Gray Discuss Teleology and Design"[346], *Perspectives on Science and Christian Faith*, **53**, pp. 196–201, retrieved 22 November 2008<templatestyles src="Module:Citation/CS1/styles.css"></templatestyles>
- Moore, James (2005), *Darwin – A 'Devil's Chaplain'?*[347] (PDF), American Public Media, retrieved 22 November 2008<templatestyles src="Module:Citation/CS1/styles.css"></templatestyles>
- Moore, James (2006), *Evolution and Wonder – Understanding Charles Darwin*[348], Speaking of Faith (Radio Program), American Public Media, archived from the original[349] on 22 December 2008, retrieved 22 November 2008<templatestyles src="Module:Citation/CS1/styles.css"></templatestyles>
- Paley, W. (1809), *Natural Theology: or, Evidences of the Existence and Attributes of the Deity*[350] (12th ed.)<templatestyles src="Module:Citation/CS1/styles.css"></templatestyles>
- Quammen, David (2006), *The Reluctant Mr. Darwin*, New York: Atlas Books, ISBN 0-393-05981-2<templatestyles src="Module:Citation/CS1/styles.css"></templatestyles>
- Sulloway, Frank J. (2006), "Why Darwin Rejected Intelligent Design"[351] (PDF), in Brockman, John, *Intelligent Thought: Science versus the Intelligent Design Movement*, New York: Vintage, pp. 107–126, retrieved 8 December 2008<templatestyles src="Module:Citation/CS1/styles.css"></templatestyles>
- van Wyhe, John (27 March 2007), "Mind the gap: Did Darwin avoid publishing his theory for many years?"[352], *Notes and Records of the Royal Society*, **61**: 177–205, doi:10.1098/rsnr.2006.0171[353], retrieved 7 February 2008<templatestyles src="Module:Citation/CS1/styles.css"></templatestyles>
- van Wyhe, John (2008), *Darwin: The Story of the Man and His Theories of Evolution*, London: André Deutsch Ltd (published 1 September 2008), ISBN 0-233-00251-0<templatestyles src="Module:Citation/CS1/styles.css"></templatestyles>
- van Wyhe, John; Pallen, Mark J. (2012), "The 'Annie Hypothesis': Did the Death of His Daughter Cause Darwin to 'Give up Christianity'?", *Centaurus*, doi: 10.1111/j.1600-0498.2012.00256.x[354]<templatestyles src="Module:Citation/CS1/styles.css"></templatestyles>

- von Sydow, Momme (2005), "Charles Darwin: A Christian Undermining Christianity?"[355] (PDF), in Knight, David M.; Eddy, Matthew D., *Science and Beliefs: From Natural Philosophy to Natural Science, 1700–1900*, Burlington: Ashgate, pp. 141–156, ISBN 0-7546-3996-7, retrieved 16 December 2008<templatestyles src="Module:Citation/CS1/styles.css"></templatestyles>
- Yates, Simon (2003), *The Lady Hope Story: A Widespread Falsehood*[356], TalkOrigins Archive, retrieved 15 December 2006<templatestyles src="Module:Citation/CS1/styles.css"></templatestyles>

Further reading

- Anonymous (1882), "Obituary: Death Of Chas. Darwin"[357], *The New York Times* (21 April 1882)<templatestyles src="Module:Citation/CS1/styles.css"></templatestyles>
- Balfour, J. H. (11 May 1882), "Obituary Notice of Charles Robert Darwin", *Transactions & Proceedings of the Botanical Society of Edinburgh* (14), pp. 284–298<templatestyles src="Module:Citation/CS1/styles.css"></templatestyles>
- Browne, E. Janet (2002), *Charles Darwin: vol. 2 The Power of Place*, London: Jonathan Cape, ISBN 0-7126-6837-3<templatestyles src="Module:Citation/CS1/styles.css"></templatestyles>
- Darwin, Charles (1837–1838), *Notebook B: [Transmutation of species]*[358], Darwin Online, CUL-DAR121<templatestyles src="Module:Citation/CS1/styles.css"></templatestyles>
- Darwin, Charles (1839), *Narrative of the surveying voyages of His Majesty's Ships Adventure and Beagle between the years 1826 and 1836, describing their examination of the southern shores of South America, and the Beagle's circumnavigation of the globe. Journal and remarks. 1832–1836. Volume 3*[359], London: Henry Colburn<templatestyles src="Module:Citation/CS1/styles.css"></templatestyles>
- Darwin, Charles (1842), "Pencil Sketch of 1842"[360], in Darwin, Francis, *The foundations of The origin of species: Two essays written in 1842 and 1844.*[361], Cambridge University Press (published 1909)<templatestyles src="Module:Citation/CS1/styles.css"></templatestyles>
- Darwin, Charles (1845), Journal of researches into the natural history and geology of the countries visited during the voyage of H.M.S. Beagle round the world, under the Command of Capt. Fitz Roy, R.N. *2d edition*[362], London: John Murray<templatestyles src="Module:Citation/CS1/styles.css"></templatestyles>
- Darwin, Charles (1859), *On the Origin of Species by Means of Natural Selection, or the Preservation of Favoured Races in the*

- *Struggle for Life*[363] (1st ed.), London: John Murray<templatestyles src="Module:Citation/CS1/styles.css"></templatestyles>
- Darwin, Charles (1872), *The Expression of the Emotions in Man and Animals*[364], London: John Murray<templatestyles src="Module:Citation/CS1/styles.css"></templatestyles>
- Darwin, Charles (2006), "Journal"[365], in van Wyhe, John, [*Darwin's personal 'Journal' (1809–1881)*][366], Darwin Online, CUL-DAR158.1–76<templatestyles src="Module:Citation/CS1/styles.css"></templatestyles>
- Eldredge, Niles (2006), "Confessions of a Darwinist"[367], *The Virginia Quarterly Review* (Spring 2006), pp. 32–53<templatestyles src="Module:Citation/CS1/styles.css"></templatestyles>
- Lamoureux, Denis O. (March 2004), "Theological Insights from Charles Darwin"[368] (PDF), *Perspectives on Science and Christian Faith*, **56** (1), pp. 2–12<templatestyles src="Module:Citation/CS1/styles.css"></templatestyles>
- Leff, David (2000), *About Charles Darwin*[369]<templatestyles src="Module:Citation/CS1/styles.css"></templatestyles>
- Leifchild (1859), "Review of 'Origin'"[370], *Athenaeum* (No. 1673, 19 November 1859)<templatestyles src="Module:Citation/CS1/styles.css"></templatestyles>
- Lucas, J. R. (1979), "Wilberforce and Huxley: A Legendary Encounter"[371], *The Historical Journal*, **22** (2), pp. 313–330<templatestyles src="Module:Citation/CS1/styles.css"></templatestyles>
- Smith, Charles H. (1999), *Alfred Russel Wallace on Spiritualism, Man, and Evolution: An Analytical Essay*[372]<templatestyles src="Module:Citation/CS1/styles.css"></templatestyles>
- Wilkins, John S. (1997), *Evolution and Philosophy: Does evolution make might right?*[373], TalkOrigins Archive<templatestyles src="Module:Citation/CS1/styles.css"></templatestyles>
- Wilkins, John S. (2008), "Darwin", in Tucker, Aviezer, *A Companion to the Philosophy of History and Historiography*, Blackwell Companions to Philosophy, Chichester: Wiley-Blackwell, pp. 405–415, ISBN 1-4051-4908-6<templatestyles src="Module:Citation/CS1/styles.css"></templatestyles>
- van Wyhe, John (2008), *Charles Darwin: gentleman naturalist: A biographical sketch*[374], Darwin Online<templatestyles src="Module:Citation/CS1/styles.css"></templatestyles>

External links

- "Darwin Correspondence Project " Darwin and Religion: an introduction"[375]. Retrieved 19 February 2013.<templatestyles src="Module:Citation/CS1/styles.css"></templatestyles> subsections include What did Darwin believe?[376] and Darwin and design[377]
- Dr Paul Marston: Charles Darwin and Christian Faith[378]
- Life and Letters of Charles Darwin (1887) ed. Francis Darwin: Chapter VIII, Religion[379],
- Charles Darwin on Religion[380] by John Hedley Brooke
- Creationism: bad science, bad religion, bad education – Derek Gillard[381]
- Talk.Origins Archive: *The Lady Hope Story: A Widespread Falsehood*[356]
- A Dog and the Mind of Newton[382] – discusses Darwin and his faith (adapted from *Evolution* by Carl Zimmer, <templatestyles src="Module:Citation/CS1/styles.css" />ISBN 0-06-019906-7)
- 2004 National Geographic article[383], which has Darwin as a deist at least at one point of his life
- SOF: Evolution and wonder – understanding Charles Darwin (Speaking of Faith from American Public Media)[384] Links to mp3, transcript, and links to supporting material.
- Eden and Evolution[385], interview with James Moore and others.
- Was Charles Darwin an Atheist?[386], article in The Public Domain Review by John van Wyhe

Evolutionary social movements

Darwinism

Darwinism is a theory of biological evolution developed by the English naturalist Charles Darwin (1809–1882) and others, stating that all species of organisms arise and develop through the natural selection of small, inherited variations that increase the individual's ability to compete, survive, and reproduce. Also called **Darwinian theory**, it originally included the broad concepts of transmutation of species or of evolution which gained general scientific acceptance after Darwin published *On the Origin of Species* in 1859, including concepts which predated Darwin's theories. It subsequently referred to the specific concepts of natural selection, the Weismann barrier, or the central dogma of molecular biology. Though the term usually refers strictly to biological evolution, creationists have appropriated it to refer to the origin of life, and it has even been applied to concepts of cosmic evolution, both of which have no connection to Darwin's work. It is therefore considered the belief and acceptance of Darwin's and of his predecessors' work—in place of other theories, including divine design and extraterrestrial origins.

English biologist Thomas Henry Huxley coined the term *Darwinism* in April 1860. It was used to describe evolutionary concepts in general, including earlier concepts published by English philosopher Herbert Spencer. Many of the proponents of Darwinism at that time, including Huxley, had reservations about the significance of natural selection, and Darwin himself gave credence to what was later called Lamarckism. The strict neo-Darwinism of German evolutionary biologist August Weismann gained few supporters in the late 19th century. During the approximate period of the 1880s to about 1920, sometimes called "the eclipse of Darwinism", scientists proposed various alternative evolutionary mechanisms which eventually proved untenable. The development of the modern synthesis in the early 20th century, incorporating natural

Figure 58: *Charles Darwin in 1868*

selection with population genetics and Mendelian genetics, revived Darwinism in an updated form.

While the term *Darwinism* has remained in use amongst the public when referring to modern evolutionary theory, it has increasingly been argued by science writers such as Olivia Judson and Eugenie Scott that it is an inappropriate term for modern evolutionary theory. For example, Darwin was unfamiliar with the work of the Moravian scientist and Augustinian friar Gregor Mendel, and as a result had only a vague and inaccurate understanding of heredity. He naturally had no inkling of later theoretical developments and, like Mendel himself, knew nothing of genetic drift, for example. In the United States, creationists often use the term "Darwinism" as a pejorative term in reference to beliefs such as scientific materialism, but in the United Kingdom the term has no negative connotations, being freely used as a shorthand for the body of theory dealing with evolution, and in particular, with evolution by natural selection.

Conceptions of Darwinism

While the term *Darwinism* had been used previously to refer to the work of Erasmus Darwin in the late 18th century, the term as understood today was introduced when Charles Darwin's 1859 book *On the Origin of Species* was

Figure 59: *As evolution became widely accepted in the 1870s, caricatures of Charles Darwin with an ape or monkey body symbolised evolution.*

reviewed by Thomas Henry Huxley in the April 1860 issue of the *Westminster Review*. Having hailed the book as "a veritable Whitworth gun in the armoury of liberalism" promoting scientific naturalism over theology, and praising the usefulness of Darwin's ideas while expressing professional reservations about Darwin's gradualism and doubting if it could be proved that natural selection could form new species, Huxley compared Darwin's achievement to that of Nicolaus Copernicus in explaining planetary motion: <templatestyles src="Template:Quote/styles.css"/>

> What if the orbit of Darwinism should be a little too circular? What if species should offer residual phenomena, here and there, not explicable by natural selection? Twenty years hence naturalists may be in a position to say whether this is, or is not, the case; but in either event they will owe the author of "The Origin of Species" an immense debt of gratitude.... And viewed as a whole, we do not believe that, since the publication of Von Baer's "Researches on Development," thirty years ago, any work has appeared calculated to exert so large an influence, not only on the future of Biology, but in extending the domination of Science over regions of thought into which she has, as yet, hardly penetrated.

These are the basic tenets of evolution by natural selection as defined by Darwin:

1. More individuals are produced each generation that can survive.
2. Phenotypic variation exists among individuals and the variation is heritable.
3. Those individuals with heritable traits better suited to the environment will survive.
4. When reproductive isolation occurs new species will form.

Another important evolutionary theorist of the same period was the Russian geographer and prominent anarchist Peter Kropotkin who, in his book *Mutual Aid: A Factor of Evolution* (1902), advocated a conception of Darwinism counter to that of Huxley. His conception was centred around what he saw as the widespread use of co-operation as a survival mechanism in human societies and animals. He used biological and sociological arguments in an attempt to show that the main factor in facilitating evolution is cooperation between individuals in free-associated societies and groups. This was in order to counteract the conception of fierce competition as the core of evolution, which provided a rationalization for the dominant political, economic and social theories of the time; and the prevalent interpretations of Darwinism, such as those by Huxley, who is targeted as an opponent by Kropotkin. Kropotkin's conception of Darwinism could be summed up by the following quote:

<templatestyles src="Template:Quote/styles.css"/>

> *In the animal world we have seen that the vast majority of species live in societies, and that they find in association the best arms for the struggle for life: understood, of course, in its wide Darwinian sense—not as a struggle for the sheer means of existence, but as a struggle against all natural conditions unfavourable to the species. The animal species, in which individual struggle has been reduced to its narrowest limits, and the practice of mutual aid has attained the greatest development, are invariably the most numerous, the most prosperous, and the most open to further progress. The mutual protection which is obtained in this case, the possibility of attaining old age and of accumulating experience, the higher intellectual development, and the further growth of sociable habits, secure the maintenance of the species, its extension, and its further progressive evolution. The unsociable species, on the contrary, are doomed to decay.*
>
> —Peter Kropotkin, Mutual Aid: A Factor of Evolution (1902), Conclusion

19th-century usage

"Darwinism" soon came to stand for an entire range of evolutionary (and often revolutionary) philosophies about both biology and society. One of the more prominent approaches, summed in the 1864 phrase "survival of the fittest" by Herbert Spencer, later became emblematic of Darwinism even though Spencer's own understanding of evolution (as expressed in 1857) was more similar to that of Jean-Baptiste Lamarck than to that of Darwin, and predated the publication of Darwin's theory in 1859. What is now called "Social Darwinism" was, in its day, synonymous with "Darwinism"—the application of Darwinian principles of "struggle" to society, usually in support of anti-philanthropic political agenda. Another interpretation, one notably favoured by Darwin's half-cousin Francis Galton, was that "Darwinism" implied that because natural selection was apparently no longer working on "civilized" people, it was possible for "inferior" strains of people (who would normally be filtered out of the gene pool) to overwhelm the "superior" strains, and voluntary corrective measures would be desirable—the foundation of eugenics.

In Darwin's day there was no rigid definition of the term "Darwinism", and it was used by opponents and proponents of Darwin's biological theory alike to mean whatever they wanted it to in a larger context. The ideas had international influence, and Ernst Haeckel developed what was known as *Darwinismus* in Germany, although, like Spencer's "evolution", Haeckel's "Darwinism" had only a rough resemblance to the theory of Charles Darwin, and was not centered on natural selection.[387] In 1886, Alfred Russel Wallace went on a lecture tour across the United States, starting in New York and going via Boston, Washington, Kansas, Iowa and Nebraska to California, lecturing on what he called "Darwinism" without any problems.

In his book *Darwinism* (1889), Wallace had used the term *pure-Darwinism* which proposed a "greater efficacy" for natural selection.[388,389] George Romanes dubbed this view as "Wallaceism", noting that in contrast to Darwin, this position was advocating a "pure theory of natural selection to the exclusion of any supplementary theory."[390,391] Taking influence from Darwin, Romanes was a proponent of both natural selection and the inheritance of acquired characteristics. The latter was denied by Wallace who was a strict selectionist.[392] Romanes' definition of Darwinism conformed directly with Darwin's views and was contrasted with Wallace's definition of the term.[393]

Other uses

The term *Darwinism* is often used in the United States by promoters of creationism, notably by leading members of the intelligent design movement, as an epithet to attack evolution as though it were an ideology (an "ism") of philosophical naturalism, or atheism.[394] For example, UC Berkeley law professor and author Phillip E. Johnson makes this accusation of atheism with reference to Charles Hodge's book *What Is Darwinism?* (1874).[395] However, unlike Johnson, Hodge confined the term to exclude those like American botanist Asa

Gray who combined Christian faith with support for Darwin's natural selection theory, before answering the question posed in the book's title by concluding: "It is Atheism."[396] Creationists use the term *Darwinism*, often pejoratively, to imply that the theory has been held as true only by Darwin and a core group of his followers, whom they cast as dogmatic and inflexible in their belief. In the 2008 documentary film *Expelled: No Intelligence Allowed*, which promotes intelligent design (ID), American writer and actor Ben Stein refers to scientists as Darwinists. Reviewing the film for *Scientific American*, John Rennie says "The term is a curious throwback, because in modern biology almost no one relies solely on Darwin's original ideas... Yet the choice of terminology isn't random: Ben Stein wants you to stop thinking of evolution as an actual science supported by verifiable facts and logical arguments and to start thinking of it as a dogmatic, atheistic ideology akin to Marxism."

However, *Darwinism* is also used neutrally within the scientific community to distinguish the modern evolutionary synthesis, sometimes called "neo-Darwinism", from those first proposed by Darwin. *Darwinism* also is used neutrally by historians to differentiate his theory from other evolutionary theories current around the same period. For example, *Darwinism* may be used to refer to Darwin's proposed mechanism of natural selection, in comparison to more recent mechanisms such as genetic drift and gene flow. It may also refer specifically to the role of Charles Darwin as opposed to others in the history of evolutionary thought—particularly contrasting Darwin's results with those of earlier theories such as Lamarckism or later ones such as the modern evolutionary synthesis.

In political discussions in the United States, the term is mostly used by its enemies. "It's a rhetorical device to make evolution seem like a kind of faith, like 'Maoism,'" says Harvard University biologist E. O. Wilson. He adds, "Scientists don't call it 'Darwinism'." In the United Kingdom the term often retains its positive sense as a reference to natural selection, and for example British ethologist and evolutionary biologist Richard Dawkins wrote in his collection of essays *A Devil's Chaplain*, published in 2003, that as a scientist he is a Darwinist.

In his 1995 book *Darwinian Fairytales*, Australian philosopher David Stove used the term "Darwinism" in a different sense than the above examples. Describing himself as non-religious and as accepting the concept of natural selection as a well-established fact, Stove nonetheless attacked what he described as flawed concepts proposed by some "Ultra-Darwinists." Stove alleged that by using weak or false *ad hoc* reasoning, these Ultra-Darwinists used evolutionary concepts to offer explanations that were not valid (e.g., Stove suggested that sociobiological explanation of altruism as an evolutionary feature was presented in such a way that the argument was effectively immune to any criticism). Philosopher Simon Blackburn wrote a rejoinder to Stove, though a subsequent essay by Stove's protegee James Franklin's suggested that Blackburn's response actually "confirms Stove's central thesis that Darwinism can 'explain' anything."

References

<templatestyles src="Template:Refbegin/styles.css" />

- Bowler, Peter J. (2003). *Evolution: The History of an Idea* (3rd completely rev. and expanded ed.). Berkeley, CA: University of California Press. ISBN 0-520-23693-9. LCCN 2002007569[397]. OCLC 49824702[398].<templatestyles src="Module:Citation/CS1/styles.css"></templatestyles>
- Browne, Janet (2002). *Charles Darwin: The Power of Place*. **2**. London: Jonathan Cape. ISBN 0-679-42932-8. LCCN 94006598[399]. OCLC 733100564[400].<templatestyles src="Module:Citation/CS1/styles.css"></templatestyles>
- Hodge, Charles (1874). *What is Darwinism?*[401]. New York: Scribner, Armstrong, and Company. LCCN 06012878[402]. OCLC 11489956[403]. Retrieved 2015-11-16.<templatestyles src="Module:Citation/CS1/styles.css"></templatestyles>
- Kropotkin, Peter (1902). *Mutual Aid: A Factor of Evolution*. New York: McClure Phillips & Co. LCCN 03000886[404]. OCLC 1542829[405].<templatestyles src="Module:Citation/CS1/styles.css"></templatestyles> Mutual aid; a factor of evolution (1902)[406] on the Internet Archive Retrieved 2015-11-17.
- Petto, Andrew J.; Godfrey, Laurie R., eds. (2007) [Originally published 2007 as *Scientists Confront Intelligent Design and Creationism*]. *Scientists Confront Creationism: Intelligent Design and Beyond*. New York: W. W. Norton & Company. ISBN 978-0-393-33073-1. LCCN 2006039753[407]. OCLC 173480577[408].<templatestyles src="Module:Citation/CS1/styles.css"></templatestyles>
- Stove, David (1995). *Darwinian Fairytales*. Avebury Series in Philosophy. Aldershot, Hants, England; Brookfield, VT: Avebury. ISBN 1-85972-306-3. LCCN 95083037[409]. OCLC 35145565[410].<templatestyles src="Module:Citation/CS1/styles.css"></templatestyles>

Further reading

- (in Russian) Danilevsky, Nikolay. 1885-1889 *Darwinism: A Critical Study*[411] (Дарвинизм. Критическое исследование) at Runivers.ru in DjVu format.
- Fiske, John. (1885). *Darwinism, and Other Essays*[412]. Houghton Mifflin and Company.
- Huxley, Thomas Henry. (1893). *Darwiniana: Essays*[413]. Macmillan and Company.
- Mayr, Ernst. (1985). *The Growth of Biological Thought: Diversity, Evolution, and Inheritance*. Harvard University Press.
- Romanes, John George. (1906). *Darwin and After Darwin: An Exposition of the Darwinian Theory and a Discussion of Post-Darwinian Questions*[414]. *Volume 2: Heredity and Utility*. The Open Court Publishing Company.
- Wallace, Alfred Russel. (1889). *Darwinism: An Exposition of the Theory of Natural Selection, with Some of Its Applications*[415]. Macmillan and Company.

External links

Look up *darwinism* in Wiktionary, the free dictionary.

- Lennox, James (26 May 2015). "Darwinism"[416]. In Zalta, Edward N. *Stanford Encyclopedia of Philosophy* (Summer 2015 ed.). Stanford, CA: The Metaphysics Research Lab, Center for the Study of Language and Information (CSLI), Stanford University. Retrieved 2015-11-16.<templatestyles src="Module:Citation/CS1/styles.css"></templatestyles>

Eugenics

This article is part of a series on
Fringe medicine and medical conspiracy theories
• v • t • e[417]

Eugenics (/juːˈdʒɛnɪks/; from Greek εὐγενής *eugenes* 'well-born' from εὖ *eu*, 'good, well' and γένος *genos*, 'race, stock, kin')[418] is a set of beliefs and practices that aims at improving the genetic quality of a human population. The exact definition of *eugenics* has been a matter of debate since the term was coined by Francis Galton in 1883. The concept predates this coinage, with Plato suggesting applying the principles of selective breeding to humans around 400 BCE.

Frederick Osborn's 1937 journal article "Development of a Eugenic Philosophy" framed it as a social philosophy—that is, a philosophy with implications for social order. That definition is not universally accepted. Osborn advocated for higher rates of sexual reproduction among people with desired traits (positive eugenics), or reduced rates of sexual reproduction and sterilization of people with less-desired or undesired traits (negative eugenics).

Alternatively, gene selection rather than "people selection" has recently been made possible through advances in genome editing, leading to what is sometimes called new eugenics, also known as neo-eugenics, consumer eugenics, or liberal eugenics.

While eugenic principles have been practiced as far back in world history as ancient Greece, the modern history of eugenics began in the early 20th century when a popular eugenics movement emerged in the United Kingdom and spread to many countries including the United States, Canada and most European countries. In this period, eugenic ideas were espoused across the political spectrum. Consequently, many countries adopted eugenic policies with

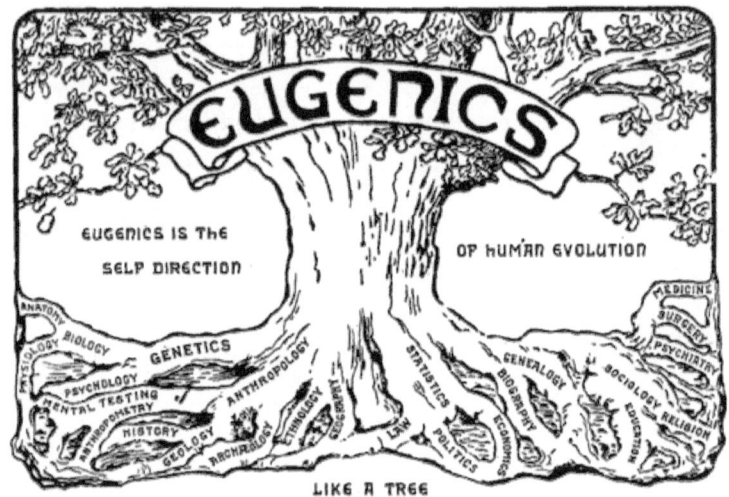

Figure 60: *Logo from the Second International Eugenics Conference, 1921, depicting eugenics as a tree which unites a variety of different fields*

the intent to improve the quality of their populations' genetic stock. Such programs included both "positive" measures, such as encouraging individuals deemed particularly "fit" to reproduce, and "negative" measures such as marriage prohibitions and forced sterilization of people deemed unfit for reproduction. People deemed unfit to reproduce often included people with mental or physical disabilities, people who scored in the low ranges of different IQ tests, criminals and deviants, and members of disfavored minority groups. The eugenics movement became negatively associated with Nazi Germany and the Holocaust when many of the defendants at the Nuremberg trials attempted to justify their human rights abuses by claiming there was little difference between the Nazi eugenics programs and the U.S. eugenics programs. In the decades following World War II, with the institution of human rights, many countries gradually began to abandon eugenics policies, although some Western countries, among them the United States and Sweden, continued to carry out forced sterilizations.

Since the 1980s and 1990s, when new assisted reproductive technology procedures became available such as gestational surrogacy (available since 1985), preimplantation genetic diagnosis (available since 1989), and cytoplasmic transfer (first performed in 1996), fear has emerged about a possible revival of eugenics.

A major criticism of eugenics policies is that, regardless of whether "negative" or "positive" policies are used, they are susceptible to abuse because the criteria of selection are determined by whichever group is in political power at the time. Furthermore, negative eugenics in particular is considered by many to be a violation of basic human rights, which include the right to reproduction. Another criticism is that eugenic policies eventually lead to a loss of genetic diversity, resulting in inbreeding depression due to lower genetic variation.

History

Origin and development

<templatestyles src="Template:Quote_box/styles.css" />

We put down mad dogs; we kill the wild, untamed ox; we use the knife on sick sheep to stop their infecting the flock; we destroy abnormal offspring at birth; children, too, if they are born weak or deformed, we drown. Yet this is not the work of anger, but of reason - to separate the sound from the worthless

Seneca the Younger

The concept of positive eugenics to produce better human beings has existed at least since Plato suggested selective mating to produce a guardian class. In Sparta, every Spartan child was inspected by the council of elders, the Gerousia, which determined if the child was fit to live or not. In the early years of ancient Rome, a Roman father was obliged by law to immediately kill his child if it was physically disabled.[419] Among the ancient Germanic tribes, people who were cowardly, unwarlike or "stained with abominable vices" were put to death, usually by being drowned in swamps.[420]

The first formal negative eugenics, that is a legal provision against birth of inferior human beings, was promulgated in Western European culture by the Christian Council of Agde in 506, which forbade marriage between cousins.[421]

This idea was also promoted by William Goodell (1829–1894) who advocated the castration and spaying of the insane.

The idea of a modern project of improving the human population through a statistical understanding of heredity used to encourage good breeding was originally developed by Francis Galton and, initially, was closely linked to Darwinism and his theory of natural selection.[422] Galton had read his half-cousin Charles Darwin's theory of evolution, which sought to explain the development of plant and animal species, and desired to apply it to humans. Based on his biographical studies, Galton believed that desirable human qualities were hereditary traits, though Darwin strongly disagreed with this elaboration of his theory. In 1883, one year after Darwin's death, Galton gave his research a

Figure 61: *Francis Galton was an early eugenicist, coining the term itself and popularizing the collocation of the words "nature and nurture".*

name: *eugenics*. With the introduction of genetics, eugenics became associated with genetic determinism, the belief that human character is entirely or in the majority caused by genes, unaffected by education or living conditions. Many of the early geneticists were not Darwinians, and evolution theory was not needed for eugenics policies based on genetic determinism. Throughout its recent history, eugenics has remained controversial.[423]

Eugenics became an academic discipline at many colleges and universities and received funding from many sources. Organizations were formed to win public support and sway opinion towards responsible eugenic values in parenthood, including the British Eugenics Education Society of 1907 and the American Eugenics Society of 1921. Both sought support from leading clergymen and modified their message to meet religious ideals. In 1909 the Anglican clergymen William Inge and James Peile both wrote for the British Eugenics Education Society. Inge was an invited speaker at the 1921 International Eugenics Conference, which was also endorsed by the Roman Catholic Archbishop of New York Patrick Joseph Hayes.

Three International Eugenics Conferences presented a global venue for eugenists with meetings in 1912 in London, and in 1921 and 1932 in New York City. Eugenic policies were first implemented in the early 1900s in the United

Eugenics 283

Figure 62: *G. K. Chesterton, an opponent of eugenics, in 1905, by photographer Alvin Langdon Coburn*

States. It also took root in France, Germany, and Great Britain. Later, in the 1920s and 1930s, the eugenic policy of sterilizing certain mental patients was implemented in other countries including Belgium, Brazil, Canada, Japan and Sweden.

In addition to being practiced in a number of countries, eugenics was internationally organized through the International Federation of Eugenics Organizations.[424] Its scientific aspects were carried on through research bodies such as the Kaiser Wilhelm Institute of Anthropology, Human Heredity, and Eugenics,[425] the Cold Spring Harbour Carnegie Institution for Experimental Evolution,[426] and the Eugenics Record Office.[427] Politically, the movement advocated measures such as sterilization laws.[428] In its moral dimension, eugenics rejected the doctrine that all human beings are born equal and redefined moral worth purely in terms of genetic fitness.[429] Its racist elements included pursuit of a pure "Nordic race" or "Aryan" genetic pool and the eventual elimination of "unfit" races.[430,431]

Early critics of the philosophy of eugenics included the American sociologist Lester Frank Ward, the English writer G. K. Chesterton, the German-American anthropologist Franz Boas, who argued that advocates of eugenics greatly over-estimate the influence of biology, and Scottish tuberculosis pioneer and author Halliday Sutherland. Ward's 1913 article " Eugenics, Euthenics, and Eudemics[432]", Chesterton's 1917 book *Eugenics and Other Evils*, and Boas' 1916 article "Eugenics" (published in *The Scientific Monthly*) were all harshly critical of the rapidly growing movement. Sutherland identified eugenists as a major obstacle to the eradication and cure of tuberculosis in his 1917 address "Consumption: Its Cause and Cure",[433] and criticism of eugenists and Neo-Malthusians in his 1921 book *Birth Control* led to a writ for libel from the eugenist Marie Stopes. Several biologists were also antagonistic to the eugenics movement, including Lancelot Hogben.[434] Other biologists such as J. B. S. Haldane and R. A. Fisher expressed skepticism in the belief that sterilization of "defectives" would lead to the disappearance of undesirable genetic traits.[435]

Among institutions, the Catholic Church was an opponent of state-enforced sterilizations. Attempts by the Eugenics Education Society to persuade the British government to legalize voluntary sterilization were opposed by Catholics and by the Labour Party. The American Eugenics Society initially gained some Catholic supporters, but Catholic support declined following the 1930 papal encyclical *Casti connubii*. In this, Pope Pius XI explicitly condemned sterilization laws: "Public magistrates have no direct power over the bodies of their subjects; therefore, where no crime has taken place and there is no cause present for grave punishment, they can never directly harm, or tamper with the integrity of the body, either for the reasons of eugenics or for any other reason."

As a social movement, eugenics reached its greatest popularity in the early decades of the 20th century, when it was practiced around the world and promoted by governments, institutions, and influential individuals. Many countries enacted various eugenics policies, including: genetic screenings, birth control, promoting differential birth rates, marriage restrictions, segregation (both racial segregation and sequestering the mentally ill), compulsory sterilization, forced abortions or forced pregnancies, ultimately culminating in genocide.

Nazism and the decline of eugenics

The scientific reputation of eugenics started to decline in the 1930s, a time when Ernst Rüdin used eugenics as a justification for the racial policies of Nazi Germany. Adolf Hitler had praised and incorporated eugenic ideas in *Mein Kampf* in 1925 and emulated eugenic legislation for the sterilization of "defectives" that had been pioneered in the United States once he took

Eugenics

Figure 63: *Hartheim Euthanasia Centre in 2005*

Figure 64: *A Lebensborn birth house in Nazi Germany. Created with the intention of raising the birth rate of "Aryan" children from the extramarital relations of "racially pure and healthy" parents.*

power.[436] Some common early 20th century eugenics methods involved identifying and classifying individuals and their families, including the poor, mentally ill, blind, deaf, developmentally disabled, promiscuous women, homosexuals, and racial groups (such as the Roma and Jews in Nazi Germany) as "degenerate" or "unfit", and therefore led to segregation, institutionalization, sterilization, euthanasia, and even mass murder.[437] The Nazi practice of euthanasia was carried out on hospital patients in the Aktion T4 centers such as Hartheim Castle.

By the end of World War II, many discriminatory eugenics laws were abandoned, having become associated with Nazi Germany.[437,438] H. G. Wells, who had called for "the sterilization of failures" in 1904, stated in his 1940 book *The Rights of Man: Or What are we fighting for?* that among the human rights, which he believed should be available to all people, was "a prohibition on mutilation, sterilization, torture, and any bodily punishment". After World War II, the practice of "imposing measures intended to prevent births within [a national, ethnical, racial or religious] group" fell within the definition of the new international crime of genocide, set out in the Convention on the Prevention and Punishment of the Crime of Genocide.[439] The Charter of Fundamental Rights of the European Union also proclaims "the prohibition of eugenic practices, in particular those aiming at selection of persons". In spite of the decline in discriminatory eugenics laws, some government mandated sterilizations continued into the 21st century. During the ten years President Alberto Fujimori led Peru from 1990 to 2000, 2,000 persons were allegedly involuntarily sterilized. China maintained its one-child policy until 2015 as well as a suite of other eugenics based legislation to reduce population size and manage fertility rates of different populations. In 2007 the United Nations reported coercive sterilizations and hysterectomies in Uzbekistan. During the years 2005 to 2013, nearly one-third of the 144 California prison inmates who were sterilized did not give lawful consent to the operation.

Modern resurgence of interest

Developments in genetic, genomic, and reproductive technologies at the end of the 20th century have raised numerous questions regarding the ethical status of eugenics, effectively creating a resurgence of interest in the subject. Some, such as UC Berkeley sociologist Troy Duster, claim that modern genetics is a back door to eugenics. This view is shared by White House Assistant Director for Forensic Sciences, Tania Simoncelli, who stated in a 2003 publication by the Population and Development Program at Hampshire College that advances in pre-implantation genetic diagnosis (PGD) are moving society to a "new era of eugenics", and that, unlike the Nazi eugenics, modern eugenics is consumer driven and market based, "where children are increasingly regarded as made-to-order consumer products". In a 2006 newspaper article, Richard Dawkins said that discussion regarding eugenics was inhibited by the shadow of Nazi misuse, to the extent that some scientists would not admit that breeding humans for certain abilities is at all possible. He believes that it is not physically different from breeding domestic animals for traits such as speed or herding skill. Dawkins felt that enough time had elapsed to at least ask just what the ethical differences were between breeding for ability versus training athletes or forcing children to take music lessons, though he could think of persuasive reasons to draw the distinction.

Lee Kuan Yew, the Founding Father of Singapore, started promoting eugenics as early as 1983.

In October 2015, the United Nations' International Bioethics Committee wrote that the ethical problems of human genetic engineering should not be confused with the ethical problems of the 20th century eugenics movements. However, it is still problematic because it challenges the idea of human equality and opens up new forms of discrimination and stigmatization for those who do not want, or cannot afford, the technology.

Transhumanism is often associated with eugenics, although most transhumanists holding similar views nonetheless distance themselves from the term "eugenics" (preferring "germinal choice" or "reprogenetics") to avoid having their position confused with the discredited theories and practices of early-20th-century eugenic movements.

Prenatal screening can be considered a form of contemporary eugenics because it may lead to abortions of children with undesirable traits.

Meanings and types

The term eugenics and its modern field of study were first formulated by Francis Galton in 1883, drawing on the recent work of his half-cousin Charles Darwin. Galton published his observations and conclusions in his book *Inquiries into Human Faculty and Its Development*.

The origins of the concept began with certain interpretations of Mendelian inheritance and the theories of August Weismann.[440] The word *eugenics* is derived from the Greek word *eu* ("good" or "well") and the suffix *-genēs* ("born"), and was coined by Galton in 1883 to replace the word "stirpiculture", which he had used previously but which had come to be mocked due to its perceived sexual overtones. Galton defined eugenics as "the study of all agencies under human control which can improve or impair the racial quality of future generations".[441]

Figure 65: *Karl Pearson (1912)*

Historically, the term eugenics has referred to everything from prenatal care for mothers to forced sterilization and euthanasia. To population geneticists, the term has included the avoidance of inbreeding without altering allele frequencies; for example, J. B. S. Haldane wrote that "the motor bus, by breaking up inbred village communities, was a powerful eugenic agent." Debate as to what exactly counts as eugenics continues today.[442]

Edwin Black, journalist and author of *War Against the Weak*, claims eugenics is often deemed a pseudoscience because what is defined as a genetic improvement of a desired trait is often deemed a cultural choice rather than a matter that can be determined through objective scientific inquiry. The most disputed aspect of eugenics has been the definition of "improvement" of the human gene pool, such as what is a beneficial characteristic and what is a defect. Historically, this aspect of eugenics was tainted with scientific racism and pseudoscience.

Early eugenists were mostly concerned with factors of perceived intelligence that often correlated strongly with social class. Some of these early eugenists include Karl Pearson and Walter Weldon, who worked on this at the University College London.

Eugenics also had a place in medicine. In his lecture "Darwinism, Medical Progress and Eugenics", Karl Pearson said that everything concerning eugenics fell into the field of medicine. He basically placed the two words as equivalents. He was supported in part by the fact that Francis Galton, the father of eugenics, also had medical training.

Eugenic policies have been conceptually divided into two categories. Positive eugenics is aimed at encouraging reproduction among the genetically advantaged; for example, the reproduction of the intelligent, the healthy, and the successful. Possible approaches include financial and political stimuli, targeted demographic analyses, *in vitro* fertilization, egg transplants, and cloning. The movie Gattaca provides a fictional example of a dystopian society that uses eugenics to decided what you are capable of and your place in the world. Negative eugenics aimed to eliminate, through sterilization or segregation, those deemed physically, mentally, or morally "undesirable". This includes abortions, sterilization, and other methods of family planning. Both positive and negative eugenics can be coercive; abortion for fit women, for example, was illegal in Nazi Germany.

Jon Entine claims that eugenics simply means "good genes" and using it as synonym for genocide is an "all-too-common distortion of the social history of genetics policy in the United States." According to Entine, eugenics developed out of the Progressive Era and not "Hitler's twisted Final Solution".

Implementation methods

According to Richard Lynn, eugenics may be divided into two main categories based on the ways in which the methods of eugenics can be applied.[443]

- Classical eugenics
  - Negative eugenics by provision of information and services, i.e. reduction of unplanned pregnancies and births.[444]
    - Advocacy for sexual abstinence.[445]
    - Sex education in schools.[446]
    - School-based clinics.[447]
    - Promoting the use of contraception.[448]
    - Emergency contraception.[449]
    - Research for better contraceptives.[450]
    - Voluntary sterilization.[451]
    - Abortion.[452]
  - Negative eugenics by incentives, coercion and compulsion.[453]
    - Incentives for sterilization.[454]
    - The Denver Dollar-a-day program, i.e. paying teenage mothers for not becoming pregnant again.[455]
    - Incentives for women on welfare to use contraceptions.[456]
    - Payments for sterilization in developing countries.[457]

- Curtailment of benefits to welfare mothers.[458]
- Compulsory sterilization of the "mentally retarded".[459]
- Compulsory sterilization of female criminals.[460]
- Compulsory sterilization of male criminals.[461]
  - Licences for parenthood.[462,463]
  - Positive eugenics.[464]
    - Financial incentives to have children.[465]
    - Selective incentives for childbearing.[466]
    - Taxation of the childless.[467]
    - Ethical obligations of the elite.[468]
    - Eugenic immigration.[469]
- New eugenics
  - Artificial insemination by donor.[470]
  - Egg donation.[471]
  - Prenatal diagnosis of genetic disorders and pregnancy terminations of defective fetuses.[472]
  - Embryo selection.[473]
  - Genetic engineering.[474]
  - Gene therapy.[475]
  - Cloning.[476]

Arguments

Efficacy

The first major challenge to conventional eugenics based upon genetic inheritance was made in 1915 by Thomas Hunt Morgan. He demonstrated the event of genetic mutation occurring outside of inheritance involving the discovery of the hatching of a fruit fly (*Drosophila melanogaster*) with white eyes from a family with red eyes.[477] Morgan claimed that this demonstrated that major genetic changes occurred outside of inheritance and that the concept of eugenics based upon genetic inheritance was not completely scientifically accurate.[477] Additionally, Morgan criticized the view that subjective traits, such as intelligence and criminality, were caused by heredity because he believed that the definitions of these traits varied and that accurate work in genetics could only be done when the traits being studied were accurately defined. Despite Morgan's public rejection of eugenics, much of his genetic research was absorbed by eugenics.

The heterozygote test is used for the early detection of recessive hereditary diseases, allowing for couples to determine if they are at risk of passing genetic defects to a future child. The goal of the test is to estimate the likelihood of passing the hereditary disease to future descendants.

Recessive traits can be severely reduced, but never eliminated unless the complete genetic makeup of all members of the pool was known, as aforementioned. As only very few undesirable traits, such as Huntington's disease, are dominant, it could be arguedWikipedia:Manual of Style/Words to watch#Unsupported attributions from certain perspectives that the practicality of "eliminating" traits is quite low.Wikipedia:Citation needed

There are examples of eugenic acts that managed to lower the prevalence of recessive diseases, although not influencing the prevalence of heterozygote carriers of those diseases. The elevated prevalence of certain genetically transmitted diseases among the Ashkenazi Jewish population (Tay–Sachs, cystic fibrosis, Canavan's disease, and Gaucher's disease), has been decreased in current populations by the application of genetic screening.

Pleiotropy occurs when one gene influences multiple, seemingly unrelated phenotypic traits, an example being phenylketonuria, which is a human disease that affects multiple systems but is caused by one gene defect. Andrzej Pękalski, from the University of Wrocław, argues that eugenics can cause harmful loss of genetic diversity if a eugenics program selects a pleiotropic gene that could possibly be associated with a positive trait. Pekalski uses the example of a coercive government eugenics program that prohibits people with myopia from breeding but has the unintended consequence of also selecting against high intelligence since the two go together.

Loss of genetic diversity

Eugenic policies could also lead to loss of genetic diversity, in which case a culturally accepted "improvement" of the gene pool could very likely—as evidenced in numerous instances in isolated island populations —result in extinction due to increased vulnerability to disease, reduced ability to adapt to environmental change, and other factors both known and unknown. A long-term, species-wide eugenics plan might lead to a scenario similar to this because the elimination of traits deemed undesirable would reduce genetic diversity by definition.[478]

Edward M. Miller claims that, in any one generation, any realistic program should make only minor changes in a fraction of the gene pool, giving plenty of time to reverse direction if unintended consequences emerge, reducing the likelihood of the elimination of desirable genes. Miller also argues that any appreciable reduction in diversity is so far in the future that little concern is needed for now.

While the science of genetics has increasingly provided means by which certain characteristics and conditions can be identified and understood, given the complexity of human genetics, culture, and psychology, at this point no agreed objective means of determining which traits might be ultimately desirable or undesirable. Some diseases such as sickle-cell disease and cystic fibrosis respectively confer immunity to malaria and resistance to cholera when a single copy of the recessive allele is contained within the genotype of the individual. Reducing the instance of sickle-cell disease genes in Africa where malaria is a common and deadly disease could indeed have extremely negative net consequences.

However, some genetic diseases cause people to consider some elements of eugenics.

Ethics

Societal and political consequences of eugenics call for a place in the discussion on the ethics behind the eugenics movement. Many of the ethical concerns regarding eugenics arise from its controversial past, prompting a discussion on what place, if any, it should have in the future. Advances in science have changed eugenics. In the past, eugenics had more to do with sterilization and enforced reproduction laws. Now, in the age of a progressively mapped genome, embryos can be tested for susceptibility to disease, gender, and genetic defects, and alternative methods of reproduction such as in vitro fertilization are becoming more common. Therefore, eugenics is no longer *ex post facto* regulation of the living but instead preemptive action on the unborn.

With this change, however, there are ethical concerns which lack adequate attention, and which must be addressed before eugenic policies can be properly implemented in the future. Sterilized individuals, for example, could volunteer for the procedure, albeit under incentive or duress, or at least voice their opinion. The unborn fetus on which these new eugenic procedures are performed cannot speak out, as the fetus lacks the voice to consent or to express his or her opinion. Philosophers disagree about the proper framework for reasoning about such actions, which change the very identity and existence of future persons.

Opposition

A common criticism of eugenics is that "it inevitably leads to measures that are unethical".[479] Some fear future "eugenics wars" as the worst-case scenario: the return of coercive state-sponsored genetic discrimination and human rights violations such as compulsory sterilization of persons with genetic defects, the killing of the institutionalized and, specifically, segregation and genocide of *races* perceived as inferior. Health law professor George Annas and technology law professor Lori Andrews are prominent advocates of the position that the use of these technologies could lead to such human-posthuman caste warfare.

Figure 66: *In the decades after World War II, the term "eugenics" had taken on a negative connotation and became increasingly unpopular within academic science. Many organizations and journals that had their origins in the eugenics movement began to distance themselves from the philosophy, as when Eugenics Quarterly became Social Biology in 1969.*

In his 2003 book *Enough: Staying Human in an Engineered Age*, environmental ethicist Bill McKibben argued at length against germinal choice technology and other advanced biotechnological strategies for human enhancement. He writes that it would be morally wrong for humans to tamper with fundamental aspects of themselves (or their children) in an attempt to overcome universal human limitations, such as vulnerability to aging, maximum life span and biological constraints on physical and cognitive ability. Attempts to "improve" themselves through such manipulation would remove limitations that provide a necessary context for the experience of meaningful human choice. He claims that human lives would no longer seem meaningful in a world where such limitations could be overcome with technology. Even the goal of using germinal choice technology for clearly therapeutic purposes should be relinquished, since it would inevitably produce temptations to tamper with such things as cognitive capacities. He argues that it is possible for societies to benefit from renouncing particular technologies, using as examples Ming China, Tokugawa Japan and the contemporary Amish.

Endorsement

Some, for example Nathaniel C. Comfort from Johns Hopkins University, claim that the change from state-led reproductive-genetic decision-making to individual choice has moderated the worst abuses of eugenics by transferring the decision-making from the state to the patient and their family. Comfort suggests that "the eugenic impulse drives us to eliminate disease, live longer and healthier, with greater intelligence, and a better adjustment to the conditions of society; and the health benefits, the intellectual thrill and the profits of genetic bio-medicine are too great for us to do otherwise." Others, such as bioethicist Stephen Wilkinson of Keele University and Honorary Research Fellow Eve Garrard at the University of Manchester, claim that some aspects of modern genetics can be classified as eugenics, but that this classification does not inherently make modern genetics immoral. In a co-authored publication by Keele University, they stated that "[e]ugenics doesn't seem always to be immoral, and so the fact that PGD, and other forms of selective reproduction, might sometimes technically be eugenic, isn't sufficient to show that they're wrong."

In their book published in 2000, *From Chance to Choice: Genetics and Justice*, bioethicists Allen Buchanan, Dan Brock, Norman Daniels and Daniel Wikler argued that liberal societies have an obligation to encourage as wide an adoption of eugenic enhancement technologies as possible (so long as such policies do not infringe on individuals' reproductive rights or exert undue pressures on prospective parents to use these technologies) in order to maximize public health and minimize the inequalities that may result from both natural genetic endowments and unequal access to genetic enhancements.

Original position, a hypothetical situation developed by American philosopher John Rawls, has been used as an argument for *negative eugenics*.[480]

References

Notes

Bibliography

- Anomaly, Jonathan (2018). *Defending Eugenics*[481]. Monash Bioethics Review.<templatestyles src="Module:Citation/CS1/styles.css"></templatestyles>
- Buchanan, Allen (2017). *Better than Human: The Promise and Perils of Deliberate Biomedical Enhancement*[482]. Oxford University Press.<templatestyles src="Module:Citation/CS1/styles.css"></templatestyles>

- Gyngell, Christopher; Selgelid, Michael (2016). *Twenty-First Century Eugenics*[483]. Oxford University Press.<templatestyles src="Module:Citation/CS1/styles.css"></templatestyles>
- Larson, Edward J. (2004). "Evolution". Modern Library. ISBN 0-679-64288-9.<templatestyles src="Module:Citation/CS1/styles.css"></templatestyles>
- Lynn, Richard (30 June 2001). *Eugenics: a reassessment* (Hardcover). 88 Post Road West, Westport, Connecticut 06881: Praeger Publishers. ISBN 0-275-95822-1. ISSN 1063-2158[484]. LCCN 00052459[485]<templatestyles src="Module:Citation/CS1/styles.css"></templatestyles>
- Savulescu, Julian; Kahane, Guy (2009). *The Moral Obligation to Have Children with the Best Chance of the Best Life*[486] (PDF). Bioethics.<templatestyles src="Module:Citation/CS1/styles.css"></templatestyles>
- Shaw, David (2006). *Genetic Morality*. Bern, Switzerland: Peter Lang. ISBN 3-03911-149-3.<templatestyles src="Module:Citation/CS1/styles.css"></templatestyles>

Histories of eugenics (academic accounts)

- Black, Edwin (2003). *War Against the Weak: Eugenics and America's Campaign to Create a Master Race*[487]. Four Walls Eight Windows. ISBN 1-56858-258-7.<templatestyles src="Module:Citation/CS1/styles.css"></templatestyles>
- Carlson, Elof Axel (2001). *The Unfit: A History of a Bad Idea*. Cold Spring Harbor, New York: Cold Spring Harbor Press. ISBN 0-87969-587-0.<templatestyles src="Module:Citation/CS1/styles.css"></templatestyles>
- Engs, Ruth C. (2005). *The Eugenics Movement: An Encyclopedia*. Westport, Connecticut: Greenwood Publishing. ISBN 0-313-32791-2.<templatestyles src="Module:Citation/CS1/styles.css"></templatestyles>
- Farrall, Lyndsay (1985). *The Origins and Growth of the English eugenics movement, 1865–1925*. Garland Pub. ISBN 978-0-8240-5810-4.<templatestyles src="Module:Citation/CS1/styles.css"></templatestyles>
- Kevles, Daniel J. (1985). *In the Name of Eugenics: Genetics and the Uses of Human Heredity*[488]. University of California Press. ISBN 978-0-520-05763-0.<templatestyles src="Module:Citation/CS1/styles.css"></templatestyles>

- Largent, Mark (2008). *Breeding Contempt: The History of Coerced Sterilization in the United States*. New Brunswick: Rutgers University Press. ISBN 978-0-8135-4183-9.<templatestyles src="Module:Citation/CS1/styles.css"></templatestyles>
- Leon, Sharon M. (2013). *An Image of God: The Catholic Struggle with Eugenics*. Chicago: University of Chicago Press.
- Redman, Samuel J. (2016). *Bone Rooms: From Scientific Racism to Human Prehistory in Museums*. Cambridge: Harvard University Press. ISBN 9780674660410.<templatestyles src="Module:Citation/CS1/styles.css"></templatestyles>
- "Deadly Medicine: Creating the Master Race"[489]. *USHMM.org*. United States Holocaust Memorial Museum. 2004. Archived from the original[490] on 4 September 2013.<templatestyles src="Module:Citation/CS1/styles.css"></templatestyles>
- Wyndham, Diana (2003). *Eugenics in Australia: Striving for national fitness*. London: Galton Institute. ISBN 978-0-9504066-7-1.<templatestyles src="Module:Citation/CS1/styles.css"></templatestyles>

Histories of hereditarian thought

- Barkan, Elazar (1992). *The Retreat of Scientific Racism: Changing Concepts of Race in Britain and the United States Between the World Wars*. New York: Cambridge University Press.<templatestyles src="Module:Citation/CS1/styles.css"></templatestyles>
- Ewen, Elizabeth; Ewen, Stuart (2006). *Typecasting: On the Arts and Sciences of Human Inequality* (1st ed.). New York: Seven Stories Press. ISBN 978-1-58322-735-0.<templatestyles src="Module:Citation/CS1/styles.css"></templatestyles>
- Gould, Stephen Jay (1981). *The Mismeasure of Man*. New York: Norton. ISBN 0-393-01489-4.<templatestyles src="Module:Citation/CS1/styles.css"></templatestyles>
- Gillette, Aaron (2007). *The Nature–Nurture Debate in the Twentieth Century*. New York: Palgrave Macmillan. ISBN 978-0-230-10845-5.<templatestyles src="Module:Citation/CS1/styles.css"></templatestyles>

Criticisms of eugenics

- Blom, Philipp (2008). *The Vertigo Years: Change and Culture in the West, 1900–1914*. Toronto: McClelland & Stewart. pp. 335–336. ISBN 978-0-7710-1630-1.<templatestyles src="Module:Citation/CS1/styles.css"></templatestyles>

- D'Souza, Dinesh (1995). *The End of Racism: Principles for a Multicultural Society*. New York: Free Press. ISBN 0-02-908102-5.<templatestyles src="Module:Citation/CS1/styles.css"></templatestyles>
- Galton, David (2002). *Eugenics: The Future of Human Life in the 21st Century*. London: Abacus. ISBN 0-349-11377-7.<templatestyles src="Module:Citation/CS1/styles.css"></templatestyles>
- Goldberg, Jonah (2007). *Liberal Fascism: The Secret History of the American Left, from Mussolini to the Politics of Meaning* (1st ed.). New York: Doubleday. ISBN 0-385-51184-1.<templatestyles src="Module:Citation/CS1/styles.css"></templatestyles>
- Joseph, Jay (2004). *The Gene Illusion: Genetic Research in Psychiatry and Psychology Under the Microscope*[491]. New York: Algora. ISBN 978-0-87586-343-6. Archived from the original[492] on 12 May 2009.<templatestyles src="Module:Citation/CS1/styles.css"></templatestyles>
- Joseph, Jay (June 2005). "The 1942 'euthanasia' debate in the *American Journal of Psychiatry*"[493]. *History of Psychiatry*. **16** (62 Pt. 2): 171–179. doi:10.1177/0957154x05047004[494]. PMID 16013119[495].<templatestyles src="Module:Citation/CS1/styles.css"></templatestyles>
- Joseph, Jay (2006). *The Missing Gene: Psychiatry, Heredity, and the Fruitless Search for Genes*[496]. New York: Algora. ISBN 978-0-87586-410-5. Archived from the original[497] on 17 April 2009.<templatestyles src="Module:Citation/CS1/styles.css"></templatestyles>
- Kerr, Anne; Shakespeare, Tom (2002). *Genetic Politics: from Eugenics to Genome*. Cheltenham: New Clarion. ISBN 978-1-873797-25-9.<templatestyles src="Module:Citation/CS1/styles.css"></templatestyles>
- Maranto, Gina (1996). *Quest for perfection: the drive to breed better human beings*. New York: Scribner. ISBN 0-684-80029-2.<templatestyles src="Module:Citation/CS1/styles.css"></templatestyles>
- Ordover, Nancy (2003). *American Eugenics: Race, Queer Anatomy, and the Science of Nationalism*. Minneapolis: University of Minnesota Press. ISBN 0-8166-3559-5.<templatestyles src="Module:Citation/CS1/styles.css"></templatestyles>
- Shakespeare, Tom (1995). "Back to the Future? New Genetics and Disabled People". *Critical Social Policy*. **46** (44–45): 22–35. doi: 10.1177/026101839501504402[498].<templatestyles src="Module:Citation/CS1/styles.css"></templatestyles>
- Smith, Andrea (2005). *Conquest: Sexual Violence and American Indian Genocide*. Cambridge, Massachusetts: South End Press. ISBN 978-0-89608-743-9.<templatestyles

src="Module:Citation/CS1/styles.css"></templatestyles>
- Wahlsten, D. (1997). "Leilani Muir versus the philosopher king: Eugenics on trial in Alberta"[499] (PDF). *Genetica*. **99** (2–3): 185–198. doi: 10.1007/BF02259522[500]. PMID 9463073[501].<templatestyles src="Module:Citation/CS1/styles.css"></templatestyles>

External links

 Wikimedia Commons has media related to *Eugenics*.

- Media related to Eugenics at Wikimedia Commons
- Quotations related to Eugenics at Wikiquote

Social Darwinism

Social Darwinism is the application of the evolutionary concept of natural selection to human society. The term itself emerged in the 1880s, and it gained widespread currency when used after 1944 by opponents of these ways of thinking. The majority of those who have been categorized as social Darwinists did not identify themselves by such a label.

Scholars debate the extent to which the various social Darwinist ideologies reflect Charles Darwin's own views on human social and economic issues. His writings have passages that can be interpreted as opposing aggressive individualism, while other passages appear to promote it. Some scholars argue that Darwin's view gradually changed and came to incorporate views from other theorists such as Herbert Spencer. Spencer published his Lamarckian evolutionary ideas about society before Darwin first published his hypothesis in 1859, and both Spencer and Darwin promoted their own conceptions of moral values. Spencer supported *laissez-faire* capitalism on the basis of his Lamarckian belief that struggle for survival spurred self-improvement which could be inherited. An important proponent in Germany was Ernst Haeckel, who popularized Darwin's thought (and personal interpretation of it) and used it as well to contribute to a new creed, the monist movement.

Origin of the term

The term Darwinism was coined by Thomas Henry Huxley in his March 1861 review of *On the Origin of Species*, and by the 1870s it was used to describe a range of concepts of evolution or development, without any specific commitment to Charles Darwin's theory of natural selection.

The first use of the phrase "social Darwinism" was in Joseph Fisher's 1877 article on *The History of Landholding in Ireland* which was published in the *Transactions of the Royal Historical Society*. Fisher was commenting on how a system for borrowing livestock which had been called "tenure" had led to the false impression that the early Irish had already evolved or developed land tenure; <templatestyles src="Template:Quote/styles.css"/>

> *These arrangements did not in any way affect that which we understand by the word " tenure", that is, a man's farm, but they related solely to cattle, which we consider a chattel. It has appeared necessary to devote some space to this subject, inasmuch as that usually acute writer Sir Henry Maine has accepted the word " tenure " in its modern interpretation, and has built up a theory under which the Irish chief " developed " into a feudal baron. I can find nothing in the Brehon laws to warrant this theory of social Darwinism, and believe further study will show that the Cain Saerrath and the Cain Aigillue relate solely to what we now call chattels, and did not in any way affect what we now call the freehold, the possession of the land.*
>
> —*Fisher 1877.*

Despite the fact that Social Darwinism bears Charles Darwin's name, it is also linked today with others, notably Herbert Spencer, Thomas Malthus, and Francis Galton, the founder of eugenics. In fact, Spencer was not described as a social Darwinist until the 1930s, long after his death.[502] The social Darwinism term first appeared in Europe in 1880, the journalist Emilie Gautier had coined the term with reference to a health conference in Berlin 1877.[503] Around 1900 it was used by sociologists, some being opposed to the concept. The term was popularized in the United States in 1944 by the American historian Richard Hofstadter who used it in the ideological war effort against fascism to denote a reactionary creed which promoted competitive strife, racism and chauvinism. Hofstadter later also recognized (what he saw as) the influence of Darwinist and other evolutionary ideas upon those with collectivist views, enough to devise a term for the phenomenon, "Darwinist collectivism".[504] Before Hofstadter's work the use of the term "social Darwinism" in English academic journals was quite rare. In fact,

<templatestyles src="Template:Quote/styles.css"/>

> ... there is considerable evidence that the entire concept of "social Darwinism" as we know it today was virtually invented by Richard Hofstadter. Eric Foner, in an introduction to a then-new edition of Hofstadter's book published in the early 1990s, declines to go quite that far. "Hofstadter did not invent the term Social Darwinism", Foner writes, "which originated in Europe in the 1860s and crossed the Atlantic in the early twentieth century. But before he wrote, it was used only on rare occasions; he made it a standard shorthand for a complex of late-nineteenth-century ideas, a familiar part of the lexicon of social thought."
>
> —Jeff Riggenbach[505]

Usage

Social Darwinism has many definitions, and some of them are incompatible with each other. As such, social Darwinism has been criticized for being an inconsistent philosophy, which does not lead to any clear political conclusions. For example, *The Concise Oxford Dictionary of Politics* states:

> Part of the difficulty in establishing sensible and consistent usage is that commitment to the biology of natural selection and to 'survival of the fittest' entailed nothing uniform either for sociological method or for political doctrine. A 'social Darwinist' could just as well be a defender of laissez-faire as a defender of state socialism, just as much an imperialist as a domestic eugenist.

The term "Social Darwinism" has rarely been used by advocates of the supposed ideologies or ideas; instead it has almost always been used pejoratively by its opponents. The term draws upon the common meaning of *Darwinism*, which includes a range of evolutionary views, but in the late 19th century was applied more specifically to natural selection as first advanced by Charles Darwin to explain speciation in populations of organisms. The process includes competition between individuals for limited resources, popularly but inaccurately described by the phrase "survival of the fittest", a term coined by sociologist Herbert Spencer.

Creationists have often maintained that Social Darwinism—leading to policies designed to reward the most competitive—is a logical consequence of "Darwinism" (the theory of natural selection in biology).[506] Biologists and historians have stated that this is a fallacy of appeal to nature and should not be taken to imply that this phenomenon ought to be used as a moral guide in human society. While there are historical links between the popularization of Darwin's theory and forms of social Darwinism, social Darwinism is not a necessary consequence of the principles of biological evolution.

Figure 67: *Herbert Spencer*

While the term has been applied to the claim that Darwin's theory of evolution by natural selection can be used to understand the social endurance of a nation or country, Social Darwinism commonly refers to ideas that predate Darwin's publication of *On the Origin of Species*. Others whose ideas are given the label include the 18th century clergyman Thomas Malthus, and Darwin's cousin Francis Galton who founded eugenics towards the end of the 19th century.

The expansion of the British Empire fitted in with the broader notion of social Darwinism used from the 1870s onwards to account for the remarkable and universal phenomenon of "the Anglo-Saxon overflowing his boundaries", as phrased by the late-Victorian sociologist Benjamin Kidd in *Social Evolution*, published in 1894.[507] The concept also proved useful to justify what was seen by some as the inevitable extermination of "the weaker races who disappear before the stronger" not so much "through the effects of ... our vices upon them" as "what may be called the virtues of our civilisation."

Proponents

Herbert Spencer's ideas, like those of evolutionary progressivism, stemmed from his reading of Thomas Malthus, and his later theories were influenced by those of Darwin. However, Spencer's major work, *Progress: Its Law and*

Figure 68: *Thomas Malthus*

Cause (1857), was released two years before the publication of Darwin's *On the Origin of Species*, and *First Principles* was printed in 1860.

In *The Social Organism* (1860), Spencer compares society to a living organism and argues that, just as biological organisms evolve through natural selection, society evolves and increases in complexity through analogous processes.[508]

In many ways, Spencer's theory of cosmic evolution has much more in common with the works of Lamarck and Auguste Comte's positivism than with Darwin's.

Jeff Riggenbach argues that Spencer's view was that culture and education made a sort of Lamarckism possible and notes that Herbert Spencer was a proponent of private charity. However, the legacy of his social Darwinism was less than charitable.

Spencer's work also served to renew interest in the work of Malthus. While Malthus's work does not itself qualify as social Darwinism, his 1798 work *An Essay on the Principle of Population*, was incredibly popular and widely read by social Darwinists. In that book, for example, the author argued that as an increasing population would normally outgrow its food supply, this would result in the starvation of the weakest and a Malthusian catastrophe.

According to Michael Ruse, Darwin read Malthus' famous *Essay on a Principle of Population* in 1838, four years after Malthus' death. Malthus himself

Figure 69: *Francis Galton*

anticipated the social Darwinists in suggesting that charity could exacerbate social problems.

Another of these social interpretations of Darwin's biological views, later known as eugenics, was put forth by Darwin's cousin, Francis Galton, in 1865 and 1869. Galton argued that just as physical traits were clearly inherited among generations of people, the same could be said for mental qualities (genius and talent). Galton argued that social morals needed to change so that heredity was a conscious decision in order to avoid both the over-breeding by less fit members of society and the under-breeding of the more fit ones.

In Galton's view, social institutions such as welfare and insane asylums were allowing inferior humans to survive and reproduce at levels faster than the more "superior" humans in respectable society, and if corrections were not soon taken, society would be awash with "inferiors". Darwin read his cousin's work with interest, and devoted sections of *Descent of Man* to discussion of Galton's theories. Neither Galton nor Darwin, though, advocated any eugenic policies restricting reproduction, due to their Whiggish distrust of government.

Friedrich Nietzsche's philosophy addressed the question of artificial selection, yet Nietzsche's principles did not concur with Darwinian theories of natural selection. Nietzsche's point of view on sickness and health, in particular, opposed him to the concept of biological adaptation as forged by Spencer's "fitness". Nietzsche criticized Haeckel, Spencer, and Darwin, sometimes under the same banner by maintaining that in specific cases, sickness was necessary and even helpful.[509] Thus, he wrote:

> *Wherever progress is to ensue, deviating natures are of greatest importance. Every progress of the whole must be preceded by a partial weakening. The strongest natures retain the type, the weaker ones help to advance it.*
>
> *Something similar also happens in the individual. There is rarely a degeneration, a truncation, or even a vice or any physical or moral loss without an advantage somewhere else. In a warlike and restless clan, for example, the sicklier man may have occasion to be alone, and may therefore become quieter and wiser; the one-eyed man will have one eye the stronger; the blind man will see deeper inwardly, and certainly hear better. To this extent, the famous theory of the survival of the fittest does not seem to me to be the only viewpoint from which to explain the progress of strengthening of a man or of a race.*[510]

Ernst Haeckel's recapitulation theory was not Darwinism, but rather attempted to combine the ideas of Goethe, Lamarck and Darwin. It was adopted by emerging social sciences to support the concept that non-European societies were "primitive" in an early stage of development towards the European ideal, but since then it has been heavily refuted on many fronts Haeckel's works led to the formation of the Monist League in 1904 with many prominent citizens among its members, including the Nobel Prize winner Wilhelm Ostwald.

The simpler aspects of social Darwinism followed the earlier Malthusian ideas that humans, especially males, require competition in their lives in order to survive in the future. Further, the poor should have to provide for themselves and not be given any aid. However, amidst this climate, most social Darwinists of the early twentieth century actually supported better working conditions and salaries. Such measures would grant the poor a better chance to provide for themselves yet still distinguish those who are capable of succeeding from those who are poor out of laziness, weakness, or inferiority.

Hypotheses relating social change and evolution

"Social Darwinism" was first described by Oscar Schmidt of the University of Strasbourg, reporting at a scientific and medical conference held in Munich in 1877. He noted how socialists, although opponents of Darwin's theory, used it to add force to their political arguments. Schmidt's essay first appeared in

English in *Popular Science* in March 1879. There followed an anarchist tract published in Paris in 1880 entitled "Le darwinisme social" by Émile Gautier. However, the use of the term was very rare—at least in the English-speaking world (Hodgson, 2004)[511]—until the American historian Richard Hofstadter published his influential *Social Darwinism in American Thought* (1944) during World War II.

Hypotheses of social evolution and cultural evolution were common in Europe. The Enlightenment thinkers who preceded Darwin, such as Hegel, often argued that societies progressed through stages of increasing development. Earlier thinkers also emphasized conflict as an inherent feature of social life. Thomas Hobbes's 17th century portrayal of the state of nature seems analogous to the competition for natural resources described by Darwin. Social Darwinism is distinct from other theories of social change because of the way it draws Darwin's distinctive ideas from the field of biology into social studies.

Darwin, unlike Hobbes, believed that this struggle for natural resources allowed individuals with certain physical and mental traits to succeed more frequently than others, and that these traits accumulated in the population over time, which under certain conditions could lead to the descendants being so different that they would be defined as a new species.

However, Darwin felt that "social instincts" such as "sympathy" and "moral sentiments" also evolved through natural selection, and that these resulted in the strengthening of societies in which they occurred, so much so that he wrote about it in *Descent of Man*:

> *The following proposition seems to me in a high degree probable—namely, that any animal whatever, endowed with well-marked social instincts, the parental and filial affections being here included, would inevitably acquire a moral sense or conscience, as soon as its intellectual powers had become as well, or nearly as well developed, as in man. For, firstly, the social instincts lead an animal to take pleasure in the society of its fellows, to feel a certain amount of sympathy with them, and to perform various services for them.*[512]

Regional distribution

United States

Spencer proved to be a popular figure in the 1880s primarily because his application of evolution to areas of human endeavor promoted an optimistic view of the future as inevitably becoming better. In the United States, writers and thinkers of the gilded age such as Edward L. Youmans, William Graham Sumner, John Fiske, John W. Burgess, and others developed theories of social evolution as a result of their exposure to the works of Darwin and Spencer.

In 1883, Sumner published a highly influential pamphlet entitled "What Social Classes Owe to Each Other", in which he insisted that the social classes owe each other nothing, synthesizing Darwin's findings with free enterprise Capitalism for his justification.Wikipedia:Citation needed According to Sumner, those who feel an obligation to provide assistance to those unequipped or under-equipped to compete for resources, will lead to a country in which the weak and inferior are encouraged to breed more like them, eventually dragging the country down. Sumner also believed that the best equipped to win the struggle for existence was the American businessman, and concluded that taxes and regulations serve as dangers to his survival. This pamphlet makes no mention of Darwinism, and only refers to Darwin in a statement on the meaning of liberty, that "There never has been any man, from the primitive barbarian up to a Humboldt or a Darwin, who could do as he had a mind to."

Sumner never fully embraced Darwinian ideas, and some contemporary historians do not believe that Sumner ever actually believed in social Darwinism.[513] The great majority of American businessmen rejected the anti-philanthropic implications of the theory. Instead they gave millions to build schools, colleges, hospitals, art institutes, parks and many other institutions. Andrew Carnegie, who admired Spencer, was the leading philanthropist in the world (1890–1920), and a major leader against imperialism and warfare.[514]

H. G. Wells was heavily influenced by Darwinist thoughts, and novelist Jack London wrote stories of survival that incorporated his views on social Darwinism.[515] Film director Stanley Kubrick has been described as having held social Darwinist opinions.

Japan

Social Darwinism has influenced political, public health and social movements in Japan since the late 19th and early 20th century. Social Darwinism was originally brought to Japan through the works of Francis Galton and Ernst Haeckel as well as United States, British and French Lamarkian eugenic written studies of the late 19th and early 20th centuries. Eugenism as a science was hotly debated at the beginning of the 20th century, in *Jinsei-Der Mensch*, the first eugenics journal in the empire. As Japan sought to close ranks with the west, this practice was adopted wholesale along with colonialism and its justifications.

China

Social Darwinism was formally introduced to China through the translation by Yan Fu of Huxley's *Evolution and Ethics*, in the course of an extensive series of translations of influential Western thought.[516] Yan's translation strongly impacted Chinese scholars because he added national elements not found in the original. He understood Spencer's sociology as "not merely analytical and descriptive, but prescriptive as well", and saw Spencer building on Darwin, whom Yan summarized thus:

> Peoples and living things struggle for survival. At first, species struggle with species; they as [people] gradually progress, there is a struggle between one social group and another. The weak invariably become the prey of the strong, the stupid invariably become subservient to the clever."[517]

By the 1920s, social Darwinism found expression in the promotion of eugenics by the Chinese sociologist Pan Guangdan. When Chiang Kai-shek started the New Life movement in 1934, he

> . . . harked back to theories of Social Darwinism, writing that "only those who readapt themselves to new conditions, day by day, can live properly. When the life of a people is going through this process of readaptation, it has to remedy its own defects, and get rid of those elements which become useless. Then we call it new life."[518]

Germany

Social evolution theories in Germany gained large popularity in the 1860s and had a strong antiestablishment connotation first. Social Darwinism allowed people to counter the connection of *Thron und Altar*, the intertwined establishment of clergy and nobility, and provided as well the idea of progressive change and evolution of society as a whole. Ernst Haeckel propagated both Darwinism as a part of natural history and as a suitable base for a modern Weltanschauung, a world view based on scientific reasoning in his Monist League. Friedrich von Hellwald had a strong role in popularizing it in Austria. Darwin's work served as a catalyst to popularize evolutionary thinking. Darwin himself called Haeckel's connection between Socialism and Evolution through Natural Selection *a foolish idea prevailing* in Germany.

A sort of aristocratic turn, the use of the struggle for life as base of social darwinism *sensu stricto* came up after 1900 with Alexander Tilles 1895 work Entwicklungsethik (ethics of evolution) which asked to move *from Darwin till Nietzsche*. Further interpretations moved to ideologies propagating a racist and hierarchical society and provided ground for the later radical versions of social Darwinism.

Criticism

Social Darwinism is often cited as an ideological justification for much of 18th/19th century European enslavement and colonization of Third World countries; it has often even found its way into the intellectual foundations of public education in neo-colonized countries.

References

Primary sources

- *Darwinism: Critical Reviews from Dublin Review (Catholic periodical)|Dublin Review*[519], Edinburgh Review, Quarterly Review *(1977 edition) reprints 19th century reviews and essays*
- Darwin, Charles (1859). "On the Origin of Species by Means of Natural Selection, or the Preservation of Favoured Races in the Struggle for Life" (1st ed.). London: John Murray.<templatestyles src="Module:Citation/CS1/styles.css"></templatestyles>
- Darwin, Charles (1882). "The Descent of Man, and Selection in Relation to Sex"[520] (2nd ed.). London: John Murray.<templatestyles src="Module:Citation/CS1/styles.css"></templatestyles>
- Fisher, Joseph (1877). "The History of Landholding in Ireland"[521]. London: Transactions of the Royal Historical Society: 249–50.<templatestyles src="Module:Citation/CS1/styles.css"></templatestyles>
- Fiske, John. *Darwinism and Other Essays* (1900)[522]

Secondary sources

- Bannister, Robert C. *Social Darwinism: Science and Myth in Anglo-American Social Thought*[523] (1989)
- Bannister, Robert C. *Sociology and Scientism: The American Quest for Objectivity, 1880–1940*[524] (1987)
- Bernardini, J.-M. *Le darwinisme social en France (1859–1918). Fascination et rejet d'une idéologie*, Paris, CNRS Edition, 1997.
- Boller, Paul F. Jr. *American Thought in Transition: The Impact of Evolutionary Naturalism, 1865–1900* (1969)[525]

- Bowler, Peter J. (2003). *Evolution: The History of an Idea* (3rd ed.). University of California Press. ISBN 0-520-23693-9.<templatestyles src="Module:Citation/CS1/styles.css"></templatestyles>
- Crook, D. Paul. *Darwinism, War and History : The Debate over the Biology of War from the 'Origin of Species' to the First World War*[526] (1994)
- Crook, Paul (1999). "Social Darwinism in European and American Thought, 1860–1945"[527]. *The Australian Journal of Politics and History*. **45**.<templatestyles src="Module:Citation/CS1/styles.css"></templatestyles>
- Crook, Paul. *Darwin's Coat-Tails: Essays on Social Darwinism* (Peter Lang, 2007)
- Degler, Carl N. *In Search of Human Nature: The Decline and Revival of Darwinism in American Social Thought*[528] (1992).
- Desmond, Adrian; Moore, James (1991). *Darwin*. London: Michael Joseph, Penguin Group. ISBN 0-7181-3430-3.<templatestyles src="Module:Citation/CS1/styles.css"></templatestyles>
- Dickens, Peter. *Social Darwinism: Linking Evolutionary Thought to Social Theory* (Philadelphia: Open University Press, 2000).
- Gossett, Thomas F. *Race: The History of an Idea in America* (1999) ch 7[529]
- Hawkins, Mike (1997). *Social Darwinism in European and American Thought 1860-1945: Nature and Model and Nature as Threat*. London: Cambridge University Press. ISBN 0-521-57434-X.<templatestyles src="Module:Citation/CS1/styles.css"></templatestyles>
- Hodge, Jonathan and Gregory Radick. *The Cambridge Companion to Darwin* (2003)[530]
- Hodgson, Geoffrey M. (December 2004). "Social Darwinism in Anglophone Academic Journals: A Contribution to the History of the Term"[531] (PDF). *Vol. 17 No. 4*. Journal of Historical Sociology: 428–63. ISSN 0952-1909[532]. Retrieved 2010-02-17. <q>Social Darwinism, as almost everyone knows, is a Bad Thing.</q><templatestyles src="Module:Citation/CS1/styles.css"></templatestyles>
- Hofstadter, Richard (1944). *Social Darwinism in American Thought*[533]. Philadelphia: University of Pennsylvania Press.<templatestyles src="Module:Citation/CS1/styles.css"></templatestyles>
  - Hofstadter, Richard (1992). Eric Foner, ed. *Social Darwinism in American Thought* (with a new introduction ed.). Boston: Beacon Press. ISBN 0807055034.<templatestyles src="Module:Citation/CS1/styles.css"></templatestyles>
- Jones, Leslie, *Social Darwinism Revisited* History Today, Vol. 48, August 1998[534]

- Kaye, Howard L. *The Social Meaning of Modern Biology: From Social Darwinism to Sociobiology*[535] (1997).

Further reading

- Sammut-Bonnici, T. & Wensley, R. (2002), 'Darwinism, Probability and Complexity: Transformation and Change Explained through the Theories of Evolution', ' 'International Journal of Management Reviews' ', 4(3) pp. 291–315.

External links

- Social Darwinism on ThinkQuest[536]
- *In the name of Darwin*[537] – criticism of social Darwinism
- Descent of Man on Alibris[520]

Works

Charles Darwin bibliography

This is a partial list of the writings of Charles Darwin, including his main works.

All of his writings are available at The Complete Works of Charles Darwin Online[538]: the Table of Contents[539] provides a complete bibliography of his works, including alternative editions, contributions to books & periodicals, correspondence, life, and a complete catalogue of his manuscripts. This is free to read, but not public domain, and includes work still under copyright. For public-domain plain text unauthoritative versions of his major works, see Works by Charles Darwin[540] at Project Gutenberg.

There is a collected printed edition, the standard for scholarly use: *The Works of Charles Darwin*, edited by Paul H Barrett and Richard Broke Freeman. New York University Press, 1987–89. 29 vols. <templatestyles src="Module:Citation/CS1/styles.css" />ISBN 0-8147-1796-9 LC[541]

Published works

- 1829–1832. [Records of captured insects, in] Stephens, J. F., *Illustrations of British entomology*[542]
- 1835: *Extracts from Letters to Henslow* (Read at a meeting of the Cambridge Philosophical Society on 16 November 1835, with comments by John Stevens Henslow and Adam Sedgwick, and printed for private distribution dated 1 December 1835.[543] Selected remarks had been read by Sedgwick to the Geological Society of London on 18 November 1835, and these were summarised in *Proceedings of the Geological Society* published in 1836.[544] Further extracts were published in the *Entomological Magazine* and, with a review, in the *Magazine of Natural History*. A reprint was issued in 1960, again for private distribution.)

- 1836: *A LETTER, Containing Remarks on the Moral State of TAHITI, NEW ZEALAND, &c. – BY CAPT. R. FITZROY AND C. DARWIN, ESQ. OF H.M.S. 'Beagle.'*[545]
- 1838–1843: *Zoology of the Voyage of H.M.S. Beagle*: published between 1839 and 1843 in five Parts (and nineteen numbers) by various authors, edited and superintended by Charles Darwin, who contributed sections to two of the Parts:
  - 1838: *Part 1 No. 1 Fossil Mammalia*, by Richard Owen (*Preface* and *Geological introduction* by Darwin)
  - 1838: *Part 2 No. 1 Mammalia*, by George R. Waterhouse (*Geographical introduction* and *A notice of their habits and ranges* by Darwin)
- 1839: *Journal and Remarks* (The Voyage of the Beagle)
- 1842: *The Structure and Distribution of Coral Reefs*
- 1844: *Geological Observations on the Volcanic Islands visited during the voyage of H.M.S. Beagle*
- 1846: *Geological Observations on South America*
- 1849: *Geology* from *A Manual of scientific enquiry; prepared for the use of Her Majesty's Navy: and adapted for travellers in general.*, John F.W. Herschel ed.
- 1851: *A Monograph of the Sub-class Cirripedia, with Figures of all the Species. The Lepadidae; or, Pedunculated Cirripedes.*
- 1851: *A Monograph on the Fossil Lepadidae, or, Pedunculated Cirripedes of Great Britain*
- 1854: *A Monograph of the Sub-class Cirripedia, with Figures of all the Species. The Balanidae (or Sessile Cirripedes); the Verrucidae, etc.*
- 1854: *A Monograph on the Fossil Balanidæ and Verrucidæ of Great Britain*
- 1858: *On the Tendency of Species to form Varieties; and on the Perpetuation of Varieties and Species by Natural Means of Selection* (*Extract from an unpublished Work on Species*)
- 1859: *On the Origin of Species by Means of Natural Selection, or the Preservation of Favoured Races in the Struggle for Life*
- 1862: *On the various contrivances by which British and foreign orchids are fertilised by insects*
- 1865: *The Movements and Habits of Climbing Plants* (Linnean Society paper, published in book form in 1875)
- 1868: *The Variation of Animals and Plants under Domestication*
- 1871: *The Descent of Man, and Selection in Relation to Sex*
- 1872: *The Expression of the Emotions in Man and Animals*
- 1875: *Insectivorous Plants*
- 1876: *The Effects of Cross and Self Fertilisation in the Vegetable Kingdom*

- 1877: *The Different Forms of Flowers on Plants of the Same Species*
- 1879: "Preface and 'a preliminary notice'" in Ernst Krause's *Erasmus Darwin*
- 1880: *The Power of Movement in Plants*
- 1881: *The Formation of Vegetable Mould through the Action of Worms*

Autobiography

- 1887: *Autobiography of Charles Darwin* (edited by his son Francis Darwin)
- 1958: *Autobiography of Charles Darwin* (Barlow, unexpurgated)

Correspondence

- Correspondence of Charles Darwin
- 1887: *Life and Letters of Charles Darwin* (ed. Francis Darwin)
- 1903: *More Letters of Charles Darwin* (ed. Francis Darwin and A.C. Seward)

Appendix

References

[1] Milner, 1.
[2] A Guide to Churchill College, Cambridge: text by Dr. Mark Goldie, pages 62 and 63 (2009)
[3] https://web.archive.org/web/20120831214731/http://www.havant.gov.uk/PDF/Belmont%20Park%20September%201.pdf
[4] http://www.montyhistnotes.com/genealogy/getperson.php?personID=I6709&tree=MontyHistNotes_II
[5] "Hugh Massingberd" https://web.archive.org/web/20080226212158/https://www.telegraph.co.uk/news/main.jhtml?xml=/news/2007/12/27/db2701.xml (obituary). *The Telegraph*. 27 December 2007.
[6] http://www-bcf.usc.edu/~wedgwood/framesetpronunciation.html
[7] //doi.org/10.1111%2Fj.1095-8312.1982.tb02010.x
[8] http://onlinelibrary.wiley.com/doi/10.1111/j.1095-8312.2010.01529.x/abstract
[9] //doi.org/10.1111%2Fj.1095-8312.2010.01529.x
[10] From Charles Darwin: a life in pictures http://darwin-online.org.uk/life1b.html at Darwin Online, the parish register of St. Chad's gives Darwin's date of baptism as 15 November 1809, a date supported by "England, Births and Christenings, 1538–1975," index, FamilySearch, accessed 18 July 2012), Charles Robt. Darwin https://familysearch.org/pal:/MM9.1.1/J362-MP8, 1809. The date is given as 17 November in Freeman (2007) p. 106 http://darwin-online.org.uk/content/frameset?itemID=A27b&viewtype=text&pageseq=113, and Desmond & Moore p. 12.
[11] Jameson, Robert ed. (1826) *Edinburgh New Philosophical Journal*, A. and C. Black, Edinburgh, pp. 296–297 https://books.google.com
[12] describes the incident and states that the insect Darwin popped into his mouth was a bombardier beetle.
*They cite Darwin's correspondence and his *Autobiography* ()
* quotes the *Autobiography*, and while its illustration shows a bombardier beetle, it says "Many beetles, including the *Brachinus crepitans* and the *Stenaptinus insignis*, release irritating chemicals as a defense."
* Letter 1009 — Darwin, C. R. to Jenyns, Leonard, 17 Oct (1846) http://www.darwinproject.ac.uk/darwinletters/calendar/entry-1009.html describes the two beetles as unidentified *carabi*, or ground beetles.
*
[13] Darwin Correspondence Cambridge 1828-1831 http://www.turtlereader.com/authors/charles-darwin/the-life-and-letters-of-charles-darwin-day-13-of-188/
[14] http://www.hti.umich.edu/cgi/p/pd-modeng/pd-modeng-idx?type=header&id=PaleyNatur
[15] http://darwin-online.org.uk/darwin.html
[16] https://web.archive.org/20090326070105/http://www.psych.uni-goettingen.de/abt/1/sydow/von_Sydow_(2005)_Darwin_A_Christian_Undermining_Christianity.pdf
[17] http://darwin-online.org.uk/
[18] https://www.gutenberg.org/author/Charles+Darwin
[19] http://www.darwinproject.ac.uk/
[20] van Wyhe 2013, p. 3.
[21] van Wyhe 2013, pp. 5–7.
[22] van Wyhe 2013, p. 6.
[23] Darwin, C. R. *Recollections of the development of my mind & character* [Autobiography [1876-4.1882] CUL-DAR26.1–121) Transcribed by Kees Rookmaaker. Darwin Online. p. 49 http://darwin-online.org.uk/content/frameset?pageseq=82&itemID=CUL-DAR26.1-121&viewtype=side
[24] He also collected what would in 1837 be described by John Gould as the type specimen of *Passer iagoensis*, the Cape Verde sparrow or Iago sparrow.

[25] Letter to L. Horner http://darwin-online.org.uk/content/frameset?itemID=F1548.2&viewtype=text&pageseq=146, Down, 29 August 1844
[26] ; p. 109, Keynes notes the site is now under Puerto Belgrano naval base.
[27] 'Cinnamon and port wine': an introduction to the *Rio Notebook* http://darwin-online.org.uk/EditorialIntroductions/Chancellor_fieldNotebooks1.10.html, Bahía Blanca, September—October 1832.
[28] His encounter with the natives of the Tierra del Fuego on his *Beagle* voyage made Darwin believe that civilization had evolved over time from a more primitive state.
[29] 'Banda Oriental S. Cruz.' Beagle field notebook. EH1.9, p. 36 http://darwin-online.org.uk/content/frameset?viewtype=text&itemID=EH1.9&pageseq=39, a typical Glyptodont tail.
[30] 'Banda Oriental S. Cruz.' Beagle field notebook. EH1.9, p. 37 http://darwin-online.org.uk/content/frameset?viewtype=text&itemID=EH1.9&pageseq=40
[31] Grant, K. Thalia and Estes, Gregory B. "Darwin in Galapagos: Footsteps to a New World." 2009. Princeton University Press. http://darwiningalapagos.com
[32] Grant, K. Thalia and Estes, Gregory B. "Darwin in Galapagos: Footsteps to a New World." 2009 Princeton University Press. http://darwiningalapagos.com
[33] ' '
[34] http://darwin-online.org.uk/content/frameset?viewtype=text&itemID=A25&pageseq=1
[35] http://darwin-online.org.uk/content/frameset?viewtype=text&itemID=F1566&pageseq=1
[36] http://darwin-online.org.uk/content/frameset?viewtype=text&itemID=F1571&pageseq=1
[37] http://darwin-online.org.uk/content/frameset?viewtype=text&itemID=F1577&pageseq=1
[38] http://darwin-online.org.uk/content/frameset?viewtype=text&itemID=F1598&pageseq=1
[39] http://darwin-online.org.uk/content/frameset?itemID=F1&viewtype=text&pageseq=1
[40] http://darwin-online.org.uk/content/frameset?itemID=F1642&viewtype=text&pageseq=1
[41] http://darwin-online.org.uk/content/frameset?itemID=F10.3&viewtype=text&pageseq=1
[42] http://darwin-online.org.uk/content/frameset?viewtype=text&itemID=F271&pageseq=1
[43] http://darwin-online.org.uk/content/frameset?viewtype=text&itemID=F272&pageseq=1
[44] http://darwin-online.org.uk/content/frameset?viewtype=text&itemID=F273&pageseq=1
[45] http://www.vqronline.org/articles/2006/spring/eldredge-confessions-darwinist/
[46] http://darwin-online.org.uk/content/frameset?viewtype=text&itemID=A73&pageseq=1
[47] http://darwin-online.org.uk/content/frameset?itemID=F10.2&viewtype=text&pageseq=1
[48] http://darwin-online.org.uk/content/frameset?itemID=F10.2a&viewtype=text&pageseq=1
[49] http://darwin-online.org.uk/content/frameset?viewtype=text&itemID=A27b&pageseq=1
[50] http://darwin-online.org.uk/content/frameset?viewtype=text&itemID=F8.11&pageseq=1
[51] http://darwin-online.org.uk/content/frameset?viewtype=text&itemID=A342&pageseq=1
[52] //doi.org/10.1017%2Fs0007087400027060
[53] http://darwin-online.org.uk/content/frameset?viewtype=text&itemID=F1956&pageseq=1
[54] //doi.org/10.17704%2Feshi.14.1.76570264u727jh36
[55] http://darwin-online.org.uk/content/frameset?viewtype=text&itemID=A623&pageseq=1
[56] http://darwin-online.org.uk/content/frameset?itemID=F1840&viewtype=text&pageseq=1
[57] http://darwin-online.org.uk/content/frameset?itemID=F1925&viewtype=text&pageseq=1
[58] http://darwin-online.org.uk/content/frameset?itemID=F10.1&viewtype=text&pageseq=1
[59] http://darwin-online.org.uk/content/frameset?itemID=A235&viewtype=text&pageseq=1
[60] http://darwin-online.org.uk/content/frameset?viewtype=text&itemID=F9.1&pageseq=1
[61] http://darwin-online.org.uk/content/frameset?viewtype=text&itemID=A544&pageseq=1
[62] //doi.org/10.1098%2Frsnr.2006.0171
[63] http://darwin-online.org.uk/people/2013,%20John%20van%20Wyhe,%20My%20appointment...Darwin%20was%20the%20naturalist%20of%20the%20Beagle.pdf
[64] //doi.org/10.1016%2Fj.shpsc.2013.03.022
[65] http://www.cnrs.fr/cw/dossiers/dosdarwinE/darwin.html
[66] http://www.aboutdarwin.com/voyage/voyage01.html
[67] http://darwin-online.org.uk/content/frameset?viewtype=text&itemID=A575&pageseq=1
[68] http://darwiningalapagos.com/darwins-itinerary
[69] http://darwin-online.org.uk/
[70] https://www.gutenberg.org/author/Charles+Darwin
[71] http://www.darwinproject.ac.uk/

[72] http://darwiningalapagos.com
[73] *Harriet Martineau's Autobiography. With Memorials by Maria Weston Chapman*; 2 volumes; Smith, Elder & Co, 1877, vol. I SectionII p. 268 http://oll.libertyfund.org/?option=com_staticxt&staticfile=show.php%3Ftitle=2011&chapter=140229&layout=html#a_2645190
[74]
[75] Darwin's Journal () backdated from August 1838 gives a date of 6 March 1837
[76] Herbert 1980.
[77] Darwin, C. R. 1837. A sketch of the deposits containing extinct Mammalia in the neighbourhood of the Plata http://darwin-online.org.uk/content/frameset?pageseq=1&itemID=F1646&viewtype=text. [Read 3 May] *Proceedings of the Geological Society of London* 2: 542–44.
[78] ,
Allen, Grant, (March 1882) Sir Charles Lyell, *Popular Science Monthly* Volume 20
[79] UK Retail Price Index inflation figures are based on data from Clark, Gregory (2017). "The Annual RPI and Average Earnings for Britain, 1209 to Present (New Series)" https://measuringworth.com/ukearncpi/. *MeasuringWorth*. Retrieved November 6, 2017.
[80] Bowler 1996, pp. 78–79.
[81] Desmond & Moore 1991, p. 235.
[82] Darwin, C. R. 1838. On the connexion of certain volcanic phænomena, and on the formation of mountain-chains and volcanos, as the effects of continental elevations http://darwin-online.org.uk/content/frameset?itemID=F1649&viewtype=text&pageseq=1. [Read 7 March] *Proceedings of the Geological Society of London* 2: 654–60
[83] Desmond & Moore 1991, p. 248.
[84]
Darwin, C. R. ' Work finished If not marry http://darwin-online.org.uk/content/frameset?pageseq=1&itemID=CUL-DAR210.8.1&viewtype=text' [Memorandum on marriage]. (1838) CUL-DAR210.8.1 (*Darwin Online*)
[85] Desmond & Moore 1991, p. 247.
[86] Desmond & Moore 1991, pp. 247–48.
[87] Desmond & Moore 1991, p. 252.
[88] Desmond & Moore 1991, pp. 253–54.
[89] Darwin, C. R. (7.1838) *This is the Question Marry Not Marry* http://darwin-online.org.uk/content/frameset?viewtype=side&itemID=CUL-DAR210.8.2&pageseq=1 [Memorandum on marriage]. CUL-DAR210.8.2
[90] *An Essay on the Principle of Population* 6th edition, 1826.
[91] Huxley, Thomas, 1897, *Evolution and Ethics and Other Essays"*, D. Appleton and Company, New York. Section IV, Capital – The Mother of Labour, *pp. 162–63*.
[92]
[93] Browne 1995, pp. 396–97.
[94] Desmond & Moore 1991, pp. 270–71.
[95] Litchfield, H. E. [Recollection of Darwin on Macaw cottage]. CUL-DAR112.B99 http://darwin-online.org.uk/content/frameset?viewtype=side&itemID=CUL-DAR112.B99&pageseq=1
[96] http://darwin-online.org.uk/content/frameset?itemID=F1&viewtype=text&pageseq=1
[97] http://darwin-online.org.uk/content/frameset?viewtype=side&itemID=CUL-DAR121.-&pageseq=1
[98] http://darwin-online.org.uk/content/frameset?itemID=F1645&viewtype=text&pageseq=1
[99] http://darwin-online.org.uk/content/frameset?itemID=F1646&viewtype=text&pageseq=1
[100] http://darwin-online.org.uk/content/frameset?itemID=F1647&viewtype=text&pageseq=1
[101] http://darwin-online.org.uk/content/frameset?itemID=CUL-DAR122.-&viewtype=text&pageseq=1
[102] http://darwin-online.org.uk/content/frameset?viewtype=text&itemID=CUL-DAR123.-&pageseq=1
[103] http://darwin-online.org.uk/content/frameset?viewtype=text&itemID=CUL-DAR124.-&pageseq=1
[104] http://darwin-online.org.uk/content/frameset?itemID=CUL-DAR125.-&viewtype=text&pageseq=1

[105] http://darwin-online.org.uk/content/frameset?itemID=CUL-DAR126.-&viewtype=text&pageseq=1
[106] http://darwin-online.org.uk/content/frameset?itemID=F10.3&viewtype=text&pageseq=1
[107] http://darwin-online.org.uk/content/frameset?itemID=F373&viewtype=text&pageseq=1
[108] http://darwin-online.org.uk/EditorialIntroductions/Freeman_LifeandLettersandAutobiography.html
[109] http://darwin-online.org.uk/content/frameset?viewtype=side&itemID=CUL-DAR158.1-76&pageseq=1
[110] http://darwin-online.org.uk/EditorialIntroductions/vanWyhe_JournalDAR158.html
[111] http://www.vqronline.org/articles/2006/spring/eldredge-confessions-darwinist/
[112] http://darwin-online.org.uk/content/frameset?itemID=F10.2&viewtype=text&pageseq=1
[113] http://darwin-online.org.uk/content/frameset?viewtype=text&itemID=F1583e&pageseq=1
[114] http://darwin-online.org.uk/EditorialIntroductions/Freeman_EmmaDarwin.html
[115] https://web.archive.org/web/20080227014518/http://speakingoffaith.publicradio.org/programs/darwin/moore-devilschaplain.pdf
[116] http://speakingoffaith.publicradio.org/programs/darwin/moore-devilschaplain.pdf
[117] https://web.archive.org/web/20081222020720/http://speakingoffaith.publicradio.org/programs/darwin/transcript.shtml
[118] http://speakingoffaith.publicradio.org/programs/darwin/transcript.shtml
[119] http://www.sulloway.org/Finches.pdf
[120] //doi.org/10.1007%2FBF00132004
[121] http://darwin-online.org.uk/content/frameset?viewtype=text&itemID=A544&pageseq=1
[122] //doi.org/10.1098%2Frsnr.2006.0171
[123] http://darwin-online.org.uk/darwin.html
[124] http://crisp.psi.uni-heidelberg.de/sites/default/files/vonSydow/von_sydow_2005_darwin_a_christian_undermining_christianity.pdf
[125] http://darwin-online.org.uk/
[126] https://www.gutenberg.org/author/Charles+Darwin
[127] http://www.darwinproject.ac.uk/
[128] letter to Henslow, 14 October 1837.
[129] Letter 1236 — Darwin, C. R. to Hooker, J. D., 28 Mar 1849 http://www.darwinproject.ac.uk/darwinletters/calendar/entry-1236.html. DarwinProject.ac.uk. Retrieved 15 January 2007.
[130] Letter 1234 — Darwin, C. R. to Darwin, S. E., 19 Mar 1849 http://www.darwinproject.ac.uk/darwinletters/calendar/entry-1234.html. DarwinProject.ac.uk. Retrieved 11 January 2008.
[131] Letter 1352 — Darwin, C. R. to Fox, W. D., 4 Sept 1850 http://www.darwinproject.ac.uk/darwinletters/calendar/entry-1352.html. DarwinProject.ac.uk. Retrieved 11 January 2008.
[132] page 482
[133] http://www.supportme.co.uk/history.htm
[134] http://www.ocduk.org/ocd-history
[135] O'Neill, Graeme. "Diagnosing Darwin" http://www.lifescientist.com.au/article/359136/feature_diagnosing_darwin/ , *Australian Life Scientist*, 01 September 2010. Retrieved 17 September 2010.
[136] http://www.apa.org/pubinfo/panic.html
[137] http://linkinghub.elsevier.com/retrieve/pii/0005-7967(86)90098-7
[138] //doi.org/10.1016%2F0005-7967%2886%2990098-7
[139] //www.ncbi.nlm.nih.gov/pubmed/3964189
[140] http://linkinghub.elsevier.com/retrieve/pii/0002-9343(78)90843-4
[141] //doi.org/10.1016%2F0002-9343%2878%2990843-4
[142] //www.ncbi.nlm.nih.gov/pubmed/360834
[143] //www.ncbi.nlm.nih.gov/pubmed/14674422
[144] //doi.org/10.1001%2Fjama.277.16.1275b
[145] //www.ncbi.nlm.nih.gov/pubmed/9109457
[146] http://www3.mistral.co.uk/bradburyac/dar9.html
[147] https://web.archive.org/web/20050719075058/http://omni.cc.purdue.edu/~sbenning/el102c/Darwin.html
[148] http://www.icr.org/index.php?module=articles&action=view&ID=112

[149] http://www.aboutdarwin.com/timeline/time_03.html
[150] //doi.org/10.1038%2F1841102a0
[151] //www.ncbi.nlm.nih.gov/pubmed/13791916
[152] http://www.biomedsearch.com/attachments/00/11/62/25/11622586/medhistsuppl00037-0116.pdf
[153] //doi.org/10.1017%2Fs0025727300071027
[154] //www.ncbi.nlm.nih.gov/pmc/articles/PMC2557456
[155] http://darwin-online.org.uk/content/frameset?viewtype=text&itemID=F1452.1&pageseq=1
[156] //www.ncbi.nlm.nih.gov/pubmed/2506517
[157] http://www.robertgordon.net/papers/four.html
[158] http://darwin-online.org.uk/content/frameset?itemID=F1925&viewtype=text&pageseq=1
[159] https://web.archive.org/web/20051004000953/http://www.queendom.com/articles/mentalhealth/etiolpsy.html
[160] //www.ncbi.nlm.nih.gov/pubmed/2109737
[161] //www.ncbi.nlm.nih.gov/pmc/articles/PMC1750247
[162] //www.ncbi.nlm.nih.gov/pubmed/4870694
[163] //www.ncbi.nlm.nih.gov/pmc/articles/PMC2166138
[164] //doi.org/10.1136%2Fbmj.1.5437.745
[165] //www.ncbi.nlm.nih.gov/pubmed/14248443
[166] http://www.sciam.com/article.cfm?articleID=000B62D6-7E63-1D7E-90FB809EC5880000
[167] http://sciencenow.sciencemag.org/cgi/content/full/1997/108/4
[168] http://www.talkorigins.org/indexcc/CA/CA131.html
[169] http://salwen.com/darwin.html
[170] URBANOWICZ ON DARWIN/September 1996 http://www.csuchico.edu/~curban/Darwin/DarwinSem-S95.html
[171] Desmond & Moore 1991, pp. 310–312.
[172] 15v–16v http://darwin-online.org.uk/content/frameset?viewtype=text&itemID=CUL-DAR119.-&pageseq=70
[173] Bunbury, Charles James Fox (1906) Recollections of Darwin. http://darwin-online.org.uk/content/frameset?viewtype=text&itemID=A716&pageseq=1 The life of Sir Charles J. F. Bunbury, Bart. Edited by his sister-in-law Mrs Henry Lyell [Katharine Murray Lyell]; with an introductory note by Sir Joseph Hooker. 2 vols. London: John Murray.
[174] Desmond & Moore 1991, pp. 403–406.
[175] Desmond & Moore 1991, pp. 408–409.
[176] Desmond & Moore 1991, pp. 410–411.
[177] Freeman 2007, pp. 107, 109.
[178] Desmond & Moore 1991, p. 412.
[179] https://books.google.com/books?id=IpLkEMA3FrsC&pg=PA103
[180] http://darwin-online.org.uk/content/frameset?viewtype=side&itemID=CUL-DAR158.1-76&pageseq=1
[181] http://darwin-online.org.uk/EditorialIntroductions/vanWyhe_JournalDAR158.html
[182] http://crisp.psi.uni-heidelberg.de/sites/default/files/vonSydow/von_sydow_2005_darwin_a_christian_undermining_christianity.pdf
[183] http://darwin-online.org.uk/
[184] https://www.gutenberg.org/author/Charles+Darwin
[185] http://www.darwinproject.ac.uk/
[186] van Wyhe 2013, pp. 103–105, 109.
[187] – the first edition called the relationship the "law of the succession of types";
[188] van Wyhe 2013, pp. 105–111.
[189] Brooke, James. (1856), [WCP3073.3041: Letter from Brooke, James to Wallace, Alfred Russel http://www.nhm.ac.uk/resources/research-curation/projects/wallace-correspondence/transcripts/pdf/WCP3073_L3041.pdf, Sarawak, dated 4 July 1856]. In : Beccaloni, G. W. (Ed.). *Wallace Letters Online*, accessed 20 December 2016
[190] van Wyhe 2013, p. 110.
[191] van Wyhe 2013, p. 133.

[192] van Wyhe 2013, p. 111.
[193] Desmond & Moore 1991, pp. 434–438.
[194] Desmond & Moore 1991, p. 450.
[195] Desmond & Moore 1991, p. 449.
[196] Desmond & Moore 1991, pp. 453–454.
[197] Desmond & Moore 1991, pp. 455–456.
[198] Desmond & Moore 1991, pp. 451–453.
[199] Moore & Desmond 2004, pp. xxx–xxxiii.
[200] Ball, P. (2011). Shipping timetables debunk Darwin plagiarism accusations: Evidence challenges claims that Charles Darwin stole ideas from Alfred Russel Wallace. Nature. online http://www.nature.com/news/shipping-timetables-debunk-darwin-plagiarism-accusations-1.9613
[201] J. van Wyhe and K. Rookmaaker. (2012). A new theory to explain the receipt of Wallace's Ternate Essay by Darwin in 1858. *Biological Journal of the Linnean Society* 10.1111/j.1095-8312.2011.01808.x
[202] http://darwin-online.org.uk/content/frameset?itemID=F1556&viewtype=text&pageseq=1
[203] http://darwin-online.org.uk/content/frameset?itemID=F14&viewtype=text&pageseq=1
[204] http://darwin-online.org.uk/content/frameset?itemID=F373&viewtype=text&pageseq=1
[205] http://adsabs.harvard.edu/abs/1872Natur...5..318B
[206] //doi.org/10.1038%2F005318a0
[207] http://www.gutenberg.org/catalog/world/readfile?fk_files=39003&pageno=1
[208] http://darwin-online.org.uk/content/frameset?itemID=F1497&viewtype=text&pageseq=1
[209] http://darwin-online.org.uk/EditorialIntroductions/Freeman_OntheOriginofSpecies.html
[210] http://darwin-online.org.uk/content/frameset?itemID=F1840&viewtype=text&pageseq=23
[211] https://web.archive.org/web/20081222020720/http://speakingoffaith.publicradio.org/programs/darwin/transcript.shtml
[212] http://speakingoffaith.publicradio.org/programs/darwin/transcript.shtml
[213] http://darwin-online.org.uk/darwin.html
[214] http://darwin-online.org.uk/people/van_Wyhe_2007_Mind_the_gap_did_Darwin_avoid_publishing_his_theory.pdf
[215] //doi.org/10.1098%2Frsnr.2006.0171
[216] https://books.google.com/books?id=fpi6CgAAQBAJ&pg=PA111
[217] http://darwin-online.org.uk/
[218] https://www.gutenberg.org/author/Charles+Darwin
[219] http://www.darwinproject.ac.uk/
[220] Herbert 2005, pp. 350–351.
[221] Darwin & Costa 2009, pp. 284–287.
[222] Burchfield 1974, pp. 303–304.
[223] Darwin & Costa 2009, p. 287.
[224] Darwin 1860, p. 287 http://darwin-online.org.uk/content/frameset?pageseq=305&itemID=F376&viewtype=text.
[225] Freeman 1977a.
[226] Anon (24 December 1859) [Review of] On the origin of species http://darwin-online.org.uk/content/frameset?pageseq=2&itemID=A514&viewtype=text, *Saturday Review*, pp. 775–776.
[227] Spelling and abbreviations as
[228] Harrison, Brian W., Early Vatican Responses to Evolutionist Theology http://www.rtforum.org/lt/lt93.html, *Living Tradition*, Organ of the Roman Theological Forum, May 2001 – quotation from here. See also: Artigas, Mariano; Glick, Thomas F., Martínez, Rafael A.; *Negotiating Darwin: the Vatican confronts evolution, 1877–1902*, JHU Press, 2006, , 9780801883897, Google books https://books.google.com/books?id=Q8WrXHnQf8MC&pg=PA5&dq=Darwin+Galileo+Catholic+Church&ei=f2kdSsi2MIrOM_mamcMC#PPA5,M1
[229] Darwin & Costa 2009, p. 286.
[230] Morrell 2001, pp. 87–88.
[231] Morrell 2001, p. 88.
[232] Anon (5 May 1860), " Professor Owen on the Origin of Species http://darwin-online.org.uk/content/frameset?viewtype=image&itemID=CUL-DAR226&pageseq=233", The *Saturday Review*, London, p. 579.

[233] Letter from Karl Marx to Engels dated 18 June 1862 cited in .
[234] Jenson, J. Vernon 1991. *Thomas Henry Huxley: communicating for science*. U. of Delaware Press, Newark. [Chapter 3 is an excellent survey, and its notes gives references to all the eyewitness accounts except Newton]
[235] Jenson, J. Vernon 1991. *Thomas Henry Huxley: communicating for science*. U. of Delaware Press, Newark.
[236] See also: Alfred Newton#Reception of the Origin of Species and Thomas Henry Huxley#Debate with Wilberforce
[237],
William Whewell Quotes - 38 Science Quotes - Dictionary of Science Quotations and Scientist Quotes http://www.todayinsci.com/W/Whewell_William/WhewellWilliam-Quotations.htm, Letter to James D, Forbes (24 Jul 1860)
[238] . Page 190 in the first edition.
[239] Morrell 2001, pp. 88–89.
[240] Thomson, William. (1864). " On the secular cooling of the earth http://courses.seas.harvard.edu/climate/eli/Courses/EPS281r/Sources/Earth-age-and-thermal-history/more/Kelvin-1863-excerpts.pdf", read 28 April 1862. *Transactions of the Royal Society of Edinburgh*, 23, 157–170.
[241] http://www.victorianweb.org/religion/altholz/a2.html
[242] https://books.google.com/?id=uvoTAQAAIAAJ&q=Darwin:The+Power&dq=Darwin:The+Powe
[243] https://doi.org/10.1086%2F351300
[244] //doi.org/10.1086%2F351300
[245] http://www.blc.arizona.edu/courses/schaffer/449/Soft%20Inhertance/Burchfield%20-%20Darwin%20and%20Geol.%20Time.pdf
[246] http://darwin-online.org.uk/content/frameset?itemID=A17&viewtype=text&pageseq=1
[247] https://books.google.com/books?id=C0E03ilhSz4C&pg=PA286
[248] http://darwin-online.org.uk/content/frameset?itemID=F373&viewtype=text&pageseq=1
[249] http://graphics8.nytimes.com/packages/images/nytint/docs/charles-darwin-on-the-origin-of-species/original.pdf
[250] http://adsabs.harvard.edu/abs/1872Natur...5..318B
[251] //doi.org/10.1038%2F005318a0
[252] http://darwin-online.org.uk/content/frameset?itemID=F376&viewtype=text&pageseq=1
[253] http://darwin-online.org.uk/content/frameset?itemID=F381&viewtype=text&pageseq=1
[254] http://darwin-online.org.uk/EditorialIntroductions/Freeman_LifeandLettersandAutobiography.html
[255] http://darwin-online.org.uk/EditorialIntroductions/Freeman_MoreLetters.html
[256] https://books.google.com/?id=A31Izksd2I0C&printsec=frontcover&dq=Desmond+Moore+Darwin#v=onepage&q=
[257] http://darwin-online.org.uk/content/frameset?viewtype=text&itemID=A27b&pageseq=1
[258] http://darwin-online.org.uk/EditorialIntroductions/Freeman_OntheOriginofSpecies.html
[259] https://books.google.com/?id=cyQg1DatmVwC&dq=editions%3ALCCN08020433&pg=PA336#v=onepage&q=
[260] https://books.google.com/books?id=2gF9Mkvgf_kC&pg=PA350
[261] http://darwin-online.org.uk/content/frameset?viewtype=text&itemID=A511&pageseq=1
[262] https://books.google.com/?id=cv6exPcvVD0C&printsec=frontcover&dq=letters+of+Thomas+Henry#v=onepage&q=
[263] http://darwin-online.org.uk/content/frameset?itemID=A166&viewtype=text&pageseq=1
[264] http://darwin-online.org.uk/content/frameset?itemID=A32&viewtype=text&pageseq=1
[265] http://darwin-online.org.uk/content/frameset?viewtype=image&itemID=CUL-DAR226.1.8&pageseq=1
[266] http://users.ox.ac.uk/~jrlucas/legend.html
[267] //doi.org/10.1017%2FS0018246X00016848
[268] //www.ncbi.nlm.nih.gov/pubmed/11617072
[269] https://doi.org/10.1144%2Fgsl.sp.2001.190.01.07
[270] http://adsabs.harvard.edu/abs/2001GSLSP.190...85M

[271] //doi.org/10.1144%2Fgsl.sp.2001.190.01.07
[272] http://citeseerx.ist.psu.edu/viewdoc/download?doi=10.1.1.973.6253&rep=rep1&type=pdf
[273] http://darwin-online.org.uk/content/frameset?itemID=A30&viewtype=text&pageseq=1
[274] http://darwin-online.org.uk/content/frameset?itemID=A19&viewtype=text&pageseq=1
[275] https://books.google.com/?id=d0AMAQAAIAAJ&dq=editions%3ALCCN10003703&pg=RA2-PA248#v=onepage&q=
[276] https://archive.org/details/lifeofalfrednewt00wolliala
[277] http://darwin-online.org.uk/content/frameset?viewtype=side&itemID=CUL-DAR121.-&pageseq=1
[278] http://darwin-online.org.uk/content/frameset?viewtype=side&itemID=CUL-DAR158.1-76&pageseq=1
[279] http://darwin-online.org.uk/EditorialIntroductions/vanWyhe_JournalDAR158.html
[280] http://darwin-online.org.uk/content/frameset?itemID=A1&viewtype=text&pageseq=1
[281] http://aleph0.clarku.edu/huxley/CE2/Phen.html
[282] http://darwin-online.org.uk/
[283] http://darwin-online.org.uk/reviews.html
[284] https://www.gutenberg.org/author/Charles+Darwin
[285] http://www.darwinproject.ac.uk/
[286] Darwin Correspondence Project: Introduction to the Correspondence of Charles Darwin, Volume 14. http://www.darwinproject.ac.uk/content/view/32/38/ Cambridge University Press. Retrieved on 28 November 2008
[287] http://www.darwinproject.ac.uk/index.php
[288] http://darwin-online.org.uk/EditorialIntroductions/Freeman_FertilisationofOrchids.html
[289] http://darwin-online.org.uk/content/frameset?itemID=F880.1&viewtype=text&pageseq=1
[290] http://www.juliantrubin.com/bigten/darwininvent.html
[291] http://darwin-online.org.uk/content/frameset?viewtype=text&itemID=A27b&pageseq=1
[292] http://darwin-online.org.uk/
[293] https://www.gutenberg.org/author/Charles+Darwin
[294] http://www.darwinproject.ac.uk/
[295] https://doi.org/10.1215/10407391-3696607
[296] //doi.org/10.1215%2F10407391-3696607
[297] http://darwin-online.org.uk/EditorialIntroductions/Freeman_TheDescentofMan.html
[298] http://darwin-online.org.uk/
[299] https://www.gutenberg.org/author/Charles+Darwin
[300] http://www.darwinproject.ac.uk/
[301] View original copy. https://archive.org/details/fruitsphilosoph00knogoog
 See also:
[302] Words of Anthem composed by J. Frederick Bridge. http://darwin-online.org.uk/content/frameset?pageseq=1&itemID=A204&viewtype=side Westminster Abbey, 1882.
[303] The Funeral of Mr Darwin, *The Times*, 27 April 1882. (Wikisource)
[304] Desmond & Moore 1991, p. 675.
[305] http://darwin-online.org.uk/
[306] https://www.gutenberg.org/author/Charles+Darwin
[307] http://www.darwinproject.ac.uk/
[308] Charles Darwin National Park. http://www.nt.gov.au/nreta/parks/find/charlesdarwin.html Northern Territory, Australia Government. Retrieved on 15 December 2006.
[309] Darwin College:About Darwin. http://www.dar.cam.ac.uk/visitors/history.shtml Darwin College, Cambridge University website. Retrieved on 10 December 2006.
[310] What's on? BBC Great Britons. http://www.npg.org.uk/live/greatbritop100.asp National Portrait Gallery. Retrieved on 15 December 2006.
[311] " How to join the noteworthy. http://news.bbc.co.uk/2/hi/uk_news/1009901.stm" *BBC News* (7 November 2000). Retrieved on 15 December 2006.
[312] Darwin Awards. http://www.darwinawards.com/ *DarwinAwards.com*. Retrieved on 11 December 2007.

[313] *Good religion needs good science* http://www.cofe.anglican.org/darwin/malcolmbrown.html Rev Dr Malcolm Brown, Director of Mission and Public Affairs, Church of England. Retrieved 17 September 2008.
[314] http://www.ufm.edu
[315] http://www.newmedia.ufm.edu/gsm/index.php?title=Darwin_Day
[316] http://darwin-online.org.uk/
[317] http://www.darwinproject.ac.uk/
[318] https://web.archive.org/web/20081203194842/http://www.darwin200.org/
[319] http://www.themountshrewsbury.com/subpages/darwin_2.php
[320] https://www.theguardian.com/science/interactive/2009/feb/12/charles-darwin
[321] http//www.cbc.ca
[322] http://www.stanford.edu/group/microdocs/darwinvolcano.html
[323] http://www.screenaustralia.gov.au/showcases/charlesdarwin/
[324] http://www.cnrs.fr/cw/dossiers/dosdarwinE/darwin.html
[325] Darwin, C. R. 1851 [=1852]. Living Cirripedia, A monograph on the sub-class Cirripedia, with figures of all the species. The Lepadidæ; or, pedunculated cirripedes. London: The Ray Society. Volume 1.
[326] Darwin, C. R. 1854. Living Cirripedia, The Balanidæ, (or sessile cirripedes); the Verrucidæ. London: The Ray Society. Volume 2.
[327] FitzRoy, R. 1837. Extracts from the Diary of an Attempt to Ascend the River Santa Cruz, in Patagonia, with the boats of his Majesty's sloop Beagle. By Captain Robert Fitz Roy, R.N. Journal of the Royal Geographical Society of London 7: 114–26. Images A74 http://darwin-online.org.uk/content/frameset?itemID=A74&viewtype=image&pageseq=1 (see page 115)
[328] Desmond & Moore 1991, pp. 332, 398, 461.
[329] Freeman 2007, p. 172 http://darwin-online.org.uk/content/frameset?itemID= A27b&viewtype=text&pageseq=179.
[330] Desmond & Moore 1991, pp. 525, 563–565.
[331] Desmond & Moore 1991, p. 600.
[332] Desmond & Moore 1991, pp. 605–606, 612.
[333] Desmond & Moore 1991, pp. 614, 638–639.
[334] Darwin 1871, p. 3, Vol. 1 http://darwin-online.org.uk/content/frameset?pageseq= 16&itemID=F937.1&viewtype=side.
[335] Darwin 1871, p. 65, Vol. 1 http://darwin-online.org.uk/content/frameset?pageseq= 78&itemID=F937.1&viewtype=side.
[336] Darwin 1871, pp. 394–395, Vol. 2 http://darwin-online.org.uk/content/frameset?pageseq= 411&itemID=F937.2&viewtype=side.
[337] Darwin 1887, p. 311 http://darwin-online.org.uk/content/frameset?pageseq=329&itemID= F1452.1&viewtype=side.
[338] Darwin 1958, pp. 96–97 http://darwin-online.org.uk/content/frameset?pageseq=98&itemID= F1497&viewtype=side.
[339] http://darwin-online.org.uk/content/frameset?viewtype=text&itemID=A25&pageseq=1
[340] http://darwin-online.org.uk/EditorialIntroductions/Freeman_TheDescentofMan.html
[341] http://darwin-online.org.uk/EditorialIntroductions/Freeman_ LifeandLettersandAutobiography.html
[342] http://darwin-online.org.uk/content/frameset?itemID=F10.2&viewtype=text&pageseq=1
[343] http://darwin-online.org.uk/content/frameset?itemID=A27b&viewtype=text&pageseq=299
[344] http://darwin-online.org.uk/content/frameset?viewtype=text&itemID=A342&pageseq=1
[345] http://darwin-online.org.uk/content/frameset?itemID=F1925&viewtype=text&pageseq=1
[346] http://www.asa3.org/ASA/PSCF/2001/PSCF9-01Miles.html
[347] http://worldtracker.org/media/library/Sociology/Dawkins%20-%20Devil%27s%20Chaplain.pdf
[348] https://web.archive.org/web/20081222020720/http://speakingoffaith.publicradio.org/programs/darwin/transcript.shtml
[349] http://speakingoffaith.publicradio.org/programs/darwin/transcript.shtml
[350] http://darwin-online.org.uk/content/frameset?pageseq=1&itemID=A142&viewtype=text

[351] http://www.sulloway.org/Why%20Darwin%20Rejected%20Intelligent%20Design%20(2006).pdf
[352] http://darwin-online.org.uk/content/frameset?viewtype=text&itemID=A544&pageseq=1
[353] //doi.org/10.1098%2Frsnr.2006.0171
[354] //doi.org/10.1111%2Fj.1600-0498.2012.00256.x
[355] http://www.philos.de/Momme/vSydow,%20M.%20%282005%29%20Darwin%20A%20Christian%20Undermining%20Christianity.pdf
[356] http://www.talkorigins.org/faqs/hope.html
[357] https://www.nytimes.com/learning/general/onthisday/bday/0212.html
[358] http://darwin-online.org.uk/content/frameset?viewtype=side&itemID=CUL-DAR121.-&pageseq=1
[359] http://darwin-online.org.uk/content/frameset?itemID=F10.3&viewtype=text&pageseq=1
[360] http://darwin-online.org.uk/content/frameset?viewtype=text&itemID=F1556&pageseq=33
[361] http://darwin-online.org.uk/content/frameset?itemID=F1556&viewtype=text&pageseq=1
[362] http://darwin-online.org.uk/content/frameset?itemID=F20&viewtype=text&pageseq=1
[363] http://darwin-online.org.uk/content/frameset?itemID=F373&viewtype=text&pageseq=1
[364] http://darwin-online.org.uk/content/frameset?itemID=F1142&viewtype=text&pageseq=1
[365] http://darwin-online.org.uk/content/frameset?viewtype=side&itemID=CUL-DAR158.1-76&pageseq=1
[366] http://darwin-online.org.uk/EditorialIntroductions/vanWyhe_JournalDAR158.html
[367] http://www.vqronline.org/articles/2006/spring/eldredge-confessions-darwinist/
[368] http://www.asa3.org/ASA/PSCF/2004/PSCF3-04Lamoureux.pdf
[369] http://www.aboutdarwin.com/darwin/WhoWas.html
[370] http://darwin-online.org.uk/content/frameset?viewtype=image&itemID=CUL-DAR226.1.8&pageseq=1
[371] http://users.ox.ac.uk/~jrlucas/legend.html
[372] http://www.wku.edu/~smithch/essays/ARWPAMPH.htm
[373] http://www.talkorigins.org/faqs/evolphil/social.html
[374] http://darwin-online.org.uk/darwin.html
[375] http://www.darwinproject.ac.uk/darwin-and-religion
[376] https://web.archive.org/web/20120612015341/http://www.darwinproject.ac.uk/what-did-darwin-believe-article
[377] https://web.archive.org/web/20141021101910/http://www.darwinproject.ac.uk/darwin-and-design-article
[378] https://archive.is/20071206173947/http://scibel.gospelcom.net/content/scibelarticles.php?id=3
[379] http://darwin-online.org.uk/content/frameset?itemID=F1452.1&viewtype=text&pageseq=1
[380] http://theologie-naturwissenschaften.de/startseite/leitartikelarchiv/darwin-on-religion.html
[381] http://www.educationengland.org.uk/articles/20creationism.html
[382] http://www.corante.com/loom/archives/2005/08/11/a_dog_and_the_mind_of_newton.php
[383] http://magma.nationalgeographic.com/ngm/0411/feature1/fulltext.html
[384] https://web.archive.org/web/20061002124015/http://speakingoffaith.publicradio.org/programs/darwin/index.shtml
[385] https://www.washingtonpost.com/wp-dyn/content/article/2006/02/03/AR2006020300822_pf.html
[386] http://publicdomainreview.org/2011/06/28/was-charles-darwin-an-atheist/
[387] Schmitt S. (2009). *Haeckel: A German Darwinian?* Comptes Rendus Biologies: 332: 110-118.
[388] Wallace, Alfred Russel. (1889). *Darwinism: An Exposition of the Theory of Natural Selection, with Some of Its Applications* https://archive.org/stream/darwinismexposit00walluoft#page/n11/mode/2up. Macmillan and Company.
[389] Heilbron, John L. (2003). *The Oxford Companion to the History of Modern Science.* OUP USA. p. 203.
[390] Romanes, John George. (1906). "Darwin and After Darwin: An Exposition of the Darwinian Theory and a Discussion of Post-Darwinian Questions" https://archive.org/stream/darwinafterdarwi02romabost#page/12/mode/2up. *Volume 2: Heredity and Utility.* The Open Court Publishing Company. p. 12

[391] Costa, James T. (2014). *Wallace, Darwin, and the Origin of Species*. Harvard University Press. p. 274.
[392] Bolles, R. C; Beecher, M. D. (1987). *Evolution and Learning*. Psychology Press. p. 45.
[393] Elsdon-Baker, F. (2008). Spirited dispute: the secret split between Wallace and Romanes. Endeavour 32(2): 75-78
[394] Scott 2007, "Creation Science Lite: 'Intelligent Design' as the New Anti-Evolutionism," p. 72 https://web.archive.org/web/20100603214827/http://biology.ucf.edu/~clp/Courses/seminar/papers/07-Scott-scientists_confront-cs_lite.pdf
[395] "This paper was originally delivered as a lecture at a symposium at Hillsdale College, in November 1992. Papers from the Symposium were published in the collection *Man and Creation: Perspectives on Science and Theology* (Bauman ed. 1993), by Hillsdale College Press, Hillsdale MI 49242."
[396] Paper for CH506: American Church History, Dr. Nathan Feldmeth, Winter Quarter 1997, "written while a student in the School of World Mission at Fuller Theological Seminary, Pasadena, California."
[397] //lccn.loc.gov/2002007569
[398] //www.worldcat.org/oclc/49824702
[399] //lccn.loc.gov/94006598
[400] //www.worldcat.org/oclc/733100564
[401] http://www.gutenberg.org/files/19192/19192-h/19192-h.htm
[402] //lccn.loc.gov/06012878
[403] //www.worldcat.org/oclc/11489956
[404] //lccn.loc.gov/03000886
[405] //www.worldcat.org/oclc/1542829
[406] https://archive.org/details/cu31924030243640
[407] //lccn.loc.gov/2006039753
[408] //www.worldcat.org/oclc/173480577
[409] //lccn.loc.gov/95083037
[410] //www.worldcat.org/oclc/35145565
[411] http://new.runivers.ru/lib/book3542/
[412] https://archive.org/stream/darwinismandothe00fiskiala#page/n7/mode/2up
[413] https://archive.org/stream/b21500009#page/n3/mode/2up
[414] https://archive.org/stream/darwinafterdarwi02romabost#page/n5/mode/2up
[415] https://archive.org/stream/darwinismexposit00walluoft#page/n7/mode/2up
[416] http://plato.stanford.edu/entries/darwinism/
[417] //en.wikipedia.org/w/index.php?title=Template:Fringe_medicine_sidebar&action=edit
[418] Database includes entries from *A Greek–English Lexicon* and other English dictionaries of Ancient Greek.
[419] The Laws of the Twelve Tables, c.450 B.C. http://www.historyguide.org/ancient/12tables.html "A dreadfully deformed child shall be quickly killed"
[420] Tacitus. Germania.XII "Traitors and deserters are hanged on trees; the coward, the unwarlike, the man stained with abominable vices, is plunged into the mire of the morass, with a hurdle put over him."
[421] Giles, Frances (2010) and the Family in the Middle Ages https//books.google.co.uk New York: Harper Collins. p.ii
[422] Bowler, Peter J., *Evolution: The History of an Idea*, 3rd Ed., University of California Press, 2003, pp. 308–310.
[423] Blom 2008, p. 336.
[424] Black 2003, p. 240.
[425] Black 2003, p. 286.
[426] Black 2003, p. 40.
[427] Black 2003, p. 45.
[428] Black 2003, Chapter 6: The United States of Sterilization.
[429] Black 2003, p. 237.
[430] Black 2003, Chapter 5: Legitimizing Raceology.
[431] Black 2003, Chapter 9: Mongrelization.

⁴³²https://archive.org/details/jstor-2763324

⁴³³"Consumption: Its Cause and Cure" An Address by Dr Halliday Sutherland on 4 September 1917, published by the Red Triangle Press.

⁴³⁴"Lancelot Hogben, who developed his critique of eugenics and distaste for racism in the period...he spent as Professor of Zoology at the University of Cape Town". Alison Bashford and Philippa Levine, *The Oxford Handbook of the History of Eugenics*. Oxford; Oxford University Press, 2010 (p.200)

⁴³⁵"Whatever their disagreement on the numbers, Haldane, Fisher, and most geneticists could support Jennings's warning: To encourage the expectation that the sterilization of defectives will "solve the problem of hereditary defects, close up the asylums for feebleminded and insane, do away with prisons, is only to subject society to deception". Daniel J. Kevles, *In the Name of Eugenics*. University of California Press, 1985. (p. 166).

⁴³⁶Black 2003, pp. 274–295.

⁴³⁷Black 2003.

⁴³⁸Lynn 2001. p. 18 "By the middle decades of the twentieth century, eugenics had become widely accepted throughout the whole of the economically developed world, with the exception of the Soviet Union."

⁴³⁹Article 2 of the Convention defines genocide as any of the following acts committed with the intent to destroy, in whole or in part, a national, ethnic, racial or religious group, as such as:
• Killing members of the group; • Causing serious bodily or mental harm to members of the group; • Deliberately inflicting on the group conditions of life calculated to bring about its physical destruction in whole or in part; • Imposing measures intended to prevent births within the group; • Forcibly transferring children of the group to another group. See the Convention on the Prevention and Punishment of the Crime of Genocide.

⁴⁴⁰Blom 2008, pp. 335–336.

⁴⁴¹Cited in

⁴⁴²A discussion of the shifting meanings of the term can be found in

⁴⁴³Lynn 2001. *Part III. The Implementation of Classical Eugenics* pp. 137–244 *Part IV. The New Eugenics* pp. 245–320

⁴⁴⁴Lynn 2001. pp. 165–186

⁴⁴⁵Lynn 2001. pp. 169–170

⁴⁴⁶Lynn 2001. pp. 170–172

⁴⁴⁷Lynn 2001. pp. 172–174

⁴⁴⁸Lynn 2001. pp. 174–176

⁴⁴⁹Lynn 2001. pp. 176–178

⁴⁵⁰Lynn 2001. pp. 179–181

⁴⁵¹Lynn 2001. pp. 181–182

⁴⁵²Lynn 2001. pp. 182–185

⁴⁵³Lynn 2001. pp. 187–204

⁴⁵⁴Lynn 2001. pp. 188–189

⁴⁵⁵Lynn 2001. pp. 189–190

⁴⁵⁶Lynn 2001. pp. 190–191

⁴⁵⁷Lynn 2001. pp. 191–192

⁴⁵⁸Lynn 2001. pp. 194–195

⁴⁵⁹Lynn 2001. pp. 196–199. Quote: "There is, nevertheless, a good case for reviving the sterilization of the mentally retarded and criminals. It is indisputable on both empirical and theoretical ground that many of these people transmit their characteristics to their children by both genetic and environmental processes."

⁴⁶⁰Lynn 2001. pp. 199–201. First quote: "The rationale for this sentencing policy was that the judges considered these women unfit to rear children and that they should therefore be prevented from having more, at least for a few years." Second quote: "In these and similar cases many people will no doubt accept that the judges were right in deciding that the women were unfit mothers and likely to cause harm to any future children and that it would be desirable to prevent further pregnancies. It is preferable for these women to be put on probation conditional on temporary sterilization than to send them to prison, which in most cases would serve little useful purpose. These judges' decisions were not made ostensibly on eugenic grounds, but they

furthered the eugenic objective of preventing these women from having children, at least for a limited period. The eugenic objective should be to support these judicial sentences and to promote their use more often, together with the stipulation of longer periods of contraception and, preferably, permanent sterilization"

[461] Lynn 2001. pp. 201–203. Quote: "A better alternative, from the point of view of reducing future criminal offending and the promotion of eugenics, would be for judges to offer convicted male criminals the alternatives of imprisonment or castration accompanied by probation."

[462] Lynn 2001. pp. 205–214

[463] Lynn 2001. pp. 211–213. Richard Lynn argued that to have an effective licensing program, reversible sterilization methods should be used. Those who wish to have children would obtain the licence and have the sterilization reversed. Lynn stated that the proposals made by Francis Galton, Hugh LaFollette and John Westman would not be effective from the eugenicists' viewpoint, since those without licences could still have children. The proposal by David Lykken would be only slightly effective.

[464] Lynn 2001. pp. 215–224

[465] Lynn 2001. pp. 215–217

[466] Lynn 2001. pp. 217–219

[467] Lynn 2001. p. 219

[468] Lynn 2001. pp. 220–221. Quote: "While it can be confidently expected that elites would respond to financial incentives to have children and to penalties for childlessness by increasing their fertility, they might not do this to the extent that would be desired. Ideally a program of positive eugenics would increase the fertility of the elite to perhaps around four children per couple; and at the same time a complementary program of negative eugenics would reduce the fertility of those with low intelligence and psychopathic personality to zero.

[469] Lynn 2001. pp. 222–224. Quote: "The final strategy for the promotion of positive eugenics would consist of the acceptance of good-quality immigrants."

[470] Lynn 2001. p. 246

[471] Lynn 2001. p. 247

[472] Lynn 2001. pp. 248–251

[473] Lynn 2001. p. 252

[474] Lynn 2001. p. 253

[475] Lynn 2001. p. 254

[476] Lynn 2001. pp. 254–255

[477] Blom 2008, pp. 336–7.

[478] (Galton 2001, 48)

[479] Lynn 2001. *The Ethical Principles of Classical Eugenics – Conclusions* P. 241 Quote: "A number of the opponents of eugenics have resorted to the slippery slope argument, which states that although a number of eugenic measures are unobjectionable in themselves, they could lead to further measures that would be unethical. This argument is unpersuasive because all sorts of measures that are acceptable might, if taken to extremes, lead to other measures that are unacceptable."

[480] Shaw, p. 147. Quote: "What Rawls says is that "Over time a society is to take steps to preserve the general level of natural abilities and to prevent the diffusion of serious defects." The key words here are "preserve" and "prevent". Rawls clearly envisages only the use of negative eugenics as a preventative measure to ensure a good basic level of genetic health for future generations. To jump from this to "make the later generations as genetically talented as possible," as Pence does, is a masterpiece of misinterpretation. This, then, is the sixth argument against positive eugenics: the Veil of Ignorance argument. Those behind the Veil in Rawls' Original Position would agree to permit negative, but not positive eugenics. This is a more complex variant of the Consent argument, as the Veil of Ignorance merely forces us to adopt a position of hypotethical consent to particular principles of justice."

[481] https://link.springer.com/article/10.1007/s40592-018-0081-2

[482] https://global.oup.com/academic/product/better-than-human-9780190664046?cc=us&lang=en&

[483] http://www.oxfordhandbooks.com/view/10.1093/oxfordhb/9780199981878.001.0001/oxfordhb-9780199981878-e-7

484 //www.worldcat.org/issn/1063-2158
485 //lccn.loc.gov/00052459
486 http://faculty.smu.edu/jkazez/PAP/savulescu-kahane.pdf
487 http://www.waragainsttheweak.com/
488 https://books.google.com/?id=8esnhRxBomMC
489 https://web.archive.org/web/20130904043526/http://www.ushmm.org/museum/exhibit/online/deadlymedicine/
490 http://www.ushmm.org/museum/exhibit/online/deadlymedicine
491 https://web.archive.org/web/20090512075255/http://www.jayjoseph.net/GeneIllusion.html
492 http://www.jayjoseph.net/GeneIllusion.html
493 http://hpy.sagepub.com/cgi/pmidlookup?view=long&pmid=16013119
494 //doi.org/10.1177%2F0957154x05047004
495 //www.ncbi.nlm.nih.gov/pubmed/16013119
496 https://web.archive.org/web/20090417170900/http://www.jayjoseph.net/MissingGene.html
497 http://www.jayjoseph.net/MissingGene.html
498 //doi.org/10.1177%2F026101839501504402
499 http://libres.uncg.edu/ir/uncg/f/D_Wahlsten_Leilani_1997.pdf
500 //doi.org/10.1007%2FBF02259522
501 //www.ncbi.nlm.nih.gov/pubmed/9463073
502 Hodgson
503
504 Leonard, Thomas C. (2009) Origins of the Myth of Social Darwinism: The Ambiguous Legacy of Richard Hofstadter's Social Darwinism in American Thought http://www.princeton.edu/~tleonard/papers/myth.pdf Journal of Economic Behavior & Organization 71, pp. 37–51
505 Riggenbach, Jeff (2011-04-24) The Real William Graham Sumner https://mises.org/daily/5206/The-Real-William-Graham-Sumner, Mises Institute
506 Paul, Diane B. in
507 Benjamin Kidd, *Social Evolution*, Kessinger Publishing, LLC, 2007, 400 pages, , p. 47.
508 Spencer, Herbert. 1860. 'The Social Organism', originally published in *The Westminster Review*. Reprinted in Spencer's (1892) *Essays: Scientific, Political and Speculative*. London and New York.
509 Barbara Stiegler, *Nietzsche et la biologie*, PUF, 2001, p. 90. See, for ex., *Genealogy of Morals*, III, 13 here http://malaspina.edu/~johnstoi/Nietzsche/genealogy3.htm#13
510 Friedrich Nietzsche, *Human, All Too Human*, §224
511 but see
512 Descent of Man, chapter 4
513 "A careful reading of the theories of Sumner and Spencer exonerates them from the century-old charge of social Darwinism in the strict sense of the word. They did not themselves advocate the application of Darwin's theory of natural selection." The Social Meaning of Modern Biology: From Social Darwinism to Sociobiology https://books.google.com/books?id=7BJUIOnC534C&pg=PA33&lpg=PA33&dq=bannister+social+darwinism
514 "At least a part—and sometimes a generous part" of the great fortunes went back to the community through many kinds of philanthropic endeavor, says
515 "Borrowing from Charles Darwin's theory of evolution, social Darwinists believed that societies, as do organisms evolve over time. Nature then determined that the strong survive and the weak perish. In Jack London's case, he thought that certain favored races were destined for survival, mainly those that could preserve themselves while supplanting others, as in the case of the White race." The philosophy of Jack London http://sunsite.berkeley.edu/London/Essays/philosophy.html
516 Jonathan D. Spence. *The Search for Modern China"*. W.W. Norton, 1990, p. 301 https://books.google.com/books?id=vI1RRslLNSwC&q=social+darwinism#v=snippet&q=social%20darwinism&f=false.
517 *Ibid.*
518 *Ibid.*, 414–15.
519 https://www.questia.com/PM.qst?a=o&d=93577330

[520] http://library.alibris.com/booksearch.detail?invid=11529157550&browse=1&qwork=1595131&first=1&mtype=B&qsort=p&page=1
[521] https://archive.org/stream/transactions05royauoft/transactions05royauoft_djvu.txt
[522] https://www.questia.com/PM.qst?a=o&d=57831077
[523] https://books.google.com/books?id=bzANHSAo60cC&printsec=frontcover#v=onepage&q&f=false
[524] https://www.questia.com/PM.qst?a=o&d=61860931
[525] https://www.questia.com/PM.qst?a=o&d=96294585
[526] https://books.google.com/books?id=iZoEyJB6rx0C&printsec=frontcover#v=onepage&q&f=false
[527] https://www.questia.com/PM.qst?a=o&d=5001247998
[528] https://books.google.com/books?id=_D3nCwAAQBAJ&printsec=frontcover#v=onepage&q&f=false
[529] https://www.questia.com/PM.qst?a=o&d=98417918
[530] https://www.questia.com/PM.qst?a=o&d=107191131
[531] http://www.geoffrey-hodgson.info/user/image/socialdarwinism.pdf
[532] //www.worldcat.org/issn/0952-1909
[533] https://books.google.com/books?id=Ty8aEmWc_ekC&printsec=frontcover#v=onepage&q&f=false
[534] https://www.questia.com/PM.qst?a=o&d=5001362323
[535] https://books.google.com/books?id=-aDpwfE9DO0C&printsec=frontcover#v=onepage&q=%22Social%20Darwinism%22&f=false
[536] http://library.thinkquest.org/C004367/eh4.shtml
[537] https://www.pbs.org/wgbh/evolution/darwin/nameof/
[538] http://darwin-online.org.uk/
[539] http://darwin-online.org.uk/contents.html
[540] https://www.gutenberg.org/author/Charles+Darwin
[541] http://lccn.loc.gov/87007695
[542] Darwin Online: Darwin's insects in Stephens' Illustrations of British entomology (1829–32) http://darwin-online.org.uk/EditorialIntroductions/vanWyhe_Stephens.html
[543] Extracts from letters addressed to Professor Henslow http://darwin-online.org.uk/content/frameset?viewtype=side&itemID=F1&pageseq=1. Cambridge: [privately printed]
[544] Proceedings of the Geological Society 2: 210–212 http://darwin-online.org.uk/content/frameset?viewtype=side&itemID=F1642&pageseq=6
[545] South African Christian Recorder 2 (4) (Sept. 1836): 221–238 http://darwin-online.org.uk/content/frameset?itemID=F1640&viewtype=text&pageseq=1

Article Sources and Contributors

The sources listed for each article provide more detailed licensing information including the copyright status, the copyright owner, and the license conditions.

Darwin–Wedgwood family *Source:* https://en.wikipedia.org/w/index.php?oldid=856958249 *License:* Creative Commons Attribution-Share Alike 3.0 *Contributors:* *Kat*, A1 Aardvark, Alansohn, Alexjohnson1994, Anaxial, Anon685, Avram, BD2412, BU Rob13, Ben MCR, Bender235, Betacommand, Bgwhite, Bluemin, Bob Jim, Brightland, Britannicus, Brograve, C. A. Russell, Carbon Caryatid, Charles Matthews, Choess, Chris the speller, ChrisGualtieri, Chrisportelli, ClueBot NG, Corvus cornix, Cyndrel, Danmateju, Dave souza, Davepape, Dawkeye, Demully, Deville, DocWatson42, Download, Dumpty17, Dusti, EchetusXe, Ekvcpa, Eluchil404, Ema–or, Erp, Fbv65edel, Firsfron, Florian Blaschke, Francis Hoar, Frietjes, Gary, Gilgamesh4, Glacialfox, Grook Da Oger, Gurch, Hydrogen Iodide, Icairns, Icairns 2, Iridescent, Isnow, Itc editor2, JLaTondre, JackyR, Johnuniq, Kelisi, Kevin Dewitt, Kikichugirl, Kittybrewster, Kiwi Kousin, Klilidiplomus, Koavf, KraRi, Lampman, Lavateraguy, Lockesdonkey, Lrippers, Macdonald-ross, Magioladitis, MarmadukePercy, Mhardcastle, Mogism, Nedrutland, Nickovs, Noha307, Nwbeeson, Oceancetaceen, Ohconfucius, Oshwah, Petri Krohn, Petropoxy (Lithoderm Proxy), Philip Cross, Phoe, Pigsonthewing, Redrose64, Regan123, Rettetast, Richiebful, RickstaDaBest123, Riom, Rogerd, STBotD, Saga City, Schmloof, Sergeant Cribb, Shuffleman117, Softlavender, Sun Creator, Targaryen, Tassedethe, Teb728, Tide rolls, Tom.Reding, Topbanana, Tpbradbury, Ulric1313, Vancouveriensis, Vanished user, Victuallers, Waacstats, Wanstep, Wedgwoodpound, Wikianon, WilliamPryor, Zanimum, Векочел, 166 anonymous edits 3

Charles Darwin's education *Source:* https://en.wikipedia.org/w/index.php?oldid=863397544 *License:* Creative Commons Attribution-Share Alike 3.0 *Contributors:* AdjustShift, Alexjohnc3, Arch dude, Atomician, Aunt Entropy, AxG, Barbara Shack, Barticus88, Basement12, Ben Argon, Ben Ben, Bender235, Big iron, Bobo192, CLCStudent, CLW, Charles Matthews, Chris the speller, Citation bot 1, ClueBot NG, Colin MacLaurin, CommonsDelinker, Dave souza, DavidJ710, Deadbeef, Deeptrivia, Deuterostome, Dthomsen8, Duncharris, EdChem, Epbr123, Erp, Fortheloveofknowledge, Gabriel Yuji, Gaius Cornelius, Gilliam, Glane23, GreenC, Gustavb, HamburgerRadio, Haruth, Horselover Frost, IW.HG, Icairns, Ilovedegrassi17, Inwind, James086, Jamesontai, Jerodlycett, John of Reading, Johnuniq, Join Tile, Karppinen, Kim Traynor, Leonard^Bloom, Lugia2453, M4r10699, MONGO, MarcoTolo, Mathsci, Mets501, Mild Bill Hiccup, Mpallen, Mumia-w-18, Nsaa, Nymf, Ohconfucius, Onel5969, Ottava Rima, Panama1958, PlyrStar93, Professor marginalia, Recognizance, Rjwilmsi, SA 13 Bro, SchreiberBike, Sheriff Bernard, Silence, Simon12, SpK, Suffusion of Yellow, Szquirrel, Te Karere, The Thing That Should Not Be, Tmol42, Trappist the monk, Tresiden, Uncle G, Versus22, Vsion, Wavelength, Wen D House, Widr, Wikipeditor, Wknight94, Yuckfoo, Zsinj, 140 anonymous edits 25

Second voyage of HMS Beagle *Source:* https://en.wikipedia.org/w/index.php?oldid=861777653 *License:* Creative Commons Attribution-Share Alike 3.0 *Contributors:* 1exec1, Aa77zz, Againme, AlternoBreak, Andrewrp, Aymatth2, BD2412, Bender235, Boneyard90, Brian A Schmidt, CAPTAIN RAJU, Cambalachero, Ccgrimm, Charles Matthews, Chenxlee, Chiton magnificus, Citation bot 1, ClueBot NG, Crispulop, Dalek Supreme X, Dave souza, Dawnseeker2000, Dl2000, Dragonblade629, Elbazza, Ethan Danes, Fnielsen, Fratrep, Funsoman, Gaius Cornelius, Gary, Geospiza, Giftlite, Good Olfactory, Graeme Bartlett, GregorB, Headbomb, JVollenhoven, Jamesontai, Jaraalbe, Jgrahamc, Jrtayloriv, Kablammo, Kenneth Wills, Khazar2, Lightmouse, Maias, Mamayuco, MiG, Mikenorton, MrOllie, Nakeidra, Narky Blert, Niceguyedc, Njahnke, NqZooArchive1969, Old Moonraker, Onel5969, OttRider, Paul A, Pecopteris, Petter Bøckman, PigFlu Oink, Plantdrew, Pragmaticstatistic, Rcsprinter123, Remotelysensed, Rich Farmbrough, Richigi, Rikf australia, Rjcflyer, Rjwilmsi, Robert FitzRoy, SchnitzelMannGreek, SchreiberBike, ShelfSkewed, Skier Dude, Smallman12q, Soerfm, Spicemix, Spinningspark, Squids and Chips, SusanLesch, Swid, Tabletop, Targaryen, The Rambling Man, The Thing That Should Not Be, Thomas Craven, Tim!, Tutthoth-Ankhre, Tuxedo junction, Umbertoumm, Vsmith, Warichrb29, Wavelength, Wee Curry Monster, Widr, Winemedineme, Woohookitty, Writtenonsand, Вальдимар, 65 anonymous edits 45

Inception of Darwin's theory *Source:* https://en.wikipedia.org/w/index.php?oldid=844099514 *License:* Creative Commons Attribution-Share Alike 3.0 *Contributors:* 1exec1, Allenmyers, Ann-Kathrin Born, Artichoker, BD2412, Barticus88, Bender235, Bgwhite, Brandmeister, BreakfastJr, CLW, Canterbury Tail, Causa sui, Charles Matthews, Choess, Chris the speller, Circeus, Citation bot 1, ClueBot NG, Correogsk, DARTH SIDIOUS 2, Dave souza, Derild4921, Dialectric, DoctorCaligari, Ettrig, Fastfission, Forbsey, Fuhghettaboutit, Garion96, Gephart, Grafen, Grover cleveland, Jagged 85, Jamesmcmahon0, Jandalhandler, Jhbdel, John of Reading, Johnuniq, Jonesey95, Lenthe, Lexor, Lilipatina, Matthew Yeager, Minglex, Mom123456789, Munibert, MusikAnimal, Neelix, Ntsimp, Ohconfucius, Orangemarlin, PBS, PKT, Phettyplace, Philly jawn, Phoe, Plucas58, Proxima Centauri, Quebec99, Qviri, Rjcflyer, Rjwilmsi, Scewing, Sietse Snel, Signalhead, Silence, Skinmeister, Srich32977, Steven Walling, Sunrise, Szquirrel, TestPilot, That Guy, From That Show!, Tillerh11, Tmol42, TongueSpeaker, VoABot II, Vsmith, Wikididact, Woland37, 45 anonymous edits 81

Health of Charles Darwin *Source:* https://en.wikipedia.org/w/index.php?oldid=857021590 *License:* Creative Commons Attribution-Share Alike 3.0 *Contributors:* ARUNKUMAR P.R, Abanima, Against the current, Ahoerstemeier, Aitias, Anthony Appleyard, Armchair info guy, Arsene, Arthena, Avenue, BD2412, BananaFiend, Barjammar, Barticus88, Bbi5291, Belovedfreak, Ben Ben, Bender235, Brunton, Bryan Derksen, CALR, CLW, CSWarren, CaTi0604, CambridgeBayWeather, Certes, Charles Matthews, Chris55, Cinnbunn, Clobberdonk, ClueBot NG, Cobi, Comp.arch, Complainer, Coz 11, DanaUllman, Dave souza, Dcirovic, Diabolo devil, Doc James, Egmonster, Elysianfields, Emersoni, Epbr123, Epicgenius, Fastfission, Gaius Cornelius, Giftlite, Grafen, Haymanj, Headbomb, Hessamnia, Ira Leviton, Iridescent, JaGa, JackofOz, JamesBurns, Jlittlet, Johnuniq, Jprg1966, Jwy, Kdbuffalo, KenBailey, Khazar2, Layraud, Lockesdonkey, Lucien leGrey, MRSC, ManbeerDrunkachola, Marianocecowski, Mattarata, Me, Myself, and I are Here, Mel Etitis, Mgumn, Mr. Guye, Nealmcb, Neelix, Norm mit, Omnipaedista, Packer1028, Pak21, Pgan002, Pharos, Quale, Quebec99, R'n'B, RDBrown, RainbowOfLight, Reconsider the static, Redwolf24, RentEdits, Richerman, Rjwilmsi, Robofish, Rowellcf, Rsabbatini, RunnyAmiga, Saimhe, Sam Medany, SamX, Sannse, Schmiteye, SebastianHelm, Sionus, Snezzy, Splash, Suslindisambiguator, Tczuel, TestPilot, The Thing That Should Not Be, Tinchoman, Tmol42, Upsala, Vanished user, Versus22, Vikionwikirocks679, VolatileChemical, Weydonian, Widr, Wikipelli, Will Beback, WolfmanSF, Woohookitty, Xezbeth, 190 anonymous edits 105

Development of Darwin's theory *Source:* https://en.wikipedia.org/w/index.php?oldid=824216483 *License:* Creative Commons Attribution-Share Alike 3.0 *Contributors:* 22crabtreewe, Aircorn, Alafarge, Allenmyers, Ann-Kathrin Born, Anne drew Andrew and Drew, Arathald, Barticus88, BenB4, Bender235, CLW, Charles Matthews, Charlie84281, Christofurio, Circeus, Citation bot 1, ClueBot NG, Dave souza, Doug Weller, Drmies, DuncanHill, Ecemaml, Egel, Fastfission, FunkMonk, Gaius Cornelius, GreatWhiteNortherner, Guettarda, Hetar, Jackol, JamesAM, Johnuniq, Khazar2, Kiandush, Koavf, Kralizec!, KylieTastic, Lexor, Logophile, MRSC, Monty845, Moonriddengirl, Munibert, Nizam Ibrahim, Numbersnow, OccamzRazor, Ohconfucius, Oshwah, Rezma90, Richard001, RotubirtnoC, Seb26, Serols, Silence, Stemonitis, SusanLesch, Syncategoremata, Tothebarricades.tk, 54 anonymous edits 123

Publication of Darwin's theory *Source:* https://en.wikipedia.org/w/index.php?oldid=847851441 *License:* Creative Commons Attribution-Share Alike 3.0 *Contributors:* Adirlanz, Alansohn, Allenmyers, Appraiser, Arado, Avoided, Ayyeitskrysan, Bueller 007, Charles Matthews, Circeus, Citation bot 1, Cleared as filed, ClueBot NG, DGG, Dalahäst, Dave souza, DavidLeighEllis, Doubting thomas, Fastfission, Gauri, Howcheng, I dream of horses, Ikanbasung, Iridescent, Jason Quinn, Johnbibby, Jonesey95, Jpbowen, Jrmccall, Kaldari, Khazar2, Koavf, Kzollman, Lexor, Logan, MAMSMACHI, MRSC, Macdonald-ross, MapReader, Metamagician3000, Mikker, MrLinkinPark333, Neelix, Norm mit, Ohconfucius, Orangemarlin, Rich Farmbrough, Richard001, Richardob, Rjwilmsi, Robert Stevens, Rrburke, Samsara, ScottSteiner, Silence, Stemonitis, Strobilomyces, SusanLesch, TableManners, The Thing That Should Not Be, Tim bates, Trappist the monk, UESPArules, Ulric1313, WLU, Widr, Wikipelli, Wobble, 53 anonymous edits 141

Reactions to On the Origin of Species *Source:* https://en.wikipedia.org/w/index.php?oldid=846811795 *License:* Creative Commons Attribution-Share Alike 3.0 *Contributors:* Aa77zz, Anarchangel, Andrew c, Apperceptions, Arbeiter, Aunt Entropy, BD2412, Bender235, Charles Matthews, Charvex, Chiswick Chap, Citation bot 1, Cleared as filed, ClueBot NG, Colonies Chris, Cosans, Crosbiesmith, Dave souza, Delta x, Doug Weller, DuncanHill, Egel, Ettrig, Fastfission, Finn Froding, Garas, Gilliam, Ginsuloft, Headbomb, Hrafn, Intercalate, Iridescent, Ironist, IsaacGS, J 1982, J.delanoy, Jefffire, Jim1138, Johnbod, Johnuniq, Keith D, Lacrimosus, Leinad-Z, Lexor, Loodog, MRSC, Macdonald-ross, Magioladitis, Mark Foskey, Markbassett, McSly, Measure, Mlaffs, Moaznfady, Multi-AC, Narky Blert, Neelix, NerriTunn, Niceguyedc, Nickst, Ohconfucius, PaperTruths, Philip J.1987qazwsx, Pinkshrimp, Plumbago, Pm1971, PrimeHunter, R'n'B, Rjwilmsi, Roshu Bangal, Seraphimblade, Sideshow Bob Roberts, Silence, Skamecrazy123, Sunrise, Thirdright, Timrollpickering, Tmol42, Trappist the monk, TrickyApron, TylzaeL, Ukt-zero, Urselius, Vanished User 0001, Vestbors, Viscious81, Vitovino, VoABot II, Weregerbil, Yintan, [illegible], 91 anonymous edits 159

Darwin from Orchids to Variation *Source:* https://en.wikipedia.org/w/index.php?oldid=784022954 *License:* Creative Commons Attribution-Share Alike 3.0 *Contributors:* Aa77zz, Barticus88, Bhadani, Bobo192, CLW, CV9933, Charles Matthews, Chris the speller, Dave souza, DuncanHill, Edward, Fastfission, Hiplibrarianship, Ixfd64, Johnuniq, Khazar2, Kross, Lilipatina, Lucyintheskywithdada, Macdonald-ross, Mattisse, Mitsukai, Mystique, Neelix, Neurolysis, NuclearWarfare, Ohconfucius, Pawyilee, Qero, RJHall, Randy Kryn, Rettetast, Rich Farmbrough, Richard001, Samsara, Silence, Squids and Chips, Stemonitis, Strobilomyces, The Vintage Feminist, Truth is relative, understanding is limited, Tuxedo junction, Vicjoe, Woohookitty, 11 anonymous edits 183

Darwin from Descent of Man to Emotions *Source:* https://en.wikipedia.org/w/index.php?oldid=851743269 *License:* Creative Commons Attribution-Share Alike 3.0 *Contributors:* Aa77zz, Brianyoumans, CLW, Charles Matthews, Colonies Chris, CommonsDelinker, Dave souza, Dewritech, Doodle77, DuncanHill, EdJohnston, Favonian, Hiplibrarianship, J heisenberg, Jack Frost, John of Reading, Johnuniq, Mets501, Ohconfucius, Phoenix-forgotten, RA0808, Richard001, Samsara, ShelfSkewed, Silence, SusanLesch, Tagishsimon, Truth is relative, understanding is limited, Underwaterbuffalo, Vanished User 0001, Vitovino, YUL89YYZ, 5 anonymous edits 196

Darwin from Insectivorous Plants to Worms *Source:* https://en.wikipedia.org/w/index.php?oldid=851743004 *License:* Creative Commons Attribution-Share Alike 3.0 *Contributors:* Aa77zz, Alai, Barticus88, Bender235, Blacklegendx, CLW, Charles Matthews, Citation bot 1, Dave souza,

Dawkeye, Denis Barthel, Everyking, Ground Zero, Hiplibrarianship, Johnuniq, Klemen Kocjancic, Lambiam, Lucyintheskywithdada, Lyttle-Wight, Macdonald-ross, Mgiganteus1, NeciFiX, Neelix, Nihiltres, Ohconfucius, OttomanReference, PKT, Pegua, Phoenix-forgotten, Ragesoss, Rich Farmbrough, Richard001, Rkitko, Samsara, Silence, Sun Creator, Tassedethe, The Vintage Feminist, TimBentley, Topstar, Trappist the monk, Truth is relative, understanding is limited, Tvtrojan20, 13 anonymous edits 209

Commemoration of Charles Darwin *Source:* https://en.wikipedia.org/w/index.php?oldid=820542852 *License:* Creative Commons Attribution-Share Alike 3.0 *Contributors:* Animalparty, BD2412, Bender235, Bjh21, Bradka, Casilva, Chris the speller, CreativeWorld2, Crusoe8181, DadaNeem, Daniel Mietchen, Dave souza, Dcirovic, Drbogdan, Droll, Fromthevaults, Indiasummer95, JustAGal, Myasuda, Ohconfucius, Pkhun, Rjwilmsi, Sadads, Sean.hoyland, Someone65, Tom.Reding, Δ, 2 anonymous edits 231

List of things named after Charles Darwin *Source:* https://en.wikipedia.org/w/index.php?oldid=842871305 *License:* Creative Commons Attribution-Share Alike 3.0 *Contributors:* AlistairMcMillan, Animalparty, Antipoeten, Antiqueight, Dave souza, Fastfission, Flyer22 Reborn, Grahamec, Jespinos, Johnuniq, Katieh5584, Loooke, Matchups, Myasuda, Neutrality, Pengemann, Qwerty Binary, Randy Kryn, Rjwilmsi, Tim!, 9 anonymous edits 237

List of taxa described by Charles Darwin *Source:* https://en.wikipedia.org/w/index.php?oldid=848322487 *License:* Creative Commons Attribution-Share Alike 3.0 *Contributors:* Chiswick Chap, Look2See1, Randy Kryn, 1 anonymous edits 239

Religious views of Charles Darwin *Source:* https://en.wikipedia.org/w/index.php?oldid=861480894 *License:* Creative Commons Attribution-Share Alike 3.0 *Contributors:* loddbins1, Aa77zz, Afterwriting, Andrewa, Andycjp, Ann-Kathrin Born, Another berean, Armchair info guy, Barticus88, Bender235, Bigmandad, Blankslatestudios, Bobblehead, CAPTAIN RAJU, CCFS, CLW, Can't sleep, clown will eat me, CatherineMunro, Celestialteapot, Charles Matthews, Chowbok, Chris the speller, Closedmouth, ClueBot NG, Colonies Chris, CommonsDelinker, ConfuciusOrnis, Cy Guy, DARTH SIDIOUS 2, DadaNeem, Dave souza, Davril2020, Deerdo, Dimadick, Doulos Christos, Download, Edward, Electricmaster, Eloquence, Ericdn, Fedayee, Federicoaolivieri, Feeeshboy, Finnusertop, Frosty, G0T0, Gdfusion, Gorthian, Gregbard, Ground Zero, Guettarda, Hackbac, Hateless, Hello71, Icairns, Ilkali, Instaurare, Iridescent, JHunterJ, Jack1956, Jamoche, JimWae, Johnuniq, Jonesey95, Joseph Solis in Australia, JuWiki2, Kylemanuel, LOL, La marts boys, Larkusix, Lewibops14, Lucyintheskywithdada, MBlaze Lightning, Macdonald-ross, Mais oui!, Makeemlighter, Materialscientist, Mcoupal, Munibert, NawlinWiki, Neelix, Niceguyedc, Nicolae Coman, O.Koslowski, Octavian history, Oddbodz, Ohconfucius, Patstuart, Perceval, Pharos, Pinethicket, Pmanderson, Popsicelz37, Procureur2014, PvOberstein, Quebec99, Racky, Red Director, Remember the dot, Rich Farmbrough, Richard001, Ritchy, Rocket000, Rreagan007, Satanael, Shawnc, Sjö, SmilesALot, Tassedethe, The Almighty Drill, The Last Arietta, Tiborh, Tmol42, Trappist the monk, Truth is relative, understanding is limited, Vanished User 0001, Vanished user, VoABot II, Vsmith, Wavelength, WickerGuy, Widr, Zazpot, 144 anonymous edits 243

Darwinism *Source:* https://en.wikipedia.org/w/index.php?oldid=864021821 *License:* Creative Commons Attribution-Share Alike 3.0 *Contributors:* -glove-, A little angry, Acroterion, Ailenus, Alan G. Archer, Alexnmartin2011, Alpha200123456o7ipo75i432ytrtr4iu5u4y33, Ameen kp, Anaxial, Animalparty, AntiCompositeNumber, Ap042905, BD2412, BRyAnJ.sIngletary, BolderBoulder, Bongwarrior, Bosley John Bosley, Bulton37, C.Fred, CLCStudent, Cahk, Cardpower, CataracticPlanets, Charles Siebrin Darwinv, Chiswick Chap, ClueBot NG, Colonel Wilhelm Klink, Crystallizedcarbon, D Eaketts, DVdm, Dave souza, Davenru, Dcirovic, DemocraticLuntz, Dl2000, DoABarrelRoll.dev, Don4of4, Donner60, Doug Weller, DrStrauss, Drewmutt, Ebyabe, Egsan Bacon, Eingtyuk, Entranced98, Excirial, Faptasm, Fares Castro02, Flyer22 Reborn, Fyddlestix, Gap9551, Gilliam, Gogo Dodo, Hayman30, Hubhubhubhubhubhub, I am One of Many, I dream of horses, Jandalhandler, Jess, Jim1138, Johnuniq, JuhaJGamer, Julietdeltalima, Jun12, KH-1, KNHaw, Kbseah, Kinetic37, Kobegetzbuckets, Lamigogta, Longhair, MBlaze Lightning, Malaras, Mann jess, MassiveYR, Materialscientist, Matt5334, Me, Myself and I are Here, Metiscus, Midnight-Blue766, Moms Spaghetti, Nathanlad355, NeilN, Neko-chan, Non-dropframe, Noyster, OSCAR08, Onel5969, Orphan Wiki, Oshwah, Peter-T, Petrb, Poconor, Pohranicniиstraze, Puffin, Qzd, Rjwilmsi, Samf4u, Samv123456789, ScrumpyGames, Seraphim System, Sergifonti95, Serols, Simplexity22, Skeptic from Britain, Smalljim, Sminthopsis84, Sowmiya9000, Stemonitis, Supercell121, TAnthony, Terrariola, Theinstantmatrix, This lousy T-shirt, Thomas.W, Tillerh11, ToBeFree, Tom.Reding, Vsmith, Widr, Wikih101, Wikipelli, Wikiprodude, Wikishovel, Xdtryhard, Yamaguchi先生, Yintan, Yobol, Yogipanda, Younusyazdani007, உலோர்.செந்தமிழ்க்கோதை, 204 anonymous edits 271

Eugenics *Source:* https://en.wikipedia.org/w/index.php?oldid=861508040 *License:* Creative Commons Attribution-Share Alike 3.0 *Contributors:* AManWithNoPlan, Akhenaten0, Alenux1, Alexb102072, Amusecilo, AnnonJung, AntiVan, AsiaNidyraThomas, Baileyj1299, Bbb23, BeenAroundAWhile, Bender235, Beyond My Ken, Bill de Bugbee, Bilsonius, BlankenburgerKeyer, BreakfastJr, CFCF, Carrite, Catlemur, Chchjesus, Chiswick Chap, Clockwise Djinn, Clr324, ClueBot NG, Conovaloff, Cynulliad, DanielRigal, Dave souza, DavidLeighEllis, Dcirovic, Ddcm8991, Derek R Bullamore, Dewerth, Dimadick, DisillusionedBitterAndKnackered, DocWatson42, Doug Weller, Dr.Koo, Ecalma, Edaen, Edaham, Editor2020, El C, Ennex Lives, EvergreenFir, Fgrieves, First past the post, Flyer22 Reborn, FourViolas, Frmorrison, GangofOne, Genetics4good, Gmlew77t, GreenMeansGo, Grj23, Grtewh, Headbomb, Ihardlythinkso, Iridescent, James Joseph P. Smith, Jim1138, Jonasisbae, Jytdog, KAP03, Kbog, Kbseah, Kcloughe, Keith D, Kilometers to Verona, Kinetic37, Kleuske, Kosarf, Krakkos, LarryBoy79, Lastratony, Lear419, Liberatus, LilyKitty, LizardJr8, Lynn4, Manofgun, Marcemmanuel29, Mark Ironie, Mark v1.0, Masblast, Mathesci, Maunus, Maxwell Verbeek, Mean as custard, Michillo, Mummbo Yumoto Soga, Motivação, MrX, Nemo bis, Nevlis, Niceguyedc, Nick Moyes, Nikolas Ojala, Nokkenbuer, On and off, One-state solution, Paine Ellsworth, PaleoNeonate, Patl, PerfectlyIrrational, Qzd, RA0808, Radioactive Pixie Dust, Raimundo Pastor, Randallsmith, RandomScholar30, Rathfelder, Reecgyb, RetroAuth, Rhododendrites, Rich Farmbrough, Richard Keatinge, RichardWeiss, Rjweather, Rjwilmsi, McCandlish, Sakura Cartelet, ScienceDawns, SgtDaws5, Sheila Ki Jawani, Shellwood, Simpsonguy1987, Smalljim, Sombe19, StartTerminal, SweetLight, SyntheticAnomaly, TAnthony, Tassedethe, TeeVeeed, That man from Nantucket, TheDragonFire, Theladyinviolet, Thevideodrome, TienShan0, Tony85poon, Torvalu4, Tyree999, Tyrone8371, UY Scuti, Unreal7, User000name, Voidxor, Volunteer Marek, Waters.Justin, WeijiBaikeBianji, Wikid77, Wikipedia nitin, Wildcat75, WinTakeAll, Wsiegmund, Wtmitchell, Yaris678, Yopienso, Zezen, 131 anonymous edits 279

Social Darwinism *Source:* https://en.wikipedia.org/w/index.php?oldid=862717888 *License:* Creative Commons Attribution-Share Alike 3.0 *Contributors:* 2000Researcher, 78.26, AKS.9955, Adam9389, Addisnog, AfroLiberal, Aikenware, Alan G. Archer, Alara46677, AlterBerg, Anonymous from the 21st century, Apophaticlogos, AvalerionV, Avoided, Atlas, BD2412, Bender235, Bobdog54, Brustopher, CanadianLinuxUser, Chiswick Chap, Chris troutman, Chris55, ClueBot NG, Cogijl, Crystallizedcarbon, Cush, Danlaycock, Dave souza, DavidBrooks, DavidLeighEllis, Demize, DferDaisy, Doug Weller, Download, Dr.Lao999, Espoo, Excirial, Eyesnore, Fgnievinski, Finnusertop, Flyer22 Reborn, Frosty, Gap9551, Gilliam, Gilo1969, Goose friend, Greedy Gungan, GregorB, H.dryad, Hctrmycss, Hello71, Helvetius, HiLo48, Hmains, Hohum, Huon, Ian.thomson, Its.brisa, JSpung, Jacobemelms, Jahelistbro, Jandalhandler, Jarble, JaydeXO, Jiten D, Jjazzabell, John Cline, Johnuniq, Jossin13, Jusdafax, K6ka, Karelian P., Kckranger, Kndimov, LeadSongDog, Lepricavark, Lndon, Lubiesque, Marcianus251, Mark Arsten, Materialscientist, Mcc1789, Me, Myself, and I are Here, MelbourneStar, Mnemosientje, Mr. Guye, MusikAnimal, Muuliapinaysksisarvinen, Mx. Granger, NIKVRANOS, Niceguyedc, Nihiltres, North Shoreman, NotJansIdea, Numeratrix, ORANSIGLOT, Oalhenaki, Omnipaedista, Onel5969, Oshawh, P. S. Burton, Pangguanzhe, Panghileri, Panoply1976, Patience62003, Paul Jonesy, Peaksnary, Peregrine981, Philip Trueman, Phoenix 123 abc, PlyrStar93, Polentarion, Reddogsix, Renamed user jC6jAXNBCg, Researchassist, RileyBugz, Rjwilmsi, Rodw, Scampo, Schmoobie, Seaphoto, Shellwood, SheriffIsInTown, Shoopdawoopymccheese, Skeptic from Britain, Skyb0x, Sminthopsis84, Spicemix, Srich32977, Sro23, Sturgeontransformer, Sunrise, Surv1v4l1st, TAnthony, Technicalpyro414, The Blade of the Northern Lights, The Wicked Twisted Road, ThePlatypusofDoom, TomS TDotO, Topbanana, Tschild, Tuchiel, Unbuttered Parsnip, User000name, User1961914, Volunteer1234, Wavelength, X-factor, Xdtryhard, Yopienso, YourLocalRamen, Zyxw, 185 anonymous edits 298

Charles Darwin bibliography *Source:* https://en.wikipedia.org/w/index.php?oldid=833989264 *License:* Creative Commons Attribution-Share Alike 3.0 *Contributors:* Aa77zz, ChrisGualtieri, ClueBot NG, DGG, Dave souza, Dave.Dunford, Gallowolf, GermanJoe, Good Olfactory, Grahamfitchett, JanSuchy, Johnsna2, Johnuniq, Jordi Roqué, Koavf, Orchi, Paul A, Pegship, Snalwibma, Stbalbach, The Man in Question, Tinymonty, Vicenarian, Xanchester, 14 anonymous edits 311

331

Image Sources, Licenses and Contributors

The sources listed for each image provide more detailed licensing information including the copyright status, the copyright owner, and the license conditions.

Figure 1 *Source:* https://en.wikipedia.org/w/index.php?title=File:JosiahWedgwood.jpeg *Contributors:* AndreasPraefcke, BotMultichill, Ecummenic, Hiart, Ja till euron∼commonswiki, Leyo, Materialscientist, Ranveig, Shakko, Sir Gawain, Un1c0s bot∼commonswiki 4
Figure 2 *Source:* https://en.wikipedia.org/w/index.php?title=File:Erasdarwin1.jpg *License:* Public Domain *Contributors:* Bukk, Conscious, Daderot, Madmedea, 竹麦魚 (Searobin) 5
Figure 3 *Source:* https://en.wikipedia.org/w/index.php?title=File:Samuel_Galton.jpg *License:* Public Domain *Contributors:* GeorgHH, Grook Da Oger, Man vyi, Mdd, OgreBot 2, 2 anonymous edits 6
Figure 4 *Source:* https://en.wikipedia.org/w/index.php?title=File:Robert_Darwin.jpg *License:* Public Domain *Contributors:* James Pardon 7
Figure 5 *Source:* https://en.wikipedia.org/w/index.php?title=File:Josiah_Wedgwood_II.jpg *License:* Public Domain *Contributors:* GeorgHH, Grook Da Oger, Man vyi, OgreBot 2, WayneRay, 2 anonymous edits 8
Figure 6 *Source:* https://en.wikipedia.org/w/index.php?title=File:Samuel_Tertius_Galton.jpg *License:* Public Domain *Contributors:* GeorgHH, Grook Da Oger, Man vyi, OgreBot 2, WayneRay, 2 anonymous edits 9
Figure 7 *Source:* https://en.wikipedia.org/w/index.php?title=File:Francis_S_Darwin.jpg *License:* Public Domain *Contributors:* Haynes 10
Figure 8 *Source:* https://en.wikipedia.org/w/index.php?title=File:Charles_Darwin_by_G._Richmond.jpg *License:* Public Domain *Contributors:* ArséniureDeGallium, Blurpeace, Infrogmation, Jdx, Judithcomm, Kilom691, Lecen, Marco Cristo∼commonswiki, NeverDoING, Shakko, Tohma, 4 anonymous edits 11
Figure 9 *Source:* https://en.wikipedia.org/w/index.php?title=File:Emma_Darwin.jpg *License:* Public Domain *Contributors:* BotMultichill, D-Kuru, Duncharris∼commonswiki, Fastfission∼commonswiki, OgreBot 2, Richard001, 2 anonymous edits 12
Figure 10 *Source:* https://en.wikipedia.org/w/index.php?title=File:William_Darwin_Fox.jpg *License:* Public Domain *Contributors:* Blackcat, GeorgHH, Grook Da Oger, Infrogmation, Kaganer, Man vyi, Materialscientist, Nikkimaria, SunOfErat, Victuallers 13
Image *Source:* https://en.wikipedia.org/w/index.php?title=File:Darwin_Arms.svg *License:* Creative Commons Attribution-Sharealike 3.0 *Contributors:* A1 Aardvark 22
Figure 11 *Source:* https://en.wikipedia.org/w/index.php?title=File:Darwin_cutout.png *License:* GNU Free Documentation License *Contributors:* GifJournal 26
Figure 12 *Source:* https://en.wikipedia.org/w/index.php?title=File:Charles_Darwin_1816.jpg *Contributors:* ALE!, Anne97432, ArséniureDeGallium, Boo-Boo Baroo, Craigboy, Dave souza, Ecummenic, Finavon, Hystrix, Jonnie Nord, Laura1822, Leyo, LongLiveRock, Matt314, Mogelzahn, Mr.Rosewater, Richard001, Rotational∼commonswiki, Wst, 5 anonymous edits 27
Figure 13 *Source:* https://en.wikipedia.org/w/index.php?title=File:Edinburgh_University_1827.jpg *License:* Public Domain *Contributors:* Dave souza, Jonathan Oldenbuck, Tatata 29
Figure 14 *Source:* https://en.wikipedia.org/w/index.php?title=File:Charles_Darwin_plaque,_Lothian_Street,_Edinburgh.JPG *License:* Creative Commons Attribution-Sharealike 3.0 *Contributors:* User:Kim Traynor 29
Figure 15 *Source:* https://en.wikipedia.org/w/index.php?title=File:Christs_shield.png *License:* GNU Free Documentation License *Contributors:* Lupin 33
Figure 16 *Source:* https://en.wikipedia.org/w/index.php?title=File:Young-Charles-Darwin-statue-by-Anthony-Smith-(Christ's-College-Cambridge)-3.jpg *Contributors:* User:Fortheloveofknowledge 39
Figure 17 *Source:* https://en.wikipedia.org/w/index.php?title=File:HMS_Beagle_by_Conrad_Martens.jpg *License:* Public Domain *Contributors:* Conrad Martens (1801 - 21 August 1878) 46
Figure 18 *Source:* https://en.wikipedia.org/w/index.php?title=File:British_Museum_Marine_Chronometer.jpg *License:* Creative Commons Zero *Contributors:* User:BabelStone 47
Figure 19 *Source:* https://en.wikipedia.org/w/index.php?title=File:Voyage_of_the_Beagle-en.svg *License:* Creative Commons Attribution-Share Alike *Contributors:* Sémhur 53
Figure 20 *Source:* https://en.wikipedia.org *License:* Public Domain *Contributors:* JVollenhoven, Soerfm 57
Figure 21 *Source:* https://en.wikipedia.org/w/index.php?title=File:Fuegian_BeagleVoyage.jpg *License:* Public Domain *Contributors:* Dave souza, Fastfission∼commonswiki, Goustien, Kaidor, Kürschner, Lotje, Shadygrove2007, Soerfm, Themightyquill, Uyvsdi, Wolfmann, Wst 59
Figure 22 *Source:* https://en.wikipedia.org/w/index.php?title=File:Image-Rhea_Darwinii1.jpg *Contributors:* John Gould 61
Figure 23 *Source:* https://en.wikipedia.org/w/index.php?title=File:Cerro_La_Campana.jpg *License:* Creative Commons Attribution-Share Alike *Contributors:* Carlos yo 63
Figure 24 *Source:* https://en.wikipedia.org/w/index.php?title=File:Remains_of_the_Cathedral_of_Conception_-_1835.png *License:* Public Domain *Contributors:* Drawing: Robert Clements Wickham (1798–1864); Engraving: S. Bull fl. 1838 - 1846 64
Figure 25 *Source:* https://en.wikipedia.org/w/index.php?title=File:Galapagos_mockingbird_-_Santa_Cruz_-_Charles_Darwin_Research_Centre.jpg *License:* Creative Commons Attribution-Sharealike 2.0 *Contributors:* putneymark 66
Figure 26 *Source:* https://en.wikipedia.org/w/index.php?title=File:HMSBeagle.jpg *License:* Public Domain *Contributors:* Bukk, Chase me ladies, I'm the Cavalry, Dave souza, Interpretix, Kresspahl, Makthorpe, Poppy, Un1c0s bot∼commonswiki, 1 anonymous edits 72
Figure 27 *Source:* https://en.wikipedia.org/w/index.php?title=File:Scelidotherium_leptocephalum_side.jpg *License:* Public Domain *Contributors:* LadyofHats 74
Figure 28 *Source:* https://en.wikipedia.org/w/index.php?title=File:Darwin_Tree_1837.png *Contributors:* Scewing 90
Figure 29 *Source:* https://en.wikipedia.org/w/index.php?title=File:Charles_Darwin.jpg *License:* Public Domain *Contributors:* Maull&Polyblank 106
Figure 30 *Source:* https://en.wikipedia.org/w/index.php?title=File:Darwins_first_tree.jpg *License:* Public Domain *Contributors:* Charles Darwin 124
Figure 31 *Source:* https://en.wikipedia.org/w/index.php?title=File:Gower_Street_London.jpg *License:* Public Domain *Contributors:* User:Mahlum 127
Figure 32 *Source:* https://en.wikipedia.org/w/index.php?title=File:Approaching_Down_House_-_geograph.org.uk_-_1196017.jpg *License:* Creative Commons Attribution-Share Alike 2.0 Generic *Contributors:* Trevor Harris 127
Figure 33 *Source:* https://en.wikipedia.org/w/index.php?title=File:Darwins_Thinking_Path.JPG *License:* Public domain *Contributors:* Cayambe, File Upload Bot (Magnus Manske), OgreBot 2, Richard001, Spellcast 131
Figure 34 *Source:* https://en.wikipedia.org/w/index.php?title=File:Darwin's_barnacles.jpg *License:* Creative Commons Attribution-Sharealike 3.0 *Contributors:* FunkMonk (Michael B. H.) 132
Figure 35 *Source:* https://en.wikipedia.org/w/index.php?title=File:Charles_Darwin_aged_51.jpg *License:* Public Domain *Contributors:* DL5MDA, Deadstar, Diwas, Ecummenic, FSII, Fastfission∼commonswiki, GreenMeansGo, Infrogmation, Jack1956, Jdx, Kurpfalzbilder.de, Ragesoss, Ryz, Sand-piper, Shakko, Stephenlarson, Un1c0s bot∼commonswiki, Wolfmann, 12 anonymous edits 142
Figure 36 *Source:* https://en.wikipedia.org/w/index.php?title=File:Origin_of_Species_title_page.jpg *License:* Public Domain *Contributors:* AEMoreira042281, Aleator, Alex6122, Aristeas, Fastfission∼commonswiki, Gveret Tered, Inductiveload, Jappalang, Jayarathina, Juiced lemon, Mogelzahn, Ragesoss, Taterian, Vanished user fijtji34toksdckqrjn54yoimascj, Wikiklaas, 10 anonymous edits 154
Figure 37 *Source:* https://en.wikipedia.org/w/index.php?title=File:Charles_Darwin_aged_51.jpg *License:* Public Domain *Contributors:* DL5MDA, Deadstar, Diwas, Ecummenic, FSII, Fastfission∼commonswiki, GreenMeansGo, Infrogmation, Jack1956, Jdx, Kurpfalzbilder.de, Ragesoss, Ryz, Sand-piper, Shakko, Stephenlarson, Un1c0s bot∼commonswiki, Wolfmann, 12 anonymous edits 161
Figure 38 *Source:* https://en.wikipedia.org/w/index.php?title=File:TH_Huxley_41.5_KB.jpg *License:* Public Domain *Contributors:* BotMultichill, Deadstar, Macdonald-Ross, Rcbutcher, Ruthven, Thomas Gun, WFinch, Wolfgang giock 168
Figure 39 *Source:* https://en.wikipedia.org/w/index.php?title=File:T.H.Huxley(Woodburytype).jpg *License:* Public Domain *Contributors:* print by Lock & Whitfield 169
Figure 40 *Source:* https://en.wikipedia.org/w/index.php?title=File:Oxf-uni-mus-nh.jpg *License:* GNU Free Documentation License *Contributors:* DrJunge, Ilm06, Kane5187, Kurpfalzbilder.de, MGA73bot2, Man vyi, OgreBot 2, Siebrand, 1 anonymous edits 173
Figure 41 *Source:* https://en.wikipedia.org/w/index.php?title=File:WilberforceVanityFair.jpg *License:* Public Domain *Contributors:* Lokal Profil, Rcbutcher 174
Figure 42 *Source:* https://en.wikipedia.org/w/index.php?title=File:Ch_Darwin-Emile_Littré_by_André_Gill.jpg *License:* Public Domain *Contributors:* Charvex, Infrogmation, Philip J.1987qazwsx, Pmx, 1 anonymous edits 178
Figure 43 *Source:* https://en.wikipedia.org/w/index.php?title=File:Charles_Darwin_photograph_by_Julia_Margaret_Cameron,_1968.jpg *License:* Public Domain *Contributors:* Kaidor, Ragesoss 192

332

Figure 44 *Source*: https://en.wikipedia.org/w/index.php?title=File:Charles_Darwin_by_Julia_Margaret_Cameron_2.jpg *License*: Public Domain *Contributors*: User:Davepape 198
Figure 45 *Source*: https://en.wikipedia.org/w/index.php?title=File:FrancesPowerCobb.jpg *License*: Public Domain *Contributors*: Believed to be Elliott & Fry 201
Figure 46 *Source*: https://en.wikipedia.org/w/index.php?title=File:Editorial_cartoon_depicting_Charles_Darwin_as_an_ape_(1871).jpg *License*: Public Domain *Contributors*: Aschroet, Avatar, Daniel 1992, DragonflySixtyseven, Fma12, Infrogmation, Jappaleng, Juiced lemon, Kaldari, Lobo, Ranveig, Richard001, Spellcast, Stw, Tony Wills, Wolfmann, Wutsje, 4 anonymous edits 203
Figure 47 *Source*: https://en.wikipedia.org/w/index.php?title=File:Insectivorous_Plants_Figure_1.png *License*: Public Domain *Contributors*: Made by Charles Darwin's son George Darwin, "reproduced on wood by Mr Cooper" 214
Figure 48 *Source*: https://en.wikipedia.org/w/index.php?title=File:Darwin_restored2.jpg *License*: Public Domain *Contributors*: Bain News Service, publisher 222
Figure 49 *Source*: https://en.wikipedia.org/w/index.php?title=File:Charles_Robert_Darwin_by_John_Collier.jpg *License*: Public Domain *Contributors*: User:Dcoetzee 232
Figure 50 *Source*: https://en.wikipedia.org/w/index.php?title=File:Habitus_of_the_holotype_of_Darwinilus_sedarisi_Chatzimanolis_-_ZooKeys-379-029-g001.jpg *Contributors*: Auntof6, Daniel Mietchen, Erfil, Johnbod, Livermore 233
Figure 51 *Source*: https://en.wikipedia.org/w/index.php?title=File:Charles_Darwin_statue_5661r.jpg *License*: Creative Commons Attribution-Sharealike 3.0 *Contributors*: Patche99z 234
Figure 52 *Source*: https://en.wikipedia.org/w/index.php?title=File:Quantum_Leap_-_the_sculpture_-_geograph.org.uk_-_1708891.jpg *License*: Creative Commons Attribution-Share Alike 2.0 Generic *Contributors*: Richard Law 236
Image *Source*: https://en.wikipedia.org/w/index.php?title=File:Commons-logo.svg *License*: logo *Contributors*: Anomie, Callanecc, CambridgeBayWeather, Jo-Jo Eumerus, RHaworth 237
Figure 53 *Source*: https://en.wikipedia.org/w/index.php?title=File:Darwin's_barnacles_Proteolepas_and_Balanus.jpg *License*: Public Domain *Contributors*: Chiswick Chap, Ruff tuff cream puff 240
Figure 54 *Source*: https://en.wikipedia.org/w/index.php?title=File:Balanus_improvisus_on_Mya_arenaria_shell.jpg *License*: Creative Commons Attribution-Sharealike 3.0 *Contributors*: User:Butko 240
Figure 55 *Source*: https://en.wikipedia.org/w/index.php?title=File:Charles_Darwin_01.jpg *License*: Public Domain *Contributors*: J. Cameron 244
Figure 56 *Source*: https://en.wikipedia.org/w/index.php?title=File:Shrewsbury_Unitarian_Church.jpg *Contributors*: User:The Almightey Drill 245
Figure 57 *Source*: https://en.wikipedia.org/w/index.php?title=File:Charles_Darwin_1880.jpg *License*: Public Domain *Contributors*: Afansavich, Claus Obana, D-Kuru, Dave souza, Foroa, Helix84, Herbythyme, Jochen Burghardt, Man vyi, Owen, RoyBoy, Santosga, Scewing, Taric25, 5 anonymous edits 259
Figure 58 *Source*: https://en.wikipedia.org/w/index.php?title=File:Charles_Darwin_by_Julia_Margaret_Cameron_2.jpg *License*: Public Domain *Contributors*: User:Davepape 272
Figure 59 *Source*: https://en.wikipedia.org/w/index.php?title=File:Editorial_cartoon_depicting_Charles_Darwin_as_an_ape_(1871).jpg *License*: Public Domain *Contributors*: Aschroet, Avatar, Daniel 1992, DragonflySixtyseven, Fma12, Infrogmation, Jappaleng, Juiced lemon, Kaldari, Lobo, Ranveig, Richard001, Spellcast, Stw, Tony Wills, Wolfmann, Wutsje, 4 anonymous edits 273
Image *Source*: https://en.wikipedia.org/w/index.php?title=File:Wiktionary-logo-en-v2.svg *Contributors*: User:Dan Polansky, User:Smurrayinchester 278
Figure 60 *Source*: https://en.wikipedia.org/w/index.php?title=File:Eugenics_congress_logo.png *License*: Public Domain *Contributors*: Allforrous, Beao, Fastfission~commonswiki, Kintetsubuffalo, Mattes, Nilfanion, Pmsyyz, 1 anonymous edits 280
Image *Source*: https://en.wikipedia.org/w/index.php?title=File:Outline-body-aura.svg *License*: Creative Commons Zero *Contributors*: Artoria2e5, Cathy Richards, 1 anonymous edits 281
Figure 61 *Source*: https://en.wikipedia.org/w/index.php?title=File:Francis_Galton_1850s.jpg *License*: Public Domain *Contributors*: not stated 282
Figure 62 *Source*: https://en.wikipedia.org/w/index.php?title=File:Gilbert_Keith_Chesterton01.jpg *License*: Public Domain *Contributors*: Coburn, Alvin Langdon, (1882 - 1966), photographer 283
Figure 63 *Source*: https://en.wikipedia.org/w/index.php?title=File:Alkoven_Schloss_Hartheim_2005-08-18_3589.jpg *License*: Creative Commons Attribution-Sharealike 2.5 *Contributors*: Dralon 285
Figure 64 *Source*: https://en.wikipedia.org/w/index.php?title=File:Bundesarchiv_Bild_146-1973-010-11,_Schwester_in_einem_Lebensbornheim.jpg *License*: Creative Commons Attribution-Sharealike 3.0 Germany *Contributors*: BotMultichill, KaterBegemot, SpiderMum, Wolfmann, 2 anonymous edits 285
Figure 65 *Source*: https://en.wikipedia.org/w/index.php?title=File:Karl_Pearson,_1912.jpg *License*: Public Domain *Contributors*: Materialscientist, Struthious Bandersnatch, 1 anonymous edits 288
Figure 66 *Source*: https://en.wikipedia.org/w/index.php?title=File:Eugenics_Quarterly_to_Social_Biology.jpg *License*: Public Domain *Contributors*: User:Fastfission~commonswiki 293
Image *Source*: https://en.wikipedia.org/w/index.php?title=File:Wikiquote-logo.svg *License*: Public Domain *Contributors*: Rei-artur 298
Figure 67 *Source*: https://en.wikipedia.org/w/index.php?title=File:Herbert_Spencer.jpg *License*: Public Domain *Contributors*: Animalparty, Chico, FSII, Jarekt, Piotrus, Speck-Made, Sven-steffen arndt, Thierry Caro, Zolo, 1 anonymous edits 301
Figure 68 *Source*: https://en.wikipedia.org/w/index.php?title=File:Thomas_Robert_Malthus_Wellcome_L0069037_-crop.jpg *Contributors*: Daderot, Scewing 302
Figure 69 *Source*: https://en.wikipedia.org/w/index.php?title=File:Francis_Galton_1850s.jpg *License*: Public Domain *Contributors*: not stated 303

License

Creative Commons Attribution-Share Alike 3.0
//creativecommons.org/licenses/by-sa/3.0/

Index

Abbeville, 185
Abinger, 219
Abiogenesis, 271
Abrolhos Archipelago, 46, 56
Abstinence-only sex education, 289
Abstract art, 235
Abstract (summary), 141, 196
Acasta cyathus, 239
Acasta fenestrata, 239
Acasta purpurata, 241
Accessdate missing url, 76, 265
Acton Smee Ayrton, 207
Adam Cornford, 19
Adam Sedgwick, 35, 40, 50, 54, 82, 83, 130, 164, 166, 202, 247, 249, 311
Adaptation, 40, 91, 243, 248
A Devils Chaplain, 36, 276
Ad hoc, 87, 276
A Dictionary of English Etymology, 8
Admiralty, 46, 48, 53, 55, 68, 130
Adolf Hitler, 284
Adrian Desmond, 43, 76, 102, 119, 139, 156, 179, 195, 207, 230, 309
Advowson, 256
Age of Enlightenment, 25, 305
Age of the Earth, 249
Aging, 293
Agnosticism, 113
Agoraphobia, 110
A Greek–English Lexicon, 325
Aktion T4, 286
Alan Barlow, 14, 16
Albert Einstein, 118
Alberto Fujimori, 286
Albert, Prince Consort, 167
Albin Roussin, 46, 56
Albury, Surrey, 205
Alcide dOrbigny, 86
Alcohol (drug), 111
Alexander Adie, 48
Alexander Monro (tertius), 30
Alexander Tille, 308
Alexander von Humboldt, 39, 40, 248
Alfred Newton, 152

Alfred Russel Wallace, 12, 138, 141, 144, 150, 161, 184, 210, 229, 237, 254, 275, 278
Alfred Tennyson, 147
Allele frequency, 288
Allopatric speciation, 90
Alphonse Pyrame de Candolle, 125
Alternative medicine, 279
Alternatives to Darwinism, 271
Altruism, 276
Alvin Langdon Coburn, 283
Amalek, 173
American Civil War, 189
American Museum of Natural History, 235
American Public Media, 266
Amish, 293
Amphibalanus amphitrite, 239
Amphibalanus cirratus, 241
Amyl nitrite, 227
Anaesthetic, 30
Ancestry, 184
Ancient Greece, 279
Ancient Greek, 279
Ancient Rome, 281
Andes, 63, 105, 114, 231
Andrew Carnegie, 306
Andrew Dalmahoy Barlow, 16
Andrew Huxley, 21
Andrew Ramsay (geologist), 163
Andrew Smith (zoologist), 69
Anelasma squalicola, 239
An Essay Concerning Human Understanding, 38
An Essay on the Principle of Population, 97, 317
Aneurysm, 114
Anger, 112
Angina pectoris, 226, 228
Anglican, 38, 82, 83, 100, 113, 130, 167, 171, 190, 211, 243, 245, 254, 256
Anglicanism, 26, 87, 245
Animal husbandry, 125, 138
Animal shell, 27
Anne Darwin, 11, 108, 217, 253
Annie Besant, 218

Anteater, 73, 85
Antediluvian, 65
Anthem, 229
Anthony Smith (sculptor), 39, 236
Anthropological Society of London, 189
Anthropology, 251
Anti-Jacobin, 174
Antispasmodic, 227
Antlion, 67, 249
Anxiety, 107
A. P. de Candolle, 97, 125
Ape, 203, 273
Appeal to nature, 300
Appearances in the nineteenth century, 39
Arabella Buckley, 223
Archaeopteryx, 188
Archbishop of Canterbury, 174, 259
Archetype, 87
Argentina, 59, 105, 114
Armadillo, 57, 60, 85, 91
Armatobalanus allium, 241
Arsenic, 116
Arsenicosis: chronic arsenic poisoning from drinking water, 116
Arthur Wellesley, 1st Duke of Wellington, 83
Artificial insemination, 290
Artificial selection, 167, 183
Aryan, 283
Aryan race, 285
Asa Gray, 148, 149, 151, 155, 165, 175, 184, 188, 189, 199, 210, 214, 219, 254, 261, 276
Ascension Island, 71
Ascension Parish Burial Ground, Cambridge, 14, 15
Asexual reproduction, 89
Ashkenazi Jew, 291
Aspergers syndrome, 110
Assisted reproductive technology, 280
Asteroid, 239
Atheism, 32, 244, 275
Atheists, 83
Athenaeum (British magazine), 69, 162, 176, 180, 268
Athenaeum Club, London, 95
Atlantic, 71
Atlantic Monthly, 175
Atlantic Ocean, 45
Atlantis, 138
Atoll, 47, 67, 68, 85, 123, 125, 126
Auguste Comte, 97, 302
Augustin de Candolle, 33
Augustinians, 272
Augustus Earle, 48, 52, 57, 67
August Weismann, 271, 287
Australia, 45, 47, 67, 72

Autobiography of Charles Darwin, 313
Autobiography on gradually increasing disbelief, 264
Autonomic nervous system, 114
Azores, 71

Baboon, 150
Baby bonus, 290
Bachelor of Arts, 33, 50
Bachelor of Medicine, 34
Baden Powell (mathematician), 137, 171
Bahia, 71
Bahia Blanca, 57
Bahía Blanca, 57, 60
Bahia, Brazil, 56
Bahia coastal forests, 56
Balanus, 239
Balanus decorus, 239
Balanus glandula, 239
Balanus improvisus, 239, 240
Balanus nubilus, 239
Balanus poecilus, 241
Balanus trigonus, 239
Balanus venustus, 239
Balanus vestitus, 239
Bank of England, 234
Bank of England notes, 234
Baobab, 55
Baptism, 26, 245
Baptists, 211, 257
Barmouth, 35, 41, 42
Barmouth valley, 200
Barnacle, 123, 132, 143, 239
Barometer, 48
Barrister, 8
Barry Marshall, 117
Bartholomew Sulivan, 48, 107, 202
Bas Pease, 21
Battle of Jutland, 17
Battle of Sedan, 202
BBC, 234
BBC Darwin Season, 235
BBC News, 322
Beagle Channel, 231
Bedford, Bedfordshire, 185
Beetle, 34, 52
Belfast, 33, 220
Belgium, 283
Benefice, 199
Benjamin Bynoe, 55, 56
Benjamin Jowett, 160
Benjamin Kidd, 301, 328
Ben Stein, 276
Bernard Darwin, 14, 15
Bilious fever, 108
Bill McKibben, 293

Bills and resolutions, 235
Bioethics, 294
Biogeography, 70
Biographical novel, 236
Biology, 243, 271
Biopolitics, 292
Birdwatching, 28
Birmingham, 135
Birth control, 284
Bishop of Oxford, 159, 167, 174
Bismuth, 109
Bittern, 37
Bivalve shell, 264
Blackjack, 37
Blasphemy, 87, 247
Blister, 107
Bloating, 107
BMJ, 116
Boarding school, 245
Body-snatching, 30
Bolas, 57
Bombardier beetle, 315
Book of Proverbs, 229
Booth baronets, 6
Borneo, 141, 144, 189
Botafogo, 56
Botanist, 4
Botany, 36, 37, 165, 199
Boxing Day, 164
Brachinus crepitans, 315
Brain, 114
Brazil, 56, 71, 197, 283
Brazilian tuco-tuco, 73
Brine, 138
British Association, 190
British Association for the Advancement of Science, 107, 133, 138, 159, 172, 198
British Empire, 301
British Geological Survey, 63
British House of Commons, 216, 222, 228, 261
British Journal for the History of Science, 265
British Museum, 49, 51, 55, 83, 89, 188, 207
British undergraduate degree classification, 34
British Whig Party, 38, 51, 83, 84, 87, 97, 218, 245
Brixham, 185
Brooklyn, 205
Bryozoa, 31
Buddhism, 264
Buenos Aires, 57, 58, 60, 105
Buenos Aires Province, 57
Builders Old Measurement, 48
Burke and Hare, 30
Burlington House, 148

Cabin boy, 56

Caerdon, 200
Caerostris darwini, 233
Callus, 117
Calvinism, 252
Cambridge, 36, 55, 71, 83, 147, 202, 223
Cambridge Apostles, 229
Cambridge Philosophical Society, 52, 72, 311
Cambridgeshire, 34
Cambridge University, 20
Cambridge University Press, 267, 309
Camel, 74, 85
Camilla Wedgwood, 8, 19
Canada, 279
Canary Islands, 40, 54
Canavans disease, 291
Cannes, 202
Canute the Great, 167
Capel Curig, 42
Cape of Good Hope, 68
Cape San Antonio, Argentina, 57
Cape Town, 68, 99, 250
Cape Verde, 54
Capybara, 73, 84
Carcarañá River, 60, 73
Cardiomegaly, 114
Caribbean, 138
Caricature, 273
Carnivorous plant, 213
Carnivorous plants, 209
Carola Darwin, 19
Carrier testing, 290
Caste, 292
Casti connubii, 284
Castration, 281
Catasetum, 187
Catastrophism, 25, 64, 69, 221, 249, 250
Category:Alternative medicine, 279
Caterpillar, 243, 252
Catherine Darwin, 95
Catholic Church, 284
Celestial navigation, 46
Central dogma of molecular biology, 271
Centrostomum incisum, 241
Cerro La Campana, 63
Chagas disease, 63, 106, 110, 114, 117
Chancellor of the Exchequer, 89
Chapter ignored, 75
Chapter IV, 328
Charles Babbage, 75, 86, 87, 99
Charles Bell, 31, 94, 206
Charles Bradlaugh, 218, 222, 261
Charles Colyear, 2nd Earl of Portmore, 5, 9
Charles Darwin, 3, 6–8, 11, 12, 16, 25, 43, 45, 50, 75, 76, 81, 101, 105, 119, 123, 124, 141, 156, 159, 183, 196, 207, 209, 210,

231, 237, 240, 243, 244, 271, 272, 281, 287, 298, 300, 308, 311
Charles Darwin (1758–1778), 4, 25
Charles Darwin bibliography, **311**
Charles Darwin Foundation, 234, 237
Charles Darwin National Park, 234, 237
Charles Darwin Research Station, 234, 237
Charles Darwins education, **25**, 82, 113
Charles Darwins health, 63
Charles Darwins illness, 82, 183, 209
Charles Darwins views on religion, 26, 209, 217, 226
Charles Darwin University, 234, 237
Charles Daubeny, 54
Charles Dickens, 95, 234
Charles Edward Mudie, 155
Charles Eliot Norton, 199
Charles Galton Darwin, 14, 15
Charles Hodge, 277
Charles H. Smith (historian of science), 268
Charles James Fox Bunbury, 131
Charles Kingsley, 155, 161, 195, 254, 261
Charles Knowlton, 218
Charles Lyell, 41, 45, 52, 54, 58, 61, 70, 72, 82, 84, 87, 99, 125, 141, 142, 144, 149, 160, 183, 184, 210, 249, 253
Charles Murray (author and diplomat), 145
Charles Robert Darwin, 4, 7
Charles Waring Darwin (infant), 146, 151
Charter of Fundamental Rights of the European Union, 286
Chartism, 126
Chauncey Wright, 205
Chemistry, 28
Cherokee class brig-sloop, 48
Chile, 66, 85
Chilean mockingbird, 66
Chiloé Archipelago, 62
Chiloé Island, 62
Chimpanzee, 235
China, 286
Chloroform, 175
Cholera, 54, 292
Chris Darwin, 20
Christian Konrad Sprengel, 186
Christopher Cornford, 17
Christs College, Cambridge, 11, 33, 34, 82, 235, 246
Chronic fatigue syndrome, 110
Chthamalus fragilis, 239
Church of England, 25, 26, 34, 113, 142, 159, 160, 184, 190, 235, 243, 245, 256
Cicely Veronica Wedgwood, 8, 19
Cidade Velha, 55
Cilia, 31
CITEREFBlack2003, 325, 326

CITEREFBlom2008, 325–327
CITEREFBowler1996, 317
CITEREFBrowne1995, 317
CITEREFBurchfield1974, 320
CITEREFDarwin1860, 320
CITEREFDarwin1871, 323
CITEREFDarwin1887, 323
CITEREFDarwin1958, 323
CITEREFDarwinCosta2009, 320
CITEREFDesmondMoore1991, 317, 319, 320, 322, 323
CITEREFFreeman1977a, 320
CITEREFFreeman2007, 319, 323
CITEREFHerbert1980, 317
CITEREFHerbert2005, 320
CITEREFMooreDesmond2004, 320
CITEREFMorrell2001, 320, 321
CITEREFvan Wyhe2013, 315, 319, 320
Civilization, 316
Clairvoyance, 107
Clement Wedgwood, 17
Cockney, 212
Cocos (Keeling) Islands, 68
Coevolution, 221
Colic, 107
Collectivist, 299
Colorhamphus parvirostris, 239
Colwyn, 42
Commemoration of Charles Darwin, **231**
Common ancestor, 91
Common descent, 32, 82, 88
Commons:Category:Eugenics, 298
Commons:Category:Things named after Charles Darwin, 237
Competition (biology), 274
Compulsory sterilisation in Sweden, 283
Compulsory sterilization, 283, 284, 290, 292
Compulsory sterilization in Canada, 283
Concepción, Chile, 64, 92
Conglomerate (geology), 57
Conrad Martens, 46, 60, 63
Continent, 72
Convention on the Prevention and Punishment of the Crime of Genocide, 286, 326
Coping (psychology), 111
Copley Medal, 183, 190
Copyright, 165, 311
Coral, 68, 123, 125
Coral reef, 68
Cordillera Darwin, 238
Corn Laws, 132
Coronula barbara, 241
Coronula reginae, 239
Correspondence of Charles Darwin, 159, 313
Corroboree, 68
Cosmological argument, 244

Council of Agde, 281
County Down, 128
Cousin marriage, 22
Cramps, 107
Crash diet, 191
Cream, 116
Creation (2009 film), 236
Creation-evolution controversy, 243
Creationism, 271, 275, 300
Credo quia absurdum, 246
Creed, 246
Cretaceous, 163
Crimean war, 138
Crohns disease, 110
Crustacean, 132
Crying, 107
Crystallography, 28
Curator, 115
Cuttlefish, 30
Cuvieronius, 74
Cyclic vomiting syndrome, 110, 116, 117
Cystic fibrosis, 291, 292
Cytoplasmic transfer, 280

Daguerreotype, 224
Daily Telegraph, 315
Daniel Kevles, 295
D. Appleton & Company, 165
Darwin Awards, 235, 238
Darwin College, Cambridge, 22, 234, 237
Darwin Day, 231, 235
Darwinella, 238
Darwin (ESA), 238
Darwin, Falkland Islands, 237
Darwin — Wedgwood family, 25, 136, 196, 202, 205, 206, 210, 213, 214, 216, 222
Darwin–Wedgwood family, **3**, 113, 245
Darwin from Descent of Man to Emotions, 184, 195, **196**, 209
Darwin from Insectivorous plants to Worms, 196, 207, **209**
Darwin from Orchids to Variation, **183**, 196
Darwin Glacier (California), 238
Darwinhydrus, 238
Darwinian Fairytales, 276, 277
Darwini (disambiguation), 233, 238
Darwinii (disambiguation), 233, 238
Darwinilus, 233, 238
Darwin Industry, 231
Darwiniothamnus, 233
Darwin Island, 238
Darwin Island (Antarctica), 238
Darwinism, 159, 168, 177, 183, 203, 238, **271**, 275, 278, 300
Darwinism (book), 275
Darwinismus, 262

Darwinius, 232, 233, 238
Darwinivelia, 238
Darwin (lunar crater), 239
Darwin (Martian crater), 239
Darwin Medal, 238
Darwin, Northern Territory, 231, 237
Darwinomya, 238
Darwin Online, 268
Darwin (operating system), 238
Darwinopterus, 233, 238
Darwinsaurus, 238
Darwins development of theory of evolution, 90
Darwins finches, 66, 85, 232, 238
Darwins fox, 90
Darwins frog, 232, 238
Darwin Sound, 231, 238
Darwin Sound (Canada), 231, 238
Darwins rhea, 60, 61, 88, 232
Darwinula, 233, 238
Darwinulidae, 233
Darwinulocopina, 233
Darwinuloidea, 233
Darwin (unit), 238
Darwin-Wallace Medal, 234
Darwinysius, 238
David Hume, 25, 40, 248
David Lack, 232
David Livingstone, 164
David Quammen, 266
David Stove, 276, 277
David Suzuki, 237
Dayak people, 144, 151
Debate with Wilberforce, 321
Defendants, 280
Deism, 35, 254
Deist, 269
Delamere, Cheshire, 13, 143
Demandasaurus, 233
Denis Lamoureux, 268
Depression (mood), 107
Desert Campaign (1833–34), 59
Development of Darwins theory, 82, 100, **123**
Devil, 247
Devonport, Devon, 52
Diagnosis, 105
Diarrhea, 117
Differences (journal), 196
Dike (geology), 70
Diluvium, 249
Dinosaur, 199, 233
Discovery Health Channel, 115
Divinity, 34, 246
Division of Darwin, 238
Dizziness, 106, 115
DjVu, 278

DNA, 115
Doctor of Medicine, 6
Doctrine, 252, 264
Dogma, 276
Domestication, 88, 143
Domestic pigeon, 143
Douglas Strutt Galton, 6
Dove, 199
Downe, 111, 126, 152, 199, 209, 252, 256
Down House, 107, 109, 111, 123, 126, 127, 131, 176, 216, 222, 224
Dragons Den, 21
Drosera, 175, 214
Drosera rotundifolia, 214
Drosophila melanogaster, 290
Drug therapy, 109
Dublin, 33
Duke University Press, 196
Dunboyne, 17
Düsseldorf, 185
Dysautonomia, 107
Dyspepsia, 107, 109, 115
Dyspnea, 107

Early Cretaceous, 220
Earths internal heat budget, 170
Earthworm, 92, 209
E. B. Pusey, 259
Ecuador, 65
Eczema, 107, 116
Edgar Leopold Layard, 143, 145
Edinburgh, 96, 113, 187, 200
Edinburgh New Philosophical Journal, 31, 315
Edinburgh Review, 130, 169, 180
Edinburgh University, 82, 105

Édouard Lartet, 88

Edward Aveling, 222, 226, 261, 262, 265
Edward Bagnall Poulton, 78
Edward Blyth, 138, 143, 144
Edward Forbes, 131, 144
Edward Frankland, 190
Edward Henry Stanley, 15th Earl of Derby, 229
Edward Herbert, 1st Baron Herbert of Cherbury, 35
Edward J. Larson, 295
Edward John Ash, 34
Edward Levett Darwin, 10
Edward L. Youmans, 205, 306
Edward M. Miller, 291
Edward N. Zalta, 278
Edward Sabine, 190
Edward VII, 16
Edwin Black, 288, 295

Egg (biology), 27
Egg donation, 290
Electrical stimulation, 109
Elizabeth Cotton, Lady Hope, 265
Elliott & Fry, 222
Elminius modestus, 239
Elrington and Bosworth Professor of Anglo-Saxon, 20
Emberizidae, 232
Embryo quality, 290
E. M. Forster, 226

Émile Gautier, 299, 305
Émile Littré, 178

Emily Langton Massingberd, 20
Emma Darwin, 8, 12, 16, 72, 82, 92, 95, 106, 112, 118, 125, 149, 166, 185, 196, 210, 251, 252, 256, 262, 263
Emma Darwin (Novelist), 20
Emma Wedgwood, 22, 243
Emotion, 112
Emotional conflict, 112
En:Bibcode, 156, 179, 180
En:Digital object identifier, 23, 77, 78, 103, 118–120, 156, 157, 178–180, 196, 266, 297, 298
Endnote 1, 111–113
Endnote 2, 111
Endnote 3, 111
Endnote 4, 111
Endnote 5, 111, 117
Endnote 6, 112
Endnote 7, 112
Endnote 8, 112
England, 71
England and France, 26
English, 279
En:International Standard Serial Number, 295, 309
En:Library of Congress Control Number, 277, 295
En:OCLC, 277
En:PubMed Central, 119, 120
Entomological Magazine, 311
Entomology, 34
Environmental ethics, 293
E. O. Wilson, 276
Epopella eosimplex, 241
Equator, 55
Equus curvidens, 74
Erasmus Alvey Darwin, 7, 28, 83, 87, 136, 166, 193, 204, 213, 225, 260
Erasmus Darwin, 3–6, 9, 25, 26, 30, 31, 40, 82, 113, 174, 187, 209, 220, 245, 246, 248, 272

Erasmus Darwin Barlow, 16, 17, 19
Eric Foner, 300
Ermengard Maitland, 14
Ernst Haeckel, 183, 193, 199, 221, 259, 275, 298, 304, 307
Ernst Krause, 220, 221, 313
Ernst Mayr, 278
Ernst Rüdin, 284
Essay on the Principle of Population, 252
Essays and Reviews, 159, 171, 173, 174, 190, 254
Estuary, 60
Ethanol, 4
Ethnological Society of London, 189
Ethology, 276

Étienne Geoffroy Saint-Hilaire, 31, 82, 87

Etiology, 110
Eton College, 196
Etty Darwin, 12, 102, 185, 186, 198, 253
Etymologist, 8
Euacasta sporillus, 241
Euclid, 38, 248
Eugenics, 14, 209, 210, 275, **279**, 298
Eugenics in Japan, 283
Eugenics in the United States, 279, 280, 283
Eugenics Record Office, 283
Eugenie Scott, 272
Euraphia intertexta, 241
Europe, 279
European hare, 90
Euthanasia, 286, 292
Evangelicalism, 69, 160, 250
Evidence as to Mans Place in Nature, 183
Evolution, 3, 6, 11, 45, 70, 123, 141, 159, 196, 243, 244, 271, 273, 281, 301
Evolution and the Roman Catholic Church, 167
Evolutionary, 298
Evolutionism, 4, 31, 99, 113, 177, 203, 300
Evolution of the eye, 165
Evolution of the horse, 74
Existence of God, 244
Ex nihilo, 25
Expelled: No Intelligence Allowed, 276
Experimental Evolution, 283
Exposition of the Creed, 246
Extinction, 25, 88
Extracts from Letters to Henslow, 311
Extra-marital affair, 4

Fainting, 107
Falkland Islands, 47, 59
Falkland Islands wolf, 70, 90
Falmouth, Cornwall, 71
Fancy pigeon, 167

Fanny Wedgwood, 136
Farewell Discourse, 98
Farnham, 108
Fathom, 68
Fatigue (medical), 115
Fault (geology), 70
Fellow, 3
Fernando de Noronha, 46, 56
Fertilisation of Orchids, 183, 187, 312
Ffestiniog, 42
Field Museum, 235
Film director, 306
Final Solution, 289
Finch, 232
First Sea Lord, 134
First World War, 16, 17
Firth of Forth, 30, 31, 52
Fissure vent, 70
Fistulobalanus pallidus, 239
Fitness (biology), 289
Flatulence, 107
Fleeming Jenkin, 194
Flood geology, 249
Floreana Island, 65, 234
Floreana mockingbird, 66
Florence Henrietta Darwin, 14
Flowering plant, 220
Flustra, 31
Fly fishing, 35
Food allergy, 116
Forced abortion, 284
Forced pregnancies, 284
Forres, 256
Fort William, Scotland, 96
Fossil, 25, 45, 81
Founding Father, 287
Fox terrier, 205
France, 83
Frances Cornford, 14, 15
Frances Julia Wedgwood, 8
Frances Power Cobbe, 200, 201, 216
Francis Abbott, 206
Francis Beaufort, 42, 48–50, 130
Francis Cornford, 15
Francis Darwin, 12, 14, 15, 102, 119, 156, 179, 202, 211, 214, 216, 262, 263, 265, 267, 313
Francis Galton, 3, 5, 6, 9, 197, 201, 209, 210, 213, 216, 275, 279, 281, 282, 287, 299, 301, 303
Francis Sacheverel Darwin, 5, 9, 16
Francis Wedgwood (1800–1888), 8
Francis William Newman, 136, 252, 253
François Jules Pictet de la Rive, 144
Franco-Prussian war, 202
Frank Sulloway, 103, 266

Franz Boas, 283
Frasers Magazine, 197
Fredegond Shove, 14
Frederic Farrar, 228, 229
Frederick Bridge, 229
Frederick Osborn, 279
Frederick Watkins (clergyman), 34
Frederick William Hope, 35
Freedom of religion, 38, 248
Freethought, 26, 87, 113, 245, 246, 262
French National Centre for Scientific Research, 79, 237
Friar, 272
Friedrich Nietzsche, 303, 308, 328
Friedrich Von Hellwald, 307
Fritz Müller, 197
Fuegians, 47, 58
Fuller Theological Seminary, 325
Funeral of Charles Darwin, 322

Galapagos Islands, 238
Galápagos Islands, 47, 65, 81, 85, 130, 144, 232, 234, 249
Galapagos land iguana, 66
Galápagos mockingbird, 66
Galápagos tortoise, 65, 70
Galileo Galilei, 167
Galley proof, 89
Gallipoli Campaign, 16
Galton Institute, 282
Gattaca, 289
Gauchers disease, 291
Gaucho, 57, 59, 92
Gemmules, 216
Gene, 291
Genealogy, 81, 91
Genealogy of Morals, 328
Gene flow, 276
Gene pool, 235, 275
Genesis creation myth, 246
Gene therapy, 290
Genetic determinism, 282
Genetic discrimination, 292
Genetic disorder, 292
Genetic divergence, 90
Genetic diversity, 281, 291
Genetic drift, 272
Genetic engineering, 286, 290
Genetics, 279, 282
Genetic testing, 286
Genetic variability, 90
Genetic variation, 90
Genocide, 284, 292
Genocide as a crime, 326
Genome editing, 279
Genovesa Island, 66

Gentleman, 42, 49
Genus, 232
Geoffrey Chaucer, 147
Geoffrey Keynes, 14, 15
Geoffrey Tindal-Carill-Worsley, 18
Geological Evidences of the Antiquity of Man, 183, 188
Geological Observations on South America, 312
Geological Observations on the Volcanic Islands visited during the voyage of H.M.S. Beagle, 312
Geological Society of London, 52, 68, 69, 72, 81, 83, 85, 99, 124, 170, 247, 311
Geologic time scale, 163
Geology, 45, 49, 50, 60, 81, 82, 106
George Annas, 292
George Bellas Greenough, 41
George Bentham, 213
George Busk, 190
George Campbell, 8th Duke of Argyll, 200
George Combe, 30, 160
George Douglas Campbell, 8th Duke of Argyll, 194, 197, 210, 223
George Erasmus Darwin, 18
George FitzRoy, 4th Duke of Grafton, 47
George Frideric Handel, 229
George Granville Bradley, 228, 229
George Graves (biologist), 30
George Holyoake, 166
George Howard Darwin, 12, 14, 15, 196, 210–214, 217, 219, 260
George III, 9
George IV of the United Kingdom, 9
George Jackson Mivart, 197, 210, 214–216, 221
George John Douglas Campbell, 8th Duke of Argyll, 229
George M. Dawson, 231
George Peacock, 42, 49, 50, 52, 247
George Robert Waterhouse, 85, 128, 132, 312
George Romanes, 214, 216, 220, 261, 275, 278
Georges Cuvier, 58, 73
George Sketchley Ffinden, 211
Georges-Louis Leclerc, Comte de Buffon, 82
Georg Wilhelm Friedrich Hegel, 305
Geranium, 37
Germanic peoples, 281
Germinal choice, 287
Germinal choice technology, 293
Gerousia, 281
Gestational surrogacy, 280
Gilbert White, 28, 34
Gilded age, 306
Giovanni Battista Brocchi, 64, 249

344

G. K. Chesterton, 283
Glaciation, 249
Glacier, 231
Glen Roy, 96, 97
Glossotherium, 74
Glyptodon, 73, 85, 91
Glyptodontidae, 73, 316
Gorilla, 138
Gospel, 113
Gospel of John, 98, 251
Gospels, 264
Gout, 115
Gower Street (London), 127
Gower Street, London, 100
Gradualism, 273
Greater rhea, 88
Great Exhibition, 136
Great Malvern, 11
Greek language, 287
Gregor Mendel, 272
Ground beetle, 35, 315
Ground sloth, 85
Guanaco, 60, 85, 88
Gunwale, 48
Guyana, 30
Gwen Darwin, 14
Gwen Raverat, 15, 21

Halliday Sutherland, 284
Hampshire College, 286
Harriet Martineau, 8, 84, 87, 134, 166
Hartheim Castle, 286
Hartheim Euthanasia Centre, 285
Harvard, 164, 199
Harvard University, 276
H. Charlton Bastian, 206
Headache, 107
Health of Charles Darwin, **105**
Hearing loss, 115
Hebrew University, 114
Helicobacter pylori, 116, 117
Henry Allen Wedgwood, 8
Henry Colburn, 265
Henry Foster (scientist), 46
Henry Galton Darwin, 18
Henry George, 225
Henry John Temple, 3rd Viscount Palmerston, 167
Henry Nicholas Ridley, 260
Henry Walter Bates, 183
Hensleigh Wedgwood, 8, 72, 86, 94, 95, 125, 211, 213
Herbert Spencer, 137, 143, 150, 160, 189, 190, 271, 298–301
Heredity, 118, 272, 281
Hermann Schaaffhausen, 185

Hermit crab, 68
Heteralepas cornuta, 239
Heterosis, 209
Hewett Watson, 164
H. G. Wells, 286, 306
Higher criticism, 159, 160, 243, 254
Hillwalking, 35
Himalaya, 135
Hindu, 264
Hindu scripture, 251
Hippopotamus, 84
Historical radicalism, 113
History of Birmingham, 37
History of creationism, 25, 82, 124, 246
History of Darwin, 231
History of eugenics, 279, 287
History of evolutionary thought, 124, 276
Hives, 116
HMNB Devonport, 48
HMS Aid (1809), 47
HMS Beagle, 42, 45, 72, 141, 147, 172, 191, 217, 220, 231, 250
HMS Chanticleer (1808), 48
HMS Prince George (1895), 16
HMY Victoria and Albert III, 16
Hobart, 68
Holocaust, 280
Holotype, 233
Holy See, 167
Homeopathy, 107
Homoeopathic, 134
Homology (biology), 32, 82, 87
Hoplophorus, 73
Horace Barlow, 16, 17
Horace Basil Barlow, 16
Horace Darwin, 12, 14, 16, 202, 210, 221
Horse riding, 115
House of Lords, 216
Hugh Falconer, 88, 132, 188
Hugh Massingberd, 20
Human, All Too Human, 328
Human cloning, 286, 290
Human evolution, 167, 184
Human genetic engineering, 287
Human population, 279
Human rights, 280, 286
Human rights violations, 292
Human society, 298
Hummingbird, 194
Hybrid (biology), 90
Hydrographic survey, 45, 46
Hydrography, 49
Hydropathy, 172
Hydropathy, 172
Hydrotherapy, 107, 134
Hyperpigmentation, 117
Hypotension, 116

Iain McCalman, 237
Ichneumonidae, 165
Ichneumon wasp, 243, 252
Ilkley, 109, 154, 161, 162
Immanuel Kant, 200
Immigration, 290
Inbreeding, 118, 288
Inbreeding depression, 281
Incarnation (Christianity), 251
Inception of Darwins theory, 3, 6, 25, **81**, 106, 113, 123, 141
Inclinometer, 41
India, 134
Indian Ocean, 68
Indies, 42
Indigenous peoples in Argentina, 59
Indonesia, 147
Inductive reasoning, 40, 248
Influenza, 135
Ingerana charlesdarwini, 233, 238
Inheritance of acquired characteristics, 275
In Memoriam A.H.H., 147
Inosculation, 88, 90
Inquiries into Human Faculty and Its Development, 287
Insanity, 281
Insect, 114
Insectivorous Plants, 215
Insectivorous Plants (book), 312
Insect pollination, 183, 186
Insomnia, 107
Instinct, 305
Intelligence (trait), 288
Intelligent design, 276
Intelligent design movement, 275
International Bioethics Committee, 287
International Brigades, 17
International Eugenics Conference, 282
International Federation of Eugenics Organizations, 283
International Standard Book Number, 16, 23, 43, 75, 76, 100, 102, 103, 119, 120, 139, 155–157, 177–179, 195, 207, 230, 265–269, 277, 295–297, 309, 311
Internet Archive, 277
Introduction, **1**
IQ, 280
Irving Stone, 236
Isaac Newton, 118, 166, 210, 229
Isabela Island (Ecuador), 66
Islam, 264
Isle of Man, 40
Isle of Wight, 40, 152, 191, 198
Israel, 114

Jack London, 306

Jacques Raverat, 15
Jamaica, 193
James Boswell, 30
James Brooke, 144
James David Forbes, 173
James De Carle Sowerby, 87
James Francis Stephens, 35, 36, 311
James Franklin (philosopher), 277
James G. Lennox, 278
James Hutton, 32
James Mackintosh, 8
James Manby Gully, 107, 134, 188
James Martineau, 252
James Moore (biographer), 43, 76, 102, 103, 119, 139, 156, 157, 179, 195, 207, 230, 265, 266, 309
James Peile, 282
James Russell Lowell, 229
Janet Browne, 43, 75, 100, 119, 139, 155, 178, 230, 265, 267, 277
Japetus Steenstrup, 132
Jared Diamond, 237
J. B. S. Haldane, 284, 288
Jean Baptiste Bory de Saint-Vincent, 58
Jean-Baptiste Lamarck, 4, 26, 82, 91, 94, 113, 144, 164, 246, 275, 302
Jeffries Wyman, 164
Jemmy Button, 58, 61, 202, 220
Jena, 193
Jesus the Logos, 251
Jews in Nazi Germany, 286
J. I. Wedgwood, 8
Joan Helen Barlow, 16
Johan Georg Forchhammer, 132
Johann Kaspar Lavater, 51
Johann Wolfgang von Goethe, 82, 304
John 15, 98
John Allen Wedgwood, 100
John Barclay (anatomist), 94
John Bird Sumner, 34, 247
John Brodie Innes, 199, 203, 209, 211, 256, 259, 262
John Burdon-Sanderson, 213
John Burgess (political scientist), 306
John Chadwick, 230
John Chapman (publisher), 107, 109, 136, 150, 191
John Clements Wickham, 48, 64, 231
John Coldstream, 30
John Collier (Pre-Raphaelite painter), 225
John Cornford, 17
John Edmonstone, 30
John Fiske (philosopher), 212, 278, 306
John Gould, 61, 77, 81, 85, 88, 99, 232, 315
John Graham (bishop), 34
John Hedley Brooke, 269

John Herschel, 39, 40, 69, 82, 86, 99, 134, 163, 210, 229, 243, 248, 250, 312
John Hunter Padel, 16
John Hunter (surgeon), 91
John Hutton Balfour, 267
John James Audubon, 31
John James Tayler, 252
John Joseph Bennett, 152
John Judd, 226
John Leifchild, 162
John Locke, 38
John Lort Stokes, 51, 231
John Lubbock, 1st Baron Avebury, 190, 229
John Maurice Herbert, 35
John Maynard Keynes, 15
John Murray (publisher), 130, 153, 161, 187, 197, 213–215, 222, 265
John Pearson (bishop), 246
John Phillips (geologist), 170, 175, 177
John Rawls, 294
John Rennie (editor), 276
John Ruskin, 221
Johns Hopkins University, 294
John Stevens Henslow, 35–37, 50, 52, 55, 62, 65, 71, 82, 83, 155, 166, 179, 185, 202, 247, 311
John Stuart Mill, 200
John Tyndall, 137, 148, 190, 198, 210, 214, 215
John van Wyhe, 78, 266, 269
John Vaughan Thompson, 54
John White Chadwick, 263
John William Draper, 172
Joint European Torus, 21
Jonathan Cape, 265, 277
Jon Entine, 289
Joseph Dalton Hooker, 63, 108, 128, 142, 145, 148, 159, 179, 184, 190, 210, 220, 229, 253
Joseph Henry Green, 87
Joseph Hooker, 237
Joseph Shaw (Christs College), 34
Josiah Wedgwood, 3, 4, 6–8, 22
Josiah Wedgwood, 1st Baron Wedgwood, 8, 16, 19
Josiah Wedgwood 2, 166
Josiah Wedgwood and Sons, 3
Josiah Wedgwood II, 4, 7, 8, 11, 33, 42, 50, 92
Josiah Wedgwood III, 7, 16
Journal of Natural History, 144, 311
Journal of the Royal Geographical Society of London, 323
Juan Manuel de Rosas, 59
Julia Margaret Cameron, 191, 192, 198
Julian Trevelyan, 18
Justice of the Peace, 149

J. W. C. Fegan, 257

Kaiser Wilhelm Institute of Anthropology, Human Heredity, and Eugenics, 283
Kaitaia, 67
Kangaroo, 249
Karl Marx, 171, 211
Karl Pearson, 288
Keele University, 294
Kelp forest, 62
Kent, 127, 209
Kew, 132, 199, 207, 213, 225
Keynes family, 15
King George Sound, 68
Knight, 167
Kropotkin, 277

Labour Party (UK), 16, 284
Lactose intolerance, 110, 116
Lake District, 166, 221, 224
Lamarckism, 31, 58, 129, 200, 246, 271, 298, 302
Lancashire, 205
Lancelot Hogben, 284
Land tenure, 299
Las Piedras, Uruguay, 60
Laudanum, 109
Lebensborn, 285
Leech, 31
Lee Kuan Yew, 287
Legion of Honour, 16
Leith Hill, 219
Leonard Darwin, 12, 14, 196, 206
Leonard Darwin 1899, 14
Leonard Huxley (writer), 180
Leonard Jenyns, 42, 50, 128
Lepas australis, 239
Leptoplana formosa, 241
Leptoplana notabilis, 241
Lester Frank Ward, 283
Liberal Christianity, 40, 159, 171, 247, 252, 254
Liberal Party (UK), 16
Life of Samuel Johnson, 30
Lightning rod, 48
Lignite, 62
Lima, 65
Lincolnshire, 130
Lineage (evolution), 91
Line-crossing ceremony, 55
Linnaean Society, 141
Linnean Society, 187
Linnean Society of London, 12, 83, 137, 148, 151, 161, 185, 188, 216, 234, 312
List of chronometers on HMS Beagle, 46, 48
List of taxa described by Charles Darwin, **239**

List of things named after Charles Darwin, **237**
Liver failure, 4
Livestock, 299
Llama, 74, 85
Llangollen, 41
Llanymynech, 41
Logical consequence, 300
London, 72, 83
London Waterloo station, 165
Longitude, 46, 56
Longitude by chronometer, 46
Lord Chancellor, 193
Lord Lieutenant of Meath, 17
Lord of the Manor, 9
Lords of the Admiralty, 48
Lori Andrews, 292
Louis Agassiz, 96, 135, 155
Loxton, North Somerset, 9
Lucy Rawlinson, 21
Ludwig Büchner, 226, 262
Lung edema, 114
Lupus erythematosus, 110
Lychgate, 136
Lych gate, 253
Lyell Island, 231
Lygaeidae, 238

Macacu River, 56
Macellum of Pozzuoli, 54
Macrauchenia, 74, 85, 88, 92
Madagascar, 233
Madeira, 54
Madrid, 58
Maer Hall, 42, 84, 92, 98, 100, 126
Maer, Staffordshire, 28, 100
Magistrate, 149
Magnetic anomaly, 55
Maidstone, 202
Malaise, 106, 115
Maldonado, Uruguay, 86
Malthusian, 82, 225, 248
Malthusian catastrophe, 302
Malthusianism, 87, 284
Malvern, Worcestershire, 107, 134, 188
Mammal, 57
Mans Place in Nature, 187
Maoism, 276
Māori people, 67, 189
Marchena Island, 66
Marcus Bourne Huish, 10
Margaret Elizabeth Darwin, 14
Margaret Keynes (née Darwin), 14
Mariano Artigas, 320
Marie Stopes, 284
Marine chronometer, 46
Marine iguana, 65

Marine invertebrate, 31
Mark Goldie, 315
Marriage restrictions, 284
Marsupial, 249
Martin T. Barlow, 19
Marxism, 276
Mary Anne Schimmelpenninck, 5
Mass murder, 286
Mastodon, 60, 64, 73, 74, 85
Materialism, 30, 31, 94, 113, 225, 246, 251
Matlock Bath, 10
Matriculation, 34
Matthew Chapman (author), 19
Mauritius, 68
Maximum life span, 293
Meaning of life, 293
Medical Journal of Australia, 116
Medicine, 105, 279
Megabalanus coccopoma, 239
Megabalanus crispatus, 241
Megabalanus decorus, 241
Megabalanus occator, 239
Megabalanus stultus, 239
Megabalanus vesiculosus, 241
Megabalanus vinaceus, 241
Megacolon, 114
Megaesophagus, 114
Megalith, 219
Megalonyx, 58, 73
Megatherium, 58, 64, 73
Mein Kampf, 284
MELAS syndrome, 116
Member of Parliament, 16
Membranobalanus declivis, 239
Mendelian inheritance, 272, 287
Mendoza, Argentina, 64, 106, 114
Ménières disease, 110, 115
Mental breakdown, 32
Mercedes, Uruguay, 60, 73, 84
Mercury (element), 48
Meridian arc, 46
Mesmerism, 107, 134
Mess, 51
Metaphysical naturalism, 272
Metaphysics, 204
Meteorology, 47
Michael Joseph (publisher), 265
Michael Ruse, 302
Midshipman, 56
Milk, 116
Milo Keynes, 15
Mimus, 66
Mind, 246
Mineralogy, 35, 49
Ming Dynasty, 293
Miocene, 88

Mises Institute, 328
Mitochondria, 116
Mitochondrial disease, 116
Mitochondrial DNA, 116
Mockingbird, 66, 70, 86, 90, 234, 249
Modern eugenics, genetic engineering, and ethical re-evaluation, 286
Modern synthesis (20th century), 271
Mollusc, 132
Monism, 298
Monkey, 273
Monte Hermoso, 58, 73
Montevideo, 46, 57, 60, 84
Moor Park, Farnham, 108
Morality, 250
Moral philosophy, 305
Moravia, 272
Moresby Island, 231
Motion sickness, 115
Mountain hare, 90
Mount Darwin (Andes), 231, 238
Mount Darwin (California), 238
Mount Darwin (Tasmania), 238
Mount Edgcumbe Country Park, 53
Museum of Science, Boston, 235
Mussel, 64
Mutant, 91
Mutation, 290
Mutilation, 286
Mutual Aid: A Factor of Evolution, 274
Mya arenaria, 240
Mylodon, 73
Myopia, 291

Nancy Armstrong, 196
Napoleonic Wars, 245
Napoleon I of France, 69
Nathaniel C. Comfort, 294
National Portrait Gallery (United Kingdom), 322
National Review (1855), 164, 178
Natural history, 3, 4, 6, 25, 27, 30, 34, 45, 49, 81, 82, 105, 243, 246
Natural History Museum, London, 234, 235, 237
Natural History Review, 175
Naturalism (philosophy), 25, 273
Natural philosophy, 40, 49, 248
Natural selection, 11, 25, 45, 82, 123, 141, 159, 196, 210, 221, 243, 244, 252, 254, 257, 271, 275, 281, 298, 300
Natural Selection (manuscript), 146, 147, 150
Natural theology, 86, 87, 243, 247, 254
Natural Theology or Evidences of the Existence and Attributes of the Deity, 39, 248
Nature and nurture, 282

Nature (journal), 201, 214
Naturphilosophie, 87
Nausea, 115
Nautical chart, 46
Nazi eugenics, 280
Nazi Germany, 280, 286
Neanderthal, 185
Neo-Darwinism, 271
Neogene, 88
Neptune (mythology), 55
Neptunism, 32
Nesochthamalus intertextus, 239
Neurosis, 111
Neutering, 281
New eugenics, 279, 290
New South Wales, 67
Newt, 197
New Testament, 37, 264
New York University, 172
New Zealand, 67, 189
Niagara Falls, 84
Nicene Creed, 252
Nicholas Lawson, 65
Nicola Mary Elizabeth Darwin, 15
Nicolas Tindal-Carill-Worsley, 18
Nicolaus Copernicus, 273
Nikolay Danilevsky, 278
Niles Eldredge, 76, 102, 268
Ninth Bridgewater Treatise, 87
Noahs ark, 249
Nobel Prize, 304
Nobia conjugatum, 239
Non-conformist, 243, 245
Nora Barlow, 43, 75, 76, 102, 156, 181, 263, 265
Nora Barlow (née Darwin), 14
Nordic race, 283
Northampton, 222
North Downs, 219
Northern Territory, 231
Norway, 138
Norwich, 198
Notes and Records of the Royal Society, 266
Notomegabalanus decorus, 239
Nottingham, 192
Nuremberg trials, 280

Obsessive–compulsive disorder, 111
Octolasmis lowei, 239
Oedipal complex, 112
Old College, University of Edinburgh, 29
Old Red Sandstone, 42
Old Testament, 250
Olivia Judson, 272
One-child policy, 286
Oneida stirpiculture, 287

349

On the Origin of Species, 82, 109, 126, 141, 153, 159, 184, 196, 210, 231, 235, 244, 254, 255, 271, 299, 301, 308, 312
On the Tendency of Species to form Varieties; and on the Perpetuation of Varieties and Species by Natural Means of Selection, 108, 141, 152, 161, 312
Open University Press, 309
Operating system, 238
Orangutan, 81
Orang-utan, 93
Orb-weaver spider, 233
Orchid, 186, 196
Organism, 300
Original position, 294
Orthodoxy, 250
Orthogenesis, 91, 183
Orthostatic intolerance, 107, 111
Osmaston, Derby, 13
Osorno (volcano), 63
Ostracod, 238
Otter, 92
Ottoman Empire, 218, 225
Otto von Bismarck, 193
Oxford, 133, 172
Oxford University, 38, 248
Oxford University Museum of Natural History, 173
Oyster, 31

Pachydermata, 74
Pachylasma auranticacum, 241
Pacific Ocean, 47
Packet trade, 51
Palaeotherium, 74
Palazzo delle Esposizioni, 235
Palmerston, Northern Territory, 231
Pampa, 114
Pampas, 59, 106
Panagaeus cruxmajor, 35
Panegyric, 219
Pangenesis, 216
Pan Guangdan, 307
Panic disorder, 110
Panspermia, 271
Pantheism, 97
Param has ext link, 156
Paraná River, 60, 74
Parasitoid, 165
Paris Commune, 204
Parodies of the ichthys symbol, 238
Parson, 34, 45, 50, 246
Partridge, 199
Passer iagoensis, 315
Patagonia, 57, 85, 88, 250, 323
Patricide, 112

Patrick Joseph Hayes, 282
Paul Kenna, 17
PCR, 115
Pedogenesis, 92
Peerage, 16, 34
Pejorative, 272
Penal colony, 65
Penguin Group, 265
Penny (British pre-decimal coin), 263
Penrhyn Quarry, 41
Period Piece (book), 15
Pernambuco, 71
Perspectives on Science and Christian Faith, 266, 268
Pervasive developmental disorder, 110
Peter J. Bowler, 100, 139, 277
Peter Kropotkin, 274
Peter Medawar, 117
Petersham, London, 109, 172
Peter Wilhelm Lund, 73
Petrifaction, 62
Petto & Godfrey 2007, 325
Phenotypic trait, 291
Phenylketonuria, 291
Philadelphia, 14
Philanthropy, 275
Philately, 27
Philipp Blom, 296
Philip Trevelyan, 18
Phillip E. Johnson, 275
Phillip Parker King, 47, 51, 78
Philologist, 8
Philosophical naturalism, 275
Phrenology, 30, 51
Phyllida Barlow, 19
Physical cosmology, 271
Physical disability, 281
Physical law, 69, 87, 97, 250
Physician, 112
Physiognomy, 51
Physiologist, 18
Piccadilly, 148
Pigeon, 138
Pigeon keeping, 143
Pinguicula, 214
Pinguicula vulgaris, 214
Pinta Island, 66
Plankton, 249
Plankton net, 54
Plato, 279, 281
Platonic idealism, 87
Platyhelminth, 241
Platypus, 67, 91, 148
Pleiotropy, 291
Plinian Society, 30, 246
Plutonism, 32

Plymouth, 105
Plymouth Sound, 53
Poecilasma kaempferi, 239
Pollination syndrome, 187
Poorhouse, 87
Poor Law, 83, 97
Poor Law Amendment Act 1834, 87
Pope Pius XI, 284
Popular Science, 305
Population genetics, 272, 288
Port Darwin, 231
Port Jackson, 47
Positivism, 302
Posthuman, 292
Postural orthostatic tachycardia syndrome, 107, 111
Potoridae, 67, 249
Praia, 46, 54
Pre-implantation genetic diagnosis, 286
Preimplantation genetic diagnosis, 280, 290
Prenatal care, 288
Prenatal diagnosis, 287
Presbyterianism, 254
President of France, 16
Prestonpans, 31
Primate, 88, 232
Primula, 27
Primula veris, 187
Primula vulgaris, 187
Prince of Wales, 225
Prince Philip, 236
Principles of Geology, 45, 54, 58, 61, 69, 70, 144, 163
Pringle Stokes, 47, 49
Problem of evil, 40, 248, 255
Proby Cautley, 88
Proctor, 36
Progressive Era, 289
Project Gutenberg, 43, 79, 104, 139, 157, 181, 195, 208, 230, 311
Project Prevention, 289
Promiscuous women, 286
Protestant Reformation, 167
Pseudoscience, 288
Psychiatric hospital, 303
Psychoanalysis, 112
Psychological repression, 112
Psychosomatic, 108, 111
Pteroptochos, 70
Pterosaur, 233
Publication of Darwins theory, 12, 108, 114, 123, 138, **141**, 254, 275
Public domain, 311
Public health, 294
Public house, 212, 257
Public school (England), 245

PubMed Identifier, 118–120, 180, 297, 298
Puerto Baquerizo Moreno, 65
Puerto Belgrano, 316
Puerto Deseado, 60
Puerto San Julián, 60, 74, 85
PUF, 328
Pugwash Conferences on Science and World Affairs, 21
Puka-Puka, 67
Punitive expedition, 59
Punta Alta, 45, 57, 73

Quackery, 109
Quarantined, 54
Quarterly Review, 174, 180
Queen Charlotte Islands, 231
Quentin Keynes, 15, 18
Quinarian system, 128

Race (biology), 153
Race (classification of human beings), 153, 286
Race (classification of humans), 61
Racial policy of Nazi Germany, 284
Racial segregation, 284, 292
Radicalism (historical), 25, 84, 87, 94, 97, 245–247
Radicals (UK), 186
Rainbow in the Bible, 250
Raised beach, 250
Ralph L. Wedgwood, 17, 21
Ralph Vaughan Williams, 3, 7, 16
Ralph Wedgwood (philosopher), 21
Randal Keynes, 20, 235
Rationalization (psychology), 274
Reactions to On the Origin of Species, 155, **159**
Reaction to Darwins theory, 196, 254
Rebbachisauridae, 233
Recapitulation theory, 304
Reception, 177
Reception of the Origin of Species, 321
Recessive trait, 290
Rede Lecture, 170, 175
Red Notebook, 89
Reduviidae, 106
Re-establishment of British rule on the Falklands (1833), 59
Ref 2, 118
Ref 3, 118
Ref 4, 118
Ref 5, 119
Ref 6, 119
Ref 7, 119
Ref 8, 119
Ref 9, 119
Relations between the Catholic Church and the state, 307

Religious skepticism, 247
Religious Society of Friends, 129
Religious text, 252
Religious views of Charles Darwin, **243**
Remission (medicine), 115
Reproduction, 88, 89, 271
Reproductive isolation, 90
Reproductive rights, 294
Reprogenetics, 287
Retail Price Index, 317
Revolution, 57
Revolution of the Restorers, 60
Rhea (bird), 57, 86, 90
Rhinoceros, 58, 73
Rhinodermatidae, 232
Richard Carlile, 36, 247
Richard Darwin Keynes, 18
Richard Dawkins, 237, 276, 287
Richard Hofstadter, 299
Richard Keynes, 15, 78, 114, 120
Richard Litchfield, 205
Richard Lynn, 289, 295
Richard Owen, 73, 78, 81, 84, 87, 99, 103, 125, 131, 148, 151, 155, 159, 162, 167, 180, 184, 207, 221, 230, 312
Richmond, London, 109, 172
Rio de Janeiro, 46, 56
Río de la Plata, 46, 88
Río Negro (Argentina), 59
Río Negro (Uruguay), 60
Robert Brown (botanist, born 1773), 51
Robert Brown (Scottish botanist from Montrose), 89, 152, 186
Robert Chambers (journalist), 129, 133, 172, 193
Robert Darwin, 6–8, 25, 26, 112, 149
Robert Edmond Grant, 31, 51, 87, 91
Robert Edmund Grant, 52, 82, 83, 99, 125, 164, 246
Robert FitzRoy, 42, 45, 47, 77, 78, 102, 147, 172, 191, 231, 249, 265
Robert George Darwin, 19
Robert Jameson, 31, 32, 41, 82, 315
Robert Knox, 146
Robert McCormick (explorer), 49, 55, 56
Robert Taylor (Radical), 36, 147, 247
Robert Vere Darwin, 15
Robert Waring Darwin, 4, 96
Robin Darwin, 18
Robin Warren, 117
Rodent, 58, 84
Roderick Murchison, 87
Rolleston on Dove, 8
Roman Catholic, 204
Romani people, 286
Ronald Fisher, 14, 284

Rostratoverruca nexa, 239
Rote learning, 28
Royal Air Force, 18
Royal Botanic Gardens, Kew, 137
Royal College of Surgeons of England, 83, 84, 87, 185
Royal Geographical Society, 250
Royal Historical Society, 299
Royal Institution, 137, 150, 167
Royal Military Academy, Woolwich, 196
Royal Museum, 32
Royal Navy, 16, 17
Royal Netherlands Academy of Arts and Sciences, 206
Royal Ontario Museum, 235
Royal School of Mines, 137, 176
Royal Society, 3, 82, 100, 111, 137, 148, 150, 183, 190, 209
Rugby School, 136, 171
Runivers.ru, 278
Rustication (academia), 36
Ruth C. Engs, 295
Ruth Padel, 16, 20

Saint Peter and Paul Rocks, 55
Saltation (biology), 88
Salvador, Bahia, 56
Samborombón Bay, 57
Samuel Butler (1835-1902), 220, 221
Samuel John Galton, 5, 6
Samuel Smiles, 218
Samuel Stevens (naturalist), 145
Samuel Tertius Galton, 5, 6, 9
Samuel Wilberforce, 130, 133, 159, 167, 172, 174, 180, 190, 211
San Cristóbal Island, 65
San Cristobal mockingbird, 65
Sansan, Gers, 88
Santa Cruz de Tenerife, 54
Santa Cruz River (Argentina), 62
Santa Fe, Argentina, 60, 74
Santa Maria Island, Cape Verde, 54
Santiago, Cape Verde, 54
Santiago, Chile, 63
Santiago Island (Galápagos), 66
São Domingos, Cape Verde, 55
Sarah Darwin, 20
Sara Sedgwick, 199
Sarawak, 144
Saturday Review (London), 163, 170, 320
Saul Adler, 114
Sauropod, 233
Savanna, 164
Savignium dentatum, 241
Savilian chair of geometry, 171
Scalp, 107

Scarlet fever, 12, 151
Scelidotherium, 73, 74, 85
Schooner, 59
Scientific American, 276
Scientific method, 86
Scientific racism, 288
Scientific theory, 271
Scolopacidae, 91
Scottish Highlands, 199, 256
Sea mouse, 30
Séance, 260
Seasickness, 115
Second Boer War, 16
Second International Eugenics Conference, 280
Second voyage of HMS Beagle, 25, 37, 42, **45**, 81, 82, 105, 113, 114, 123, 124, 141, 142, 231, 243, 249, 263
Selective breeding, 279, 281
Self-help, 298
Seneca the Younger, 281
Separation anxiety, 111
S:Eugenics, 284
S:Eugenics and other Evils, 284
Sex education, 289
Sexual reproduction, 89, 279
Sexual selection, 11, 138, 149, 184, 189, 194, 196, 197
Shilling, 60, 155
Ship commissioning, 48
Ships chronometer from HMS Beagle, 47
Ships doctor, 49
Shrewsbury, 6, 26, 126, 235, 236
Shrewsbury School, 28, 245
Shrewsbury, Shropshire, 33, 36, 71, 83
Shrewsbury Unitarian Church, 245
Shropshire, 28, 41
Sic, 52
Sickle-cell disease, 292
Simon Blackburn, 277
Simon Keynes, 20
Simon Mangan, 17
Singapore, 287
Sirach, 229
Sir Charles James Fox Bunbury, 8th Baronet, 83
Sir Henry Holland, 1st Baronet, 166
Sir John Lubbock, 3rd Baronet, 131
Sir John Sebright, 7th Baronet, 93
Sir Ralph Wedgwood, 1st Baronet, 19
Sir William Lawrence, 1st Baronet, 87
Sivalik Hills, 88
Skandar Keynes, 21
Skin, 107
Smyrna, 9
Social Darwinism, 238, 275, **298**

Social Darwinism in European and American Thought 1860-1945, 309
Social equality, 38, 248
Social interpretations of race, 292
Social order, 279
Social philosophy, 279
Social welfare provision, 303
Society for Biodemography and Social Biology, 282, 284
Sociobiology, 276
Sociocultural evolution, 305
Sociologist, 300
Sociology, 274
Sophie Pryor, 15
Sounding line, 68
South America, 45–47, 85
Southampton, 11, 193, 214, 219
Soviet Union, 326
Spanish Civil War, 17
Sparta, 281
Spasm, 106
Spa town, 134, 161
Speaking of Faith, 266
Speciation, 300
Species, 123, 143, 232, 271
Species description, 315
Spiritualism, 213
Spiritualism (religious movement), 183, 193, 260
Staffordshire, 65
Stagecoach, 71
Stanford Encyclopedia of Philosophy, 278
Stanford University, 278
Stanley Kubrick, 306
Staphylinidae, 233
State of nature, 305
Stationers Hall, 155
St Chads Church, Shrewsbury, 26
Steamboat, 96
Stenaptinus insignis, 315
Stephen Jay Gould, 296
Stephen Keynes, 15
Sterilization (medicine), 279, 289
St. George Jackson Mivart, 257
St. Gregorys Bay, 60
St. Helena, 69
Stoke-on-Trent, 7
Stomach, 114
Stonehenge, 219
Straits of Magellan, 60, 62
Stratigraphy, 32, 54, 82, 170
Stratum, 41, 70, 249
Stress (medicine), 111
Sudbrook Park, Petersham, 109
Suffrage, 38, 248
Surrey, 108, 109

Survival of the fittest, 275, 300
Susannah Darwin, 26, 116
Susannah Wedgwood, 4, 6–8
Sussex, 152
Swaffham Bulbeck, 50
Swan River Colony, 68
Sweden, 280
Sydney, 67
Sympiesometer, 48
Symptom, 105
Syms Covington, 57, 59, 72, 89
Syncope (medicine), 228

Tachycardia, 107, 115
Tacitus, 325
Tahiti, 45, 67
TalkOrigins Archive, 267, 268
Tanager, 232
Tania Simoncelli, 286
Tasmania, 68, 99
Taxidermy, 30
Taxonomy (biology), 73
Tay–Sachs disease, 291
Teaching hospital, 87
Teleological argument, 40, 82, 113, 243, 248, 254, 255, 271
Teleology, 90, 97
Temnaspis fissum, 239
Template:Fringe medicine sidebar, 279
Template talk:Fringe medicine sidebar, 279
Tenerife, 40, 54
Tetraclita rubescens, 239
Tetraclita serrata, 239
The Age of Enlightenment, 245
The Autobiography of Charles Darwin, 76, 119, 156, 224, 255, 263, 315
The Chronicles of Narnia (film series), 21
The Complete Works of Charles Darwin Online, 43, 79, 104, 139, 157, 179, 181, 195, 208, 230, 237, 265, 315
The Constitution of Man, 160
The Daily Telegraph, 20
The Darwin Adventure, 236
The Descent of Man, 58, 210, 258
The Descent of Man and Selection in Relation to Sex, 197
The Descent of Man, and Selection in Relation to Sex, 76, 196, 201, 204, 312
The Different Forms of Flowers on Plants of the Same Species, 313
The eclipse of Darwinism, 271
The Effects of Cross and Self Fertilisation in the Vegetable Kingdom, 312
The Establishment, 72
The Expression of the Emotions in Man and Animals, 31, 94, 196, 206, 312

The Formation of Vegetable Mould through the Action of Worms, 224, 313
The Guardian, 198, 237
The Historical Journal, 268
Theism, 25, 244, 252, 255
The Lancet, 87
The Mount, Shrewsbury, 26, 41, 42, 71, 83, 96, 134
The Movements and Habits of Climbing Plants, 312
The Naturalist on the River Amazons, 183
The New York Times, 267
Theodicy, 40, 243, 248, 252
Theology, 165, 273
The Origin (novel), 236
The Origin of Species, 156, 161
Theory of criminal justice, 36
The Parsons Prologue and Tale, 147
The Power of Movement in Plants, 209, 313
The Quantum Leap, 235, 236
Thermodynamics, 177
The Scientific Monthly, 284
The Structure and Distribution of Coral Reefs, 47, 65, 68, 89, 123, 126, 312
The Subjection of Women, 200
The Times, 164, 174, 180, 204, 224, 228, 322
The Variation of Animals and Plants under Domestication, 175, 183, 196, 216, 312
The Virginia Quarterly Review, 102, 268
The Voyage of the Beagle, 6, 45, 54, 72, 76, 81, 88, 123, 125, 141, 144, 153, 160, 184, 312
Thirty-nine Articles, 38, 211, 245, 248, 257
Thomas Archer Hirst, 190
Thomas Bell (zoologist), 84, 152
Thomas Bentley (manufacturer), 3
Thomas Carlyle, 86
Thomas Charles Hope, 30, 32
Thomas Erasmus Barlow, 16
Thomas Henry Huxley, 145, 152, 159, 183, 190, 229, 271, 278, 299
Thomas Hobbes, 305
Thomas Hunt Morgan, 290
Thomas Huxley, 137, 142, 147, 148, 160, 168, 180, 184, 210, 237
Thomas Jefferson University, 116, 117
Thomas Malthus, 82, 83, 97, 124, 166, 243, 248, 252, 299, 301, 302
Thomas Spring Rice, 1st Baron Monteagle of Brandon, 89
Thomas Theta Farrer, 211, 221
Thomas Vernon Wollaston, 145
Thomas Wakley, 87
Thomas Wedgwood (1771–1805), 4, 8
Tick-borne disease, 110
Tide, 68

Tierra del Fuego, 42, 46, 48, 58, 59, 93, 151, 202, 316
Tinnitus, 107, 115
Tiredness, 107
Tobacconists, 34
Tokugawa shogunate, 293
Tom Shakespeare, 297
Torquay, 186
Torture, 286
Tory, 38, 51, 83, 84, 172, 204, 218, 245, 248
Tower of Babel, 250
Toxodon, 73, 74, 84, 88
Tradesman, 49
Transactions & Proceedings of the Botanical Society of Edinburgh, 267
Transhumanism, 287
Transitional fossil, 232
Transmutation of species, 32, 66, 70, 81, 87, 106, 123, 124, 141, 243, 251, 271
Tree of life (science), 81, 90, 91
Tremor, 106
Triatoma infestans, 106, 114
Tribe, 244
Trinity, 252
Tripos, 34
Tropical medicine, 114
Troy Duster, 286
Trypanosoma cruzi, 114
Tuamotus, 67
Twelve Tables, 281
Two pounds (British decimal coin), 235
Type specimen, 315
Typhoid, 185

UC Berkeley, 286
Unicellular organism, 32
Uniformitarianism, 170, 177
Uniformitarianism (science), 41, 82, 84, 141, 249
Unintended consequences, 291
Unitarianism, 25, 26, 82, 87, 113, 129, 164, 230, 245, 252, 253, 263
United Kingdom, 279
United Nations, 286
United States Congress, 235
University College London, 87, 164, 213, 288
University of California, Berkeley, 275
University of California Press, 277, 309
University of Cambridge, 11, 28, 33, 34, 49, 105, 113, 128, 164, 195, 196, 219, 235, 243, 245
University of Edinburgh, 25, 28, 29, 52, 164, 246
University of Manchester, 294
University of Maryland, Baltimore, 117
University of Melbourne, 116

University of Oxford, 137, 171, 245
University of Strasbourg, 304
University of Wrocław, 291
Unsupported attributions, 291
Ursula Mommens, 15, 18
Uruguay, 60
Uruguay River, 60
Utopia, 189
Uzbekistan, 286

Valdivia, Chile, 64
Vale of Clwyd, 42
Valparaiso, 63, 106
Vector (epidemiology), 114
Vegetative reproduction, 209
Vertigo (medical), 106, 115
Vestiges of Creation, 159, 162
Vestiges of the Natural History of Creation, 123, 129, 144, 160, 253
Vices, 281
Victor Carus, 224
Victoria Cross, 17
Victorian era, 89
Victoria of the United Kingdom, 96, 167
Villegagnon Island, 46, 56
Vine, 183, 209
Viscount Castlereagh, 49
Visual perception, 107
Vitalism, 87
Vladimir Kovalevsky, 194
Volcanic cone, 65
Vomiting, 107, 115
Voyage on the Beagle, 50

Wales, 28, 35, 41, 82
Walford House, 31
Walter Bagehot, 197
Walter Weldon, 288
Wanella milleporae, 239
Water treader, 238
Weald, 163, 170, 175, 177
Wedgwood, 28
Weight loss, 117
Weismann barrier, 271
Wernerian Natural History Society, 31
West Indies, 227
Westminster Abbey, 115, 210, 215, 228, 263
Westminster Review, 136, 137, 150, 168, 180, 273
White Rajahs, 144
Whitworth rifle, 169, 273
Wikipedia:Avoid weasel words, 118
Wikipedia:Citation needed, 160, 199, 244, 291, 306
Wikipedia:Link rot, 43
Wikipedia:No original research, 92

Wikipedia:Vagueness, 160
Wiktionary:blackamoor, 30
Wikt:savant, 50
Wikt:supernumerary, 45, 48
Wikt:victuals, 52
Wiley-Blackwell, 268
Wilhelm Ostwald, 304
William A. F. Browne, 30, 246
William Allingham, 198
William Benjamin Carpenter, 129, 164, 178, 230, 263
William Bernhard Tegetmeier, 143
William Bernhardt Tegetmeier, 145
William Broderip, 72, 84
William Buckland, 62, 84, 89, 92, 249
William Cavendish, 7th Duke of Devonshire, 229
William Clift, 62
William Cobbett, 87
William Darwin Fox, 13, 34, 35, 95, 107, 137, 143, 146
William Erasmus Darwin, 11, 199, 229
William Ewart Gladstone, 218
William Fitzwilliam Owen, 46
William Goodell (gynecologist), 281
William Graham Sumner, 306
William Inge (priest), 282
William Kirby (entomologist), 34
William Paley, 35, 37, 39, 113, 243, 247, 264
William Pryor (writer), 21
William Rathbone Greg, 197
William Robert Darwin, 14
William Snow Harris, 48
William Spence (entomologist), 34
William Spottiswoode, 190, 209, 228, 229
William Thiselton-Dyer, 213
William Thomson, 1st Baron Kelvin, 177, 194, 200
William Whewell, 35, 86, 92, 173, 247
William Yarrell, 51, 93, 143
Womens Royal Naval Service, 17
Woodbine Parish, 58, 87
Workhouse, 83
World view, 307
World War II, 17, 280, 286, 293, 305
Wren, 86
W.R.Grove, 192
W. W. Norton & Company, 277
Wyville Thomson, 223

X Club, 183, 190, 198, 201, 210
Xenarthra, 58
XII, 325

Yaghan, 58
Yan Fu, 307

Zoological Museum of Copenhagen, 132
Zoological Society of London, 51, 52, 83, 85, 86, 151
Zoology of the Voyage of H.M.S. Beagle, 126, 128, 312
Zoönomia, 30, 89, 246
Zygosity, 290

www.ingramcontent.com/pod-product-compliance
Lightning Source LLC
Chambersburg PA
CBHW021340300426
44114CB00012B/1014